BOLLINGEN SERIES XCI:2

HENRY CORBIN

Spiritual Body and Celestial Earth

From Mazdean Iran to Shīʿite Iran

Translated from the French by
NANCY PEARSON

BOLLINGEN SERIES XCI: 2

PRINCETON UNIVERSITY PRESS

Published by Princeton University Press,
Princeton, New Jersey

THIS IS PART TWO OF THE NINETY-FIRST IN A SERIES OF WORKS
SPONSORED BY
BOLLINGEN FOUNDATION

Published in French as
*Terre céleste et corps de résurrection:
de l'Iran mazdéen a l'Iran shî'ite*
(Collection "La Barque du Soleil"),
Buchet-Chastel, Paris, 1960.

Part One was originally published in French (in slightly different form) in *Eranos-Jahrbuch* XXII (1953) by Rhein-Verlag, Zurich.

Library of Congress Cataloging in Publication Data will be found on the last printed page of this book

Printed in the United States of America
by Princeton University Press, Princeton, New Jersey

CONTENTS

PROLOGUE

It may be that the world which our authors here describe in symbolic language as the "eighth climate" will be seen by Western people as the "lost continent." Should some of them be searching for it, the Spiritual Masters whom the present book seeks to interpret will perhaps serve as their guides.

The spatial distances between humans are being more and more reduced in our day, at least if measured in terms of time; concurrently we hear talk of an "acceleration of history." On the other hand, the *real* universes—those by which and for which men live and die, which can never be reduced to empirical data because their secret reality exists before all our projects and predetermines them—those universes, it would seem, have never been so far from being able to communicate with each other, from being penetrable by one another. It may be that the first and last reason for this impenetrability is to be sought in the loss of the *interworld*, in the vanished consciousness of this assembly of universes which our authors call the "world of Hūrqalyā."

How does the cultured man of today represent to himself the spirituality of Islam? What picture can he form of the spiritual world of Iran on the two poles of which, before and after Islam, we will try here to apply our attention? People are generally absorbed in political or sociological considerations and lose sight of the essential. We ask questions without even ascertaining what meaning, if any, they have for the man addressed and, for the same reason, the sense or non-sense of his answers for ourselves.

It is a great and formidable adventure to be the guest of a culture to the point of communicating in its language and participating in its problems. But he who remains on the shore will never foretaste the secrets of the high seas. How can he know, for example, what it might be to read the Qur'ān as a Bible (like that Bible from which the Qur'ān partially stems) unless, like those whose Bible it is, he perceives the *spiritual meaning* that they perceive in it, and as they perceive it in the traditions which unfold it. But how can we keep company with the Ṣūfīs and Spiritual Masters of Islam if we ourselves have forgotten the language of symbols, if we are blind and deaf to the *spiritual meaning* of the ancient writings, while, on the other hand, we take such pride in showing how favorably they compare with other historical or archeological documents?

Among other symptoms indicative of a "lost continent," we should note the unusual insistence with which certain contemporary theologians have taken the "immortality of the soul" as opposed to the "resurrection of the dead," as though it were a great triumph to abandon the philosophers, the impenitent Platonists, to their vain pretensions, while they themselves, as perfect realists, stand ready to condone the concessions necessary in order to "keep up with the times." For in truth there has been a great destruction of hopes in the West, and there is no telling where this will end. Its most alarming symptom is the pious agnosticism that is paralyzing excellent minds and inspiring in them a panic terror before everything with the suspect aroma of "gnosis."

Let us be clear about one thing: the dilemma we have just mentioned is utterly and justifiably foreign to the thoughts and the thinkers assembled here in this book. There is no question of "demonstrating" something such as the immortality of the soul or resurrection of the dead, and above all not to someone who is denying them or rejecting the idea. If it is true that rational demonstration fails to support either the thesis or the antithesis, it is for a fundamental reason that emerges from our texts themselves. Neither the rejection nor the hope that challenges it is a matter of theoretical proof. It has to do with the judgment which each one bears in himself of himself and thanks to which he takes on the entire responsibility for himself. This is why it would be ineffective to try to impose immortality or resurrection on anyone who does not want it—the more so in that there could be no "resurrection of bodies" without a "resurrection of souls," that is, without having overcome the peril of the "second death," so clearly discerned by the most ancient Hermetism, and which postulates the "descent to Hell." For it is from the soul itself, from the celestial Earth of the soul, that the "spiritual flesh" is constituted—the suprasensory and at the same time perfectly concrete *caro spiritualis*. A "dead soul," in the sense that a soul can die, could not be its substance. This connection will be the central thought of the texts and of the authors studied in this book.

These texts together form a progression from one octave to the other of the Iranian spiritual universe, repeating and amplifying the same theme. Here exactly lay the difficulty of the task to which we felt called, because, until now, very little has been written in an attempt to open up a view of the unity of this universe and to show how its component parts are connected. First of all, we had to outline a phenomenology of Mazdean consciousness or, more exactly, of Mazdean angelology, with the personal Figures and archetypes that are its hierophanies. Then, by means of the theme studied here, we had to clear the way leading from Mazdean Iran to Islamic Iran.

Finally, in the second part of the book, in allowing certain authors, whose names and works have remained until now almost totally unknown in the West, to speak for themselves, our intention was to show how certain problems could be shared and a common terminology established. Without such participation, we could not hope for much even from exchanges undertaken with the best will in the world. The pages that have been translated here, both from Persian and Arabic, are extracts from eleven authors, who together cover the period from the twelfth century up to the present day. Their names are well known in Iran, but what can be said for our knowledge of man, of *homo sapiens*, so long as we know nothing of the invisible regions that have been explored nor of the explorers themselves?

Normally, the work of "diffusion" would be preceded by a preliminary study of the material, but unfortunately, in view of the rarity of works in this field, the philosopher-orientalist will in fact be bound for some time to come to take these two tasks on himself. That is why it is impossible to construct an investigation of this nature without furnishing what are commonly called "notes" and which are, in fact, the commentaries without which the whole structure would remain hanging in the air. Nevertheless, we wished to write a book that would be of general interest —that is, to the prepared seeker, who will find in it many themes to study in depth, as well as to him who in eighteenth-century France was called the "honnête homme," the open-minded man to whom the scholar owes consideration, the more so in that his kind is perhaps doomed, owing to contemporary conditions, to disappear.

In what follows there will be a constant recurrence of certain terms that to one reader or another will be a source of irritation; they may be assured that their irritation is shared. However, this irritation has no longer any foundation if we take the terms in question with the genuine simplicity of the texts from which they are translated. The word "theosophy," for example, is a translation of the Arabic *ḥikma ilāhīya* and the Persian *khūdā-dānī*, which themselves are the exact equivalent of the Greek *theosophia.* The terms "esotericism" and "initiation" do not imply any exclusive claim to teach by some self-instituted authority. They refer, respectively, to hidden, suprasensory things, to the discretion which the words themselves suggest in regard to those who, not understanding, scorn them, and to the spiritual birth that causes the perception of those hidden things to open. These terms may have been abused, but we shall be reminded of their rightful use in the context of what follows.

As for the word "Imām," meaning "spiritual guide," this word dominates the form of Islam which will especially concern us here, namely, Shīʿism (also called *Imāmism*) and, above all, Shīʿite Iran. If it is already true to say that cultivated people in the West usually have only an approximate idea of Islamic theology in general, when it comes to Shīʿism, it is to be feared that we are speaking of *terra incognita.* Some pages in the present book (Ch. II, § 1), as well as the translated texts, may suggest what constitutes its essence. But we could not include here an outline of the history of Shīʿism or explain how and why it became the form of Iranian Islam.

Actually, Iranian Islam belies the opinion according to which Islam is too often identified with an ethnic concept, with the past history of a race. Islam is primarily a religious concept. For centuries, and from his youth up, the Iranian has known his national epic poem contained in the "Book of Kings" by Firdawsī. He is aware that there were great kings and even a prophet, Zarathustra-Zoroaster, before Islam. Yet the Shīʿite Imāmology professed by Iran represents the supreme homage that can be paid to the Arabic Prophet and to the members of his Household. The question is one neither of race nor of nation but of religious vision. Again, that is why we would have liked to stress (but cannot do so here) how the relationship between Shīʿism and the principal phenomenon of spiritual Islam, known under the name of Ṣūfism, is regarded in Iran. In any case, suffice it to say that the conditions of the dialogue between Christianity and Islam change completely as soon as the interlocutor represents not legalistic Islam but this spiritual Islam, whether it be that of Ṣūfism or of Shīʿite gnosis.

Even so, the difficulties of approach remain considerable. A Westerner usually takes the terms *muslim* and *mu'min* as synonymous. They are, however, by no means synonymous for a Shīʿite: one can be a *muslim* and profess Islam without yet (nor for that reason alone) being a *mu'min*, that is, a true believer, an adept of the holy Imāms and their doctrine. On his side, the *mu'min* will find it hard to understand immediately the reasons for and import of religious terminology current in the West, where we speak, for example, of the "difficulties of belief"—using the phrase, almost always, with a confessional connotation. This is because the "difficulties" in question depend on a certain concept of philosophy and theology that has accrued during several centuries and, ultimately, on an opposition that is not experienced at all in a milieu where such terms as *ʿārif* and *ʿirfān* are in current use. The latter can be translated respectively as "mystical theosophy" and "mystical gnosis," but these technical equivalents do not exactly preserve the familiar shade of meaning in Arabic of these words, which connote a specific type of spiritual knowledge. But does not the very fact that we have no adequate terminology reveal that we are dealing with something which, for us, is not current?

And this, among other things, is what motivates the use of the term "esotericism" because, in this perspective, the polemics between Western believers and unbelievers are seen to have taken place on a plane of knowledge above which neither side was able to rise. For example, there have been arguments about the miracles described in the New Testament. One side acknowledges, the other rejects the possibility of a "breach of natural laws." Belief and unbelief become locked in the dilemma—history or myth? The only way out is to realize that the first and greatest miracle is the irruption of another world into our knowledge, an irruption that rends the fabric of our categories and their necessities, of our evidences and their norms. But it should be understood that the other world in question is one that cannot be perceived by the organ of ordinary knowledge; that it can be neither proven nor disputed by means of ordinary argumentation; that it is a world so different that it can neither be seen nor perceived except by the organ of "Hūrqalyān" perception.

This other world, with the mode of knowledge it implies, is the one which, as we shall see, has been meditated upon tirelessly throughout the centuries as the "world of Hūrqalyā." It is the "Earth of visions," the Earth which confers on visionary apperceptions their truth, the world through which resurrection comes to pass. This is what will be re-echoed by all our authors. Indeed, this is the world in which real spiritual events "take place," real, however, not in the sense that the physical world is real, nor yet in the sense that events chronologically recorded to "make history" are real, because here the event transcends every historical materialization.

It is an "external world," and yet it is not the physical world. It is a world that teaches us that it is possible to emerge from measurable space without emerging from extent, and that we must abandon homogeneous chronological time in order to enter that qualitative time which is the history of the soul. Finally, it is the world in which we perceive the *spiritual sense* of the written word and of beings—that is, their suprasensory dimension, that meaning which most often seems to us an arbitrary extrapolation, because we confuse it with allegory. We cannot penetrate the "Earth of Hūrqalyā" by rational abstraction nor yet by empirical materialization; it is the place where spirit and body are one, the place where spirit, taking on a body, becomes the *caro spiritualis*, "spiritual corporeity." Everything suggested here by our authors goes, perhaps, very much against the current of contemporary thinking and may well be entirely misunderstood. We might find their brothers in soul, however, among those who have been called the Protestant *Spirituales*, such as Schwenckfeld, Boehme, the Berleburg circle, Oetinger, and others, whose line has been continued to the present day.

But there is a further point to make clear: it was not our intention here, in studying the two complementary aspects, Mazdean Iran and Shī'ite Iran (more exactly, up to the Shaikhī school), to treat this theme from a historical point of view. We shall do no more here than indicate it as a possibility, since we hope later to make it the subject of the fuller study it calls for. If we try to consider what is suggested to us in the following extracts in the light of our accustomed historical dimension, we shall, with the best intentions in the world, be bound to falsify the perspective. For our historical, evolutionary, and linear viewpoint is the result of a one-dimensional mental structure, which serves for determining causes inherent in this level alone, which explains things by reducing them all to this same level; it is limited to a homogeneous time and space in which it places events.

Our authors see things from a different point of view. They postulate several planes of projection. The passage of time is viewed as a cycle; beings and events themselves qualitatively situate their time and space. This being so, we should pay particular attention to *structures* and homologies of structure; what has to emerge is the law of their *isomorphism*. In comparison, discussions conducted on the level of pure historicism are almost always irritating and sterile, for invariably one comes up against a possible "counterexplanation." For example, the question is sometimes raised as to whether Shīʿism is or is not an Iranian phenomenon. There is in any case a Shīʿism with a specifically Iranian structure. We are not concerned to label objects in a showcase or to identify photographs, but to search for a mode of understanding that we have described as a *progressio harmonica.* Any musician, any Gestaltist, will immediately grasp what we mean.

For example, in Mazdaism there is the *var* of Yima, the "hyperborean paradise," and in Ṣūfism and Shīʿism there is the Earth of Hūrqalyā, also in the celestial "Far North." In Mazdaism there are traces of a mystical physiology and the same, vastly amplified, in Shaikhism. Both in Mazdaism and in Suhrawardī's theosophy there are Angels of the Earth, Spenta Armaiti and Daēnā, Figures respectively representing the eternal Sophia; in Shīʿite gnosis we find Fāṭima, person of Light, Daughter of the Prophet, who is also a Figure representing Sophia and the supracelestial Earth. In Mazdaism there is the Saoshyant, or Savior-to-come, surrounded by his companions, while in Shīʿism there is the hidden Imām, surrounded by a mystical body of knights, whose *parousia* will herald the completion of our *Aeon.* This sequence of themes is already an outline of the curve described by the present book. However, this should not be taken to mean that the one version and the other are purely and simply identical. The terms are not identical, but there is an analogy of relationships. Because the Figures exemplify the same archetypes, their identity lies in the function they assume in the midst of homologous wholes.

To pass from one octave to a higher octave is not the same as to pass from one date in time to another, but is a progression to a height or pitch that is qualitatively different. All the elements are changed, yet the form of the melody is the same. Something in the nature of harmonic perception is needed in order to perceive a world of many dimensions.

A philosopher, to whom we were explaining the concept and function of the world of Hūrqalyā according to our authors, remarked: "Finally, then, all phenomenology of the spirit takes place in Hūrqalyā?" It seems certainly that it must be something like that. But we should still add one more remark: as a rule, when discussing past events, we fix them in the dimension of the past and are unable to agree on their nature or their significance. Our authors suggest that if the past were really what we believe it to be, that is, completed and closed, it would not be the grounds of such vehement discussions. They suggest that all our *acts of understanding* are so many recommencements, re-*iterations* of events still unconcluded. Each one of us, willy-nilly, is the initiator of events in "Hūrqalyā," whether they abort in its hell or bear fruit in its paradise. While we believe that we are looking at what is past and unchangeable, we are in fact consummating our own future. Our authors will show us how a whole region in Hūrqalyā is peopled, *post mortem*, by our imperatives and wishes—that is to say, by that which directs our acts of understanding as well as our behavior. It follows that the whole of the underlying metaphysics is that of an unceasing recurrence of the Creation (*tajaddud*); not a metaphysics of the *ens* and the *esse*, but of the *esto*, of *being* in the imperative. But the event is put, or put again, in the imperative only because it is itself the *iterative* form of *being* by which it is raised to the reality of an event. Perhaps, then, we shall glimpse the full gravity of a spiritual event and of the spiritual sense of events "perceived in Hūrqalyā," when at last consciousness rediscovers the Giver of what is given. Everything is strange, say our authors, when one sets foot on that Earth where the Impossible is in fact accomplished. For all our mental constructions, all our imperatives, all our wishes, even the love which is the most consubstantial with our being—all that would be nothing but *metaphor* without the interworld of Hūrqalyā, the world in which our symbols are, so to speak, taken literally.

March 1960

Publisher's Note

The system of transliteration in this volume conforms to the style of the Library of Congress catalogue, and differs from that used in the other two volumes by Henry Corbin published in this series.

NOTE ON ILLUSTRATIONS

The design of the Frontispiece is reproduced from a silk textile in the collection of the Cleveland Museum of Art, purchased from the J. H. Wade Fund. It also appears in a book by Gaston Wiet entitled *Soieries persanes* (Mémoires de l'Institut d'Egypte, Vol. 52, Cairo, 1947, Pl. XI and pp. 55–63). The original figure on silk was discovered in 1925, together with many other extraordinary pieces, when certain graves accidentally came to light in the hills adjoining the sanctuary of Shahr-Bānū, not far from Ray (the Rhages of the Book of Tobias), a few miles to the south of Teheran.

It can be inferred from the place of the discovery that this was a precious material offered by friends or relatives for wrapping the body of a deceased person (cf. Issa Behnam, in *Revue de la Faculté des Lettres de l'Université de Téhéran*, October 1956). It is said to date from the fifth century (eleventh century C.E.) and was found in a state of perfect preservation. Iconographically, it is interesting as a motif in the Sāsānid style on material dating from the great Islamic period. The site of the discovery makes it even more interesting, for, according to Iranian tradition, the princess Shahr-Bānū, daughter of the last Sāsānid ruler, Yazdgard III, became the wife of Ḥusayn ibn ʿAlī, the Third Imām of the Shīʿites, and here we find an expression, iconographic and topographic, of this union of Mazdean Iran and Shīʿite Iran.

Beyond doubt the design represents the theme of the ascent to Heaven: a youth, with a royal head of hair as a halo, is carried off into space by a great, fantastic bird that holds him enclosed in its breast. Certain stylized details suggest that this bird be identified, not merely as a two-headed eagle, but as the *ʿanqā'* (the phoenix) or sīmurgh which, already in the Avesta as in the later Persian mystical epics, assumes so many symbolic functions, even becoming the emblem of the Holy Spirit. It would be useless to multiply examples based on outer analogies (which would lead us far afield, even to the abduction of Ganymede, for instance). But it is of direct interest to draw attention to an episode in the heroic epic of Iran, namely, the abduction of Zāl, son of Sām, who was nurtured and reared by the bird Sīmurgh. Suhrawardī developed at great length in one of his mystical romances the spiritual meaning of this episode. And in this sense it comes finally into full accord with the *ḥadīth* which, without further reference, can best lead us to meditation on the symbolism of this image. The *ḥadīth* in question alludes to the *green Bird* whose breast offers shelter, in the other world, to the spirits of the "witnesses of truth." As interpreted by Simnānī, one of the Iranian Ṣūfī masters, this is an allusion to the formation and the birth of the "resurrection body." Thus the hieratic movement of being taken up to Heaven, which the Iranian artist has represented here, reveals the meaning of what Wiet so rightly calls its "triumphant gravity."

We should not omit pointing out that exactly the same motif, with all the features justifying reference to the *ḥadīth* interpreted by Simnānī, figures among the paintings adorning the ceiling of the Palatine chapel at Palermo (cf. Ugo Monneret de Villard, *Le Pitture musulmane al soffito della Cappella Palatina in Palermo*, pp. 47–48 and figs. 52–55, 245). Whether or not the Palermo painters came from Fāṭimid Egypt, it is known that they were inspired by themes originating for the most part in Iran, and often, as in the present case, did no more than reproduce them.

The plate facing page 32 is from a Persian anthology, a manuscript dated Shiraz A.D. 1398 in the Türk ve Islam Müzesi, Istanbul, and is reproduced from Basil Gray, *Persian Painting* (Geneva: Skira, 1956) by permission of the publisher. It is discussed on p. 31.

PART ONE

SPIRITUAL BODY AND CELESTIAL EARTH

I THE MAZDEAN *IMAGO TERRAE*

1. "*The Earth Is an Angel*"

In a book entitled *On the Question of the Soul*, G. T. Fechner tells how on a spring morning, while a transfiguring light cast a halo over the face of the earth, he was struck not merely by the esthetic idea, but by the vision and concrete evidence that "the Earth is an Angel, such a gorgeously real Angel, so like a flower!" But, he added with melancholy, nowadays an experience like this is dismissed as *imaginary*. It is taken for granted that the earth is a spherical body; as for getting to know more about what it is, this is just a matter of research in the mineralogical collections.[1]

This brief lyrical confession prompts us to reflect on two points. In the first place, we have to remember that Fechner himself wrote a *Zend-Avesta*, which is his most important philosophical work; in it he displays throughout the resources of analogical reasoning, counter perhaps to the demands of strict philosophy, but manifesting in this way his aptitude for perceiving symbols. Although the book, with the exception of its title, has nothing in common with the sacred book of Zoroastrian Mazdaism, it is nevertheless a fact that the *cognitio matutina* by which the Earth is revealed to our philosopher as an "Angel" is completely in accord with the doctrine and practice of the Avesta, in which, for example, we read the following (in the ritual of the twenty-eighth day of the month): "We are celebrating this liturgy in honor of the Earth which is an Angel."[2]

There remains, of course, a certain lack of precision in Fechner's vision. He seems to have identified the face of the earth, haloed by the spring light, with the actual effigy of the Angel, when in fact the telluric glory is the liturgical creation, the hierurgy of that Earth Angel whose features are perceived as a glorified human image. But such exact perception presupposes the perfect exercise of this faculty, the degradation and neglect of which is exactly what Fechner deplores. And this is the second point to remember. The fact that the perception of the Earth as an Angel can be classed as imaginary, as unreal, signifies and indicates that this way of perceiving and meditating the Earth is, on the contrary, linked with a psycho-spiritual structure which we have to rediscover in order to bring out the value of the means of knowledge it offers.

Essentially this mode of perception implies an intellectual faculty that is not limited to the sole use of conceptual abstraction nor to the sensory perception of physical data. That is why Fechner's avowal, to the very extent that it is a valid reminder of the Mazdean angelology, calls on us to link together two equally inseparable questions: that of the Mazdean perception of the Earth, as it arises in the perspective of an angelology, and correlatively, that of the mode of apprehension of beings and things which it presupposes and which differs entirely from the only one acknowledged by our positive science and, incidentally, by our geography.

To come face to face with the Earth not as a conglomeration of physical facts but in the person of its Angel is an essentially psychic event which can "take place" neither in the world of impersonal abstract concepts nor on the plane of mere sensory data. The Earth has to be perceived not by the senses, but through a primordial Image and, inasmuch as this Image carries the features of a personal figure, it will prove to "symbolize with" the very Image of itself which the soul carries in its innermost depths. The perception of the Earth Angel will come about in an intermediate universe which is neither that of the Essences of philosophy nor that of the sensory data on which the work of positive science is based, but which is a universe of archetype-Images, experienced as so many personal presences. In recapturing the intentions on which the constitution of this universe depend, in which the Earth is represented, meditated, and encountered in the person of its Angel, we discover that it is much less a matter of answering questions concerning essences ("what is it?") than questions concerning persons ("who is it?" or "to whom does it correspond?"), for example, *who* is the Earth? *who* are the waters, the plants, the mountains? or, *to whom* do they correspond? The answer to these questions causes an Image to appear and this Image invariably corresponds to the presence of a certain state. This is why we have to recapture here the phenomenon of the Earth as an angelophany or mental apparition of its Angel in the fundamental angelology of Mazdaism as a whole, in that which gives its cosmology and its physics a structure such that they include an answer to the question, "who?"

To forestall any misunderstanding and make clear the full significance of the term angelology, which we require in order to think the Mazdean hierophany of the Earth, we have also to remember this. Angelology is one of the characteristic features of Zoroastrian Mazdaism, for which reason it can neither be reduced to an abstract and monolithic type of monotheism, nor invalidated by what people have tried to interpret as a return to the "ancient gods," or a restoration of pre-Zoroastrian polytheism. A spiritual morphology, the aim of which is to restore and to valorize effectively lived devotion, demands that we comprehend the canonical Avesta as a whole, or at least that part of it which has reached us, namely, the ritual which preserves in its center the Psalms (*Gāthās*) of Zarathustra, and is completed by the commentaries and traditions in middle Iranian (Pahlavi) and in Persian. Here again, when the believer is reciting his Bible or when the liturgy is being celebrated, the objections justified by historical stratifications would appear to be wide of the mark. In always wanting to know "where" things "come from" one wanders about finally in vain pursuit of a succession of hypotheses.

If, on the other hand, we ask ourselves, "to what does this lead?" the soul, on being questioned, can at least give us irrefutable evidence of what it wished. The soul cannot be explained; it is the soul itself which is the principle of every explanation and the key to it. This is why, for many centuries, Mazdean piety has recognized the equivalent of its *Yazatas* (the "Adorable Ones") in the figures of Angels and Archangels (*firishtagān* in Persian). Of course, their ontological status is quite different from that of the biblical or Qur'ānic angels; they are neither servants nor messengers, but rather figures homologous to the *Dii-Angeli* of Proclus. On this point I am convinced that Neoplatonism (which it has long been fashionable to disparage) was infinitely closer to Iranian angelology, and to a better understanding of the theurgical and demiurgical role of its heavenly entities than the philsophical improvisations in which religious historians are apt to indulge when they are short of categories. We have an exact tradition to follow if we wish to understand, for example, what the Angels of the Earth proclaim to Mazdean piety.

Here it is absolutely necessary that we recall the general schema of Mazdean cosmology, that is, the general schema that is the structure of the heavenly pleroma of light. Unfortunately, we can only restate it here in broad outline. The Mazdean vision divides thinkable totality into an infinite *height* of Light in which there dwells, for all eternity, Ohrmazd (the Avestan Ahura Mazda), the "Lord Wisdom"; and an unfathomable *abyss* of Darkness that conceals the Antagonist, the Counterpower of negation, disintegration, and death, Ahriman (the Avestan Angra Mainyu). Between the Power of Light and the Counterpower of Darkness there is no common ground, no compromise of coexistence, but a merciless battle of which our Earth, together with all visible Creation, is the field, until the consummation of the *Aeon*, the *apokatastasis* or "restoration" which will put an end to the mixture (*gumechishn*) by the separation (*vicharishn*) that will cast the demonic Counterpowers back into their abyss.

To be sure, this view of things is by no means the childish concept to which, as we frequently see nowadays, certain writers, pressed for time or ill-informed, reduce something they believe to be now Mazdaism, now Manicheism, describing it as incomplete and rudimentary. This view has nothing at all to do with professing that the beings who surround us are either "white" or "black." The state in which we live is precisely one of "mixture." What is in question is a certain way of understanding this "mixture" and a way of being toward it, which differs profoundly from that which is inspired in us by our ready-made and rarely challenged judgments.

Now, it is a characteristic feature of the Zoroastrian view that the Lord Wisdom should always appear surrounded by six Powers of Light with which he himself (as the first, or as the seventh) forms the supreme divine Heptad. On the pretext that what is in question is a so-called "primitive" thought, there have been occasional attempts to reduce these Powers to "aspects" of the supreme divinity, without taking into account that such a modalism would, on the contrary, imply highly developed theological speculation, and that in any case the impulse of piety has nothing to do with these subtle abstractions and distinctions, but is directed toward heavenly Persons, the fascination of whose beauty has been experienced and whose power has been acknowledged as effective. These are the Seven Powers who are designated as the *Amahraspands* (the Avestan *Amerta Spenta*), a name that is currently translated as "the Holy Immortals"; their holiness is understood not as a canonical attribute, but as a transitive, active, and activating Energy that communicates being, establishes it, and causes it to superabound in all beings.[3] These are the Seven Powers who are also generally designated as the Zoroastrian Archangels.

Yasht XIX of the Avesta (that is, one of the liturgical hymns with a characteristic antiphonal structure) describes in wondrous terms their splendor and the mystery of their relationship. The hymn celebrates these Archangels, "all Seven of whom have the same thought, the same word, the same action . . . they see each others' souls engaged in meditating thoughts of righteousness, in meditating words of righteousness, in meditating actions of righteousness, in meditating the Abode of Hymns,[4] and they have paths of light by which to travel to the liturgies [celebrated in their honor] . . . who created and govern the creatures of Ahura Mazda, who formed them and direct them, who are their protectors and their liberators."[5]

So there is, among the Seven Archangels, a sort of *unio mystica*, which makes the divine Heptad as different from the current ways of describing monotheism as from those referring to polytheism; we would do better to speak of a *kathenotheism*, in the sense that *each* of the Figures of the Heptad can be meditated in turn as actualizing the totality of the relations common to the others. In the texts we can follow a certain oscillation which sometimes enhances the primacy of the Lord Wisdom among the Seven, and sometimes stresses his *unio mystica* with the (six) other Powers of Light.[6] Thus, in the Pahlavi texts, the frequency with which Ohrmazd, initiating Zarathustra his prophet, refers to: "We, the Archangels"[7] corresponds, in the Avesta itself, to the use of the word *Mazda* in the plural, "the Lords Wisdom,"[8] to designate the Amahraspands as a whole. In comparison, we can recall how, in Philo, the Logos—if not God Himself—is called by the name of Archangel, because he is Ἄρχον Ἀγγέλων.[9]

Traditionally, in mental iconography, as also no doubt in real iconography,[10] the divine Heptad is figured as divided into two groups: three Archangels represented as masculine on the right of Ohrmazd, three feminine Archangels on his left. Ohrmazd himself reunites their twofold nature, since it is said of him that he was at one and the same time the father and the mother of Creation.[11] All the Seven together produced created beings by a liturgical act, that is, by celebrating the heavenly Liturgy.[12] Each of the Seven Powers of Light, by virtue of the Energy that overflows from its being, brings forth the fraction of the beings that in the totality of creation represents its personal hierurgy, and which for this reason can be designated by its own name.

As his own hierurgy, as the object of his creative and provident activity, Ohrmazd has taken the human being, or more precisely that part of humanity that has chosen to respond on earth for the beings of Light.[13] Of the three masculine Archangels: *Vohu Manah* (excellent thought, Vohuman in *Pahlavi*, Bahman in *Persian*) has undertaken the protection of the whole animal creation; *Arta Vahishta* (perfect existence, Artvahisht, Urdībihisht), the government of Fire in all its different manifestations; *Xshathra Vairya* (desirable reign, Shathrīvar, Shahrīvar), the government of the metals. As for the three feminine Archangels: *Spenta Armaiti* (Spendarmat, Isfandārmuz) has as her own hierurgy the Earth as a form of existence whose Image is Wisdom, and woman regarded as a being of light; to *Haarvatat* (integrity, Khurdād) belong the Waters, the aquatic world in general; to *Amertāt* (immortality, Murdād) belong the plants, the entire vegetable kingdom. These are the hierurgical relations that indicate to human beings precisely where and how to meet the invisible Powers of Light, that is, by cooperating with them for the salvation of the creatural region which is dependent on their particular providence.[14]

In this work the supreme Archangels are helped in the first place by the many Yazatas (*Īzad* in Persian, literally the "Adorable Ones," who are the objects of a liturgy, a *Yasna*); these are the Angels proper to Mazdaism, and the notion of their cooperation with the Amahraspands suggests a striking convergence with the angelology of Neoplatonism.[15] Among them is Zamyāt, the feminine Angel of the Earth, as *Dea Terrestris* and telluric Glory, who cooperates with the Archangel Amertāt. Some people have regarded her as a mere doublet of Spenta Armaiti; in the end we shall see that their functions and their persons are distinct.[16] Moreover, all the Celestials are Yazatas, including Ohrmazd and the Amahraspands, although all the Yazatas are not Amahraspands, with respect to whom they form a kind of subordinate hierarchy. Finally, there are the countless multitude of feminine celestial entities called *Fravarti* (literally, "those who have chosen," meaning those who have chosen to fight in order to come to the help of Ohrmazd),[17] who are at one and the same time the heavenly archetypes of beings and their respective tutelary angels; metaphysically they are no less necessary than the Yazatas, since without their help Ohrmazd could not have defended his creation against the destructive invasion of the demonic Powers.[18] They presuppose a universal structure of being and of beings according to Mazdean ontology. Every physical or moral entity, every complete being or group of beings belonging to the world of Light, including Ohrmazd, the Amahraspands, and the Īzads, has its Fravarti.[19]

What they announce to earthly beings is, therefore, an essentially dual structure that gives to each one a heavenly archetype or Angel, whose earthly counterpart he is.[20] In this sense, there is a *dualitude* even more essential to Mazdean cosmology than is the *dualism* of Light-Darkness, which is its most commonly remembered aspect; this dualism merely expresses the dramatic phase undergone by the Creation of Light when invaded and blemished by the demonic Powers, and is a dualism which interprets this negativity without compromise, without reducing the evil to a *privatio boni*. As for the essential dualitude, it conjoins one being of light with another being of light; but never can a being of light be complemented by a being of darkness, were it its own shadow: the property of bodies of light on the transfigured Earth is precisely not to "cast a shadow" and in the pleroma it is always "midday."[21]

This dual structure establishes a personal relationship that parallels that other basic relationship expressed in Mazdean cosmology by the distinction between the *mēnōk* state and the *gētīk* state of beings. This distinction is not exactly between the intelligible and the sensory, nor simply between the incorporeal and the corporeal (for the Celestial Powers have very subtle bodies of light);[22] the distinction is rather a matter of the relationship between the invisible and the visible, the subtle and the dense, the heavenly and the earthly, provided it is clearly understood that the *gētīk* state (earthly, material) in itself by no means implies a degradation of being, but that it was itself, before the Ahrimanian invasion, as it will be thereafter, a glorious state of light, peace, and incorruptibility. Every being can be thought of in its *mēnōk* state, as well as in its *gētīk* state (for example, in its heavenly state, the earth is called *zam*; in its empirical, material, ponderable state it is called *zamīk*, or *zamīn* in Persian).[23]

Here precisely we arrive at that particular mode of perception of beings and things which, by reaching the possibility of understanding no longer simply *what* they are, but *who* they are, will allow us to meet them in the person of their Angel. It is quite evident that the mental vision of the Angel of the Earth, for example, is not a sensory experience. If, by logical habit, we classify this fact as imaginary, the question nonetheless remains as to what can justify an identification of what is imaginary with what is arbitrary and unreal, the question as to whether representations deriving from physical perception are the only ones to be considered as *real* knowledge, whether physically verifiable events alone can be evaluated as facts. We must ask ourselves whether the invisible action of forces that have their purely physical expression in natural processes may not bring into play psychic energies that have been neglected or paralyzed by our habits, and directly touch an Imagination which, far from being arbitrary invention, corresponds to that Imagination which the alchemists called *Imaginatio vera* and which is the *astrum in homine*.[24]

The active Imagination thus induced will not produce some arbitrary, even lyrical, construction standing between us and "reality," but will, on the contrary, function directly as a faculty and organ of knowledge just as *real* as—if not more real than—the sense organs. However, it will perceive in the manner proper to it: The organ is not a sensory faculty but an *archetype-Image* that it possessed from the beginning; it is not something derived from any outer perception. And the property of this Image will be precisely that of effecting the transmutation of sensory data, their resolution into the purity of the subtle world, in order to restore them as symbols to be deciphered, the "key" being imprinted in the soul itself. Such perception through the Imagination is therefore equivalent to a "dematerialization"; it changes the physical datum impressed upon the senses in a pure mirror, a spiritual transparency; thus it is that the Earth, and the things and beings of the Earth, raised to incandescence, allow the apparition of their Angels to penetrate to the visionary intuition. This being so, the authenticity of the Event and its full reality consist essentially of this visionary act and of the apparition vouchsafed by it. And this is the profound meaning of what, in the history of dogma, is called *docetism*, concerning which the same errors have been tirelessly and monotonously repeated.

Thus is constituted this intermediary world, a world of archetypal celestial Figures which the active Imagination alone is able to apprehend. This Imagination does not *construct* something unreal, but *unveils* the hidden reality; its action is, in short, that of the *ta'wīl*, the spiritual exegesis practised by all the Spirituals of Islam, whose special quality is that of alchemical meditation: to occultate the apparent, to manifest the hidden.[25] It is in this intermediary world that those known as the *'urafā'*, the mystical gnostics, have meditated tirelessly, *gnosis* here being taken to mean that perception which grasps the object not in its objectivity, but as a sign, an intimation, an announcement that is finally the soul's annunciation to itself.

When Suhrawardī, in the twelfth century, restored in Iran the philosophy of Light and the angelology of ancient Persia, his schema of the world was structured on the world of archetypal Images, an intermediary world in which transmutations of the ephemeral into spiritual symbols take place and which, by virtue of this, is the world where the resurrection of bodies is effected.[26] Indeed, just as the body of the mortal Adam was created from the material Earth, so the soul "substantiates" its resurrection body from the heavenly Earth, which it projects and meditates upon. The connection is rigorous. The active Imagination is the organ of metamorphoses: the transmutation of the Earth into the substance of the resurrection body depends upon its manner of meditating upon the Earth. Such meditation, as the source of the soul's activities, is the organ of this birth. The very idea of *body* having thus been made independent of representations of the body of perishable flesh, leads inevitably to the idea of this mystical Earth of Hūrqalyā which we shall see as governing the spirituality of *Shaikhism*. The latter is a school that arose in the midst of Iranian Shī'ism at the end of the eighteenth century, and this idea remains without doubt the truly creative contribution of that school in our time.

The task now will be to seek out how and under what conditions the figure of the Angel takes shape exactly at the point where the data of sensory perception are raised, as it were, to the diaphanous state by the active Imagination (when the *gētīk* is perceived in its *mēnōk*). This task is chiefly to make it clear what kind of an organ this archetype-Image is, through which the active Imagination, by perceiving things directly, effects their transmutation; how it is that once this transmutation is effected, things reflect its own Image to the soul, and how this self-recognition of the soul brings into being a spiritual science of the Earth and of earthly things, so that these things are known in their Angel, as foreseen by the visionary intuition of Fechner.

Here there comes into play an Energy that sacralizes both the *mēnōk* state and also the *gētīk* state of being; the representation of this Energy is so basic to the entire Mazdean view of the world that it was wholly incorporated into the philosophical restoration that was the work of Suhrawardī.[27] This Energy is operative from the initial instant of the formation of the world until the final act announced and forecast in the technical term *Frashkart*, which designates the transfiguration to be accomplished at the end of the *Aeon* by the Saoshyants or Saviors issuing from the race of Zarathustra. This is the Energy that is designated by the term *Xvarnah* in the Avesta (*khurrah*, *farrah* in Persian). Several translators have attempted to define it, to convey all its shades of meaning.[28] The term "Light of Glory" seems to us to restore what is essential, if at the same time we keep in mind the Greek equivalents, already given above: Δόξα and Τύχη, Glory and Destiny.[29] It is the all-luminous substance, the pure luminescence of which Ohrmazd's creatures were constituted at their origin. "From it Ahura Mazda has created the many and good . . . beautiful, marvelous . . . creatures, full of life, resplendent" (Yasht XIX, 10). It is the Energy of sacral light which gives coherence to their being, which measures at the same time the power and the destiny imparted to a being, which ensures victory to the beings of light over the corruption and the death introduced into the Ohrmazdean creation by the demonic Powers of darkness.[30] This energy is thus associated essentially with eschatological hopes; so, in the liturgical chant dedicated to *Zamyāt*, the Angel of the Earth, the mention of the creatures of light, whose attribute is this Light of Glory, calls forth each time, in refrain, the following doxology: "Of such a kind that they will make a new world, freed from old age and death, from decomposition and corruption, eternally living, eternally growing, possessing power at will, when the dead will rise again, when immortality will come to the living, and when the world will renew itself as desired" (Yasht XIX, 11 ff.).

In iconography it is represented by the luminous halo, the *Aura Gloriae*, which haloes the kings and priests of the Mazdean religion, and later by transference, the figures of Buddhas and Bodhisattvas, as well as the heavenly figures of primitive Christian art. Finally, a passage in the great *Bundahishn*, the Mazdean book of Genesis, fixes as precisely as one could wish the direction in which this imagery is tending, when it identifies *Xvarnah*, that Light which is Glory and Destiny, with the *soul* itself.[31] So this, finally and essentially, is the fundamental Image, in which and by which the soul understands itself and perceives its energies and its powers. In Mazdeism it represents what depth psychology has taught us to distinguish as the archetypal Image; here it is the *Imago Animae.* And perhaps we are thus approaching the secret structure revealed and made possible by the vision of the Earth in its Angel.

That Light of Glory, which is the archetype-Image of the Mazdean soul, is in fact the organ by which the soul perceives the world of light that is of the same nature as itself, and through which, originally and directly, the soul effects the transmutation of physical data, the very data which for us are "positive," but which for the soul would be "insignificant." This is the very Image that the soul projects into beings and things, raising them to the incandescence of that victorial Fire with which the Mazdean soul has set the whole of creation ablaze, and which it has perceived above all in the dawns flaming on the mountain peaks, in the very place where it was expecting the revelation of its own destiny, and the Transfiguration of the Earth.

In short, it is by this projection of its own Image that the soul, in effecting the transmutation of the material Earth, also establishes from the beginning an *Imago Terrae* that reflects and announces its own Image to the soul, that is to say, an Image whose *Xvarnah* is also the soul's own *Xvarnah*. It is at that point —in and by this double reflection of the same Light of Glory— that the Angel of the Earth is revealed to the mental sight, that is to say, that the Earth is perceived in the *person* of its Angel. And this is what is admirably and profoundly expressed in a feature of Mazdean angelology, barely pondered upon until now, when it is pointed out that the Amahraspand Spenta Armaiti, the feminine Archangel of earthly existence, is the "mother" of *Daēnā*.

Daēnā is, in fact, the feminine Angel who typifies the transcendent or celestial "I"; she appears to the soul at the dawn following the third night after its departure from this world; she is its Glory and its Destiny, its *Aeon*. The meaning of this indication, therefore, is that the substance of the celestial "I" or Resurrection Body is engendered and formed from the celestial Earth, that is, from the Earth perceived and meditated in its Angel. What it also means is that the destiny of the Earth entrusted to the transfigurative power of the souls of light leads to the fulfillment of these souls, and that this is reciprocal. And such is the profound meaning of the Mazdean prayer, many times repeated in the course of the liturgies: "May we be among those who are to bring about the Transfiguration of the Earth" (Yasna XXX, 9).

The mystery of this *Imago Animae* projecting the *Imago Terrae*, and reciprocally the mystery of this archetype-Image of the Earth "substantiating" the formation of the future total I, is expressed, therefore, in angelological terms in the relationship referred to above. Spenta Armaiti, who in the Pahlavi texts is interpreted as perfect Thought, silent Meditation, and whose name, excellently translated by Plutarch as *Sophia*, lights the path of Mazdean sophiology—Spenta Armaiti is the "mother" of Daēnā, and at the same time the one concerning whom the Mazdean believer, on his initiation at the age of fifteen, is taught to profess: "My mother is Spendarmat, Archangel of the Earth, and my father is Ohrmazd, the Lord Wisdom."[32] In what is here the *principium relationis* we can perceive something like a Mazdean *sacramentum Terrae*; in its essence, and from the very name Spenta Armaiti Sophia, it can be described as a *geosophy*, that is to say as being the *Sophianic* mystery of the Earth, whose consummation will be its eschatological Transfiguration (*Frash-*

kart). What we still have to formulate precisely here in bold outline is the metamorphosis of the face of the Earth as seen by the organ of the Mazdean active Imagination.

The perception of the Sophianic mystery of the Earth, of geosophy, obviously cannot take place in the framework of positive geography. It presupposes a visionary geography, what has been rightly called a "landscape of *Xvarnah*," that is, a landscape prefiguring the *Frashkart*. This is not spread over profane, previously determined space, but is concentrated or concentrates a sacral space *in medio mundi*, in the center of the vision contemplated in the presence of the visionary soul (or of the visionary community), and this space does not need to be *situated*, since it is of itself *situative*. Geographical features, mountains for instance, are here no longer merely physical features; they have a significance for the soul; they are psycho-cosmic aspects. The events that take place there consist in the very seeing of these aspects; they are psychic events. So the paradise of Yima, the paradise of the archetypes, exists in this center because it is the meeting place of the Heavenly Beings and the Earthly Beings.

Such is the Image of the Earth that the cartographical method of the ancient Iranians will reveal to us. Just as a landscape of *Xvarnah* cannot be expressed by representative art, but has essentially to do with symbolic art, so this map making does not lead to reproducing the outlines of a continent. Rather, it shapes an instrument for meditation that makes it possible mentally to reach the center, the *medium mundi*, or rather to take position there directly. Only a visionary geography can be the scene of visionary events, because it itself takes part in them; plants, water, mountains are transmuted into symbols, that is, perceived by the organ of an Image which itself *is* the presence of a visionary state. Like the heavenly Figures, the earthly landscapes then appear haloed with the Light of Glory, restored to their paradisal purity, and the visions of Zarathustra, his meetings with Ohrmazd and the Archangels, take place and are "Imagined" in a setting of mountains blazing in the dawn and of heavenly waters in which grow the plants of immortality.

2. *The Earth of the Seven Keshvars*

The schema of the surface of the earth, as projected here by the active Imagination, is as follows.[33] In the beginning, the Earth was established as a continuous whole, but, because of oppression by the demonic Powers, it was divided into seven *keshvars* [*kishvar*] (Avestan *karshvar*). This word should be understood as representing something analogous to the Latin *orbis*: these keshvars are *zones* of *Terra firma*, rather than "climates." Not only is the image not the same etymologically, but it is advisable to forestall confusion with the division into climates properly so called, which will come later.

There is the central keshvar, called Xvaniratha (which means something like "luminous wheel"),[34] the extent of which in itself alone is equal to that of all the six other keshvars, which are arranged around it and separated one from another by the cosmic ocean that surrounds them. There is one eastern keshvar, one western keshvar, two to the north, two to the south. The keshvar on the eastern side is called Savahi; the one on the western side, Arezahi; the two keshvars to the south are Fradadhafshu and Vidadhafshu; the two to the north are Vourubareshti and Vourjareshti. The mythical ocean surrounding and dividing them is called Vourukasha. As to their situation, this is deduced astronomically in relation to the keshvar which *is* the center, whose presence, therefore, has the quality of *situating* space, before itself being *situated in* that space. In other words, it is not a matter of a preexisting, homogeneous, and *quantitative* space *in* which regions are distributed but the typical structure of a *qualitative* space.

The eastern keshvar, Savahi, extends from the point where the sun rises on the longest day to the point where it rises on the shortest day. The two southern keshvars extend from this last point to the point where the sun sets on the shortest day. From there to the point where the sun sets on the longest day extends the western climate, Arezahi. Finally the two northern keshvars extend from this last point to where the sun rises on the longest day. The names of the six keshvars that surround the central climate of Xvaniratha actually correspond to *mythical* regions (Fig. 1). For this reason it has been possible to take

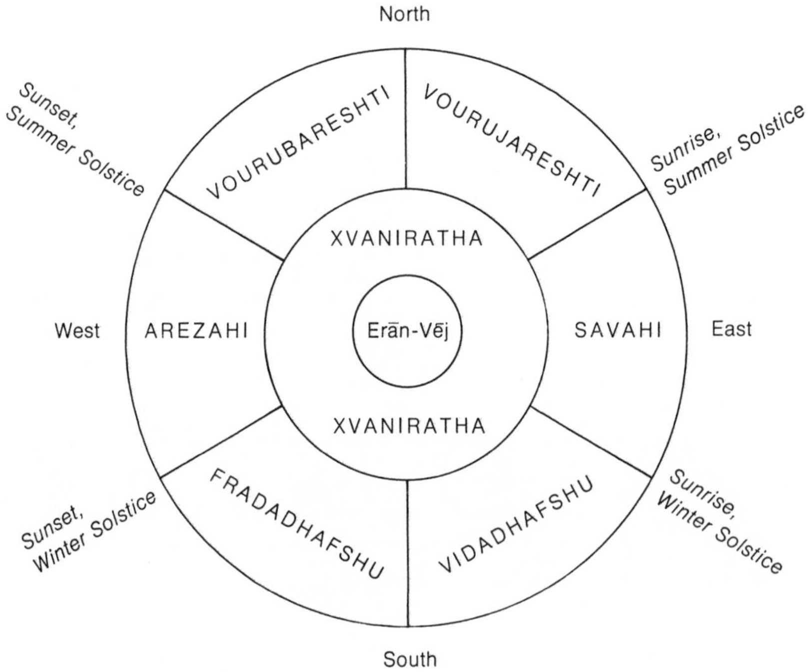

Figure 1. Diagram of the seven mythic *keshvars.*

them as originally referring to a celestial topography later applied to terrestrial localities; thus lakes and mountains of the Earth would be named after their celestial archetypes. As for the significance of the names of these keshvars, we can divine it from the names of the six Saoshyants (Saviors) that correspond to them symmetrically, that is, from the names of the six heroes who, each in his own respective keshvar, will cooperate with the last of the Saoshyants in the transfiguration of the world.[35]

§2. *The Seven Keshvars*

As we have just said, the arrangement of these keshvars corresponding to mythical regions does not confirm the data of positive geography, but gives shape to the *Imago Terrae* projected by the imaginative perception. This being so, it is no longer possible today, as it was in the beginning, for humans to pass from one keshvar to another.[36]

Airyanem Vaejah (Pahlavi *Ērān-Vēj*), the cradle or seed of the Aryans (= Iranians), is in Xvaniratha at the center of the central keshvar. There it was that the Kayānids, the heroes of legend, were created; there, the Mazdean religion was founded and from there spread into the other keshvars; there will be born the last of the Saoshyants, who will reduce Ahriman to impotence and bring about the resurrection and the existence to come.

In its turn, Xvaniratha, which represents the totality of geographic space now accessible to man, although it is only one of the seven parts of the inhabited Earth,[37] was later divided into seven regions, according to a plan in which a central circle represents the land of Iran, around which are grouped six other circles, but this time tangent to one another and of equal radius. This was the method of circular representation that the Iranian geographers of the Sassanid period transmitted to the Arabs; Yāqūt, for instance, working from ancient data, expressly attributes this method of geographical representation to Zoroaster (Fig. 2).[38]

This method is exactly what allows us to discover an entirely appropriate way of imagining and meditating the Earth.[39] In fact, it determines a structure independent of all systems of spatial coordinates: "to posit an origin is all it requires."[40] In contemplating this structure, one's attention converges toward the center and is always called back there, since the location, direction, and orientation of the other keshvars are determined by the center and originate from it (in order to grasp the contrast, it suffices to compare it with the cartographical method of Ptolemy, in which climates are represented by parallel belts ranging outward from the equator). The entire structure, therefore, is ordered in respect to this center-origin. In whatever place

I. *Mazdean* Imago Terrae

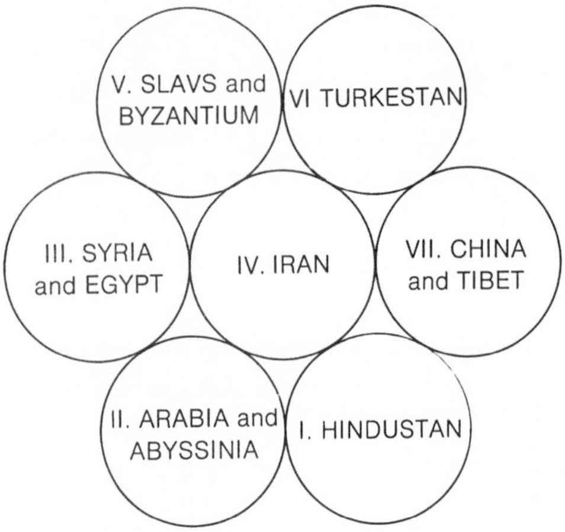

Figure 2. The seven geographic *keshvars* according to Biruni (10th century).

according to positive geography we have to situate the primitive history of the Iranians—whether to the east in central Asia or to the west in Azerbaijan—the mental process of remembering is the same: the Events took place and are remembered in Ērān-Vēj, that is, at the *center*, which is at the same time the *origin*. The presence of the subject at the center is not a *situated* presence but a *situative* presence. *In medio mundi* the soul is no longer bound to spatial coordinates. Instead of "falling into," of having to *be situated in* a predetermined space, the soul itself "spatializes," is always the origin of the spatial references and determines their structure. That is why we find here, not an empirical representation, but an archetypal figure.

There are other possible examples of this figure, which always tend to establish the soul in the center or lead it back there, because it is not in dispersion but in concentration that the *Imago Terrae* can reflect its own Image back to the soul, or reciprocally, that the soul can fix its meditation on the archetype-Image. This was, for example, the meaning of the art and structure of gardens in Iran (it is known that our word *paradise* originated from a Medean word, *pairidaeza*).[41] That is why it can be said that the representation of the Earth with its seven keshvars as an archetype-Figure is an instrument for meditation. It is offered as a *mandala*. It guides a movement of thought that travels, not on a syllogistic or dialectical track, but as in the way of the *ta'wīl*, the *exegesis* of symbols, a spiritual exegesis leading back to the origin, which is the *center*,[42] there precisely where the apparent can be occultated and the hidden manifested (just as in alchemy, as noted above). This, indeed, is the real transmutation of what is written (whether in a book or in the cosmos) into symbols; what is written is raised to incandescence and the hidden significance shines through the covering, which becomes transparent. From this point we can grasp the connection of such a cartography with the events of a visionary geography, the geography of a world that secretes its own light, like those Byzantine mosaics whose gold illumines the space they encompass, or like the icons or landscapes of some Persian school, where the red-gold background transfigures the colors; or like the paradise of Yima, *in medio mundi*, and also the Earth of Hūrqalyā, on which we shall dwell at length in the following pages.

From this point, we can pass beyond the level on which was posed one of the most irritating questions, which tormented several generations of orientalists: Where did the Zoroastrian preaching take place? Where was Ērān-Vēj, since it was in Ērān-Vēj that Zarathustra had his visions and began to teach? Today most orientalists take for granted that the place of his preaching (which we can still hear in reading the *Gāthās*), was in central Asia, somewhere in the upper Oxus region, at the eastern boundary of the Iranian world.[43] On the other hand, this prevalent scientific certainty contradicts later Iranian traditions, of the Sāsānid and post-Sāsānid period, which would place the birth and preaching of Zarathustra on the western boundary of the Iranian world, in Azerbaijan. There have been attempts to reconcile these contradictions but always with the wish to remain on the ground of positive facts: Zarathustra was probably born in the West but his preaching probably took place in the East.

A recent solution was clearly inspired by the system of the keshvars. In this case it is suggested that the sacred history of primitive Zoroastrianism took place in the East of the Iranian world; that the Zoroastrian mission then penetrated progressively toward the West of the Iranian world until one fine day the geographic orientation was simply reversed (the eastern keshvar became the western keshvar). Even the word "falsification" comes into it on the grounds that the western Magi identified the holy places of sacred history (the Arax, Mount Savalān, the holy city of Shīz) after the event, without this identification having the least "historical" value![44]

In reality, the term "falsification" is completely irrelevant, since these questions point in fact to the preservation of the structure of an essentially *qualitative* space, whose regions are ordered in relation to one another, not according to preestablished geometrical coordinates, but according to their intrinsic qualification. If there was complete transposition of the place of historical scenes, this *fact* presupposes and bears witness in the first place to the possibility of a mental operation, the verification and significance of which elude positive science, which, bound as it is to material data alone, is thereby reduced to suspecting "falsification," even if unconscious. But the schema of the seven keshvars considered as an archetypal representation clearly reveals to us this possibility and the process involved, that is, the presence that constitutes the center and which, as such, is the *origin* and not the resultant of spatial references, which is not situated but *situative*. This presence carries its space along with it without needing to change the system of spatial references as a whole. Or rather, since this center is still and at all times *the* Center, there has, in the reality of the psychic event, been no real transfer (*in* space). The significance of the Center, the *medium mundi*, as the place where psycho-spiritual events always take place, as the space of hierophanies,[45] allows us to pose the problem on a level where traditional certainty and the certainties of positive science no longer conflict.

It is by no means our intention to relegate the sacred history of Zoroastrianism to the "realm of legend." But it is essential to take into account that in whatever place a historical event (in the current meaning of the term) may have taken place in outer and material reality, verifiable by the senses of those who witnessed it, there had to be—in order that notification of the Event should reach us in its spiritual *identity*, regardless of the *diversity* of the physical localizations—an organ of remembrance functioning in a way quite different from the verifications of our positive science, which, restricted to what for it are the "facts," has thereby a one-sided understanding of the physical event. This organ of remembrance and religious meditation is precisely the archetype-Image which, by being projected onto materially diverse geographical spaces, has been able to transmute them by bringing them back to itself as Center, in such a way that the hierophanic space is always and in each case *at the center.* The active Imagination has then been able to consecrate them as holy places and *identify* them *each time* as being indeed the same Earth of vision; not the other way round, namely, that some material quality (even "historical") of spaces here and there imposes evidence of their sacredness, determines their identity, or on the contrary causes a "mistake" to be made. Hierophanies take place in the *soul*, not in *things*. And it is the event in the soul that situates, qualifies, and sacralizes the space in which it is imagined.

And so, what are the Events that take place in Ērān-Vēj? There are the memorable liturgies, celebrated by Ohrmazd himself, by the celestial beings, by the legendary heroes. It was in Ērān-Vēj that Ohrmazd himself celebrated liturgies in honor of Ardvī Sūrā Anāhitā, "the High, the Sovereign, the Immaculate," the Angel-Goddess of the celestial Waters, in order to ask her that Zarathustra be attached to him and be his faithful prophet (Yasht V, 18). Zarathustra asked the same goddess for the conversion of King Vīshtāspa (Yasht V, 105).[46] It was in Ērān-Vēj that the comely Yima, "Yima of shining beauty, the best of mortals," received the order to build the enclosure, the *Var*, where were gathered together the elect from among all beings, the fairest, the most gracious, that they might be preserved from the mortal winter unleashed by the demonic Powers, and some day repopulate a transfigured world. Indeed, the *Var* of Yima is, as it were, a city, including houses, storehouses, and ramparts. It has luminescent doors and windows that themselves secrete the light within, for it is illuminated both by uncreated and created lights. But once a year, the stars, the moon, and the sun are seen to set and rise; that is why a year seems but a day. Every forty years, each human couple gives birth to another couple, masculine and feminine. And this perhaps suggests the androgynous condition of those beings who "live the most beautiful of lives within the unchanging *Var* of Yima."[47]

Is it by meditation or by a campaign of archeological excavation that we can hope to discover the traces of this Paradise of archetypes, of this celestial Earth in the center of the world that preserves the seed of the resurrection bodies? Yima's Paradise cannot be marked on the surface of our maps, subject to a system of coordinates. What is called for here is not topographical research, but to achieve the transparency which allows the archetype-Image to appear, in the only place where this is possible, *in medio mundi*. This, therefore, is our quest: How does the visionary geography take shape, when perceived from this center of the world, and of what psycho-spiritual events does it indicate the presence?

3. *Visionary Geography*

Once again Yasht XIX, the liturgical chant dedicated expressly to Zamyāt, the Angel of the Earth, *Dea Terrestris*, is what sheds full light on the Mazdean *Imago Terrae*. The hymn characteristically opens by an evocation enumerating all the mountains,[48] in celebration of the *Xvarnah* and its distinguished possessors, amongst whom are included precisely some of these mountains. Indeed, the latter play an essential part in the composition of the visionary landscape that prefigures the Transfiguration of the Earth. They are preeminently the seat of theophanies and angelophanies. According to the ritual, on the twenty-eighth day of the month (the day of Zamyāt), the liturgy is offered to the "Earth which is an Angel, to the mountains of the dawns, to all the mountains, to the Light of Glory."[49] A connection is already outlined, the patterns in which will become clear.

The Mazdean book of Genesis (*Bundahishn*) gives a striking description of the formation of the mountains:[50] under attack by the demonic Powers of Ahriman, the Earth began to tremble, it shook in horror and rebellion. As if to set up a rampart against these powers, the Earth raised up its mountains. First the powerful chain of mountains surrounding it, which, in the Avesta, is called "Hara berezaiti." Etymologically this is the Persian *Elburz*, and it is the name given until today to the chain of mountains bordering Iran on the north, from west to east; and so it is here, amidst the peaks and high plateaus of that chain, that the Sāsānid tradition rediscovered the sites of the episodes in the sacred history of Zoroastrianism. In any case, there or elsewhere, *visionary space* presupposes the transmutation of sensory data. In order for the "real" Elburz to correspond to this visionary space, for example, the active Imagination has to recapture it in its archetypal species. That is why we can leave aside here all discussion of positive material topography, and concern ourselves only with the *Image*, insofar as it is an organ of perception, and insofar as it is itself perceived through a *psycho-geography*.

Indeed, we are far removed from the ordinary view and positive proofs. Elburz has not ceased to grow during eight hundred years: two hundred years to the station of the stars, two hundred years to the station of the Moon, two hundred years to the station of the Sun, and two hundred years to that of the infinite Lights.[51] Now, these are the four degrees of the Mazdean Heaven. Elburz is therefore indeed the *cosmic mountain*, raised up by the supreme effort made by the Earth in order not to be separated from Heaven. It is "the resplendent mountain . . . where there is neither night, nor darkness, nor sickness with a thousand deaths, nor infection created by the demons."[52] It is the seat of divine palaces created by the Archangels. And the other mountains all originate from it, as if from a gigantic tree growing and thrusting out roots from which spring other trees. The mountain system thus forms a network in which each peak is a knot.[53] People have tried to identify them on the basis of their number—the number 2244 is alluded to in the tradition: some have been pronounced "real," others "mythical." The only thing that guides us with any certainty is the *Image*, which apprehends both the "real" ones and the "mythical."

Here, then, we have a group of high peaks which present difficulties no doubt forever insoluble by those who seek to place them by the positive method. As against this, the situation of these high peaks teaches us about the Earth as an event lived by the soul, that is, it shows us in what manner the Earth has been meditated by the organ of the active Imagination. It would be difficult, indeed, to localize these mountains by means of positive topography, for the intention and aim of this meditation was quite different from that of our positive science. All the mountains where the active Imagination perceives a hierophany of the *Xvarnah* are in Ērān-Vēj, *in medio mundi*; on them, the *Xvarnah* projects the scenes of the events experienced or foreseen, giving body to them, because the active Imagination is in itself their substance and their body, that which at the same time enacts them and experiences them.

There is in Ērān-Vēj a mountain called Hūkairya (Hugar, the very high),[54] a mountain which is as high as the stars, and from which pours down the torrent of the heavenly Waters of Ardvī Sūrā Anāhitā, "the High, the Sovereign, the Immaculate,"[55] a torrent "possessing a *Xvarnah* as great as all the Waters together which flow upon the Earth."[56] There it is that the earthly abode of the goddess of the heavenly Waters is imagined. She thus appears as the paradisal source of the Water of Life. Marvelous plants and trees grow in or around this wellspring, and above all the white Haoma, "Gaokarena,"[57] of which it is said: "He who partakes of it becomes immortal."[58] That is why the Elixir of immortality will be made from this at the moment of the final Transfiguration. The tree which cures all ills and "in which are deposited the seeds of all plants,"[59] grows next to the white Haoma. Indeed, the fertility of all beings in all their forms depends on the goddess or feminine Angel Ardvī Sūrā. However, she is by no means the "*Terra Mater*" after the manner of Cybele, for example; she is far more like a Virgin of the Waters, pure, chaste, immaculate, recalling the Greek Artemis.[60]

In Ērān-Vēj, close by the mountain of Hūkairya, there is a mountain of the dawns (*Ushidarena*). The liturgical chant to the Angel Zamyāt opens with a strophe in praise of this mountain of the dawns. It is made of ruby, of the substance of heaven; it is situated in the middle of the cosmic sea Vourukasha, into which it pours the waters it receives from Hūkairya. It is the first mountain to be lighted up by the auroral fires;[61] for this reason, it is the receptacle, the treasury of the *dawns*, and likewise (by homophony) that which gives *intelligence* to men. It is said that "the mountain first lighted up by the rays of the dawn also enlightens the intelligence, since *dawn* and *intelligence* are one (*ushā* and *ushi*)."[62]

Finally, the ritual affirms the connection which is essential here between the mountain of dawn and eschatology:[63] it prescribes that an offering be made to the Angel Arshtāt at the hour of Aushahin (that is, between midnight and dawn), and the reason given is that the mountain of dawn is mentioned in order to propitiate the Angel Arshtāt. And now the connection becomes clear: it is at the dawn that rises after the third night following death that the soul has to face the ordeal of the Chinvat Bridge. Thus, the mountain of dawn is invested with the Light of Glory at the exact hour when the soul is called upon to testify concerning its earthly existence in the presence of the Angel Arshtāt and of Zamyāt, the Angel of the Earth, *both of whom* assist the Amahraspand Amertāt in the "weighing" of the souls.[64] "The souls are in the light of dawn when they go to render their account; their passing takes place through the splendid dawn." So what is perceived here in the mountain haloed by the Glory of the dawns is not an astronomical phenomenon, but the dawn of immortality: the *Imago Gloriae* being projected onto the rising dawn, this dawn appears to the soul as the anticipated presence of a state already lived, that is, as the anticipation of its personal eschatology.

Another high mountain, the Chakad-i-Daītik (the peak of

judgment), completes this same landscape of individual eschatology and is also situated in Ērān-Vēj, the middle of the world.[65] From its summit springs the Bridge of Chinvat, at the entrance to which takes place the meeting of the soul either with Daēnā, its heavenly "I," or, on the contrary, with the terrible apparition that reflects nothing but an "I," mutilated and disfigured by every kind of ugliness, cut off from its celestial archetype. So this is the situation, above all others, when the *Imago Terrae*, transfiguring the outer material data, shows the perfect soul the places and symbolic landscapes of its anticipated eternity, in which it encounters its own heavenly Image. The perfect soul crosses the Bridge of Chinvat by the impetus of its spiritual flight and the power of its actions: it moves on towards the stars, then to the Moon, then to the Sun, and then to the infinite Lights.[66] Here again we have the four stages of the growth of the Alburz. Thus the Bridge of Chinvat links the summit that is in the center of the world to the cosmic mountain; and the ascent of the latter leads to the *Garōtmān*, to the "Abode of the Hymns."

So we shall no longer be astonished to find the mountains recalled in the beginning of the hymn to Zamyāt, nor shall we see the latter as a mere list of physical features devoid of religious content.[67] In fact, none of these—the dawns blazing on the mountain tops, the torrents of spring water, the plants of immortality growing in them—belong to the empirical earth accessible to the neutral verification of sensory perception. This is the Earth perceived in Ērān-Vēj as the original Iranian Earth; this is an Earth which the Mazdean active Imagination has transmuted into the symbol and center of the soul, and which is integrated into the spiritual events of which the soul itself is the scene. Here we already glimpse that what the soul perceives through its *Imago Terrae* is actually both its own archetypal Image and the enactment of its own mental dramaturgy.

Neither the dawn, nor the running waters, nor the plants, are perceived as equivalent to what we call astronomical, geological, or botanical phenomena. The dawn in which Daēnā is revealed, the heavenly waters of Ardvī Sūrā, the plants of Amertāt, all of them—the dawns, waters, and plants—are perceived in their Angel, because beneath the *appearance* the *apparition* becomes visible to the Imagination. And this is the phenomenon of the Angel, the figure which the active Imagination reveals itself to be, which it reveals to itself beneath the appearances perceived, is the figure of the Angels of the Earth. That is why terrestrial phenomena are more than phenomena: they are the hierophanies proper to Mazdeism which, in beings and things, reveal *who* these beings and these things are, that is, *who* their *heavenly person*, the source of their *Xvarnah*, is.[68] Again, in other words, the beings and the things, having been transmuted by the Imagination into their subtle (*mēnōk*) state, are revealed as the *actions* of a personal thought, of which they are the hierurgy.

The active Imagination perceives and shows to itself an Earth which is other than that Earth which is seen in ordinary sensory experience. That other Earth is the Earth irradiated and transfigured by *Xvarnah*. But the Light of Glory is most certainly not a material quality inherent in sensory substances, perceptible by all men without distinction; phenomenologically, we should understand it as being at the same time the Light which constitutes, haloes, and enlightens the soul, and the primordial Image of itself which the soul projects. Thus it is the organ by which the soul shows to itself earthly things transfigured, or awaiting the final Transfiguration. The soul must, indeed, have an Image of itself of such a kind that, by projecting it, it can discover in its vision the figures of the Light of Glory. In the soul raised to incandescence by this Light of Glory, with which it is finally identified,[69] it becomes possible, like Fechner, to see that the "Earth is an Angel," or rather for the Earth to be *seen* in its heavenly person, and, thanks to her, at the same time for all the feminine Angels of the Earth to be *seen* as the "sisters," or as the "mother" of the Angel Daēnā, the heavenly "I," the *Anima coelestis*. The Image of the Earth is revealed here in the form of an Angel, because it is imagined in the Image of the soul; their homology is revealed in the very kinship of their Angels.

We can therefore say this: the *Imago Terrae*, while it is the organ of perception itself, also signifies those aspects and figures of the Earth that are perceived, no longer simply by the senses nor as sensory empirical data, but by the archetype-Image, the Image *a priori* of the soul itself. The Earth is then a *vision*, and geography a *visionary geography*. Hence it is the Image of itself and its own Image that the soul rediscovers and meets. This Image projected by it is at the same time the one which enlightens it and the one which reflects back to it the figures in its Image, of which reciprocally it is itself the Image, namely: the feminine Angels of the Earth that are in the likeness of Daēnā-*Anima*. That is why the Mazdean phenomenology of the Earth is, properly speaking, an angelology.

Out of geographical studies, a new line of study, described as *psychological geography*, has developed in our day:[70] The intention is to discover the psychological factors that come into play in the conformation given to a landscape. The phenomenological presupposition implicit in research of this kind is that the essential functions of the soul, the *psyche*, include the projection of a nature, a *physis*; conversely, each physical structure discloses the mode of *psycho-spiritual* activity that brings it into operation. In this sense, the categories of the *sacredness* "which possesses the soul" can be recognized in the landscape with which it surrounds itself and in which it shapes its habitat, whether by projecting the vision on an ideal iconography, or by attempting to inscribe and reproduce a model of the vision on the actual earthly ground. This is why each of the hierophanies of our visionary geography offers an example of a case of psychogeography unlike any other. We shall limit ourselves here to a rapid description of two such examples.

The first example is supplied by the iconography of what has been called the "landscape of *Xvarnah*." How can one represent an earthly landscape in which everything is transfigured by that Light of Glory which the soul projects onto it? When the Mazdean soul perceives that this Energy of sacral light is the power that causes the springs to gush forth, the plants to germinate, the clouds to sail by, human beings to be born, that it is the power that lights up their intelligence, endows them with a victorious and supernatural strength, and consecrates them as beings of light by clothing them in hieratical dignity—none of this can be expressed in *representative* painting, but only by a preeminently *symbolical* art. As the earthly splendor of the divinity, the *Xvarnah Imagined* by the soul transfigures the Earth into a heavenly Earth, a glorious landscape *symbolizing with* the paradisal landscape of the beyond. This requires, therefore, a form of expression combining all the hierophanic elements of this Glory and transmuting them into pure symbols of a transfigured nature.

Perhaps the best illustration of this which has come down to us today is to be found in a late manuscript which so far is considered unique of its kind, whose full-page paintings in fantastic colors were executed at Shiraz in southern Persia at the end of the fourteenth century (A.D. 1398).[71] (See plate facing p. 32.) And here it would be appropriate to recall the landscapes in certain Byzantine mosaics, without even pausing to consider controversial questions about material influences or historical causality.

The second example of imagination of the celestial Earth can be observed in that sacred botany that connects the cultivation of flowers and floral art with the liturgy. A characteristic feature of Mazdean angelology is to give each of its Archangels and Angels a flower as an emblem, to point out, as it were, that if one wishes mentally to contemplate each of these heavenly Figures and to become the receptacle of their Energies, then the best instrument of meditation is indeed the flower which is their respective symbol. So, for each of the Archangels or Angels to whom one day of the month is respectively consecrated, and for whom that day is named, there is a corresponding flower. For Ohrmazd, myrtle. For Vohuman, white jasmine. For Artavahisht, marjoram. For Shatrīvar, the royal plant (basil). For Spendarmāt, musk (sweet basil). For Khordāt, the lily. For Amertāt, that perfumed yellow flower called "campak" in Sanskrit.

After the Amahraspands come the feminine Angels, which are more closely related to the soul, to *Xvarnah*, and to the

Earth: Ardvī Sūrā has the iris as her emblem; Daēnā, the rose with a hundred petals; Ashi Vanuhi (Ashisang), her sister, all wild flowers (or else the chrysanthemum, *buphthalmus*); Arshtāt, the white haoma; Zamyāt, saffron,[72] and so on. These flowers played an important role in ancient Zoroastrian liturgical practise; certain flowers were used for each Angel whose liturgy was being particularly celebrated. The ancient Persians, too, had a language of flowers, which was a sacred language.[73] Moreover, this delicate and subtle symbolism offers unlimited possibilities to liturgical imagination as well as for rituals of meditation. In their turn, the art of gardens and the cultivation of a garden thus acquire the meaning of a liturgy and a mental actualization of a vision. In this art, flowers play the part of the *materia prima* for alchemical meditation. This means mentally reconstituting Paradise, keeping company with heavenly beings; contemplation of the flowers which are their emblems evoke psychic reactions, which transmute the forms contemplated into energies corresponding to them; these psychic energies are finally dissolved into states of consciousness, into states of mental vision through which the heavenly Figures appear.

In both of the examples we have just analysed, we see that the intention and effort of the soul tends to give a form to the celestial Earth and to actualize it, thus making possible the epiphany of the beings of light. The Earth of Visions has to be reached *in medio mundi*, where real events are the *visions* themselves. And such, indeed, are the events described in the Recitals concerning the prophetic investiture of Zarathustra. The *Zarātusht-Nāma* (the "Book of Zoroaster") tells us about it with sublime simplicity: "When Zarathustra had reached the age of thirty, he had the desire for Ērān-Vēj, and set out with some companions, men and women."[74] To have desire for Ērān-Vēj is to desire the Earth of Visions, to reach the center of the world, the celestial Earth, where the meeting with the Immortal Saints takes place. In fact, the episodes that mark the progress and entry of Zarathustra and his companions into Ērān-Vēj, and the moment in time when this entry is achieved, are neither outer

events nor dates that can be chronologically recorded. They are hierophanic episodes and signposts.

The landscapes and events are completely *real*, and yet they no longer depend on positive topography, nor on chronological history. An essential clue is that access to Ērān-Vēj is a rupture with the laws of the physical world. A large expanse of water stands in the way of the little group; led by Zarathustra, all of them cross it without even stripping off their clothes: "As a vessel glides over the flowing waves, so did they walk on the surface of the water" (*Zarātusht-Nāma*, ch. XVI). Corresponding to hierophanic space, Time is no longer profane time with dates which can be recorded in the calendars of history (although this has been attempted). The arrival in Ērān-Vēj, the Earth of Visions *in medio mundi*, takes place on the last day of the year (the eve of *Naw Rūz*; in Shīʿīte theosophy, the *parousia* of the hidden Imām likewise occurs on the first day of the year, the *Naw Rūz*). Now, each Mazdean month, as well as the whole year, is the homologue of the *Aeon*, the great cycle of the Time-of-long-domination. The "date" is therefore in this case a hierophanic sign: it heralds the end of a millennium, the dawn of a new age (further on we shall also see that the celestial Earth of Hūrqalyā lies on the boundary between Time and the *Aevum*). In the same way, also, the first theophany will take place on the fifteenth of the month of Ordibehesht, which corresponds to the median division of twelve millennia, that is, to the moment when the Fravarti (the celestial entity) of Zarathustra was sent on its mission to earth. Here the dates are those of a liturgical cycle commemorating and repeating the "events in Heaven."

At this point, Zarathustra leaves his companions. He reaches the river Dāitī, in the center of Ērān-Vēj (*Zarātusht-Nāma*, p. 25, n. 6; *Zāt-Spram*, II, 6), on the banks of which *he was born.* Thus he returns to the origin, to the archetypal world, the necessary prelude to the direct vision of the archetypal Powers of light. There he is, alone, on the bank of the immense, bottomless river, which is divided into four branches. He enters it fearlessly, plunging ever more deeply into each of the four branches of the river (*Zarātusht-Nāma*, ch. XX). Here the Zoroastrian tradition has captured so well the feeling of the *psycho-spiritual* importance of the event that it applies the process of the *ta'wīl* or esoteric exegesis of the Spirituals of Islam to the external date, and leads the Event back to the spiritual reality that gives it its theme and structure. The crossing of the four branches of the river Dāitī is equivalent in this context to the mental achievement of the totality of the *Aeon.* It represents Zarathustra *redivivus* in the person of the three Saoshyants issued from his *Xvarnah*, who will bring about the transfiguration of the world (*Zarātusht-Nāma*, ch. XXI; *Zāt-Spram*, XXI, 7).

And when the first theophany takes place, when the vision takes the shape of the Archangel Bahman (Vohu Manah), of prestigious beauty, "resplendent from afar like the sun and clothed in a robe of light,"[75] the Archangel orders Zarathustra to put off his dress, that is, his material body, his organs of sensory perception, and allow himself to be taken into the dazzling presence of the divine thearchy of the Seven. The dialogue opens in the manner of the dialogue between Hermes and his *Nous*, Poimandres. The Archangel asks: "Tell me your name, what you seek in the world, and to what you aspire." Accompanied by the Archangel, Zarathustra is in ecstasy in the presence of the Council of Archangels. Here a new detail of mystical physiology is given—as soon as Zarathustra entered the assembly of the Celestials, he no longer "sees the projection of his own shadow on the ground, because of the dazzling splendor of the Archangels" (*Zāt-Spram*, XXI, 13). It means that to take off the "material dress" is to foretaste the state of the Body of Light, or resurrection body, the pure diaphanous incandescence of Archangelical Lights; this pure incandescence unites with the Lights without casting a shadow, because it is itself a source of light. Not to cast a shadow is the property of the *glorious body*, is to be *at the center.* And the significance of all this is that the seat and organ of the events which take place in the land of Ērān-Vēj is the subtle body of light.[76]

Finally, the theophanies take place on the high peaks of this Earth. The Avesta mentions the mountain and the forest where the sacred conversations take place.[77] There are late traditions that identify this mountain with certain mountains of positive geography;[78] we have already tried to define the mental process that leads to such homologation. Let us rather call to mind here the indications in the Pahlavi texts referring particularly to two of these mountains, which were the *places* of these theophanies: Hūkairya, the mountain of the primordial Waters, where the white Haoma, the plant of immortality, grows,[79] and the mountain of the dawn, haloed in the Light of Glory at the exact hour when the dawn of the heavenly life rises in the soul. It is true, therefore, that the ecstasies of Zarathustra take place precisely where the inner vision preexperiences the individual eschatology. The mountain tops of the Earth of visions are the mountain tops of the soul. The two archetypal Images, the *Imago Terrae* and the *Imago Animae*, correspond to one another: *the mountain of visions is the psycho-cosmic mountain.*

Moreover, this has been confirmed by certain ancient traditions that have been preserved in the Greek texts relating to Zarathustra. For example, Porphyry describes the retreat of Zarathustra in a grotto in the mountains of Persis, adorned with flowers and gushing springs, which provided a perfect *Imago mundi*[80] for his meditation. Dion Chrysostom mentions the high peak on which Zarathustra retired in order to "live in the way that was his own," and where a ceremony of ecstasy, invisible to the eyes of the profane, unfolds in a setting of fire and supernatural splendor.[81] Retreat on the psycho-cosmic mountain actually represents an essential phase of every mysteriosophy: its final act is an ecstasy; then the heavenly Figures, as they become apparent through the organ of its own archetype-Image, are made visible to the soul. And here once more it is perhaps to a Greek text that we owe an essential detail of the sacred ecstasies in Ērān-Vēj; it was *Agathos Daimon* who directly initiated Zarathustra into wisdom. Now, earlier research allowed us to recognize *Agathos Daimon* as a figure homologous to that of Daēnā, the celestial "I," the *Anima coelestis*.[82]

So, finally, the vision of the earthly landscape haloed by the *Xvarnah*, the Light of Glory, as well as the consistent character of the events, visible only to the soul, which take place there, all of this begins to convey an eschatological orientation. It is a foretaste both of the final Transfiguration of the Earth (*Frashkart*) and the great event of individual eschatology, the auroral meeting with the heavenly "I," the Angel Daēnā, at the entrance to the Chinvat Bridge. That is why this visionary geography creates a mental iconography that offers a support for meditation on what we previously called *geosophy*, and is revealed as inseparable from eschatology, for its function is essentially to prepare the birth of the earthly human being to his celestial "I," which is Daēnā, the daughter of Spenta Armaiti-Sophia.

4. *Geosophy and the Feminine Angels of the Earth*

An exposition of this geosophy will therefore incline to take the form of an outline of Mazdean Sophiology. The very term "geosophy" suggested here is merely a translation of the name Spenta Armaiti, the *Sophia* and Feminine Angel of the Earth.[83] What this term makes apparent from the start is the striking difference between a vague feeling (and the commonplace notion) of being a "son of the earth" on the one hand and on the other the feeling and knowledge characteristically expressed in the Mazdean profession of faith, and impressed on the adept in that context, of being a human individual who is the son of Spenta Armaiti, the feminine Archangel of the Earth.[84] The second term in the filial relationship is now no longer a man imprisoned between the boundaries of terrestrial birth and death, but a human being in his totality, including the past of his preexistence and the future of his superexistence. The filial relationship with the Archangel Spenta Armaiti extends from the preexistential celestial "I" to that celestial "I" by and for whom she will engender the man. It is the consummation of a form of existence preluded in Heaven[85] at the dramatic moment when the Fravartis accept to descend to the material Earth and there wage battle on the side of the Powers of Light against all the human-faced demons. For the human soul, it is the moment of choosing to come to Earth and *answer* there *for* the Powers of Light, as the latter *will answer* for it *post mortem.*

Therefore the *choice* of the soul will also be its *judge.* Participating at each moment of the *Aeon* in the final work of the Saoshyants, each soul of light must fight for the Transfiguration of the Earth, for the expulsion of the demonic Powers from the Ohrmazdian creation. And the vision that transmutes the Earth and the things of the Earth into symbols already inaugurates the restoration of the Earth to its paradisal purity. The victory of the soul incarnated in terrestrial existence is measured by the degree of this restoration, that is, by the degree of the soul's *Xvarnah,* of its growth toward its celestial existence to come, of its resurrection body, the substance of which, reciprocally, is made of that celestial Earth which is its action and its work.

For man to undertake such a work, is precisely to undertake in his own being what the Pahlavī texts call *Spendarmatīkīh*[86] (an abstract noun derived from *Spendarmat,* the Pahlavī form of the name Spenta Armaiti), and which we can translate as *Sophianity,* the Sophianic nature of Spenta Armaiti considered as Sophia (in accordance with Plutarch's translation and with the Pahlavī texts). By assuming this nature, the human being is then, in the true sense, the son of the Angel of the Earth, and so able to have a mental vision of her. The soul then awakens also to consciousness of its celestial kinship. Around Daēnā, who is the daughter of Spenta Armaiti and who is herself Sophia, are clustered the figures of Angel-Goddesses whose hierophanies are described in the Avesta in marvellous terms (Chisti, Ashi Vanuhi, Arshtāt, Zamyāt, Ardvī Sūrā Anāhitā), which reveal the *personal* forms in which exemplifications of one and the same archetype were suggested experientially to Mazdean consciousness, this archetype being the central symbol by which the totality and completeness of his being are proclaimed to man. Here experience is schematized in conformity with the fundamental angelology of the Mazdean vision of the world. The presence of a feminine Archangel of the Earth in the celestial pleroma was recognized and experienced. This relationship establishes the Mazdean *sacramentum Terrae*, the Sophianic mystery of the Earth.

It must be admitted that very few efforts have been made to bring all the Figures of Mazdean angelology into a coherent whole. Usually, people have been content merely to put together the "facts." Rarely has an effort of meditation been applied in order to comprehend these Figures, to activate their personal characteristics, to motivate their actions and interactions. We need only stress here the principal Figures among these feminine Angels of the Avesta, insofar as their relationship with the Sophianic mystery of the Earth is concerned. As for the accomplishment of this mystery, we have just defined it as consisting, in the case of the human being, in becoming invested with Spendarmatīkīh, that is with the "Sophianity" of Spenta Armaiti-Sophia. This investiture is necessary in order to verify (make true) a twofold teaching relating to the feminine Archangel of the Earth; on the one hand, that it is she regarding whom the Mazdean believer is taught to profess from the age of fifteen: "I am the son of Spenta Armaiti," and, on the other hand, that it is she who is the "mother" of Daēnā-Anima. This is to say that the "maternal" relationship of Spenta Armaiti with the human being finally culminates in a fulfillment wherein it is then equally true to say that Daēnā is engendered in him, or to say that he is himself engendered in Daēnā. Thus the relationship with the Mother-Archangel of the Earth is fulfilled on the eschatological horizon, and the other feminine Angels cooperate in this fulfillment. Let us try briefly to indicate the process as it appears to us, pointing out that it would certainly be necessary to meditate on it at greater length than we can here.

To assume Spendarmatīkīh means that the human being will exemplify in his person the mode of being of Spenta Armaiti as the feminine Archangel of the Earth and of earthly existence, that is, of the present mode of being of the incarnate Fravarti. We can discover what such an "assumption" implies and what makes it possible, both from a study of the features that define the person of Spenta Armaiti herself, and from the rough sketch of a mystical anthropology that outlines the interiorization or appropriation of the attributes conditioning rebirth in the celestial state. Mental iconography attributes features to the person of Spenta Armaiti that relate her closely to Sophia considered as master craftsman of Yahweh's Creation.[87] She is the daughter of the "Lord Wisdom," she is the "mistress of his house" and the "mother of his creatures,"[88] she is the Dwelling place: "We offer this liturgy to thee who art the very Dwelling place, Spenta Armaiti."[89] Of course, the invocation is addressed neither to a building nor to telluric matter. It is addressed to the one who precisely is the "mistress of the Dwelling place," and to live there oneself is to assume toward the dwelling place a mode of being and responsibility conforming to the hierurgic and provident action of the feminine Archangel in whose regency and care it is. That in itself defines not a spatial relationship, but a personal one, the relationship thanks to which the task of the incarnated Fravartis is carried out, that same task which Spenta Armaiti formulated directly to Zarathustra in the course of a confidential conversation.[90]

A few indications allow us to glimpse therefore how the Sophianic nature of Spenta Armaiti is developed in the innermost being of the Ohrmazdian human creature. It is said that of the three Amahraspands or feminine Archangels: "The creatures of Ohrmazd possess *life* through Khordāt (the Archangel of aquatic nature), *immortality* through Amertāt (the Archangel of vegetal nature), *perfect thought* (*bavandak mēnishnīh*) through Spenta Armaiti."[91] As perfect thought, thought of quietude and gentleness, meditative Imagination and silent Meditation,[92] the Archangel Spenta Armaiti's antagonist is the Archdemon Taromati (unruly thought, violence, uproar, oppression). And this perfect mental activity ("perfect thought under the pure gaze of love") defines the Sophianic nature of the "daughter" of the God of Light. When the believer assumes this Spendarmatīkīh,[93] and reproduces in himself that thought of wisdom which is the essence of the Angel of the Earth, he causes Spendarmat, the daughter of Ohrmazd, to exist in his own person. He is the child, not just of the Earth Mother, but of the feminine Angel of the Earth, that is, he causes the celestial

Earth, the "house" of which Spenta Armaiti is the "mistress" to open up in himself. To the same degree that this meditation of wisdom is the organ of the birth of the celestial Earth, it becomes true to say that, for every Mazdean soul, Spenta Armaiti is the mother of *its* Daēnā, that is of its celestial "I," the *Imago Animae*, the mirror reflecting its own transfiguration, its *geosophia*, in the *Imago Terrae*.

This process in which Sophianic meditation brings the soul to its celestial "I" can be followed further thanks to the vestiges of a mystical physiology, so hard to trace in Mazdeism that no heed is paid to it, the more precious for this reason. "In the vital energy of the human being, there is a *Thought*: therein Spenta Armaiti abides. In this Thought there is a *Word*: therein abides Ashi Vanuhi (the feminine angel who is Daēnā's sister). And in this Thought, there is an *Action*: therein abides Daēnā."[94] A triad of feminine Archangelic Powers is interiorized on the plane of this sacrosanct trilogy of Zoroastrianism (Thought, Word, Action). In conformity with homologous sequences, just as realized action or professed thought gives body to the inner thought, so is Daēnā the celestial figure who appears to the mental vision to the extent that the soul realizes and activates in itself the Sophianity of Spenta Armaiti, which means that meditation or "perfect thought" is the organ that gives birth to the celestial "I," or that Spenta Armaiti is the "mother of Daēnā." Therefore this perfect thought, the active Imagination of the celestial Earth, is not a "fantasy"; it is a power capable of "substantiating" and "vivifying." This is because in the human being it is the seat of a Power which, as it has rightly been pointed out, is homologous to that other figure called, in Manicheism, *Mater Vitae*, *Mater Viventium*, Mother of Life or Mother of the Living.[95] Therefore the Sophianic form of Mazdean devotion to the Angel of the Earth ultimately tends to cause the opening up in consciousness of that archetypal Image which depth psychology calls *Anima*, and which is the secret presence of the Eternal feminine in man.[96]

For a right understanding of the activation of this Image, the preterrestrial dramaturgy to which we previously alluded must be present in thought: the prologue in Heaven, the *choice* offered to the human Fravartis ("those who have chosen"): either to remain inviolate in the celestial world, or else to descend to Earth and do battle there for the world of the Angel. And that is indeed the paradox. The Fravartis are the celestial archetypes and tutelary angels, the Guides of all beings, both Celestial and Terrestrial. What does it mean then, if the human Fravartis (representing Ohrmazdian humanity) incarnate themselves on earth? Is the essential *dualitude* which conjoins two beings of light thereby abolished? Although this problem has hardly been meditated (it is of so little interest to historical science as such), the amplification offered by its solution can be based with certainty on the data which emerge on the level of Mazdean consciousness. In fact, the incarnate Fravarti, the Angel-soul that has given up its "celestial" condition to confront the horror of Ahrimanian humanity, is not alone: the soul in its terrestrial condition, making common cause with all the beings of light, wages at their side its "battle for the Angel." The "Angel" is simultaneously its faith and its judge, its existence and its superexistence, its celestial *paredros*. This fact will be revealed to the soul only *post mortem*, and that is why Daēnā, the Angel of the incarnate soul (*for* which the Fravarti, having come "to Earth," *has chosen* to answer), is also called *ravān-i rāh*, "the soul on the path," that is, the *Anima coelestis* which the *Anima humana* meets "on the path" to the Chinvat Bridge.[97]

And this is why the soul has its prevision (see above, § 3), in the annunciatory dawns of the visionary landscape *in medio mundi*, on the peak from which projects that Chinvat Bridge, with Daēnā standing at the entrance to facilitate the passage of the being whose *Anima coelestis* she is. She herself is another figure exemplifying the archetypal Sophia; she is, likewise, the daughter of Sophia; she has also been compared more than once to the figure of Sophia in the Old Testament,[98] where Wisdom is the daughter of Yahweh and the master craftsman of his creation, appearing as a splendid maiden to whom every youth with an ardent desire for knowledge plights his troth.[99] Or with equal justification, as has been pointed out, there is an analogy with the Koré of Hermetism, as well as with the "Virgin of Light" of Manicheism and of the gnostic book *Pistis Sophia.*[100]

The very name of Daēnā brings together several aspects that should not be fragmented or opposed to one another, but should be recaptured in the unity of her "Person."[101] Etymologically (Avestan *dāy*, Sanskrit *dhī*), she is the visionary soul or the visionary organ of the soul, the light it throws and which makes it possible to see, and at the same time the light that is seen, the celestial figure that comes face to face with the soul at the dawn of its eternity. Daēnā is the *vision* of the celestial world as it is *lived*, that is, as religion and professed faith,[102] and for that very reason it is the essential individuality, the transcendent celestial "I." By the conjunction of these two aspects or ideas in her person, she proclaims that realization unfailingly corresponds to faith. In this sense, because she is the archetype, the guardian Angel who guides and inspires the life of the believer, she is also his judge,[103] she who reveals to him the degree to which his earthly existence has satisfied the most personal law of his being, in the living expression of it. When the soul in amazement asks, "Who are you?" the maiden, more resplendent than any beauty ever glimpsed in the terrestrial world, moves toward the entrance of the Chinvat Bridge and answers: "I am your own Daēnā,"[104] which means: I am *in person* the faith you have professed and she who inspired it in you, I am she for whom you answered and she who guided you, who comforted you and who now judges you, for I am in person the Image set before you since the birth of your being and the Image which, finally, you yourself desired ("I was fair, thou hast made me fairer still"). That is why Daēnā is also *Xvarnah*, personal Glory and Destiny, and as such is "thine *Aeon*, thine Eternity."[105] It is not in the power of a human being to destroy his celestial Idea; but it is in his power to betray it, to separate himself from it, to have, at the entrance to the Chinvat Bridge, nothing face to face with him but the abominable and demonic caricature of his "I" delivered over to himself without a heavenly sponsor.

And Daēnā-Sophia has "sisters," who are, as it were, her prefigurations, mediators, and heralds, from the point of view of the ideal sequence in which visionary events are ordered. There is the Angel *Chisti*, celebrated in Yasht XVI, which is specifically dedicated to Daēnā. Her name, too, conveys the idea of an active Light which illuminates and reveals a Form of Light. It is she who confers on each being the faculty of vision, particularly on the participant in the liturgy, who by her is enabled to *see* and penetrate the meaning of the words and gestures of the Ritual. As it is recalled in the Yasht (strophe 2): "Zarathustra sacrificed to her, saying: 'Rise from thy throne, come from the Abode of Hymns, O most upright Chisti, created by Mazda and holy.' " In the liturgy consecrated to Daēnā, it is therefore Chisti who reveals her presence in mental vision as mediatrix for her "sister" and as the performer of this liturgy.[106] She carries the oblations, she is the priestess in person. Since it is she who confers vision, she herself therefore *is* the vision that defines the features of her iconography: tall and slender, clothed in white and herself white.[107] She gives to the Zoroastrian trilogy its truly sacro-liturgic meaning of "thought, word, action," and that is why Daēnā, having her center or "seat" (cf. n. 94 above) in the human being, in the holy *action* activated by meditative thought (Spenta Armaiti), is visualized in the person of her "sister," her mirror-image, whose features correspond to what is experienced and lived in the course of the liturgical *action.* This action places man in Ērān-Vēj, *in medio mundi*, where heavenly beings and earthly beings can communicate. As the Angel of the liturgy, Chisti is thus the mediatrix of her sister Daēnā, that is, the one who causes the liturgical action to become vision and anticipation of the eschatological meeting.[108]

The soul is again invited to experience a similar intuitive anticipation by Daēnā's other sister, the Angel *Ashi Vanuhi*, who also, in the trilogy of powers described above, serves as mediatrix between Spenta Armaiti, whose "daughter" she is, and Daēnā, whose "sister" she is. Her attributes resemble theirs: she also is "Ahura Mazda's daughter, the sister of the Archangels";[109] she takes on the form of a proud and beautiful maiden, her girdle tied high, pure, noble, and invincible.[110] Not only do the features of her iconography reproduce those of the other feminine Angels

(Daēnā, Ardvī Sūrā), thus exemplifying the same archetypal Image, but she, like Ardvī Sūrā, assumes the prerogative of extraordinary precedence, since Ohrmazd himself, Lord of the Amahraspands and of all the Yazatas, offers sacrifices in Ērān-Vēj both to her and to Ardvī Sūrā (as possessors and dispensers of *Xvarnah*).[111] In Ērān-Vēj, that is *in medio mundi*, Zarathustra also meets the Angel Ashi Vanuhi. This event is strikingly described in Yasht XVII. The Angel-Goddess, driving her chariot of Victory, is invoked as all-powerful and as herself possessing *Xvarnah*. This Iranian *Gloria Victrix* is indeed the sister of the Nike of Greek statuary (those "Victories" who, principally owing to gnostic influence, were the origin of the first representations of the Angel in early Christian iconography). Then, erect on her triumphal chariot, she invites Zarathustra to approach, to mount and sit beside her: "Thou art beautiful, O Zarathustra, thou art very fair . . . to thy body *Xvarnah* is given and to thy soul lasting bliss. Behold, thus I proclaim it to thee."[112]

Thus, the Angel Ashi Vanuhi possesses and bestows *Xvarnah*, the Light of Glory, but at the same time she herself also *is* the Victory, the victorial Fire. In her person are concentrated the significance both of Glory and of Destiny, the *Aura Gloriae* of a being of light. Thus Mithraism took her as *τύχη* (in the sense of *Fortuna Victrix*, *Gloria-Fortuna*).[113] To meet Ashi-Vanuhi in Ērān-Vēj, to be invited to sit at her side on her chariot of victory, is indeed the psychic event which at the same time anticipates, prefigures, and makes possible the meeting *post mortem* with her "sister" Daēnā, Glory and Destiny having been fulfilled. She is the *Imago Victrix* of the soul, its sacralization by *Xvarnah*, the revelation of its celestial archetype. The vision in Ērān-Vēj prefigures the dawn rising on the Chinvat Bridge, and that is why the Pahlavī tradition recognizes Ashi Vanuhi, sister of Daēnā-Sophia, as herself being the Spirit of Wisdom that guides the beings of light toward "perfect existence," that is "paradisal"[114] existence. She is also called "the Angel of the paradisal[115] abode," an "assistant" of Spenta Armaiti, who is "our Abode."

At this point, then, the conjunction takes place of the destiny of the soul—the Fravarti incarnated in terrestrial existence—and the destiny of that terrestrial Earth to which it came solely in order to help Ohrmazd and the Powers of Light to save the Earth from the demonic Powers. Ashi Vanuhi is the Angel who radiates *Xvarnah*, the Light of Glory; but this radiation everlasting, that is to say, the perdurable radiance thus restored by vision, now becomes that other feminine Angel who is called by the name *Arshtāt*.[116] In her person she is the *Imago Gloriae* reflecting to the soul the Image of an Earth transfigured into the image of the soul that transfigures it. To understand the mental dramaturgy dominated by the figure of the Angel Arshtāt, let us remember the eschatological implications of the Image of *Xvarnah*. In Yasht XIX we hear celebrated the creatures who are to come from the world of light and, in the form of Saoshyants, renew earthly existence, making it an existence with the nature of Fire, when all creatures will possess an incorruptible body of luminous Fire.[117] But that is an event toward which all creatures of light are working now, in the present. This work and this event were the very reason, from the beginning, for the choice and the battle of the Fravartis. The creatures of light receive their capacity to fulfill or to anticipate this metamorphosis precisely thanks to the victorial Fire whose *radiance* embodied in beings is called by the personal name of the Angel Arshtāt.

The prevision of this final Transfiguration (*Frashkart*), the consciousness of belonging to the creatures of light who work together for it in every moment of the *Aeon*, are perceptions which, like the visionary geography of the landscapes mentioned above, bring into play, not simple physics originating in sensory perceptions, but a visionary physics. This transfiguring energy of which the *Imago Gloriae* is the source and organ, envelopes the whole of the soul. Perception of the Fire of earthly Glory proclaims the radiance of a spiritual Fire bringing the soul to incandescence, to the Light of saving knowledge (*gnosis*), introduces the soul to the Earth of Light, and to all the beings composing its own world, the world for which it is answerable. That is why the figure of Daēnā, the light of knowledge and the

Imago Animae,[118] is sometimes substituted for that of the Angel Arshtāt. And that is also why at the "judgment" which is the confrontation of the soul with the celestial archetypes for which it had to answer on earth, the Angel Arshtāt stands at the side of Zamyāt, the *Dea terrestris*, at the "weighing" of the soul, both of them assisting the Archangel Amertāt.[119]

For this confrontation causes the soul to ask: with what "weight" did it weigh its own *Xvarnah* which was for the transfiguration of being? To what degree was it itself a Saoshyant, thus fulfilling the vow of its own prayer: "May we be among those who are to bring about the Transfiguration of the Earth" (Yasna XXX, 9). If Arshtāt and Zamyāt are the "judges" of the soul before Amertāt (Immortality), so, by the same token is their sister Daēnā. The outcome of the struggle is either transfiguration or demonic disfiguration. To make the image of the Earth translucid to the figure of the Angel in an angelomorphic vision such as Fechner's, the form of the Angel must flower in the soul itself. Now therein consists the birth of the soul to Daēnā, to its celestial "I," and we have already indicated how, in this individual eschatology, the ultimate meaning of the profession of faith is fulfilled: "My mother is Spenta Armaiti, the Archangel of the Earth." Here is where we begin to see how Zamyāt, the Angel of earthly Glory, glimpsed in the flame of the dawn on the mountain tops of the landscapes of *Xvarnah*, is not simply a "doublet" of Spenta Armaiti. Zamyāt is only "visible" to the soul in which and by which it becomes true that Spenta Armaiti is the "mother" of Daēnā-Sophia. Giving birth to the celestial "I" and the Transfiguration of the Earth form the cycle of what we have tried to describe here as a "geosophy."

Therefore, from this "geosophy" fulfilled by the feminine Angels of the Earth, the Mazdean religious Imagination shaped a mytho-history, in which the vision of the Archangel of the Earth engendering a human being, still preterrestrial, already typifies the supernatural generation of the Savior, the final Saoshyant to come, in the name and work of whom every Fravarti participates through its own struggle.

Gayōmart, the primordial Man, was created in Ērān-Vēj, on

the banks of the river Dāitī in the center of the world. When Ahriman succeeded in getting Death to penetrate him, Gayōmart fell on his left side, and, since his body was composed of pure "metal," the absolute metal constituting the metallic totality, seven metals emerged from his body, each proceeding from the member to which it corresponded. The anthropogony that forms a bridge between the cosmic significance of primordial man and speculations concerning the microcosm, brings out very clearly the correspondence of the metals with the parts of the human body. Besides this, it gives an essential definition: *Gold*, as the *eighth* metal, and because of its preeminence, issues from the very *soul* (*Xvarnah*) of Gayōmart and from his seed. Gold, exalted by its nobility above all other metals, symbolizes here *with* the essential "I," the soul, which is super-added to the individual "members" whose totality it dominates, and to which the metals are respectively related. This Gold, as we know, is, in the alchemical tradition, the symbol above all others of the *filius regius*, of the "resurrection body," of the Self. Now, it is this Gold that Spenta Armaiti gathered together. For forty years[120] she kept it, at the end of which time an extraordinary plant germinated from the "soil"; this plant formed the first human couple, Mahryag-Mahryānag, two beings so like one another, so closely united with each other, that the male could not be distinguished from the female, much less isolated. On these two beings, or rather on this still dual being, this androgyne, descended one and the same *Xvarnah*, one and the same Light of Glory, one and the same *soul*, which existed before the physical organism.[121]

What is grasped in this vision is once again the Event of pre-Adamic humanity (Adam-Eve, not yet Adam *and* Eve). Adamic humanity really only begins from the descendants of Mahryag and Mahryānag—when masculine and feminine, distinct from one another, will become *two*. Here again, the depths of the profession of faith, its meaning, shines through: "I have Spenta Armaiti as my mother, I hold my human condition from Mahryag and Mahryānag."[122] The Earth that collects the "gold" of Gayōmart is certainly not the earth of our ordinary physics, but the "person" of the Angel of the Earth, Spenta Armaiti.

Neither the categories of our geology, nor those of natural embryology, are to be substituted for the mode of perception which is here properly that of "geosophy." Neither is the human being whom Spenta Armaiti conceives by her own son Gayōmart[123] man in our present human condition. He is the total human being, still androgynous, Mahryag-Mahryānag. However, since Ahriman had caused Death to enter into Gayōmart, the structure of this total being, of this androgyne issuing from his Gold, that is, from his *soul* or Self, of which Armaiti-Sophia is the receptacle —this structure is unstable and fragile; it is not viable on the Earth, which is the prey of demonic powers. Finally, by the scission of its internal *dualitude*, this being gives birth to its posterity, historic humanity, the condition of which is the only one we can experience, and whose emergence is therefore subsequent to the great catastrophe, to the "day after," the invasion by "Evil."

The idea of a restored dualitude is expressed in the conjunction *post mortem* of the human being with Daēnā, who is precisely the "daughter of Spenta Armaiti," just as the human being in his prehistoric or supraterrestrial condition is her "son." That is why the Event which took place in prehistory (Spenta Armaiti collecting the Gold or Self of Gayōmart, of her own son tainted by Death) prefigures typologically the Event that is the "dénouement" of history, the threshold of metahistory. In other words: when Spenta Armaiti becomes the mother of a human being in the sense and to the very degree that she is the mother of Daēnā, this "birth" refers to an eschatological conjunction, such that the Sophianic mystery inscribed in the very name of the Angel of the Earth, Armaiti-Sophia, is consummated together with the general eschatology. Only then is the profound meaning of the texts that present Ardvī Sūrā Anāhitā as the "assistant," the coworker (*hamkār*) of Spenta Armaiti, revealed.

It would be impossible truly to understand the myth of Gayōmart and to render justice to the Iranian mystery of the Anthropos if one were to isolate the figure of Gayōmart from its principle. Gayōmart, Zarathustra, and the final Saoshyant represent the beginning, the middle, and the end of Man and of the world of Man subjected to "mixture."[124] Zarathustra is also primordial Man, Gayōmart *redivivus*, just as the last Saoshyant will be Zarathustra *redivivus*, and just as Mazdean *gnosis* anticipates the exaltation of Anthropos in the person of the Saoshyant. And that is why the supernatural and virginal conception of the Saoshyant, the prototype of a humanity finally redeemed from death, represents, in relation to the "moment" of the person of Zarathustra, a process homologous but inverse to the one which brought forth from Gayōmart, through the intermediary of Spenta Armaiti, a humanity delivered over to the mortal condidition. This condition of historic humanity was heralded by the scission of the total being, constituted by the Gold or Self of Gayōmart.

The image of the Saoshyant is therefore the *antiphony* of the Image of the Anthropos ravaged by the demonic Powers. The virgin birth, through a supernatural process, abolishes biological laws, or rather transcends the physical meaning of phenomena by going beyond the duality and opposition of masculine and feminine: a single being takes on the function of both. Just as the Gold issued from Gayōmart was preserved by Spenta Armaiti under the protection of the Angels of the Earth, so, not the seed in the physiological meaning of the word, but the *Xvarnah* (Gold) of Zarathustra, his *Aura Gloriae*, was received by the Angel Neryosang, and was entrusted by him to the Glory (*Xvarnah*) of the Waters, that is, to the Angel-Goddess Ardvī Sūrā Anāhitā, "the High, the Sovereign, the Immaculate." Here also, the expectation of the Transfiguration of man and the Earth can be perceived and expressed only in terms of a geosophy. The Zarathustrian Glory is kept by Ardvī Sūrā "in person," mythically in the waters of Lake Kansaoya, from which emerges the mountain of dawns, *Mons Victorialis*;[125] a multitude of Fravartis watch over it. At the end of the twelve millennia, when our *Aeon* will come to an end, a maiden, acting as the earthly and visible typification of Ardvī Sūrā in person, will enter the waters of the mystic lake. The Light of Glory will be immanent in her body, and she will conceive "one who must master all the evil deeds of demons and men."[126] That is why the Virgin Mother, Eredhat

Fedhri, is already herself hailed by the name Vispa Taurvairi ("the all-conquering"), the *Omnivictrix*. Therefore, Ardvī Sūrā Anāhitā, preserving the *Xvarnah* of Zarathustra, from which the hero of the final restoration (*apokatastasis*) is born, is indeed, as the liturgy[127] says, the "coworker" of Spenta Armaiti, keeping the Gold issued from Gayōmart; and Vispa Taurvairi is the earthly Woman typifying both of them. Mazdean eschatology also, like the Sophianic mystery of the Earth, is fulfilled by an exaltation of Sophia.[128]

All this, of course, is fulfilled in Ērān-Vēj (where Gayōmart died, where Zarathustra was born, where the Saoshyants will be born, where the final Liturgy setting the world on fire will take place); and so this entire dramaturgy is itself perceptible only in Ērān-Vēj, at the *center of the world*, that is at the *summit of the soul.*

We have heard Fechner grieve because in our day visions of this nature are considered imaginary and unreal. Perhaps we can appreciate today, even more than in the last century, philosophies that did not confuse the Imaginary, or rather the Reality corresponding to imaginative perception, with the unreal. Between a universe constituted by a pure physics and a subjectivity which inflicts isolation on itself, we foresee the need of an intermediate world to join one with the other, something in the nature of a spiritual realm of subtle bodies. Such an intermediate world was ceaselessly meditated, particularly in Islamic Iran, both by the masters of Ṣūfism, the adepts of the Suhrawardian philosophy of light, and the adepts of Shaikhism. This intermediate world is no longer only the center of *the world*, like Ērān-Vēj, but the center of *the worlds*. The world of the Imaginable, of imaginative Reality, the world of archetype-Images, is established as mediator between the world of the pure, intelligible essences and the sensory universe. This world is the *eighth* keshvar, the eighth climate: the "Earth of the emerald cities," the mystical Earth of Hūrqalyā.

II THE MYSTICAL EARTH OF HŪRQALYĀ

1. Progressio harmonica: *Fāṭima, Daughter of the Prophet, and the Celestial Earth*

Whoever is somewhat familiar with the organ knows what are referred to as "stops." Thanks to these stops, each note can cause several pipes of different lengths to "speak" simultaneously; thus, besides the fundamental note, a number of harmonic overtones can be heard. Among the contrivances that regulate them, the *progressio harmonica* designates a combination of stops which allows more and more overtones to be heard as one ascends toward the upper register, until at a certain pitch the fundamental note also resounds simultaneously.

This is described very briefly and without any claim to technical accuracy, but for a definite purpose. It is just that this phenomenon seems to us the parallel most helpful in understanding the subtitle of this book: "From Mazdean Iran to Shīʿite Iran." As a result of the connection which was effected between the old Mazdean Iran and Shīʿite Iran—a connection in which we shall have to pay special attention to the spiritual school that has reactivated traditional Shīʿite gnosis in Iranian Islam since the end of the eighteenth century—something like a *progressio harmonica* takes place. The higher we "ascend," the more harmonics we hear. Finally, the fundamental, which gave the preceding chapter its tonality, will become audible again.

The analogy suggested may at last enable us to understand certain features of the spiritual history of Iran. So little study has thus far been devoted in the West to the philosophy of

Iranian Islam, whether Shīʿite or not, that those who specialize in the study of ancient Iran, as well as specialists in Muslim philosophy as such, sometimes seem surprised, if not annoyed, when a connection is pointed out which till then was not seen in their scheme. On the other hand, there are very few cultivated Iranians who are insensitive to this connection. To succeed in representing it adequately, we shall probably have to give up certain of our customary categories that take only outer history into account, where everything is studied with a view to discovering major currents, deducing influences and causal explanations, trying in all ways to reduce things to a common denominator. If a phenomenon does not lend itself to such reduction to identity by way of cause and effect, if it refuses to fit the preconceived label, one will readily be suspected of having been led astray by some material that is not authentic. This is what has made it so difficult to discuss *spiritual facts* as such, especially those that took place in Iran, because spiritual facts, as such, are discontinuous and irreducible; they do not succeed one another in a homogeneous time; they *are*, each of them, their own time.

We shall now consider briefly two of these "times." On the one hand, the "time" of Suhrawardī, whose work, chronologically, belongs to our twelfth century. In it, the author pursues the aim of reviving in Islam the wisdom, the *theosophia*, of ancient Persia. His metaphysical outlook is dominated, on the one hand, by the motif of the *Xvarnah*, the Light of Glory, and by the Mazdean angelology through which he interprets the Platonic Ideas; and, on the other hand, by the "time" of Shīʿism, determined as to quality by the idea of the hidden Imām and his *parousia*. This idea resounds like the harmonic of a fundamental note that we have already heard in the Zoroastrian idea of the eschatological Savior or Saoshyant. But neither Suhrawardī nor the Shīʿites are Zoroastrians. They are and intend to remain in Islam, in a spiritual Islam, to be sure, which is profoundly different from the legalistic Islam, the official religion of the majority. If one is limited to the positive history of external things, without knowing how to effect phenomenological reduction, how can one possibly give "historical" authenticity to a phenomenon that expresses, in a given world, the values and reality of certain perceptions received in a world that is foreign, even heterogeneous, to the former? Such an attempt will give rise to talk of syncretism, dialectical conciliation, artificial transposition. And that will be the end of it.

Our Spirituals, indeed, do not indulge in syncretism, nor do they have to attempt dialectical conciliation, because they have at their disposal a mode of perception different from the one to which we have been reduced by our one-dimensional historical consciousness. In the first place, they have at their disposal a world of several levels, and it is exactly one of these levels that the present book is trying to describe and to situate. In the course of this book we shall come across the following expression by one of our authors: "To see or perceive things in Hūrqalyā." Therein lies an allusion to the bringing into play of the faculty of perception, which also and necessarily is available to these Spirituals. The bringing into play of this faculty is designated by the technical term *ta'wīl*, which etymologically means "to bring back" the *data* to their origin, to their archetype, to their *donor*. For this, the same data must be recaptured at each of the degrees of being or levels through which they had to "descend" in order to reach the mode of being corresponding to the plane on which they are evident to our ordinary consciousness. This practice has the effect of causing these planes to symbolize *with* one another.

Hence, the *ta'wīl* is preeminently the hermeneutics of symbols, the ex-egesis, the bringing out of hidden spiritual meaning. Without the *ta'wīl*, Suhrawardī's *Oriental Theosophy* would not exist, nor yet that spiritual phenomenon in general, namely Shī'ite gnosis, by which the meaning of Islam is transfigured. And conversely, there would be no possibility of a *ta'wīl* without the world of Hūrqalyā, which we are at present studying; that is, without the world of archetypal Images where that imaginative perception functions and is able, by transmuting the material data of external history into symbols, to penetrate to the inner meaning. In short, this concerns the "spiritual history" whose events take place in Hūrqalyā. *Ta'wīl* presupposes the superposition of worlds and interworlds, as the correlative basis for a plurality of meanings in the same text.

This "technique," to be sure, was known at one time in the West. There, however, it rapidly degenerated into an artificial technique, but in fact for reasons which were extrinsic to its nature and which distorted its practice, both because it was cut off from the *theosophia* of which it is the correlative, and because it was deprived of spontaneity by a dogmatic authority. Today, in the eyes of the philologists and historians, it is thought of as something artificial and negligible, if not unbearable. I do not believe that there is any profit in discussion aimed at reconciling the two points of view. Regardless of what happened to this technique in the West, the fact remains that its practice in Islamic theosophy (the *ḥikma ilāhīya*) has continued to be supported by quite other means, and to preserve its spontaneity. If one does not understand from what it springs, all the spiritual facts connected with it remain incomprehensible. The *ta'wīl*, without question, is a matter of *harmonic perception*, of hearing an identical sound (the same verse, the same *ḥadīth*, even an entire text) on several levels simultaneously. One hears or one does not hear. But he who does not possess the inner ("Hūrqalyan") ear cannot be made to hear what he who does possess it is able to hear. Because, for that matter, the secret of the progression of chords, in harmony, depends upon the *ta'wīl* of a given chord.

Later in this book we shall read a few pages of Suhrawardī, the young master who died a martyr at the age of thirty-eight (587/1191) and who came later to be called the "Master of Oriental Theosophy" (Shaikh al-Ishrāq)[1] because his great aim was the renaissance of ancient Iranian wisdom. We have already mentioned his name and shall do so again, since his work is of such capital importance to our theme—the "Celestial Earth." In the present context, we intend only to draw attention to a few pages from his chief work, which explicitly mention the rank and function of the feminine Archangel of the Earth under the name that Mazdean hierosophy traditionally confers upon her,

Spenta Armaiti. This name, in Middle Iranian or Pahlavi, becomes Spendarmat, which in modern Persian gives us Isfandārmuz. In the preceding chapter we were shown how the constellation of the other Angels of the Earth were arrayed around her.

In the Suhrawardian doctrine, the schema of the spiritual universes appears in broad outline as follows: from the first "Victorial" Light (Qāhir), or first Archangel emanated from the Light of Lights, whose traditional Mazdean name is Bahman (Vohu-Manah), there issues a pleroma of innumerable beings of light, pure intelligible Lights, quite independent of any material body; this is the world of the *Jabarūt*. From it there emanates another pleroma of substances of light, some of which have to take upon themselves the guardianship of a material species, which is their "theurgy," while the others have to fill the role of Souls, which for longer or shorter periods animate a material body. The first are the archetype-Angels or Angels of species, among which the Zoroastrian Amahraspands are referred to by name: Suhrawardī interprets the Platonic Ideas on the plane of this angelology. The second are the Souls of the Spheres (*Angeli coelestes*) and human souls. These two categories together form the world of *Malakūt*, and the Earth of *Malakūt* is the celestial earth of Hūrqalyā.

Isfandārmuz figures among the Angels of the species. It is significant and confirmative that Suhrawardī, in his turn, employs the characteristic old Iranian term by which, as we have seen, the Avesta already designated the function of Spenta Armaiti, namely the *kad bānū'īya*, the function of the "mistress of the house." As the Angel of the Earth, Isfandārmuz assumes in particular the guardianship of the natural realms in which the telluric element predominates, since the Earth is the "theurgy" of its Angel. The Earth is "she who receives"; as the receptacle of the influx and effects of the celestial Spheres, it assumes the feminine role with respect to the masculine. This is one of the themes which will be further developed by Suhrawardī's profound commentator, Ṣadruddīn Shīrāzī (d. 1640, see below, Part Two, Arts. I, VI, and IX) when he was teaching at Shiraz. On the one hand, the relationship between the Earth as we know it and the other Forms that are objects of sensory perception is analogous to that which exists between the ideal Earth, that is, the Angel of the Earth, and the other separate substances or Angels of species. This does not mean, of course, that we can speak of "passivities" (*infiʿālāt*) in the world of Intelligibles: the femininity of the Angel of the Earth rests on the fact that she is "the one who receives," the one in whom is manifested the multitude of the effects and influences of the Cherubinic "active Intelligences" according to an ontological gradation and an intelligible structure, in the same way as, on this Earth, the effects of the heavenly bodies of which these Intelligences are the motive powers, through the intermediary of their Souls, are manifested according to a chronological succession and a structure perceptible to the senses. On our Earth, this is how the function of *kadbānū'īya* is seen to make our Earth symbolize with its Angel, Isfandārmuz.[2]

This simple example which we have chosen from amongst others should suffice to show how the speculative theosophy of Islamic Iran, from Suhrawardī in the twelfth century to Ṣadruddīn Shīrāzī in the seventeenth century (and we should include their successors up to the present day), preserves and continues to meditate the figure of the Angel of the Earth, whose person the ancient Iranians had been taught by the Mazdean religion to recognize. This figure, the *Gestalt*, has completely retained its identity, even though the elements of the context have changed. What is admirable is the power of the *ta'wīl* of the spiritual hermeneutics, which is able to give value to all the symbols and "bring them back" to the archetype. This is the initiatic function which spiritual Islam assumes, in the person of the "master of Oriental theosophy," and his emulators.

That is not all. When we again find Suhrawardī using the very name Isfandārmuz, the Angel of the Earth and the Sophia of Mazdaism, we have no difficulty in recognizing her features, since even the characteristic name of her function has been carried over from the Mazdean liturgy into the Islamic, Neoplatonic context of Suhrawardī. But it may happen that her name is no longer pronounced, that a Figure with an entirely different name appears in an entirely different context, and that nevertheless we can still identify the same features, the same *Gestalt.* Let us take careful note, however, of the specific nature of the spiritual phenomenon which is about to claim our attention. As it appears, we cannot simply say that this is a Figure that is merely a new exemplification of the archetype personified by Spenta Armaiti. On the height of the plane where we shall be enabled to perceive this Figure, we should rather speak of an archetype-Figure of the archetype, as though we were approaching the peak of the *progressio harmonica*, and that there at last—and only there—it were given to us to hear once more and simultaneously the fundamental sound in the base. It is the feminine Archangel of a *supracelestial* Earth, assuming the rank and privilege of the divine Sophia, that it is suggested we may perceive, on the level of the world of the *lāhūt*, the eternal reality of the dazzling Fāṭima, daughter of the Prophet, as she is meditated in Shīʿite gnosis, or more exactly, in that of the Shaikhī school.

It is true, alas, that in the absence until now of a comprehensive work on Shīʿite doctrines, and especially those of Shaikhism, to which we could refer, we may be suspected of a too easy acceptance of obscure allusions. Shīʿism—this word comes from the Arabic *shīʿa* and designates the community of the *adepts* who follow the Imāms of the Prophet's family—Shīʿism, which for five centuries has been the form of Islam in Iran, where from the beginning it had its centers of radiation, is still very little known in the West. Too often, influenced by contemporary fads, people reduce its origins to questions of political succession. By so doing, they completely overlook the important body of literature consisting of the conversations of the first adepts with successive Imāms until the ninth century of our era. These conversations bear witness that the flowering of Shīʿism was essentially the flowering, or rather the resurgence, of gnosis in Islam (if one were to go back and study the origins of the doctrines, one could not separate Twelver Shīʿism and Ismāʿīlī Shīʿism). Shīʿite gnosis is preeminently the esotericism of Islam, and when it was made the state religion by the

Ṣafavids in the sixteenth century, this resulted in the formation of a kind of official clergy almost exclusively concerned with jurisprudence. The chief effect of this ordeal was to render the Iranian adepts of Shī'ite gnosis, even today, still more rigorous in their practice of the "discipline of the arcanum."

While prophetology is an essential element of Islamic religion as such, in Shī'ite theosophy it is divided into prophetology and Imāmology. Beside the prophetic function, which delivers the message of the literal Revelation, there is the initiatic function, which initiates into the hidden meanings of revelations, and which is the function of the Imām. After the cycle of prophecy (*dā'irat al-nubūwa*) that ended with Muḥammad, the "Seal of the Prophets," there comes the cycle of Initiation (*dā'irat al-walāya*), the present cycle, placed under the spiritual rule of the Twelfth Imām, the hidden Imām, "present in the hearts but invisible to the senses."[3]

The Shaikhī school, which flourished at the end of the eighteenth century under the stimulus of the lofty and strong spiritual personality of Shaikh Aḥmad Aḥsā'ī (d. 1826), marked an extraordinary revival of primitive Shī'ite gnosis. Its literature is enormous, for the most part still in manuscript. Here we cannot even outline all the doctrines, but in the course of the following pages we shall see how and why the theme of Hūrqalyā is one of its essential themes. In it, the meaning of Imāmology has been closely examined in great depth (or height). The twelve Imāms who assumed the initiatic function subsequent to the prophetic message of Muḥammad, his person, and the person of his daughter, Fāṭima, from whom the line of the Imāms originated, this pleroma of the "Fourteen Very-Pure" is understood and meditated not only as regards the ephemeral appearance on earth of their respective persons, but in the reality of their precosmic eternal entities. Their persons are essentially theophanic; they are the Names and the divine Attributes, that which alone can be known of the divinity; they are the organs of the divinity; they are its "operant operations." From a structural point of view, in Shī'ite theology, Imāmology plays the same role as Christology in Christian theology. That is why whoever has known only Sunnite Islam, is confronted in Iran by something unexpected, and becomes involved in a dialogue the richness and consequences of which are unforeseeable.

Thus, the twelve Imāms, in their theophanic persons, together with the Prophet and the resplendent Fāṭima, form the pleroma of the "Fourteen Very-Pure"; when meditated in their substance and their preeternal person, they assume a mode of being and a position analogous to the *Aeons* of the pleroma in Valentinian gnosis. As regards the subject of our concern here, namely, the theme of the celestial Earth, the position and role of Fāṭima in this pleroma now take on a predominant significance. In the aforementioned schema of Suhrawardian "Oriental theosophy," we were shown how our Earth and its feminine Angel, Isfandārmuz, ranked in the world of the archetypes, the world of the Soul or *Malakūt*. Thus, we had a threefold universe: the earthly human world, which is the object of sensory perception; the world of the Soul or *Malakūt*, which is, properly speaking, the world of imaginative perception; and the world of pure Cherubinic Intelligences, the *Jabarūt*, which is the object of intelligible knowledge.

In the Shīʿite theosophy of Shaikhism, another universe (as in Ibn ʿArabī), is superimposed on the above three universes: the universe of the *lāhūt*, the sphere of the deity. But the characteristic of Shīʿism and Shaikhism is to conceive this *lāhūt* explicitly as constituting the pleroma of the "Fourteen Very-Pure." One might say that it allows us to hear the theme of the celestial Earth, like all the other themes, in a still higher octave. Each octave is a new world, a new beginning, where everything is rediscovered, but at a different height, that is, in a higher mode of being. This succession of octaves is what allows the *ta'wīl*, or spiritual hermeneutics, to be practiced authentically. Moreover, in the transcendent Person of Fāṭima as a member of the supreme Pleroma, we shall be hearing something like the motif of the *supracelestial Earth*; and through this supracelestial Earth, we are led to the idea of a Shīʿite Sophiology, by which we shall perceive afresh something that Mazdean Sophiology already perceived in the person of the Angel of the Earth, but this time at a new and higher level, since the *progressio harmonica* produces the resonance of harmonics which until then had remained silent.

We shall summarize here a few essential pages of a great work in Persian, in four volumes, composed, as well as many others, by the eminent Shaikh Ḥājj Muḥammad Karīm Khān Kirmānī (d. 1288/1870),[4] second in the line of succession from Shaikh Aḥmad Aḥsā'ī as head of the Shaikhī school. His "Spiritual Directory" abounds in glimpses that are opened to the reader thanks to his profound and original thought (the second part of the present book, Art. x, contains a few pages from it). In order to understand the structure of the pleroma of Shī'ite theosophy and the role in it played by Fāṭima,[5] one must be guided by the basic idea, of which we are constantly reminded in the text, that all the universes symbolize with one another. Here again we meet the Heavens and an Earth, but these are not the Heavens and the Earth of our world, nor those of *Malakūt*, nor those of *Jabarūt*, but the Heavens and the Earth of that *hypercosmos* which is the sphere of the Deity, the *lāhūt*. The rhythm that determines its architectonic structure is then developed in the dimension of terrestrial time. To discover in this historic dimension itself a structure which makes it possible to see the succession as homologous to the structure of the pleroma—this will be essentially the esoteric hermeneutic, the *ta'wīl*; it will be a discovery of the true and hidden meaning, the spiritual history that becomes visible through the recital of external events. It will mean to "see things in Hūrqalyā."

Clinging as we do in the West to the materiality of historical facts, lacking which we fear to lose our foothold, it is perhaps difficult for us to understand that the origin of all Islamic faith and hope, as well as of the responsibility on which the conscience of the believer is based, lies not in a fact of history, but in a *fact* of *metahistory*—the preeternal pact concluded when the divine Being asked the totality of human beings present in the Anthropos, the celestial Adam: "Am I not your Lord?" (*A-lastu bi-rabbikum?* 7:171). We have already seen also that the Mazdean faith and ethic are based on a *fact* of *metahistory*: the Lord

Wisdom's questioning of the Fravartis as to whether they were willing to descend to earth, there to fight against the Ahrimanian powers. But here there is still something more: the same metahistorical event in which the *spiritual history* of the Adamites originates is itself only the reappearance, on the plane of Adamic humanity, of an Event that resounds from descending octave to descending octave, but whose primordial scene is the supreme pleroma. In fact, the interrogation encodes for the imaginative perception the unfathomable mystery of the origin of origins. Ibn ʿArabī suggests the approach to this when he declares that the Divine Being was at one and the same time the questioner and the respondent.

This question is, indeed, the key to the mystery of the primordial theophany, the revelation of the Divine Being who can only be revealed to himself in *another* self, but is unable to recognize himself as *other* or to recognize that other as himself, except in that he *himself* is the other's God. The fact that the beings of the supreme pleroma appeared in an order of ontological precedence corresponding to the order in which they answered the primordial interrogation is a way, for the imaginative perception, of deciphering the structure of the pleroma as the place of the primordial theophany. Just as the visible Heavens are created by the contemplative acts of cherubinic Intelligences emanating one from another, so the "heavens of the pleroma," in the sphere of the *lāhūt*, are brought about by theophanic acts.

These theophanic acts coincide with the progressive differentiation of the drops of the primordial ocean of being, that is, of being given its imperative by the creative *Esto*.[6] The *vis formativa*, immanent in each drop, enables it to give the answer that concludes the divine preeternal pact. Since the order of ontological succession of the answers determines the structure of the pleroma of the *lāhūt*, the result is that the hierarchy of the Fourteen supreme spiritual entities will have its epiphany on earth, at the time of the cycle of Muḥammadan prophecy, in the succession of the persons who typify it, the "Fourteen Very-Pure": the Prophet Muḥammad, Fāṭima, his daughter, and the twelve Imāms.

II. *Mystical Earth of Hūrqalyā*

The first of the spiritual entities to answer is the first of the beings, the "inchoate being," he who will have his sensory manifestation on earth in the person of the Prophet Muḥammad. This is why he is the supreme Heaven of the Pleroma, and the one whose homologue in the astronomical Heavens is the Sphere of Spheres, the Throne (*ʿarsh*), the Empyrean. After him, the second of the eternal spiritual entities to answer is the one who will be manifested on earth in the person of Ḥaẓrat Amīr[7] (that is, the First Imām, ʿAlī ibn Abī-Ṭalib, a cousin of the Prophet and the husband of Fāṭima); his homologue in the astronomical heavens is the eighth Heaven, the Heaven containing the "fortresses" or constellations of the Zodiac, the Heaven of the Fixed Stars (*Kursī*), the firmament. Therefore, the empyrean of the pleroma is the Heaven of Prophecy (*nubūwa*); its firmament is the Heaven of Initiation (*walāya*). By virtue of that, this firmament is the Heaven of Integral Initiation; the First Imām, in his theophanic person, recapitulates it in its totality.

However, the totality of the Heaven of the Initiation is a conjunction of twelve Persons or primordial hypostases (the astronomical homologues of which are the twelve signs of the Zodiac), that is, of the spiritual entities that will be manifested on earth as the twelve Imāms. Each of them has his distinctive sign in the Zodiac of the pleroma, that is, in the coalescence of the Initiation recapitulated in the heaven of the First Imām. But each of them, according to his distinct ontological rank, likewise produces his own Heaven. Two of them voice their response, those two to which, on earth, will correspond that pair of brothers, the young Imāms, Ḥasan and Ḥusayn (prince of martyrs), the sons of ʿAlī and of Fāṭima; these two entities produce, respectively, the Heaven of the Sun and the Heaven of the Moon of the supreme pleroma. Then comes the one whose epiphany on earth will be the Twelfth Imām, the hidden Imām,[8] that is, the Imām of our time, whose person is to the Prophet Muḥammad as the last Saoshyant, *Zarathustra redivivus*, is to the prophet Zarathustra himself. Later the eight other Imāms utter their response in succession, in the order which in the eternal Initiation will be symbolized astronomically by the other planetary Spheres and by those imagined in order to account for the movements of the Moon.

Finally there comes the response of Ḥaẓrat Fāṭima to complete the pleroma of the *lāhūt* and give it both its plenitude and its foundation. Thus, she is the *Earth* of the supreme pleroma, and this is why it can be said that on this ontological plane she is more than the celestial Earth, she is the *supracelestial Earth.* In other words the Heavens and the Earth of the pleroma of the *lāhūt* are related to the Heavens and the Earth of Hūrqalyā, about which there will be much to say later in this book, in the same way as the Heavens and the Earth of Hūrqalyā are related to the Heavens and the Earth of the sensory world. Or again, the pleromatic person of Fāṭima is to the celestial Earth of Hūrqalyā as Spenta Armaiti is to the Mazdean Earth haloed by the light of the *Xvarnah.*

No human being can have access to the vision of the supreme pleroma; to do so, he would need to "catch up with" those spiritual entities who are eternally "ahead" of the totality of creatures. One single atom of the supracelestial Earth projected into a million of our universes would suffice—because of its beauty, its purity, and its light—to bring them into a state of incandescent fusion. The beings of the pleroma of the *lāhūt* are visible only in their apparitional forms, which are the receptacles of their theophanies. Primordial, therefore, is the function of the one who in person is the supracelestial Earth, the paradise beyond paradise, to the same extent that the celestial Earth of Hūrqalyā is the Earth of theophanic visions. In other words, as we shall see, without the person of Fāṭima there would be neither the manifestation of the Imāmate, nor Imāmic initiation. For the pleroma of these entities of light is the very *place* of the divine mystery. Their light is the divine light itself; their transparency allows it to shine through, retaining none of it as their own ipseity. Pure flaming crystals which the eye cannot gaze upon because they manifest the illuminating Sun, these "Fourteen Very-Pure" are not only the Friends and Loved Ones of God; they are the very substance of pre-eternal Love; they are the identity of love, lover, and beloved, that identity which all Ṣūfīs have aspired to live, and which, according to the Shīʿite Spirituals, is inaccessible to anyone not initiated into the secret of Imāmology. This can explain, for example, their circumspect attitude, that of Shaikhism, for example, toward non-Shīʿite Ṣūfism.

From this height, we reach a perspective in which the *Sophiology* of Shaikhism will be developed. On this earth, Fāṭima, the daughter of the Prophet, was the wife of ʿAlī ibn Abī-Ṭālib, himself the Prophet's cousin. Their exemplary union is the manifestation of an eternal syzygy originating in the eternity of the pleroma of the *lāhūt*.[9] The First Imām and Fāṭima are related to each other in the same reciprocal way as the two first hypostases, *ʿAql* and *Nafs*, Intelligence and Soul, or in terms more familiar to us (because they go back to Philo): *Logos* and *Sophia.*

The couple *ʿAli-Fāṭima* is the exemplification, the epiphany on earth, of the eternal couple *Logos-Sophia.* Hence, we can foresee the implications of their respective persons. The Logos (*ʿaql*), in Shaikhī doctrine is the hidden substance of every being and of every thing; it is the suprasensory calling for visible Form in order to be manifested. It is like the wood in which the form of the statue will appear. Better still, it is like the archetypal body, the inner astral mass of the sun, invisible to human perception, in relation to the visible Form, which is its *aura*, brilliance and splendor. The *maqām* (this word signifying state, rank, degree, plane, also the pitch of a note in music)—the *maqām* of Fāṭima corresponds exactly to this visible form of the sun, without which there would be neither radiance nor heat. And this is why Fāṭima has been called by a solar name: *Fāṭima al-Zahrā'*, the brilliant, resplendent Fāṭima. The totality of the universes consists of this light of Fāṭima, the splendor of each sun illuminating every conceivable universe.

So one could also speak here of a cosmic Sophianity, having its source in the eternal person of Fāṭima-Sophia. As such, she assumes a threefold rank, a threefold dignity and function. For she is the manifested Form, that is, the very soul (*nafs*, *Anima*) of the Imāms; she is the Threshold (*bāb*) through which the

Imāms effuse the gift of their light, just as the light of the sun is effused by the form of the sun—which is its brilliant splendor —not by the invisible substance of its "archetype-body." Thus, in the second place, she is all thinkable reality, the pleroma of meanings (*maʿānī*) of all the universes, because nothing of what *is* can be without qualification. Qualification and meaning are on the same level of being as form, and form is precisely on the level of being of the Soul, for it is the Soul-Sophia that confers qualification and meaning. This is why the whole universe of the soul and the secret of the meanings given by the Soul is the very universe and secret of Ḥaẓrat Fāṭima. She is Sophia, which is to say divine wisdom and power, embracing all the universes. That, lastly, is why her eternal Person, which is the secret of the world of the Soul, is also its manifestation (*bayān*), without which the creative Principle of the world would remain unknown and unknowable, forever hidden.

Or yet again: the ontological rank of the Imāms in their eternal entity transcends all representation and perception, all means of expression and designation by created beings, whereas the rank of Ḥaẓrat Fāṭima is the plane of their epiphany, because the rank of her being is the very rank of the Soul for each degree of being. Thus the degree of being of Fāṭima-Sophia recapitulates the whole of the degrees of knowledge, of gnosis, so very completely that the rank of the respective preeminence of the prophets in regard to their knowledge of God is measured by their knowledge of Ḥaẓrat Fāṭima. Even those who were the most eminent from among the hundred and twenty-four thousand *Nabīs*, those who, prior to Muḥammad, were entrusted with the mission of revealing a heavenly Book, even they are still below the rank of Fāṭima-Sophia, because it is she who is the source of all their knowledge, revelations, and thaumaturgical powers, for Fāṭima-Sophia is the *tabula secreta* (*lawḥ maḥfūẓ*).

Indeed, according to tradition, Gabriel is the Angel of Revelation and the Angel of Knowledge, the herald sent to the prophets. But he himself receives the divine revelation, which he communicates to them, through the intermediary of three other archangels, Azrael, Seraphiel, and Michael, who are the supports of the Throne. Only the Archangel Michael receives directly part of the knowledge concealed in the *tabula secreta*, which indicates the rank itself and the position of Fāṭima-Sophia as the heart of the transcendent spiritual world.

In the Qur'ān there are verses whose complete meaning cannot be understood except by means of the spiritual hermeneutic, the Shī'ite *ta'wīl*; for example, the verse (which we translate as required by this *ta'wīl*) in which God declares: "Yes, I swear it by the Moon, and by the night when it retires, and by the dawn when it rises, this Sign is one of the greater Signs, one of those which warn human beings" (74:35–39). This Sign among the greater Signs is Ḥaẓrat Fāṭima in the midst of the "Fourteen Very-Pure."

After recapitulating the ontological prerogatives of Ḥaẓrat Fāṭima-Sophia with our eminent Shaikh, we can say of her through whom earthly existence is transfigured into the dawn of a supracelestial Earth, that she is *the* THEOPHANY. The theme rises and expands to such magnitude that our Iranian Shaikh (to whom, moreover, we are also indebted for a treatise on colors) reaches heights foreshadowed by Goethe at the conclusion of the second Faust: an Eternally Feminine, preceding even terrestrial woman because preceding the differentiation of male and female in the terrestrial world, just as the supracelestial Earth rules over all the Earths, celestial and terrestrial, and exists before them. Fāṭima-Sophia is in fact the Soul: the Soul of creation, the Soul of each creature, that is, the constitutive part of the human being that appears essentially to the imaginative consciousness in the form of a feminine being, *Anima*. She is the eternally feminine in man, and that is why she is the archetype of the heavenly Earth; she is both paradise and initiation into it, for it is she who manifests the divine names and attributes revealed in the theophanic persons of the Imāms, that is, in the Heavens of the Pleroma of the *lāhūt*.

Here one begins to understand the resurgence of a theme of primitive Shī'ite gnosis, more exactly of Ismā'īlī gnosis, in which Fāṭima is called *Fāṭima Fāṭir*, Fāṭima the *Creator* (in the masculine). Indeed, this suggests that we can perceive, at an extraordinary height of resonance, the meaning of the name which the Shīʿite faithful give today to Ḥaẓrat Fāṭima. In Fāṭima they hail the "queen of women." But in this context it suggests that we look for its meaning far beyond and above the sexual differentiation which is the condition of earthly humanity, a meaning that we have to translate by something like "sovereign of feminine humanity" or "of humanity in the feminine." Indeed, we have to take feminine as meaning, in the first place, the totality of the beings of the universes of the Possible! All creatures have been created out of the Soul itself, out of the *Anima* of the holy Imāms; they issue from the "left side" of the latter, as Eve, the *Anima* of Adam, was created from his left side, as the light of the Sun consists of the manifested form and the qualifications of the sun.

All creatures being formed from their soul, the ontological status of the universe of creatures in relation to the holy Imāms as cosmogonic powers is a feminine status. In this sense the twelve Imāms are the "men of God" alluded to in certain verses of the Qur'ān. But at the same time the Imāms, who inaugurate on earth the cycle of Initiation into the hidden meaning of the revelations, were created from the soul of the Prophet, or rather they *are* the soul of the Prophet. This is indicated several times in the Qur'ān, as, for example, in the following verse: "He has made wives for you out of your own souls" (16:74 and 30:20). In this sense, the Imāms are the "brides" of the Prophet. And furthermore, since Initiation is nothing but the spiritual birth of the adepts, in speaking of the "mother of the believers" in the true sense, we should understand that the real and esoteric meaning of this word "mother" refers to the Imāms. Indeed, this spiritual birth is effected through them, and the following saying of the Prophet refers to this: "I and ʿAlī are the father and the mother of this community."

And so the twelve Imāms, as the instruments and effective causes of Creation, are, on the one hand, the "men of God," and masculine. But, on the other hand, and at the same time, they are the soul of the Prophet, that is the *Anima*, the Feminine aspect of the Prophet through whom Initiation, that is, spiritual creation, takes place. Now we already know that the ontological rank of the Soul and the reality of the Soul are the very rank and reality of Fāṭima-Sophia. The Imāms are masculine as agents of cosmogony, since creation is their soul; as authors of spiritual creation they are feminine, since they *are* the Soul and since the Soul is Fāṭima. This, therefore, is why we read that Fāṭima is the theophany of the supreme pleroma, and that is why the theophanic and initiatic function of the holy Imāms is precisely their "Fāṭimic" degree of being (their *fāṭimīya*, which we faithfully translate as "Sophianity"), and this is how Fāṭima comes to be called Fāṭima Fāṭir, Fāṭima the *Creator*.

Her functions *symbolize* with each other, from one universe to the other: in the pleroma of the *lāhūt*, as the supracelestial Earth which is its foundation; on the terrestrial Earth, as the daughter and Soul of the Prophet and as the one from whom issue those who in their turn are the Soul of the Prophet, the lineage of the twelve Imāms. She is *the* theophany and she is the Initiation; she is *majmaʿ al-nūrayn*, the confluence of the two lights, the light of Prophecy and the light of Initiation. Through her, creation, from the beginning, is Sophianic in nature, and through her the Imāms are invested with the Sophianity that they transmit to their adepts, because she is its *soul*. From this pleromatic height we can distinguish the fundamental sound emerging from the depths: namely, that which Mazdean Sophiology formulated in the idea of *spendar matīkīh*, the Sophianity with which Spenta Armaiti, the feminine Angel of the Earth invested the faithful believer.

However, unlike what we found in the "Oriental theosophy" of Suhrawardī, the name of Spenta Armaiti has not been mentioned in the passages we have just analyzed and commented upon. Nevertheless, if our harmonic perception makes it possible to discern spontaneously the chord produced by the Mazdean Earth transfigured by the Light of Glory and the celestial Earth transfigured in the person of Fāṭima-Sophia, this concordance will be confirmed in another way.

It was made clear earlier (Ch. I, § 4) how the link is formed between Spendarmat, the Angel of the Earth, and the person of the *Saoshyants*, the Saviors of whom the last one is destined to carry out what in Zoroastrian eschatology is called the Transfiguration and Rejuvenation of the world (*Frashkart*): the *apokatastasis*, or restoration of all things to their primordial splendor and wholeness, to the state in which they were until the invasion of the Ahrimanian Counterpowers. Unfortunately, we cannot attempt here a comparative outline that would follow from the analogy suggested, on the one hand, by the relationship between Muḥammad, Fāṭima, and the hidden Imām—the one whose *parousia* will also be a prelude to the *apokatastasis*—and, on the other hand, by the relationship between Zarathustra, the mother of the last Saoshyant and the last Saoshyant in person. But what needs to be pointed out, however, is that in the voluminous literature still produced nowadays in Shīʿite Iran, around the traditional sources dealing with the hidden Imām, there are abundant references showing that certain Shīʿite theologians have a direct knowledge of the Old and New Testaments of the Bible, as well as of Zoroastrian eschatology. Already in the seventeenth century, when Quṭbuddīn Ashkivarī, one of the most outstanding pupils of Mīr Dāmād (the great master of theology in the Iṣfahān school) was writing his spiritual history in three cycles (ancient Sages and prophets, figures of Sunnite Islam, portraits of Shīʿite Islam), he stressed the identity of the features that mark the Person of the Zoroastrian *Saoshyant*, and of the attributes according to the Shīʿite faith of the Person of the Twelfth, or hidden, Imām.

We also encounter passages of this kind in another Persian work by the same eminent Shaikh, Muḥammad Karīm Khān Kirmānī, from whose teaching we have just reaped such profit. We are thinking especially of the pages in which the Shaikh refers[10] to one of the ecstasies of Zarathustra, in the course of which Ohrmazd gives his prophet the vision of a tree with seven branches, the shadow of which reached out to every place on the Earth. The seven branches of the tree were made of gold, silver, copper, bronze, lead, steel, and iron, respectively. Ohrmazd explains to Zarathustra the meaning of each branch: each (as in the vision of Daniel) symbolizes one of the great empires.

With the seventh branch, that is, the seventh period, inaugurated by the reign of the ʿAbbāsids (indicated by their symbolic color, which is black), catastrophes follow in rapid succession, among them the whirlwind descent of the Mongols. But Ohrmazd consoles Zarathustra by announcing the advent of the eschatological hero, Bahrām Varjavand, who will come from the East, from Central Asia. Certain traditions specify that he will come from the "city of the maidens" (*shahr-i dukhtarān*), which lies in the direction of Tibet (cf. above, Ch. I, n. 126). His name defines his person: *Bahrām* is the Persian name for the planet Mars (now we have already seen that in the heavens of the pleroma of the *lāhūt*, the homologue of the Heaven of Mars is the Heaven of the Twelfth Imām); *Varjavand* means he who possesses the power and sovereignty of the Light of Glory, the *Xvarnah*.[11] The homologation of the Zoroastrian eschatological hero to the person of the hidden Imām, whose *parousia* bursts forth as the sign of the Resurrection, goes back, as we have just recalled, to much earlier Shīʿite theologians.

But other homologations can be made. The Zoroastrian hero and the Imām-Resurrector both have as their comrades in arms not only those who, in one period or another, carry on for them the battle of the spirit that brings closer the future of their reign, but also those who, preserved in a mystical sleep, wait to rise up with them when the time comes, and all those from the past who will "return" for the final battle. For the Zoroastrians, for example, there is Peshotūn, one of the sons of King Vīshtāspa who protected Zarathustra and encouraged his preaching, and for the Shīʿites, the First Imām in person. These are two great figures of "spiritual knights" (*javānmardān*) whose identical eschatological role justifies the homologation suggested by our Shaikh.

However, let us stress the fact that our authors are thinking not in terms of "historical currents" or "influences," but in the form of cycles, taking into account both the schema of universes symbolizing with one another and also the schema of periods of spiritual history. Thus the homologated forms do not have to be reduced to the same homogeneous time; each of them *is* their time. And that is precisely why they are typifications and why they can rightly be homologated to one another, and why each personage has his homologue in each cycle. To make the Saoshyant homologous to the hidden Imām is not, as we would doubtless tend to make it, a matter of weighing influences in pointing out currents, that is, in taking apart the entire mechanism of external history in order to "explain" its identity by bringing it back to a single plane. Far from it, for this way of thinking in cycles demands a kind of harmonic perception; or, again, the perception of a constant structure, just as the same melody can be produced in different registers. Each time the melodic elements are different, but the structure is the same—the same melody, the same musical figure, the same *Gestalt*.

That is why the progression, which this mode of thought makes it possible for us to conceive, is not a horizontal linear evolution, but an ascent from cycle to cycle, from one octave to a higher octave. A few pages from the same Shaikh, which have been translated here (Part Two, Art. x, § 2) illustrate this. The spiritual history of humanity since Adam is the cycle of prophecy following the cycle of cosmogony; but though the former follows in the train of the latter, it is in the nature of a reversion, a return and reascent to the pleroma. This has a gnostic flavor, to be sure, but that is exactly what it means to "see things in Hūrqalyā." It means to see man and his world essentially in a vertical direction. The *Orient-origin*, which *orients* and magnetizes the return and reascent, is the celestial *pole*, the cosmic North, the "emerald rock" at the summit of the cosmic mountain of Qāf, in the very place where the world of Hūrqalyā begins; so it is not a region situated in the East on the maps, not even those old maps that place the East at the top, in place of the North. The meaning of man and the meaning of his world are conferred upon them by this *polar dimension*[12] and not by a linear, horizontal, and one-dimensional evolution, that famous "sense of history" which nowadays has been taken for granted, even though the terms of reference on which it is based remain entirely hypothetical.

Moreover, the paradise of Yima in which are preserved the

most beautiful of beings who will repopulate a transfigured world, namely, the *Var* that preserves the seed of the resurrection bodies, is situated in the North. The Earth of Light, the *Terra Lucida* of Manicheism, like that of Mandeism, is also situated in the direction of the cosmic North. In the same way, according to the mystic ʿAbd al-Karīm Jīlī (cf. Part Two, Art. IV), the "Earth of the souls" is a region in the far North, the only one not to have been affected by the consequences of the fall of Adam. It is the abode of the "men of the Invisible," ruled by the mysterious prophet Khiẓr. A characteristic feature is that its light is that of the "midnight sun," since the evening prayer is unknown there, dawn rising before the sun has set. And here it might be useful to look at all the symbols that converge toward the paradise of the North, the souls' Earth of Light and the castle of the Grail.

Now we must try to understand how our texts unfold to show us this Earth of Light as the Earth of Visions and the Earth through which the resurrection of the bodies or, more exactly, the apparition of the "spiritual bodies," takes place. But as regards this world, described to us as the world of archetype-Images and the world of the soul, we had to have an idea *who* was its soul. By guiding us to the higher octave, to the pleroma of the *lāhūt*, Shaikhī theosophy has shown us how Fāṭima-Sophia is the supracelestial Earth, because she is the Soul, the *Anima* or manifested form of the supreme pleroma.

As our authors gradually help us to enter into the "eighth climate," we shall also be learning how the *Anima substantiva* of the adept, his "spiritual body," is the Earth of his Paradise. Now this Earth of Hūrqalyā is where the hidden Imām lives at the present time. Consequently, we shall begin to see the bond of mystical exemplification that associates the soul and person of the Shīʿite adept with Fāṭima-Sophia, prime origin of the Twelfth Imām, and invests the adept with the Sophianic function of Fāṭima. For, as we shall learn, the *parousia* or manifestation of the hidden Imām is not an external event destined suddenly to appear on the calendar of physical time; it is a *disoccultation* that gradually takes place as the pilgrim of the spirit, rising toward the world of Hūrqalyā, brings about the event of the awaited Imām in himself. The whole of the spirituality of Shī'ism is based on this, as it will become clear to us on reading the fine passages from the writings of Shaikh Sarkār Āghā given in translation in the second part of this book and which were precisely selected to help us understand why Hūrqalyā is the Earth of Visions and the Earth of Resurrection.

2. *The "Eighth Climate"*

The historian Ṭabarī (ninth century) has preserved for us some of the earliest information available about a mysterious region, which his description enables us to identify as the "Earth of the Emerald Cities." Two cities are situated there—Jābarṣā and Jābalqā[13]—to which the traditions we shall study here add a third city, Hūrqalyā; the name Hūrqalyā is then used to designate this mystic country as a whole. I regret not being able yet to provide a satisfactory etymology for these names; leaving aside several plausible hypotheses, we shall simply conform here to the traditional pronunciation still in use today in Iranian spiritual circles.

Jābarṣā and Jābalqā, Ṭabarī tells us, are two emerald cities that lie immediately beyond the mountain of Qāf. Like those of the Heavenly Jerusalem, their dimensions express quaternity, the symbol of perfection and wholeness. The surface of each is a square, the sides measuring twelve thousand parasangs. The inhabitants do not know of the existence of our Adam, nor of Iblīs, the Antagonist; their food consists exclusively of vegetables; they have no need of clothing, for their faith in God makes them like the angels, although they are not angels. Since they are not differentiated by sex, they have no desire for posterity.[14] Lastly, all their light comes to them from the mountain of Qāf, while the minerals in their soil and the walls of their towns (like those of the archetypal paradise of Yima) secrete their own light. This indication already puts us on the way to establishing the identity of the mountain with the mysterious cities. It is said, in fact, that in this mountain "there is neither sun, nor moon, nor stars." Now we know that in the Ptolemaic system a characteristic of the ninth Sphere, which comprises the totality of the celestial Spheres and communicates diurnal movement to them, is that it is a heaven without constellations.[15] Moreover, traditions specifically describe the mountain Qāf as the mountain surrounding our universe and as formed entirely of emerald, the reflection of which produces the green color (which to us looks blue) of the celestial vault.[16] Or again, it is the rock (*ṣakhra*) forming the keystone of the celestial vault and imagined as being composed of emerald and as casting a reflection on the mountain of Qāf. What the *visio smaragdina* perceives here is, therefore, the cosmic mountain encircling and overhanging our earthly habitat; the cosmic mountain was also what was perceived as encompassing the visible horizon of Ērān-Vēj, *in medio mundi*, at the very place where the Chinvat Bridge projected from a high peak to join this cosmic mountain, whose ascent led the soul to the realm of infinite Lights.

Now the geographer Yāqūt expressly affirms that the mountain of Qāf was once called the Elburz.[17] Indeed, it is the very same mountain which is the "mother" of all the mountains of the world; they are connected to it by subterranean branches and veins. And it is also the one climbed by the pilgrims of the spirit —as in Suhrawardī's "Recital of the Occidental Exile," for example—to reach the emerald rock looming before them like the translucent side of a mystical Sinai. And there, as at the entrance to the Chinvat Bridge of the Mazdean dramaturgy of the soul, the meeting with the archetypal Figure takes place, the celestial Person from whom the terrestrial "I" originates.[18] Therefore, the mountain of Qāf marks the boundary between two worlds, the one visible and the other invisible to the senses. In order to penetrate into the cities hidden on its further side, the mystical pilgrim must have passed beyond the evidence of the senses and common norms, must have faced the ordeals symbolized by the long journey in the Darkness across the distances that separate him from the Earth of the emerald cities.[19]

Of course, insofar as the mountain of Qāf only lends its name to the ancient Elburz, its primordial Image has been projected also on spaces of empirical geography (the Caucasus and its foothills on Iranian soil), which then become the theater of mythical events. On the other hand, as a primordial Image, it always marks the extremity of the world, and is inaccessible to men. To reach it, it would be necessary to walk for four months "in the Darkness"; that is why Alexander's progress through the region of Darkness is that of the archetypal spiritual hero, in Avicenna's "Recital of Ḥayy ibn Yaqẓān," as well as in the exegesis of the Qur'ānic Sūra 18:84, describing how Alexander's Quest led him to the extreme Occident and the extreme Orient of the universe. Beyond, a region begins that includes many other cities (a country white as silver, forty days' travel in length, inhabited by angels; another country, of gold, seventy countries of silver, seven countries of musk, each ten thousand days' journey in length and breadth, etc.). In short, to penetrate into these Earths is to gain access to the intermediate climate of the "celestial souls" that move the Spheres and are preeminently endowed with pure Imagination, not depending on the senses. It is the "eighth climate," into which, as into Ērān-Vēj, one does not penetrate with the organs of sensory perception, but by passing through the "Source of Life," at the psycho-cosmic center.

Here we find our direction in a brief reference to the schema of the world that takes definite shape in Avicenna's cosmology. This schema divides the totality of thinkable being into a cosmic Occident and a cosmic Orient. We have already recalled precisely that this cosmic Orient is not to be sought in the East on our maps, but in the "polar dimension." In fact, this Orient is the *celestial pole*, the "center" of all conceivable orientation. It is to be sought in the direction of the cosmic North, that of the "Earth of Light."[20]

The "Occident" represents the sensory material world, and it is twofold: there is the "climate" of sublunar terrestrial matter, that of our material Earth, subject to generation and dissolution; and there is the "climate" of celestial matter, that of the Spheres, consisting of an etheric substance, diaphanous and incorruptible, but still, however, deriving from the physical. The "Orient" begins from the climate of the soul: at the celestial pole, at the "emerald rock." There the spiritual Sun rises for the pilgrim, and this dawn reveals to him the perspective of an entirely new universe, wherein are ranked successively the souls summoned to govern human bodies for a time; then the Souls whose mission it is to communicate the movement of their desire and their love to the celestial Spheres, and who are called celestial Angels (*Angeli coelestes*); finally, the pure Intelligences, who are, respectively, the objects of this love and what are designated spiritual Angels or Cherubim (*Angeli intellectuales*). The characteristic that distinguishes Avicenna's cosmology from that of Averroes is precisely that the former includes in its structure this world of celestial Souls, in whose image the human soul is constituted, but which, unlike it, do not possess the organs of sensory knowledge. On the other hand, they are endowed with active Imagination. They even possess it in so pure and perfect a degree that their Imagination, independent, unlike ours, of sensory data, is entirely true and never weakened. Therefore, the representations that the Angels or celestial Souls may make of their universe correspond to the situation of the human soul when its active Imagination, purified and trained, has become the *Imaginatio vera*, its organ of meditation.

So what the soul shows to itself, in this case again, as in the case of the Mazdean *Imago Terrae*, is precisely its own image: the Earth it projects, the Earth of Hūrqalyā, is the phenomenon of the Earth in its pure state, since it directly reflects the Image premeditated by the soul. The universe thus imagined, free from misleading and perishable sensory data, is therefore a function of the pure transcendental Imagination and depends only on its categories, which are *a priori* archetypal Images. That is why this universe is called *ʿālam al-mithāl*, the world of archetypal Images, the world of autonomous imaginative forms, or again, the world of correspondences and symbols, that is, a world symbolizing *with* the sensory, which it precedes, and *with* the intelligible, which it imitates. It is a mixed world, mediating between the sensory and the intelligible; it is the *center of the worlds*, or again the "intermediate Orient," between the "near

Orient," which is the human soul rising to consciousness of itself, and the spiritual "far Orient," constituted by the pleroma of cherubic Intelligences. Thus, as pictured by our Spirituals in their own way, it represents this intermediate kingdom between pure matter and pure Spirit, an intermediary necessary in order to validate the visionary events, the entire dramaturgy of which the soul is both the subject and the scene, everything that sensory perceptions have no means to govern, impair, or supplement; everything to which the scepticism of rational consciousness is opposed, as it is to all essentially individual cases that can neither be classified nor gauged by ordinary standards.

The premises and structural purpose of this intermediate universe, this *mundus archetypus*, have so far been very little analyzed.[21] However, it fulfills an organic function in the scheme of the world and in the inner experience to which a whole spiritual tradition bears witness and from which, in Iran, we have already selected the two moments of time most essential for our purpose: in the twelfth century, the restoration of the philosophy of ancient Persia (based on angelology and the *Xvarnah*, the Light of Glory), insofar as this was Suhrawardī's work; closer to us, at the end of the eighteenth century, that spiritual school born in an Iranian Imāmite milieu, which was the work of Shaikh Aḥmad Aḥsā'ī (d. 1826) and his successors, and which is usually called Shaikhism. We have outlined above the fundamental Imāmology professed by this school, which entirely revalorizes the gnosis already known in the esoteric circles of Imāmism or primitive Shī'ite Islam. Later, we shall have to stress again its no less fundamental theme, the *spiritual body*. This school, still very much alive today in Iran (where its principal center is Kirmān),[22] can give us an idea of what a purely spiritual Islam would represent for our modern times.

Here now are the teachings given us by the one and the other. "When you learn in the treatises of ancient Sages," writes Suhrawardī, "that there exists a world with dimensions and extension, other than the pleroma of Intelligences and other than the world governed by the Souls of the Spheres, a world with so many cities that it is almost impossible to count their number, do not hasten to call this a lie; it so happens that the pilgrims of the spirit contemplate this world and in it find every object of their desire."[23] The author, as well as his immediate commentators, have on several occasions clearly described its ideal topography.[24] They tell us that while the world with extension perceptible to the senses includes *seven* climates (the seven *keshvars* previously mentioned), another world exists, which forms the *eighth* climate. The ancient Sages were alluding to this world when they declared that besides the sensory world there is another world with shape and dimensions also extending in space, but the shape, dimensions, and extent of this other world are not identical with those we perceive in the world of physical bodies, although what exists in the sensory world has its analogue there; it is not a question of sensory dimensions, but of exemplary imaginative dimensions (*maqādīr mithālīya*).

So here we have a threefold universe: an intelligible universe, a sensory universe, and between the two a universe for which it is difficult in our language to find a satisfactory term. If we use the word *Imaginable*, we risk suggesting the idea of eventuality, possibility. The word must be given all the force of a technical term as designating the object proper to the *imaginative perception*, everything that can be perceived by the Imagination, with as much reality and truth as the sensory can be perceived by the senses, or the intelligible by the intellect. Perhaps then it would be simpler to use the word *Imaginative*, provided the term is related both to the subject who imagines and to the Image which is imagined; moreover, the latter is the Image of this subject; the *imaginative* world is the world of the soul which is made Image by the organ of the soul, thereby revealing to it its own Image. That is the teaching tirelessly repeated by all our authors.

So this is a universe which symbolizes both *with* corporeal substance, because it possesses shape, dimensions, and extent—and *with* separated or intelligible substance, because it is essentially made of light (*nūrānī*). It is both immaterial matter and the incorporeal corporealized. It is the *limit* which separates and at the same time unites them. That is why in the speculative theosophy of Ṣūfism this universe is usually called *barzakh* (screen, limit, interval, interworld).[25] There, among other marvels, are three immense cities, Jābalqā, Jābarṣā, Hūrqalyā, peopled by innumerable creatures. And by virtue of the homology that makes the three worlds symbolize with one another, the world of the Imaginable or of the *Imaginative* also presents a division corresponding to the twofold Occident of the physical world; thus Jābarṣā and Jābalqā correspond to the terrestrial world of elementary matter, while Hūrqalyā corresponds to the Heavens of the physical world. Like them, Hūrqalyā transmits its influx to its own Earth, on which it also confers its own name. The world of Hūrqalyā therefore contains both Heavens and an Earth, not a sensory Earth and Heavens, but Earth and Heavens in the state of exemplary Images. Likewise, the Earth of Hūrqalyā also includes all the archetypal Images of individual beings and corporeal things existing in the sensory world (so our authors ask that these archetypal Images should not be confused with the Platonic Ideas which, although designated by the plural of the same word, *muthul*, are pure intelligibles).[26] This eighth climate, this world in the subtle state, which includes many degrees, and which is impenetrable by the sensory organs, is the *real* place of all psycho-spiritual events (visions, charismas, thaumaturgical actions breaching the physical laws of space and time), which are considered simply as imaginary—that is, as unreal—so long as one remains in the rational dilemma which is restricted to a choice between the two terms of banal dualism, "matter" or "spirit," corresponding to that other one: "history" or "myth."

In his turn, Shaikh Aḥmad Aḥsā'ī describes in detail the ideal topography of the Earth of Hūrqalyā.[27] It begins, he says, on the convex surface of the ninth Sphere—this is a precise and subtle way to indicate that this Earth is no longer contained in the dimensions of our physical cosmic space, since beyond the surface of the enveloping Sphere which, in the Ptolemaic system of the world, is the boundary limiting and defining the directions of space, the Sphere of Spheres, no further direction nor orientation in physical space is possible. There is a discontinuity between sensory space and the spatiality proper to the archetypal world of Images, which is transspatial in relation to the first one.[28] That is why, just as the world of the *barzakh*, this boundary-Earth "begins," that is has its "below" at the boundary of the emerald rock or mystical Sinai, the keystone of the celestial vault, the "pole"—in the same way Shaikh Aḥmad situated Hūrqalyā both at the "high point of Time" (*aʿlāʾl-zamān*) and at the lowest or first degree of eternity (*asfal al-Dahr*, more exactly of the *Aevum* or eternal Time).[29] Finally, it is, therefore, an *interworld*, limiting and conjoining time and eternity, space and transspace, just as its immaterial matter and its celestial Earth are also the sign of its *coincidentia oppositorum*,[30] the conjunction of the sensory and the intelligible in the pure space of the archetype-Images.

This theme is amplified in a most interesting way in an important work by the present leader of the Shaikhī community, Shaikh Sarkār Āghā, an eminent spiritual figure in Iran today, fifth in line from Shaikh Aḥmad Aḥsāʾī. We were struck by this central thought: the hierarchy of being is ranged in a series of universes, all of which end finally in our terrestrial Earth (*khāk*),[31] this Earth which is like the "tomb" to which they have been entrusted; it is from this tomb that they must emerge and be resurrected. But this resurrection is conceivable only if the "descent" of the eternal Forms onto this Earth is understood in its true sense. Just as the astralness of the Sun does not "descend" from its Heaven, so there is no question of an inherence or an "infusion" nor of a material incarnation, an idea which an "Oriental" philosophy definitely rejects.[32] On the contrary, the idea of *epiphany* dominates its mode of perception and that is why the comparison with a "mirror" is always suggested to us. Human souls, being eternal, do not themselves mix "in person," so to speak, with the world of material and accidental things, which are temporal. It is their silhouette, their Image, their shadow, which is projected onto it.[33] Each of them has its own particular activity and perfection, which are an effect and an influx of the universal and absolute activity of the Soul of the World.

§2. *The "Eighth Climate"*

Now this, the Shaikh says, is what is called "world," that absolute psychic activity which, taken as such, is at the same time below the Soul whose activity it is, but above those accidental terrestrial matters in which the sensory faculties perceive it. The world as absolute psychic activity is a *barzakh*, an interval. Hence, just as the material substance and the form of the mirror are neither the matter nor the form of the Image reflected and perceived in it, but simply the privileged place where this Image is epiphanized, so sensory matter is but the vehicle (*markab*), or rather the epiphanic place (*maẓhar*), for the forms produced by the absolute activity of the soul. It would be the greatest mistake to take mirror as constituting here the substance and consistency of the Images that appear in it. The mirror may no longer be there, it may be broken: the forms of the soul, being neither inherent in nor cosubstantial with the mirror, continue to subsist.

In order to grasp the Image in its *absolute* reality, that is to say *absolved*, detached, from the sensory mirror in which it is reflected, it is undoubtedly necessary to have what the Shaikh calls an "*eye of the world beyond*" (*Chashm-i barzakhī*), that is, an organ of vision which is itself a part of the absolute activity of the soul, and which corresponds to our *Imaginatio vera.* Let us emphasize then, that this does not mean knowing things as abstract idea, as philosophical concept, but as the perfectly *individuated* features of their Image, meditated, or rather premeditated, by the soul, namely their archetypal Image. That is why in this intermediate world there are Heavens and Earths, animals, plants, and minerals, cities, towns, and forests. Now, this means, in effect, that if things corresponding to all these are visible and seen in this world, here on this terrestrial Earth, it is because ultimately what we call *physis* and physical is but the reflection of the world of the Soul; there is no pure physics, but always the physics of some definite psychic activity. So, to become aware of it is to see the world of the Soul, to see all things as they are in the Earth of Hūrqalyā, the Earth of emerald cities, it is the *visio smaragdina*, which is the surrection and the resurrection of the world of the Soul. Then this reality that ordinary consciousness confers on physical things and events as if they were autonomous realities, proves in fact to be the *visionary* reality of the soul.[34]

That is why we were able to say that the mystical Earth of Hūrqalyā represents, as it were, the phenomenon of the Earth in its *absolute* state, that is, *absolved* from the empirical *appearance* displayed to the senses, and, on the other hand, the *real apparition* restored by the transcendental Imagination alone. Here all realities exist in the state of Images, and these Images are *a priori* or archetypal; in other words, they are themselves, as it were, *pre-meditant*, in the meditation of the soul whose world they are, for, since they are the world, that is the activity proper to this soul, they "give the measure" of this soul, express its structure and its energies. The awakening to consciousness of Hūrqalyā announces a new mode of relationship of the soul with extent, with everything that is corporeal and spatial, a relationship that cannot be a relation of content with container. The way of seeing the Earth and the way of seeing the soul are the very same thing, the vision in which the soul perceives itself; this can be its *paradise*, and it can be its *hell*. The "eighth climate" is the climate of the soul, and that is what the great theosophist Ibn ʿArabī (d. 1240) conveys to us in a mythical recital from which I will give here only a few striking extracts.

From the clay from which Adam was created, he says,[35] or rather from the leaven of this clay, a surplus remained. From this surplus an Earth was created whose Arabic name (*Arḍ ḥaqīqa*) can be translated both as "Earth of True Reality" and "Earth of Real Truth." It is an immense Earth, which itself includes Heavens and Earths, Paradises and Hells. A great number of things whose existence in our world has been proven rationally and validly to be impossible, nevertheless do exist without a doubt in that Earth—the prairie on which the mystical theosophists never tire of feasting their eyes. And here is the point: in the whole of the universes of this Earth of Truth, God has created for each soul a universe corresponding to that soul. *When the mystic contemplates this universe, it is himself* (*nafs*, his *Anima*), *that he is contemplating.*

§2. *The "Eighth Climate"*

Thus, the *Imago Terrae* is indeed here the very image of the soul, the image through which the soul contemplates itself, its energies and its powers, its hopes and its fears. That is why this Earth of Truth is the place where all the Images which the soul projects on its horizon really subsist and disclose to it the presence of one or another of its states. Rational or rationalistic objections cannot prevail against it. This Earth of Truth is the Earth of the flowering of symbols that the rational intellect fails to penetrate, believing as it usually does that in "explaining" a symbol it has by the same token made it disappear by rendering it superfluous. No, in this Earth of Truth the whole enchanted universe of the soul subsists because there the soul is "at home" and because its own archetypal Images have become transparent for it, while at the same time they remain necessary to it precisely in order that their esoteric quality (*bāṭin*) may show through.

Without these Images the soul would actualize neither these rituals nor these iconographies and dramaturgies whose *place* of real fulfillment is precisely the Earth of Hūrqalyā. That is also why this Earth is the *place* of visionary recitals, of prayer in dialogue; it is not, Ibn ʿArabī says, the *place* of mystical annihilations, of the abysses of negative theology, but the *place* of divine epiphanies (*tajalliyāt ilāhīya*), which do not volatilize the soul nor tear it away from the vision of itself, but on the contrary help it to be at last with itself and in itself. Every form in which these epiphanies are clothed, as well as every form in which man sees himself in dreams or in the intermediate state between waking and sleeping, or in that state of active meditation which is a state of waking while the senses are asleep—all this belongs to the *body* of this Earth of Truth. For one does not enter into it with bodies of coarse matter. The adept must know that if he happens to see there with his eyes some spiritual entity, it is because he has become qualified to clothe himself in one of those Forms assumed by Angels when they make themselves visible to nonsensory perception.[36]

We are now able to grasp the full significance of the concise and striking formulae in which a great theologian-philosopher, Muḥsin-Fayẓ, an Iranian Imāmite of the seventeenth century, condenses all that it is essential to know concerning the Earth of Hūrqalyā, the eighth climate, the world of archetype-Images: "This intermediate world," he says, "occupies in the macrocosm the same rank as the Imagination in the microcosm." And for this reason "it is the world through which spirits are embodied, and bodies spiritualized."[37] It may be said that each function is the reason for the other. The intermediate world is accessible only to the active Imagination, which is at the same time the founder of its own universe and the transmuter of sensory data into symbols. By this very transmutation a resurrection of material bodies into subtle or spiritual bodies takes place. This Earth of Hūrqalyā, which the adept's meditation feeds with his own substance, is at the same time the Earth from which his meditation extracts and develops the subtle elements of his body of resurrection. And that is why finally the mystical Earth of Hūrqalyā, the Earth of emerald cities, may be defined as the Earth of Visions *and* as the Earth of Resurrection.

3. *Hūrqalyā, Earth of Visions*

To illustrate this first aspect, we could gather here very many experimental data that can be gleaned from the works of our Spirituals. Since we must limit ourselves, we shall select only three cases: one is presented as a personal case, another refers to an ideal case, a third offers a whole spiritual teaching. The first two examples are furnished by the work of the master of Ishrāq, Suhrawardī; the third belongs to the Shaikhī teaching.

Suhrawardī relates in one of his books[38] how, during a period of overwork and spiritual ordeal brought on by meditation on the problem of Knowledge, up to then unsolved by him, one night, while still in an intermediate state between waking and sleeping, he was gratified by the apparition of the Imām of Philosophers, the *Primus Magister*, Aristotle. The beauty and the delicate light of the vision[39] are carefully described; then the author reports what was in fact a long dialogue, evoking one after another high doctrinal themes. Elsewhere, referring to this memorable conversation, he speaks of it as an event that took place in the mystical station of Jābarṣā.[40] This is both a subtle and a precise way to define the consistence of the pure psycho-spiritual event as penetration into one of the emerald cities. Precisely, the first advice given by Aristotle's apparition to his visionary, in order to free him from the problem troubling him, from which he found no relief in philosophy books, is this: "Awake to yourself." For, with this "awakening to oneself" the whole inner experience of the Ishrāq expands, that is the experience of the rising of the light, of the light in its Orient. When it awakens to *itself*, the soul is itself this rising dawn, itself the substance of the Orient Light. The "Earths" that it illuminates are no longer, for it, a collection of outer places and things, knowable only through descriptive science (*ʿilm rasmī*); they are, for the soul, its very presence to itself, its absolute activity, which it knows through "presential science" (*ʿilm ḥuḍūrī*), that is, through this "Oriental knowledge" (*ʿilm ishrāqī*) which can be characterized as *cognitio matutina.* To this day Iran has preserved this tradition.

Hermes is the ideal hero of this *cognitio matutina.* This is the second experimental datum borrowed also from Suhrawardī's works. As one can be easily convinced, the person of Hermes is there as a substitute for that of the author to thematize the personal event. It is a dramaturgy of ecstasy, the description of which is striking:[41] "One night when the sun was shining, Hermes was praying in the temple of Light. When the column of dawn burst forth, he saw an Earth being swallowed up with cities on which the divine anger had fallen, and they toppled into the abyss. Then he cried out: 'Thou who art my father, save me from being imprisoned with those who are near perdition!' And he heard a voice cry out in response: 'Grab the cable of our Irradiation and ascend to the battlements of the Throne.' So he ascended and under his feet, Lo! Earth and Heavens."

Suhrawardī's commentators have devoted themselves to deciphering the meaning of this episode;[42] it seems that it can be clearly interpreted without too much difficulty. The episode constitutes a case of celestial "inner" ascension, such as are given in visionary biographies, Zarathustra's[43] as well as that of the

Prophet of Islam during the night of the *Miʿrāj*,[44] and it is such cases which have contributed to the need, particularly in Shaikhism, for the doctrine of the "spiritual body."

Let us select the main features that here give the event its meaning for our search. There is the Earth, which is engulfed with its cities: it is the terrestrial Earth together with the faculties of sensory perception that apprehend it; they fall and vanish at dawn, that is, in the first gleam of the vision of ecstasy. Mention is then made of an Earth and of Heavens that Hermes, thereafter, has under his feet. Henceforth, Hermes is indeed on the Earth of Hūrqalyā, which implies that he has left below him all the Heavens of the physical cosmos, the "celestial Occident" of the material world. Then the synchronism of the episodes is itself significant, confirming what we had noted in the event taking place in Jābarṣā; there is a coincidence between dawn's breaking and the awakening to one's self. For, this *sun* near which, at *night*, Hermes was praying, is his very soul which, in *arising* to itself, lets the empirical facts imposed upon him by his terrestrial sojourn sink back into their darkness: this sun is the spirit's "midnight sun" or "aurora borealis." But at the moment of this breaking dawn, there is such danger that Hermes calls on his supreme recourse for assistance: the celestial *Ego* from whom he originates, to whom he returns, and who can be understood here, in the very terms of the Ishrāqī philosophy, both as "Perfect Nature," the archetypal "I" or guardian Angel of the philosopher (the "Fravarti," ἴδιος δαίμων), as well as the Angel of humanity, who is both active Intelligence and the Angel Gabriel or Holy Spirit from whom human souls emanate.[45] Rising dawn and awakening to oneself, penetration into the Earth of Hūrqalyā and meeting with the celestial *alter ego*, these are the complementary aspects of the same event that proclaims the transmutation of the soul, its birth into the intermediary world.

It would undoubtedly take a whole book to exhaust all the allusions and meanings implied by this dramaturgy of ecstasy. In any case, it allows us to understand on what experimental data the efforts of our "Oriental" (Ishrāqī) theosophists or Ṣūfīs were based to establish in its autonomy and lofty reality this intermediary world of the *Imaginalia*, so completely misconstrued through the habits of rational and positive mind, which identifies it simply with the unreal.

On the other hand, our Spirituals have diligently tried to define its ontological status. It had to be admitted that forms and figures of the "imaginative" world do not subsist like empirical realities of the physical world, otherwise they could rightfully be perceived by just anybody. It was also seen that they cannot subsist in the pure intelligible world, since they have extent and dimension, a materiality undoubtedly "immaterial" in relation to that of the sensory world, but still properly corporeal and spatial. For the same reason, they cannot have our thought alone as a substratum. And yet, they do not belong to the unreal, the void, otherwise we could neither perceive them nor have any opinion about them. Thus the existence of an intermediary world (*al-ʿālam al-khayālī al-mithālī, mundus imaginalis archetypus*) appeared metaphysically necessary. Equally dependent on it are: the validity of visionary recitals perceiving and relating "events in Heaven," the validity of dreams, of hierophanies and symbolic rituals, the reality of *places* constituted by intense meditation, the reality of inspired imaginative visions, of cosmogonic relations and of theogonies, the authenticity of the spiritual *meaning* decipherable under the imaginative data of prophetic revelations, and so on—briefly, everything that surpasses the order of common empirical perception and is individualized in a personal vision, undemonstrable by simple recourse to the criteria of sensory knowledge or rational understanding.[46]

So that, unable to attribute to these realities perceived as psycho-spiritual events either the status of permanent physical substances in sensory space or the inherence of sensory accidents in their substratum, one was led to conceive a mode of being formulated as a mode of "being in suspense" (*al-muthul al-muʿallaqa*), that is, a mode of being such that the Image or the Form, being its own "matter," is independent of a substratum in which it would be immanent in the manner of an accident (like the color black, for example, subsisting through the black object in which it is immanent). Let us imagine the form of a statue in its pure state, liberated from the marble, the wood, or the bronze. That is why we always return to the *apparitional* mode which is that of subsistence of the Images "in suspense" in a mirror. This was generalized in a doctrine of epiphanic places and forms (*maẓāhir*), which is one of the characteristic aspects of Suhrawardī's Oriental theosophy. The active Imagination (*takhayyul*) is the mirror *par excellence*, the epiphanic place (*maẓhar*) of the Images of the archetypal world. That is why its perceptions are just as real as those of the sensory faculties.

They are real even to a more eminent degree, since the *Imaginalia* of sensory things that are epiphanized there proclaim transmutation of the latter. Personal figures, forms, and landscapes, plants and animals that appear in it no longer obey the permanent laws of density nor the conditions of the perceptibility of the sensory world. Thus, it is in Hūrqalyā that Pythagoras, for example, was able to perceive the melody of the Spheres, the cosmic music—that is to say, outside of his material body and without his organs of sensory perception.[47] It is therefore necessary to conceive that there are sounds, for example, perfectly perceptible by the active Imagination, which are not conditioned by vibrations of the air; they constitute the archetype-Image of sound.[48] In short, there is a whole universe of correspondences in the image of the physical world (possessing figure, color, extension, scent, resonance) that does not depend on pure physics,[49] or rather, that presupposes the integration of physics as such into psycho-spiritual activity, their conjunction in an intermediate world rising above the dualism of matter and spirit, of senses and intellect.

The metamorphosis, which elevates our vision and situates it on a level from which everything that was offered to the ordinary consciousness as a purely physical thing or event appears from then on in its essential conjunction with the psycho-spiritual activity that conditions its very perceptibility—this metamorphosis is "to be in the Earth of Hūrqalyā." *Hūrqalyā is the Earth of the soul, because it is the soul's vision.* "To see things in Hūrqalyā" is to see them as they are as events of the soul, and not as constituted into autonomous material realities, with a meaning detached from and independent of the soul, as our positive science constitutes and "objectifies" them. Finally, it is a way of meditating the Earth and transfiguring it by this meditation.

Here we can also refer to the teaching of the eminent Shaikh Sarkār Āghā, and this is the third example that I wished to cite, because it stresses the orientation of the entire spiritual life. It is here below, on this very Earth, the Shaikh tells us, that one must become an inhabitant of the Earth of Hūrqalyā, a *Hūrqalyāvī*.[50] Immediately we glimpse the importance of this imperative, when it concerns living the fundamental hope of Imāmism or Shīʿism, its expectation of the Imām (corresponding to the expectation of Maitreya, the future Buddha, of the Saoshyant in Zoroastrianism, to the return of Christ in Christianity). It is not an outward event to be expected sometime in the far distant future; it is an Event that here and now is taking place in souls and slowly progresses and matures there. "The Imām's epiphany takes place for us," the Shaikh writes, "at the very moment when our eyes open [cf. above, "the eye of the world beyond," the "*barzakhī* eye"], the moment we contemplate the epiphany of this reign in all the universes." Then the statement of Shaikh Aḥmad Aḥsā'ī takes on its full meaning, affirming that for the Spirituals "the Imām *from this very day in Hūrqalyā* is the object of their contemplation." This is what is meant by the Sun rising (or rising again) in the West, that is the Orient, in the true sense, the corollary being the decline of the ready-made empirical evidences of the material Earth, to which the soul had declined. Furthermore, says the Shaikh, only then "you will have contemplated Hūrqalyā, and rising higher than this terrestrial Earth, will you have perceived the archetype-Image and the light of your own Imām, a light which encompasses at the same time the terrestrial world and all that is contained between Jābalqā and Jābarṣā."

With this conception of eschatology, we can understand also that the whole of *history* is "seen in Hūrqalyā."[51] That being admitted, the events of this history are seen to be much more than what we ourselves call "facts"; they are *visions*. On the other hand, everything that we call "history," and value as "historical," is not "seen in Hūrqalyā," is not an event in the Earth of Hūrqalyā, and therefore is devoid of religious interest and spiritual meaning. The orientation of the terrestrial Earth toward the Earth of Hūrqalyā, toward the celestial *pole*, confers a *polar dimension* on terrestrial existence, gives it a direction not evolutionary but vertical, ascensional. The past is not behind us, but "under our feet."[52] It is precisely there that our mental habits, not only scientific but religious, perhaps make us "lose our footing." Where these habits demand what we call historical facts, verifiable concrete realities, physical events witnessed and recorded, we are answered mildly by "visions." Perhaps the content of those books that we call Apocryphal (those of the Old and of the New Testament) can best help us to understand the matter[53] (and precisely the fact that they are set aside as "Apocryphal" has a meaning). One may call this *docetism*, but perhaps the entire East has always been profoundly docetist (there is docetism in gnosis, there is docetism in Islam, there is a Buddhist docetism, for docetism is fundamentally nothing but a "theosophical" critique of knowledge, a phenomenology of spiritual forms).

In any case, it is this idea of *physics* being simultaneously and essentially a psycho-spiritual activity, which makes possible something like a physics of Resurrection and a physiology of the "body of resurrection." It is not from the elements of the terrestrial Earth, but from the elements of the Earth of the emerald cities that the "spiritual body" originates. It is as Earth of Visions that the Earth of Hūrqalyā is the Earth of Resurrection. This is the highest point and outstanding feature of the Shaikhī doctrine, amply expounded in the work of its founder, Shaikh Aḥmad Aḥsā'ī.

4. *Hūrqalyā, Earth of Resurrection*

The specific nature of the doctrine is already indicated in the terminology that leads Shaikh Aḥmad to make a strict distinction between two terms currently used to designate body: there is the body considered as organic, animated body (*jasad*), and there is the body considered as corporeal mass or volume (*jism*).[54] In our Shaikh's anthropology it is established that the human being possesses two *jasad* and two *jism*; they represent a twofold *accidental* body and a twofold *essential* body, according to the following schema:

(1) There is the first *jasad*, which we shall call *jasad A*, and which is understood as being the *elemental body*, material and perishable. It is the apparent body of each one of us, the one that we can see, touch, weigh, recognize. It is an *accidental* and perishable formation, a compound of sublunar *physical elements*.

(2) There is a second *jasad*, which we shall call *jasad B*; it is hidden and occult from our sight in *jasad A*; it also is an elemental formation, but differs from the first in that it is not composed of perishable terrestrial elements—those, that is, of our material Earth—but of archetypal elements, the subtle elements of the "Earth of Hūrqalyā." This second *jasad* is, therefore, a formation belonging to the intermediate world, the world of the *barzakh*; consequently, it has dimensions, but, unlike the first *jasad*, it is not an accidental body but an *essential* and imperishable body; it is the subtle elemental body, the body of "spiritual flesh," *caro spiritualis*.

(3) There is the first *jism*; let us call it *jism A*. Unlike the two *jasad*, it is not an elemental body; it belongs neither to the terrestrial Elements nor to the subtle Elements. It resembles *jasad A* for, like it, it is accidental, not everlasting. It resembles *jasad B* in the sense of being, like it, a formation of the intermediate world. However, it does not arise from the subtle elements of the Earth of Hūrqalyā (from the region, that is to say, which corresponds there to the *terrestrial climate* of the cosmic Occident); it originates from the celestial matter and Heavens of Hūrqalyā (from the region, that is, corresponding to the Spheres, to the *celestial climate* of the cosmic Occident). It is the subtle celestial body, the astral body, destined to be reabsorbed.

(4) There is the second *jism*, which we shall call *jism B*, and this is the essential subtle body, archetypal, eternal and imper-

ishable (*jism aṣlī ḥaqīqī*); the spirit is never separated from it, for it is what constitutes the eternal individuality. One can say of it that it is the *corpus supracoeleste* in man.[55]

At first sight, this schema strikingly resembles what we find in the writings of the Neoplatonist, Proclus. The idea of these different bodies, in which the soul is clothed, and which correspond to different levels of being, reproduces the concept of the ὀχήματα (*okhēmata*) or "vehicles of the soul" which the Neoplatonists were so prone to meditate.[56] The doctrine of the astral body (σῶμα ἀστροειδὲς) or ὄχήματα-πνεῦμα is so fundamental in the spiritual family to which Neoplatonism belongs that it immediately calls for many other references, notably the "perfect body" (σῶμα τέλειον) of the Mithraic liturgy, the "immortal body" (σῶμα ἀθάνατον) of the Hermetic *Corpus*,[57] and finally, for this is what it suggests, this is its aim and object of aspiration, the ἴδιος δαίμον or οἴκεος δαίμον,[58] the personal divinity or guardian Angel to whom the adept is entrusted on initiation, and which makes the terrestrial human being the counterpart of a celestial being with whom it forms a whole. This, in terms of Mazdean theosophy, is Fravarti, Daēnā, the transcendent "I," the celestial *alter ego*.

We know the terms of the question in the case of a Proclus: a compromise had to be found not only between Plato and Aristotle, but also between the Peripatetic tendency of Neoplatonism and the Stoic psychology of the *pneuma*.[59] Besides, two traditions concerning the "astral body" had to be reconciled, both alive in Neoplatonism. Of these traditions, one represents the astral body as attached permanently to the soul, the other represents it as acquired or assumed by the soul during the soul's descent from the upper regions, and as having to be abandoned by the soul in the course of its reascent.[60] Proclus succeeds here in achieving a synthesis, the homologue of which is found in the Shaikhite doctrine; for him it consists in accepting the existence of two ὄχημα (*okhēma*). These are:

(1) the higher ὄχημα which is original, congenital (συμφυές), the one that is called αὔγοειδές (luminous, auroral) or ἀστροειδές (astral). It is the *proton soma* (original body) in

which the demiurge has placed the soul. It is immaterial, impassible, imperishable. What corresponds exactly to it in Shayikh Aḥmad Aḥsā'ī's terminology and concepts, is the *jism B*, which is called the archetype original, essential (*jism aṣlī ḥaqīqī*): it is the real or essential human being, man in the true sense (*insān ḥaqīqī*).[61]

(2) The ὄχημα πνευματικόν, or lower "pneumatic" vehicle, which is a temporary adjunct, composed of four elements: it is the subtle body or vehicle of the irrational soul; like the latter it survives the death of the body, but is destined to disappear or be reabsorbed. What corresponds to it is *jism A*, an accidental formation issued from the Heavens of the *barzakhī* or *hūrqalyī* intermediate world.

This question of the subtle body, of the vehicle of the soul, (Macrobius' *luminosi corporis amictus*, Boethius' *levis currus*)[62] has persisted and will persist, will always be meditated, so it seems, as long as Neoplatonic thought survives. It reappears among the Byzantine Neoplatonists (Michael Psellos, Nicephoros Gregoras), the Cambridge Neoplatonists (Ralph Cudworth, seventeenth century) and, let us now add, among our Neoplatonists of Persia.

But in Shaikhism, the themes of meditation grow more complicated. While Proclus was able to reconcile the two traditions —of an original and imperishable *okhēma* and of an *okhēma* which will end by being reabsorbed or detached from the soul— it can roughly be said that Shaikh Aḥmad Aḥsā'ī proceeds simultaneously to affirm the existence of a twofold imperishable *okhēma* (*jism B* and *jasad B*), and of an *okhēma pneumatikon* (*jism A*), a nonpermanent subtle astral body. The complication of this schema can, it seems, be attributed to the need to safeguard the exegesis of Qur'ānic data concerning eschatology in general.

These data taken literally, as they were understood by the literalist "orthodox" of Islam, presuppose that the body of terrestrial flesh, *jasad A*, is resurrected, or "returns" just as it was. For philosophical meditation, this material identity has always represented an insurmountable contradiction, all the more fruitless in that it stems from an insufficient understanding of the problem. For the physical impossibility to be proven, the question demands that one rise above the realm of empirical sensory evidence and the corresponding mode of perception. At that very point, the work to be done is to transmute the latter into its spiritual truth; it is not to find a way of escape into allegory and its abstract residuum, but to establish a "*hūrqalyī* physics." This is the very thing that makes possible the schema of the fourfold body we have just outlined. In effect, though *jism A*, the accidental astral body, is finally to disappear (like the *okhēma pneumatikon* of the Neoplatonists)—for, while being a *hūrqalyī jism*, it is nevertheless accidental—it will be replaced by another "vehicle," subtle and permanent, which is a body at the same time *elemental* and *essential*, a body of "spiritual flesh," constituted by the subtle archetype—elements of the celestial Earth of Hūrqalyā. In this way, the state of wholeness, *homo totus*, always comprises, as in Proclus' system, a twofold *okhēma.* This concept is properly that of the Iranian Neoplatonists and in a way reinforces that of the Greek Neoplatonists.

Here then, very briefly, is the Shaikhite conception of the eschatological process: everything which is *accidental* body (*jasad A* and *jism A*) will eventually disappear. Everything which is essential body (*jasad B*, and *jism B*) is assured of survival. *Jasad A* is the coarse elemental body in which the descending soul clothed itself on reaching the terrestrial world. It is not essential, merely an accidental coating. It perishes and is decomposed, each element returning to its source and blending with it—a fact of ordinary observation. Now, what leaves this perishable body at the moment when the Angel of Death comes to gather up the soul is a twofold thing: the *essential* original body (*jism B*, *okhēma symphyes*), which is the permanent basis of the eternal soul (*ḥāmil li'l-nafs*), but at this point enwrapped in that *accidental* subtle body (*jism A*, *okhēma pneumatikon*) in which the soul had clothed itself in the course of its descent towards the terrestrial Earth, on passing through the intermediate world of the *barzakh.* This also is a formation of the intermediate world; however, as we have already said, it is constituted not from the subtle matter of the *elements* of the

Earth of Hūrqalyā, but from the subtle matter of the Heavens of Hūrqalyā. It likewise is an accidental formation. These two *jism* (*A* and *B*) survive, together forming the state of eternal human individuality and experiencing in the interworld either the joy and sweetness of the "Occidental Paradise" (the flavor of this expression unexpectedly recalls the "Pure Earth" of Buddhism) or, on the contrary, the despair of a Hell immanent in itself. This applies to individual eschatology as such. But what enters at this point is an extremely complex interpretation of *general eschatology*, that is, of the events closing our *Aeon* and preluding a new cosmic cycle.

A verse in the Qur'ān (39:68) tells of the two "blasts of the trumpet" which are to be sounded by the Angel Seraphiel. This verse gave full scope to the speculative impulse of the Shaikhī theosophists. The Angel's "trumpet" is, of course, a cosmic instrument. Each of its orifices represents the "treasure," the original matrix from which each being has come forth, in this case the *jism aṣlī*, the subtle, essential, congenital body (*jism B*), the archetype of human individuality. The first sounding of the trumpet heralds the total reabsorption of the cosmos; each being reenters its source and sleeps there during an interval whose length is expressed as four centuries of our terrestrial duration (this of course does not refer to chronology or quantitative time). The second sounding of Seraphiel's trumpet proclaims the Renewal of Creation (*tajdīd al-khalq*), a new cosmic cycle that assumes the character of an *apokotastisis*, a restoration of all things in their absolute, paradisic purity.[63]

In what then does the Event of this Resurrection consist? How can it be that the Earth of Hūrqalyā is at the same time the instrument and the scene no longer of the individual eschatology alone (the entrance of subtle bodies into the "Occidental Paradise"), but of the general eschatology? What they tell us is this: when the trumpet sounds for the Resurrection, the essential, original body, which is the support of the eternal individuality (*jism aṣlī*, *jism B*), reappears in its unchangeable wholeness (*verus homo*, *insān ḥaqīqī*). As for *jism A*, *okhēma pneumatikon*, which had merely lent a degree of opacity to the perfect subtleness of the *jism B*, it does not reappear, or rather, it is completely reabsorbed into the all-luminous subtlety of *jism B*. As we have seen, these two *jism* departed together, at the moment of death, from the perishable, terrestrial, elemental body, *jasad A*. But what of the imperishable subtle elemental body, the body of "spiritual flesh" made of the elements of the Earth of Hūrqalyā, *jasad B* or *jasad hūrqalyī*?

Here Shaikhism introduces a highly original concept. This body, likewise *essential*, is made up of the subtle matter of the archetype—elements of the Earth of Hūrqalyā and is also a receptacle of the influences of the Heavens of Hūrqalyā; this means that it possesses organs of perception that are seventy times more noble and more subtle than those of the body of elemental flesh in which it is hidden and invisible. It has shape, extent, and dimension, and is nevertheless imperishable. Whereas the terrestrial elemental body, *jasad A*, perishes in the grave, *jasad B*, or *jasad hūrqalyī* does not depart from it at the moment of death in company with the essential man (*insān ḥaqīqī*), who is made up of the original subtle body enveloped in his other, provisional, subtle body. The *jasad hūrqalyī* survives, they tell us—survives "in the grave." But at this point we should refer to a striking feature of one of Maeterlinck's dialogues expressing the esoteric meaning of death, when the Shadow, a few moments before becoming the Angel of him whose death it *is*, declares: "They look for me only in the graveyards, where I never go. I do not like corpses."[64] The "grave," that is, the place where the *jasad B* continues to be, is not the "graveyard," but exactly the mystical Earth of Hūrqalyā to which it belongs, being constituted of its subtle elements; it survives there, invisible to the senses, visible only to the visionary Imagination.

Vision of this mystical subsistence is, therefore, itself a preeminent example of a psycho-spiritual event "taking place" in the Earth of Hūrqalyā. Here the difference between the schools of thought becomes apparent. Proclus held that the inhabitants of the high places of the Earth in Plato's myth, the *Phaedo* were souls still clothed in their lower *okhēma* and awaiting their complete *apokotastisis*.[65] In a way peculiarly his, Shaikh Aḥmad also rises above the dilemma which would leave no choice except between the idea of completely disembodied souls (in contradiction with the idea of soul) and the idea of complete immortality of the irrational soul (*Jamblichus*). But when we come to Shaikhism, the doctrine of *apokotastisis* is amplified. It is affirmed, not only that the lower *okhēma* is stripped, but further affirms the reassumption of this other essential body, which is also a subtle vehicle, an imperishable, paradisic body, sleeping in Hūrqalyā, the Earth of Light whence it came. That is where the Angel took it in order to "hide" it in the terrestrial body of flesh, at the moment of conception.

Therefore, at the second sounding of the trumpet, this *jasad B* or *hūrqalyī* body, the body of "spiritual flesh," is the body which the eternal, individual soul, conveyed by its original, essential, or archetypal body (*jism B*), again puts on its transfigured terrestrial raiment of glory. Now, this reunion and transfiguration take place in and through the Earth of Hūrqalyā. This celestial Earth, this "eighth climate," is, indeed, what preserves the future "Resurrection Body," since this Earth is its source; and for that reason also it plays the same role in the general eschatology, namely, that of "Earth of Resurrection." It goes without saying that "orthodox" Islam has never been able to find its way in this theosophical physics; the Shaikhīs had to face difficult situations, a mass of objections, on the feebleness of which we need not dwell, since the premises remained on the very mental level which the Shaikhīs' meditation aimed to surpass.[66]

Let us enter still more deeply into this Shaikhī meditation, which transmutes things into the substance of Hūrqalyā by contemplating them in that "Earth" and thus evolves a physics and physiology of Resurrection. We notice, then, that in this process meditation on the alchemical Work plays a capital part, and that the spiritual practice of alchemy continues in a discreet fashion even to our day in Iranian Shaikhism. The work of its founder reveals the need he exemplifies to interiorize the true practice in order to obtain from it the psychic reactions which are resolved in a mystical psychology of the Resurrection body.

II. *Mystical Earth of Hūrqalyā*

The basic idea of alchemy for the Shaikhīs[67] is that it alone makes it possible to conceive the resurrection of bodies as a consequence or corollary of the survival of Spirits. It makes it possible to pass from the one to the other and gather them into a single concept. To make this transition is to make at the same time a transposition (an "anaphora") and a transmutation, which invalidate the rationalist philosophical arguments against resurrection, because these arguments are carried on on a level lower than the level on which the question in fact arises, just as, and for the same reason, the "literalist" concepts of orthodox theologians concerning the resurrection of bodies are equally weak.

From the beginning, let us remember Shaikh Sarkār Āghā's beautiful and forceful maxim: one's first concern is to become a *Hūrqalyāvī* oneself; one must be able and one must have been initiated to see things and beings, processes and events, "in Hūrqalyā." The organ of sight is the active Imagination, which alone enters into the intermediate realm, makes the invisible within the visible visible to itself. It is thus the *quinta essentia* of all living, corporeal, and psychic energies. We hear Shaikh Aḥmad insisting strongly in his turn on the essential function of the meditant, active Imagination; as he says very definitely: "The Imagination is essential to the soul and consubstantial (*jawharānī*) with it; it is an instrument of the soul, just as the hand is an instrument of the physical body. Even sensory things are known only by means of this organ, for it is to the soul what the Soul of the Heaven of Venus is to the Soul of the Heaven of the Zodiac."[68] One can therefore also say here in Paracelsist terms that the Imagination is the "*astrum in homine*," "*coeleste sive supracoeleste corpus*."[69] And one can add likewise that the alchemical Work, because of the psychic effects it produces in him who meditates and interiorizes it, is essentially *carried out* "in the Earth of Hūrqalyā." So in that sense, it can be said of alchemy that it works with the elements of the Earth of Hūrqalyā and "transmutes" the terrestrial elements into these subtle elements.

But for this to be true, the alchemical Operation must be really perceived and mentally actualized in Hūrqalyā, and it is for this purpose that the appropriate organ of perception is necessary. This is why the alchemical Operation (*ʿamal al-ṣināʿa al-maktūm*), literally, that is, the *operatio secreta Artis*, is called the "Wise Men's Mirror" (*mirʾāt al-ḥukamāʾ*). "Of the Operation of the Elixir (*ʿamal al-iksīr*)," writes Shaikh Aḥmad, "the Wise have made a Mirror in which they contemplate all the things of this world, whether it be a concrete reality (*ʿayn*) or a mental reality (*maʿnā*). In this mirror, the resurrection of bodies is seen to be homologous to the resurrection of spirits."[70] The postulate is that one and the same spiritual Energy of light is just as much the constituent of the essence of what is qualified as material as it is of the essence of what is qualified as spiritual.[71] Briefly, how it should be expressed is by saying that "Spirits are being-light in the fluid state (*nūr wujūdī dhāʾib*) whereas bodies are being-light but in the solidified state (*nūr wujūdī jāmid*). The difference between the two is like the difference between water and snow. Proof confirming the resurrection of the one is valid in respect of the resurrection of the other." Now, the final result of the alchemical Operation is exactly this *coincidentia oppositorum*: once a body has been treated and perfected by this Operation, it is in the state of "solid (or 'congealed,' 'frozen,' *miyāh jāmida*) liquid."[72]

Here, then, are some themes for meditation which, amongst others, are suggested to us with a view to interiorizing the alchemical Work. Let us, for example, take silica and potash, opaque, dense substances corresponding to the state of the terrestrial, elemental body (*jasad A*). In the first place, having been boiled and liquefied, these two substances lose their opacity and become glass (potassium silicate), which is transparent; in this state the outer allows the inner to be seen through it; the hidden spontaneously shows through the apparent. Certainly it is still the lithoid substance, and yet it is no longer that. This state should be meditated as corresponding to the *jasad B*, which is the subtle, diaphanous body composed of the *elements* of Hūrqalyā. In refusion with the addition of a certain chemical, glass becomes crystal; crystal with the addition of the white Elixir turns into the "crystal which sets on fire" (a "lens"). At this stage it corresponds to *jism A* (*okhēma pneumatikon*), that is, to the astral body which envelopes the essential original body (*jism aṣlī*, *jism B*), or eternal individual, and which, together with the latter, enters the "celestial Earth" at the moment when death separates them from the perishable elemental body (i.e., from *jasad A*). When the crystal is fused a second time with white Elixir, it becomes diamond. This is the same crystal, the same silicate in which the crystal was hidden, the same compound of mercury and sulphur, and yet it is no longer any of these. "And diamond, freed from crystal, freed from glass, freed from stone, corresponds to the believer's bodies in this absolute Paradise."[73]

This operation is confirmed by others. That, for instance, which is performed on pewter. Pewter treated with white Elixir turns into pure silver, the stage of *jasad B*. Treated with red Elixir, the silver becomes pure gold, the stage of *jism A*, which enters the earthly Paradise or celestial Earth. Treated again with red Elixir, the pewter-become-gold itself becomes Elixir, the stage of *jism B*, which, reunited with *jasad B* (the *hūrqalyī* body) and having assimilated the latter to its own subtlety, enters into the absolute Paradise.[74]

Briefly, the meditation that interiorizes the transmutations accomplished in the course of the real operation engenders the *spiritual body*, which also is a *coincidentia oppositorum*. It enters into the intermediate realm, into the psychic realm of subtle bodies through the active meditant Imagination, which, by transmuting sensory processes or events into symbols, itself activates psychic energies which radically transmute the relationship between soul and body. There is then a state, says Shaikh Aḥmad, in which "bodies perceive through their very essence (*bi-dhātihā*) the thoughts which are thought in the celestial world, as well as angelic Forms. Reciprocally, the Spirits dependent on these bodies perceive bodies and corporeal realities through their own essence, since their bodies, when they wish it, become spirit and their spirit, when they wish it, becomes body."[75] Therefore, meditation on the alchemical operation or meditation operating alchemically reach the result the formula of which is precisely the definition we have heard, given by Moḥsen Fayẓ, of the world of the *barzakh* as "a world through which bodies are spiritualized, and spirits embodied." And this is the perfect definition of the Earth of Hūrqalyā, as well as of the Events which are accomplished there and to which this mystical Earth lends its very substance.

But, of course, this "substantiation" occurs only through the presence of the adept to this mystical Earth where spiritual bodies alone can be present. That is why the constant principle here again is: *solve et coagula.* The Wise, writes Shaikh Aḥmad, dissolve and coagulate the Stone with a part of its spirit and repeat the operation several times. When they have treated it three times with the white Elixir and nine times with the red Elixir, the Stone becomes a living spiritual Mineral (or metal) (*maʿdan ḥayawānī rūḥānī*), which exactly translates our Latin alchemists' idea of the living Stone (*lapis vivus*).[76] It is a *body*, but its operation is *spiritual*: it gives life to those "metals" which are dead. Meditate and understand this Sign, says the Shaikh, for such a body is precisely the Sign of the dwellers in Paradise, "for they have bodies in which exist all the attributes, laws, and actions of bodies, but such bodies enact the actions of Spirits and pure Intelligences; they perceive what the celestial Souls and angelic Intelligences perceive, just as the latter perceive through their own essence what Souls and bodies perceive."[77] Bodies such as these are made from the original clay (*al-ṭīna al-aṣlīya*) of the emerald cities Jābalqā and Jābarṣā, and they receive the influx, no longer of the Heavens of the physical cosmos, but of the Heavens of Hūrqalyā.[78]

Shaikh Aḥmad Aḥsā'ī's own words have, we believe, conveyed what is essential in the doctrine. At some future date, we shall publish a study of the amplification by his successors of the theme of the spiritual body which is the body of resurrection. In so doing, we shall discover the constants in what might be called the "metaphysics of ecstasy" common to all the Spirituals, and which bears witness to the permanence and identity of this *interworld* on which their similar experiences converge. The Shaikhs emphasize the idea of an essential archetype body (*jism aṣlī ḥaqīqī*) which simultaneously possesses dimension, shape, form, and color like bodies in general, but which differs from them in one radical respect, namely that the appearance of the essential body depends on actions fulfilled and the inner states manifested by these actions.[79] In our terrestrial world, our inner states are invisible and the aspect of what we do is limited to the outer, observable appearance, but in the celestial earth the same actions assume another form and inner states project visible forms. Some take the form of palaces, others the form of houris, or of flowers, plants, trees, animals, gardens, streams of running water,[80] and so on. All these forms and figures are seen and are real "outside," but they are at the same time *attributes* and *modes of being* of man. Their transfiguration is the transfiguration of man, and they form his surroundings, his celestial Earth. Hence it can be said that the action is its own reward and the reward is the action "itself."[81]

The ontological status of this celestial Earth is thus defined in terms comparable, to take but one example, to the fundamental doctrine of Swedenborg, who constantly reminds us, in formulations which vary very little, that "things outside the Angels assume an appearance corresponding to those which are within them."[82] All things that come into the Angels' field of vision correspond to their "interior" and represent it; "they vary in accordance with these inner states, and this is why they are called 'Apparitions' (*apparentiae*), but because they issue from this source they are perceived so much more vividly and distinctly than the way in which men perceive terrestrial data, that they must rather be called 'real Apparitions' (*apparentiae reales*) since they really exist."[83] And the following formulation is perhaps the essential one: "the body of each Spirit and each Angel *is* the form of its love."[84] A Shaikhī saying echoes this fundamental thesis: "The paradise of the faithful gnostic is his very *body* and the hell of the man without faith or knowledge is likewise his body itself."[85] Or again, this saying which condenses the fruit of Shaikh Aḥmad Aḥsā'ī's meditations on the "diamond body": "Every individual rises again in the very form which his Work (in the alchemical sense) has fixed in the secret (esoteric) depth of himself."[86]

One can also understand how the idea of the celestial body or resurrection body expresses the idea of the human being in his totality, *homus integer*. By representing the human person in its transfigured state, it is henceforward far more than the physical organ of personal subjectivity in opposition to the world, since it is "its" world, its "true world," that is, not a foreign, opaque reality, but a transparency, the immediate presence of itself to itself. From that point also we can understand how the representation of the original, spiritual body, the *okhēma symphyes* of Neoplatonism, came to be connected with the idea of personal divinity (*idios daïmōn*), the guardian Angel or archetypal "I" from which the terrestrial "me" originates. This again recalls an odd detail: Shaikh Aḥmad, when asked about the origin of the name Hūrqalyā, which has as strange and foreign a sound in Persian as in Arabic, answered that it was a word which came from the Syriac language (*sūryānī*) in use amongst the Sabeans of Baṣra, or more exactly, the Mandeans.[87] Now the Earth of Hūrqalyā, the intermediate world of exemplary Real Images, is the homologue, both in Suhrawardī's "Oriental theosophy" and in Shaikhism, of the Paradise of the archetypes of Yima, and it so happens that the close resemblance between the *Var* of Yima and the "second world," or world of archetypes, of Mandeism (*Mshunia Kushta*) has more than once been pointed out.

And in all cases it refers to that same world in which the liberated soul, whether in momentary ecstasy or through the supreme ecstasy of death, meets its archetypal "I," its *alter ego* or celestial Image, and rejoices in the felicity of that encounter. This reunion is celebrated in a Mandean text as follows: "I go to meet my Image and my Image comes to meet me, embraces me and holds me close when I come out of captivity."[88] Recently also, our attention was drawn to the affinity between the central hero of Mandean gnosis, Hibil Ziwa, and the young Parthian prince, the hero of the "Song of the Pearl" in the *Acts of*

Thomas.[89] In this ancient gnostic book we find again the rapture of a similar encounter, when the young Prince, on returning to the East, his fatherland, discovers the luminous raiment he had left behind: "The garment suddenly appeared when I saw it before me like unto a mirror of myself. I saw it altogether in me and I was altogether in it, for we were two, separate one from the other and yet but one of like form."[90] And the *Gospel According to Thomas* declares: "When you see your likeness, you rejoice, but when you see your Images which came into existence before you, which neither die nor are manifested, how much will you bear!"[91]

Now we must return to that which is the archetype of the individual eschatology, and which was clearly described to us in the last part of the preceding chapter. The figure of the Angel Daēnā, the celestial "I," as the daughter of Spenta Armaiti, the feminine Archangel of the Earth and of earthly existence, led us to make a connection that has seldom been pondered. It became clear to us that the filiation of the celestial "I" is verified as and when man assumes *Spendarmatīkīh*, the very nature of Spenta Armaiti, who is Wisdom-Sophia. Hence the relationship of man with the Earth, defining his present existence, was seen by us to be a *Sophianic* relationship, the full actualization of which is destined to come about in a meeting of the Earth with the "Abode of Hymns" (*Garōtmān*, the Iranian name of the celestial Paradise). Going on from there, not in the "historical direction," but according to the "polar dimension," we heard in a higher octave of the harmony of the worlds, the theme of the supracelestial Earth in the person of Fāṭima the Resplendent, Fāṭima-Sophia, who is the Earth of the pleroma of the deity because she is its Soul. We have since learned that the flowering of the spiritual body, which is the awakening and birth to the celestial "I," takes place in the form of a meditation that transfigures the Earth into a celestial Earth, because, reciprocally, it is said that "the clay of every faithful gnostic was taken from the Earth of his Paradise." Perhaps then we can begin to see no longer only *what* is the celestial Earth, but *who* is the celestial Earth.

What does all this mean for us today? Nothing more nor less

than that very thing toward which we are going, which we shape, each one of us, in the image of our own substance. We have heard it expressed in languages both remote and nearer to us, in very ancient and also in modern contexts (we went from Mazdaism to Shaikhism). Very likely, the experiences of the Iranian Spirituals evoke in each of us comparisons with certain spiritual facts known from other sources. I would like to remind you here of the words uttered in the very last moments of his life by the great musician Richard Strauss: "Fifty years ago," he managed to say, "I wrote Death and Transfiguration (*Tod und Verklärung*)." Then, after a pause: "I was not mistaken. It is indeed that."[92]

At the boundary where the boundary ceases to be a boundary and becomes a passage, there comes the overwhelming and irrefutable evidence: realization does indeed correspond to the faith professed in the innermost part of the soul. One has only to remember the last bars of this symphonic poem, and one will understand the import of that realization *in the present* at the moment when the end becomes a beginning: all that was foreglimpsed, all the struggle and secret hope borne as one faces a challenge—it is indeed that. The triumphal solemnity of the closing chorale of Mahler's Resurrection Symphony: "O my heart, believe! nothing art thou losing. What is yours remains, yes, remains forever, all that was thy waiting, thy love, thy struggle." One thing alone matters in the night in which our human lives are wrapped: that the faint gleam, the fiery light, may grow which makes us able to recognize the "Promised Land," the Earth of Hūrqalyā and its emerald cities.

PART TWO

SELECTIONS FROM TRADITIONAL TEXTS

INTRODUCTION
THE TEXTS AND THEIR AUTHORS

It seems the right moment now to let our Shaikhs speak for themselves, namely, those who have guided our research and our meditation on the theme of the celestial Earth, more particularly in Islamic Iran. This will at last provide the reader with a more direct contact, no doubt rarely available, since there are so few translations in this field. The titles of the books and the names of the authors that appear in the following pages are still, with two or three exceptions, unknown in the West, save to a few specialists. Yet the question under discussion here is not, or should not be, a problem for "specialists."

Certainly we are no longer at the stage of believing that Islamic thought is represented only by the names of the five or six great philosophers who were known to Latin Scholasticism. But how long will it still take until the cultivated Western man realizes the number of monuments of thought and spiritual masterpieces both in Arabic and in Persian which so far are almost entirely unknown? And how much longer still before the treasure of their thought enters into what is called the "cultural circuit," where it might bear fruit in conversations informed by mutual good will and open, at last, an approach to the essential? Having access, or claiming to have access, to texts of this kind, and then wrapping oneself in pseudo mystery and in a superior way withholding any references to them is simply "closing the gate of knowledge behind one"—a procedure that Suhrawardī already denounced in so many words, condemning it as a sign of imposture.

But let us be clear about one thing. The few pages translated here are just a drop in the ocean. If at least, by making it known that these books exist, they could inspire a few people with the desire to know more about them and to set to work themselves, they would already have fulfilled a part of their objective. All the passages we have given were used as the basis for Chapter II of Part One of this book. The following information concerning their authors will help to give the reader a clearer picture of the order of their succession in time. With two or three exceptions, they are Iranian authors; here we necessarily offer only very summary information about them.

I. Shihābuddīn Yaḥyā Suhrawardī, the Shaikh al-Ishrāq—that is (as we have already recalled), the "Master of Oriental Theosophy"—was born in 548/1153 or 550/1155 in northwest Iran, at Suhraward in the province of Jabal near Azerbaijan. He died a martyr's death at Aleppo, persecuted and prosecuted by the Doctors of the Law in 587/1191, at the age of thirty-six or thirty-eight. His life's work aimed to restore the theosophical wisdom of ancient Persia in Islam itself, and with the resources of the pure spiritual side of Islam. Some four centuries before the great Byzantine Gemistes Pletho, Suhrawardī's work connected the names of Plato and of Zarathustra (Zoroaster) in his metaphysic of Light, in which the Platonic Ideas are interpreted by means of the Zoroastrian angelology.

In his doctrine, the word "Orient" takes on a technical meaning. In the literal sense, it is at one and the same time the geographic East, or, more precisely, the world of Iran and the hour when the horizon is lighted by the fires of dawn. In the true sense—that is to say, in the spiritual sense—the Orient is the world of the beings of Light, from which the dawn of knowledge and ecstasy rises in the pilgrim of the spirit. There is no true philosophy which does not reach completion in a metaphysic of ecstasy, nor mystical experience which does not demand a serious philosophical preparation. And such precisely was the *dawning* wisdom of the Khusrawānids, those ancient Iranians in whose person the two meanings of the word "Orient"—*Aurora con-*

surgens, *Ishrāq*—were thus conjoined. This "Oriental theosophy" was destined to have representatives in Iran up to the present day; the entire spiritual life of Iran has been marked with its imprint. The authors of Iran are in the habit of repeating that this Oriental theosophy is to philosophy what Ṣūfism is to scholastic theology (the *Kalām*).

II. Muḥyīddīn ibn ʿArabī (born at Murcia in Andalusia, 560/1165; died in Damascus in 638/1240) was one of the greatest mystical visionaries and theosophists of all time, whose role in spiritual Islam a determinant factor, and of whom, without exaggeration, one can truly say that his work was gigantic. His most celebrated book is the *Kitāb al-futūḥāt al-Makkīya* (the *Book of the Spiritual Conquests of Mecca*), comprising some 3,000 pages printed on large in quarto. But in his doctoral thesis (a history and classification of the works of Ibn ʿArabī, 2 vols., Institut français de Damas, 1964), Osman Yahya has collated 550 titles from the extant manuscripts (over 2,000 in number), each of which he has personally examined. If we eliminate the titles of 138 works of uncertain authorship, there still remains a bibliography of 412 titles. Our previous research centered on a study of the symbols of his "life curve" and of some predominant themes in his gigantic work. Here we can only briefly refer to them, all the more so as this book, in certain respects, is a continuation of our study *Creative Imagination in the Ṣūfism of Ibn ʿArabī*. The pages that appear later on are just as relevant to that study as they are to this book.

III. Dā'ūd Qayṣarī, born in Anatolia, as his name indicates (*Qayṣariya* = *Cesarea*), later settled in Cairo and was one of the great Ṣūfī figures of the eighth century of the Hijra; he died in 751/1350. He is best known for his extensive commentary on one of the books of Ibn ʿArabī, the *Fuṣūṣ al-ḥikam*, which has been the most read and expounded in all Islamic languages. This commentary includes such a highly developed introduction on the great themes of Ṣūfism that in certain bibliographies it is considered as an independent work. The commentary, in its turn, has given rise to further exposition of the theme, even in Shīʿite Iran; among the more recent expositions were those of Mīrzā Riẓā Qumshahī (d. 1310/1892 at Teheran). His contemporary, the celebrated Avicennian, Abu'l-Ḥasan Jilvah (d. 1317/1899), added another Shīʿite commentary directly on the *Fuṣūṣ*. These two were likewise commentators of the great work of Mullā Ṣadrā Shīrāzī (see below, Art. VI).

IV. ʿAbd al-Karīm Jīlī or Jīlānī, born in 767/1365, belonged, as his name shows (Gīlān is a province on the southwest coast of the Caspian Sea), to a family of Iranian ancestry but which had long since settled in Baghdad, like so many Iranian families to this day. Curiously enough, the biographical collections make no mention of him, and we have to glean the information about his spiritual autobiography from his own works. From them we learn that in all probability he belonged to the Dervish Order of the Qādirīs, founded by ʿAbd al-Qādir Jīlānī (d. 561/1165); we can deduce from certain clues that he was a descendant of the latter. He traveled in India and then lived in the Yemen. His most famous and widely-read book is his treatise on the Perfect Man (as a microcosm recapitulating the divine cosmic energies), but he left about twenty others, most of them unpublished, though all worthy of publication. His work finds its place in the line of that of Ibn ʿArabī; he wrote a commentary on the penultimate chapter (the 559th) of the *Futūḥāt*; nonetheless, his own doctrine shows considerable personal originality. He died in 805/1403, at the age of thirty-eight.

V. Shamsuddīn Muḥammad Jīlānī Lāhījī, a native of Lāhījān, came in his turn to settle on the shores of the Caspian Sea. He was a distinguished Shaikh of the Dervish Order of the Nūrbakhshīya, and later succeeded Sayyid Nūrbakhsh as head of the order. He died and was buried at Shiraz in 869/1465. His principal work, of which there have been several editions in Iran, is a monumental example of Iranian spirituality. Written in Persian, it is a summary of Shīʿite Ṣūfism, in the form of a commentary on the "Rose Garden of the Mystery" (*Gulshan-i rāz*), a long poem of some 1,500 verses dealing in concise allusive sentences with the lofty doctrines of Ṣūfism. This poem (which, significantly, was adopted by the Ismā'īlīs) had been composed by the celebrated Ṣūfī Shaikh from Azerbaijan, Maḥmūd Shabistarī, who, after living mostly in Tabrīz, died at the age of thirty-three in 720/1320 and was entombed at Shabistar. The poem, as well as its commentary, is still very much read in Iran.

VI. *Ṣadruddīn Muḥammad Shīrāzī*, more often called by his honorific surname, Mullā Ṣadrā, is one of the greatest Iranian figures of the Ṣafavid period. He was the pupil of the famous Mīr Dāmād (master of the school that we have called the School of Iṣfahān), of Shaikh Bahā'ī, and of Mīr Findariskī, a rather mysterious personage who, in the time of Shāh Akbar and Dārā Shikūh, played some part in initiating the translation of Sanskrit texts into Persian. The work of Mullā Ṣadrā is a monumental expression of the Iranian Renaissance under the Ṣafavids. It typically represents the confluence of Avicennism and the Ishrāq of Suhrawardī, on the one hand, and of the theosophy of Ibn 'Arabī and Shī'ite gnosis, on the other. However, although Mullā Ṣadrā is an Ishrāqī, he develops a metaphysic of being and the inquietude of being, in the place of Suhrawardī's metaphysic of essence, which gives a very personal character to his synthesis. As a result of his work, he, as well as all of his people and his successors, had considerable trouble with the official clergy. His collected works consist of fifty titles and cover the field of philosophy and mysticism, as well as of the spiritual exegesis of the Qur'ān and the Shī'ite traditions. Several commentaries have been devoted to his work, and nowadays a renaissance of traditional Iranian philosophy is tending to arise around his name. Mullā Ṣadrā died at Baṣra in 1050/1662, as he was returning from a pilgrimage to Mecca.

VII. Mullā 'Abd al-Razzāq Lāhījī (d. 1072/1662) was yet another north Iranian living on the shores of the Caspian Sea and was a distinguished pupil of Mullā Ṣadrā. He even became his master's son-in-law and received from him the "pen name" *Fayyāẓ* (overflowing), just as his brother-in-law, Muḥsin, received the name *Fayẓ* (overflowing plenitude). His reputation and productivity did not equal that of his brother-in-law, but he left about a dozen solid works which are still much in use today; this is especially true of his commentary on Naṣīruddīn Ṭūsī, the great thirteenth-century Shī'ite philosopher, and the work in Persian entitled *Gawhar-i murād* (*The Desired Jewel*), written for Shāh 'Abbās II (1642–67). Doubtless his Ishrāqī and Ṣūfī bent is less pronounced than that of Muḥsin Fayẓ, but in the case of a Shī'ite writer one must always take into account the possibility that he is being deliberately reticent. Mullā Ṣadrā had two sons who were also philosophers and writers. One of them, Mīrzā Ḥasan, left a dozen works, the manuscripts of which unfortunately, like so many others, have seemingly been buried in the arcanum of some private collection.

VIII. Muḥsin Fayẓ Kāshānī, together with his brother-in-law, 'Abd al-Razzāq Lāhījī, was one of the most brilliant pupils of Mullā Ṣadrā and, after him, one of the greatest Imāmite scholars during the eleventh century of the Hijra. He was born in Kāshān, where his father, Mullā Shāh Murtaẓā, was already famed for his learning and his valuable personal library. He came to Shiraz, where he studied with the celebrated theologian Sayyid Mājid of Bahrein and then with Mullā Ṣadrā, one of whose daughters he, too, married. He was a philosopher and a Ṣūfī, deeply Shī'ite, and a great admirer of Ibn 'Arabī. He wrote a great many works; there are some 120 titles in his bibliography, in Persian as well as in Arabic, dealing with all the traditional branches of Islamic science. He was also a poet; his *Dīwān* contains some thousand verses. He died at Kāshān in 1091/1680.

IX. The Shaikhī school owes its name and its origin to its founder, Shaikh Aḥmad Aḥsā'ī, its greatest Shaikh. We have already had occasion to point out that it is the sign of a powerful revival of primitive Shī'ite gnosis and of the teaching contained in traditions that go back to the Holy Imāms. This event, which came to pass in Iran at the end of the eighteenth century, after the time of troubles that followed the collapse of the Ṣafavid dynasty, was symptomatic. We shall study this school at length at a later date and so merely allude to it here, emphasizing three principal points.

A glimpse of the basic doctrine of Imāmology developed by this school was shown in a few pages above (Part One, Ch. II, § 1). As to its doctrine of the "spiritual body," it has been discussed at length in Ch. II, § 4. Still further on there are some significant pages pointing out how the doctrine stands half way between that of the philosophers and that of the literalistic theologians. Let us also note, though we have been unable to stress it here, how important it was in developing one of the great themes upon which the Spirituals of Islam tirelessly meditated—namely, the ascent of the Prophet to Heaven, the night of the *Miʿrāj*. Lastly, the school has developed a doctrine of the spiritual community, that of the "Perfect Shīʿites," in which we can perceive—of course, in accord with the exigencies of the tonality proper to Imāmism—a resonance not only of the Ṣūfī motif of the *rijāl al-ghayb*, the "Men of the Invisible," but of the idea of an *Ecclesia Spiritualis*, upon which so many independent Spirituals in Christianity have meditated. The literalistic Orthodox have shown absolutely no understanding of all these points, among many others. If one follows the sad story of discussions and bickerings, one may well wonder whether the Orthodox made, or even could make, the slightest effort to understand the true nature of these problems. One would have to be very naive to be surprised by it. The same spiritual facts have always aroused the same human reactions.

Shaikh Aḥmad Aḥsāʾī (d. 1241/1826), founder of the school, was himself a native of Bahrein, but more than fifteen years of his life were spent in Iran, and it is probable that without an Iranian audience there would have been no "Shaikhism." The Shaikh resided principally in Yazd, where he enjoyed the friendly good will of the governor, Muḥ. ʿAlī Mīrzā, son of Fatḥ-ʿAlī Shāh. With his family he took several trips across the territory of Iran to Teheran (where the sovereign, Fatḥ-ʿAlī Shāh Qājār, wished him to settle permanently), to Mashhad, the sanctuary of the Eighth Imām, to Iṣfahān, to Qazvīn, and to Kirmānshāh. At last the Shaikh withdrew to the Shī'ite holy places in Iraq. It will not be possible here to enumerate the totality of his works (the bibliography established by Shaikh Sarkār Āghā contains 132 titles, to which, alas, must be added many works which unfortunately have been lost), or to give a biographical sketch, for which firsthand documents are available. But what we would like at least to suggest is the spiritual *aura* that casts a halo around the truly very special person of Shaikh Aḥmad Aḥsā'ī. And it was his good fortune to have a line of successors at the head of the Shaikhī school whose nobility of character and force of spiritual personality were as admirable as was their scientific productivity.

X. Shaikh Ḥājj Muḥammad Karīm Khān Kirmānī (d. 1288/1870) was the second in succession to Shaikh Aḥmad Ahsā'ī at the head of the Shaikhī school. Muḥ. Karīm Khān was a pupil of Sayyid Kāẓim Rashtī, who had been the beloved disciple of the Shaikh and the first of his successors (d. 1259/1843). Through his father, Karīm Khān was a prince of the Qājār family. To recall some day his spiritual career would require an entire book. In the breadth of this universal spirit, which embraces and outstrips the entire spiritual culture of his circle and his epoch, there is something of an Iranian Goethe. His work, both in Persian and in Arabic, totals no less than 278 books; it covers not only the field of philosophy and Shī'ite theosophy, the spiritual hermeneutics of the Qur'ān and the *ḥadīth*, but also an encyclopedia of the sciences: medicine, physics, optics, astronomy, theory of light, of music, of color, including alchemy and related sciences. The few pages that we have translated should suffice to show that the latter essentially dealt with spiritual sciences. Much of this tremendous work is still unpublished. The same is true of the equally extensive work of his two sons, Shaikh Ḥājj Muḥammad Khān Kirmānī (d. 1324/1906) and Shaikh Zayn al-'Ābidīn Khān Kirmānī (d. 1361/1942), who were the third and fourth successors of Shaikh Aḥmad. Thus, the very original production of the Shaikhī school, besides published works, still comprises tens of thousands of sheets of unpublished manuscripts.

XI. Shaikh Abu'l-Qāsim Khān Ibrāhīmī was born in Kirman in 1314/1896, the son of Shaikh Zayn al-ʿĀbidīn Khān and the grandson of Shaikh Muḥ. Karīm Khān. His people call him for short and with affectionate respect by the honorific title Sarkār Āghā. Today he is the fifth successor of Shaikh Aḥmād Aḥsā'ī to head the Shaikhī school. His works, themselves important, include a vast work that expands certain difficult themes in the work of Shaikh Muḥ. Karīm Khān Kirmānī. The closing pages of this book are composed of extracts from this work; they are the most suitable for showing the place of the theme under discussion here in the totality of Shīʿite spirituality. And it is chiefly on this score that I would like to pay tribute to the outstanding personality of Shaikh Sarkār Āghā. I have had occasion, personally, to experience his spiritual radiation on those around him and to learn things which I would never have learned from books in the course of the many conversations that by his kindness he has made possible.

Such are the men from whom we have taken our choice of "traditional" texts. We are employing this term here just as simply as they do themselves, not in any way implying some secret and vague authority to teach, which Westerners are apt to assume when they discuss these matters. It simply means the texts to which one traditionally refers when having to deal with a theme like the present one.

Finally, our authors turn out to be eleven in number, although this was not by intention on our part. It is probable, however, that no Twelver Shīʿite will accept this as the result of chance, because he will know the whereabouts of the twelfth one.

I

SHIHĀBUDDĪN YAHYĀ SUHRAWARDĪ
(d. 587/1191)

Hūrqalyā, the World of Autonomous Images and Imaginative Perception

(a) Book of Conversations*

When you learn from the writings of the ancient Sages that there exists a world possessed of dimensions and extent, other than the pleroma of Intelligences and the world governed by the Souls of the Spheres, and that in it there are cities beyond number among which the Prophet himself mentioned Jābalqā and Jābarṣā, do not hasten to proclaim it a lie, for there are pilgrims of the spirit who come to see it with their own eyes and in it find their heart's desire. As for the rabble of impostors and false priests, they will deny what you have seen even if you bring proof to expose their lie. Therefore, remain silent and have patience, for if you come eventually to our *Book of Oriental Thesophy*, no doubt you will understand something of what has just been said, provided your initiator gives you guidance. If not, be a believer in wisdom.

(b) Book of Elucidations†

A narrative and a dream: For some time I was prey to an intense obsession. I ceaselessly practiced meditation and spiritual exercises, since the problem of knowledge assailed me with insoluble difficulties. What they say about it in books brought me no light. On one particular night I experienced a dreamlike ecstasy. Suddenly I was wrapped in gentleness; there was a

* Our edition, p. 109, in the notes; quoted here according to the manuscript.[1]

† P. 70, par. 55.

blinding flash, then a very diaphanous light in the likeness of a human being. I watched attentively and there he was: Helper of souls, Imām of wisdom, *Primus Magister*, whose form filled me with wonder and whose shining beauty dazzled me. He came toward me, greeting me so kindly that my bewilderment faded and my alarm gave way to a feeling of familiarity. And then I began to complain to him of the trouble I had with this problem of knowledge.

"Come back (awaken) to yourself," he said to me, "and your problem will be solved."

"How so?" I asked.

"Is the knowledge which you have of yourself a direct perception of yourself by yourself, or do you get it from something else? . . ."[2]

Later, Suhrawardī himself alluded to the meaning of this conversation in his *Book of Conversations*, pp. 483–84, par. 208.

As for the view I personally profess concerning this problem (of knowledge), it is mentioned in my book on the "Oriental theosophy," but it is not possible for me to dwell upon it here explicitly, since in this book I intended to conduct my enquiry in such a way that it would not be too far from the program of the Peripatetics. Nevertheless, if one were to study this present book carefully, one would find that it is not devoid of precious things and treasures hidden under a thin veil. If the half-wit is unable to discover them, the fault is not mine. As for the persistent worker and persevering seeker, let him gather the teachings which are firmly established in this book, let him seize hold of that for which he had not yet dared to wish and for which I will have provided him with the necessary daring. The surest way for the seeker to follow before studying my *Oriental Theosophy* is the way I mentioned in my *Book of Elucidations*. Therein I relate what came to pass between the wise Imām of the dialecticians and myself, when his apparition talked with me in the mystical dwelling-place, Jābarṣā. For the seeker, this way consists first of all in investigating his knowledge of himself, and then in raising himself to the knowledge of that which is above him.[3]

(c) Book of Elucidations*

On a certain night when there was sunlight, Hermes was at prayers in the temple of Light. When the "column of dawn"[4] blazed forth, he saw an Earth about to be engulfed, with cities upon which the divine anger had descended and which fell into the abyss.[5]

Then Hermes shouted, "You who are my father, rescue me from the enclosure of those near to perdition!"

And he heard a voice shouting an answer, "Take hold of the cable of our Irradiation and climb up to the *battlements* of the Throne."

Then he climbed up and there, beneath his feet, was an Earth and Heavens.

Shahrazūrī: By *HERMES*, the author is symbolically referring to the noble and perfect soul. His prayer is his orientation toward the other world. The night of the sun is the Presence, there and then a reality, of that to which the Soul looks forward in its spiritual efforts and in following the mystic path. The bursting forth of the "column of dawn"[6] is the epiphany of the soul outside the material body, when the divine lights and most sacred flames suddenly come upon it. Just as the column of dawn rises for us above the earthly horizon, so this column of dawn—I refer to the thinking soul—bursts forth by rising above the Earth of the body. So it is quite true that Hermes sees an Earth being swallowed up. The pilgrim, that is, the thinking soul, which, in the lightning flash of theophany, is manifested outside the material body, sees the Earth of his body and his cities—that is his faculties—being swallowed up together. This is because, thanks to the revelation and epiphany, the soul finds itself in the space of the intelligible lights and higher entities, whereas the body and its faculties remain in the space of the lower world upon which the divine anger falls. This is a way

* P. 108, par. 83.

of pointing out that the latter represent what is furthest removed from the divine Majesty. Then the mystical pilgrim, rising from the abyss of the material body toward the zenith of the Intelligence, calls on his "father," a name which refers either to the Necessary Being itself or to the archangelical Intelligence from which the soul of the mystic emanates. "Save me," he cries, "from the enclosure of those near to perdition," that is, the bodily faculties and material attachments. A voice answers him, "Take hold of the cable of Irradiation," that is, speculative theosophy and practical theosophy, both of which lead to the higher worlds. "Climb up to the battlements of the Throne," to the angelic Intelligences separated from matter. And there beneath his feet there was an Earth and Heavens. And so Hermes was indeed raised above all the material universes, above the world of the celestial Spheres as well as above the world of the Elements. Now the ancient Sages were in the habit of referring to the spiritual entities as Spheres, because those whose light is stronger encompass the weaker, just as the celestial Spheres encompass each other. This is what Plato refers to when he says, "In a state of ecstasy I saw Spheres of light," which means Heavens which can be seen only by those who are raised from the dead, when another Earth takes the place of the Earth and when new Heavens take the place of the Heavens.

Ibn Kammūna: It is difficult to decipher these symbols in conjunction. Our conjecture is as follows:[7] The column of dawn breaking forth is the epiphany of the lights of higher knowledge. The earth is the body, or else matter in general. The cities are the souls which have become attached to material bodies, or else the faculties which have their seat in the latter. It seems, therefore, that the author is comparing the faculties to the inhabitants of these cities and is calling the inhabitants themselves cities, as when he says, "The city has sought refuge with God," meaning thereby the inhabitants. Their fall into the abyss is the fall of these souls from the rank to which the principle of their original nature would have entitled them. You know already the condition and the cause of this downfall. The enclosure is the body, those close to perdition are the bodily functions. The cable of

Article I

Irradiation is the connection with the higher world. The battlements of the Throne are the spiritual entities. Finally, the fact that under the feet of Hermes there is an Earth and Heavens means that in his ascent he has now left the world of bodies and material realities and is above their Earth as well as their Heavens.

Ibn Kammūna, like Shahrazūrī before him, proceeds here to allude to the celebrated account of ecstasy which all of our authors attribute to Plato, whereas, as we know, it comes from a spiritual autobiography in the *Enneads* of Plotinus (IV.8.1). Our authors know it through a passage from the *Theology* attributed to Aristotle, which was one of their, so to speak, "bedside books." Suhrawardī quotes the first lines in his *Oriental Theosophy*, and his commentator, Quṭbuddīn Shīrāzī, zealously transcribes the entire passage. Our commentators do not question—and they are absolutely right—that the ecstasy of Hermes means his entry into the interworld, that is, the world of Hūrqalyā. In support of this, Ibn Kammūna cites the same three passages translated above. Hermes emerged from the confines of the Earth and of the Heavens visible to astronomy and penetrated into the world of archetype-Images which has its own Earth and Heavens, and which contains, among countless other cities, Jābalqā and Jābarṣā. Ibn Kammūna concludes as follows: "The real intention of the author in this passage raises more difficulties for me than everything which came earlier in this chapter." Shahrazūrī did not experience these difficulties; but it is true that Ibn Kammūna was not a mystic.

Since the account of ecstasy as it appears in the Arabic text of the *Theology* attributed to Aristotle was a paraphrase of the text of the *Enneads*, we are not giving the translation here. Furthermore, this new Earth and these new Heavens, no longer those of the sensory world, but those of the imaginative universe, the *mundus archetypus*, are again described in the passage from the *Theology* most often used by Ṣadruddīn Shīrāzī (cf. below, Art. VI) in his lessons on Book II of the second part of the *Oriental Theosophy*. This text in itself is justification for relating the image of the Heavens or Spheres of light to the spiritual entities which Plato, according to our authors, had seen. Here we quote the translation of this passage by our colleague Georges Vajda.[8]

There are several kinds of spiritual entities. Some of them have their dwelling place in the heaven situated above the starry sky. Each of the spiritual entities living in this heaven occupies the whole of the sphere of his heaven, and yet has a fixed place, distinct from that of his companion—in contrast to the corporeal things which are in the sky—for they are not bodies, nor is the heaven in question a body. That is why each of them occupies the whole of his heaven. We say that behind this world there is a heaven, an earth, a sea, animals, plants, and celestial men; every being in that world is celestial and in it there is no earthly thing. The spiritual entities which are there correspond to the human beings who are there; none of them is different from another, and there is no opposition nor disagreement between them, but each supports the other.

(d) Book of Conversations*

The encounter with suprasensory reality can come about through a certain way of reading a written text; it can come about from hearing a voice, without the speaker being visible. Sometimes the voice is soft, sometimes it makes one tremble, at other times it is like a gentle murmur. It may be that the speaker makes himself visible in some form, either as a constellation, or in the likeness of one of the supreme celestial princes. The experience of authentic raptures in the world of Hūrqalyā depends on the magnificent prince, Hūrakhsh,[9] the most sublime of those who have assumed a body, the greatly venerated one who, in the terminology of the Oriental theosophy, is the Supreme Face of God. It is he who sustains the meditation of the soul by lavishing light upon it, and he is witness of its contemplation.[10] There are also visitations and communications from other celestial princes. Sometimes the visitation consists of the manifestation of certain of these celestial princes in epiphanic forms or places appropriate to the moment when they show themselves to the perfected recluse. Sometimes it is the souls of the past which induce an awakening or an inner call. Sometimes the apparition takes on human form, other times the form of a constellation,

* Pp. 494–96, pars. 215–26.

or again that of a work of art, a statue uttering words, or else a figure resembling the ikons seen in churches, likewise endowed with speech. Sometimes the Manifestation takes form immediately after the shock of the enrapturing light; at other times it comes only after the form of light. When the blazing light lasts long, it obliterates the form; the figures are taken away and the individual visitation is effaced. At that point one understands that what is effaced is giving way to something of a higher order. . . .

We deny the right to the Peripatetics to speak about the forms and realities which become visible to the visionary contemplatives, for what is in question is a path which scarcely any of them has followed and even in those very few cases the mystical experience remained weak and precarious. The follower of the mystical path who has received his initiation from a master with theosophical[11] experience, or thanks to the special divine assistance which guides the solitary exile—the latter case being very rare—will fully understand that the Peripatetics have entirely overlooked two sublime universes which never figure in their discussions, and that there are a number of other things that remain beyond the scope of their philosophy.

(e) From the same work*

. . . In short, the theosophist who has truly attained to mystical experience is one whose material body becomes like a tunic which he sometimes casts off and at other times puts on.[12] No man can be numbered among the mystical theosophists so long as he has no knowledge of the most holy leaven of mystical wisdom, and so long as he has not experienced this casting off and this putting on. From that point, he ascends toward the Light at will, and, if it pleases him, he can manifest himself in whatever form he chooses. This power is produced in him by the auroral Light (*nūr shāriq*) which irradiates his person. Do you not see how it is when fire causes iron to become red hot, that the iron takes on the appearance of fire; it irradiates and

* Pp. 503–505, pars. 223–24.

ignites? The same holds true for the soul whose substance is that of the spiritual world. When it has undergone the action of light and put on the robe of auroral Light,[13] it too is able to influence and to act; it makes a sign and the sign is obeyed; it imagines and what it imagines comes to pass accordingly. Impostors beguile us with trickery, but the enlightened man, the perfected man, the man in love with harmony, is immune from evil and acts through the energy and with the help of the Light because he himself is the child of the world of Light.

.If that which predominates in the essential substance of the soul is the *res victorialis* (*al-amr al-qahrī*), then the Light of dawn rises on the soul in such a way that that part of the victorial realities emanating from the constellations and from the Angels who are their theurgies, predominate in it. This is the suprasensory reality which the ancient Persians called *Xvarnah* ("Light of Glory," *Khurrah* in Persian).[14] This is something which, having arisen from astral incandescence, remains as a dominating force in the human world; he who is invested with it becomes a hero, a conqueror, a victor. If the Light of dawn arising from the *spiritual stars*—pure spiritual entities of light—corresponds to the capacity of the soul in a "dimension" of desire and love, then what remains of the *Xvarnah* which penetrates it will be manifested by causing its possessor to take joy in subtle and refined things, by awakening in souls inclination and love toward him, by bringing men to sing his praises, for the splendor communicated to his being derives from the Angels and their beneficent theurgies, worthy of glorification and of love. Finally, if there is balance and if the qualities of light received from a sublime luminary through the intermediary of the celestial prince are superabundant in him,[15] then he will become a magnificent king, surrounded by respect, favored with knowledge, perfection, and prosperity. And that alone is what is called the *royal Xvarnah* (*Kayān Khurrah*). In its plenitude this refers to the most majestic of categories, for it implies a perfect balance of light, besides the fact that the sublime Luminary is the gateway to all the greater ecstasies.[16]

As for the fact of walking on water, gliding through the air, reaching Heaven, seeing the Earth roll up like a carpet, these are experiences known to a certain number of mystics, provided that the Light which reaches them is created by the column of dawn in the cities of the intermediate Orient.[17] To be sure, all this can be met with on the way followed by the mystics. Those among them who are still only moderately advanced stop at that point, but the perfected ones attach no importance to it. At all events, we know no one in the sect of the Peripatetics who has ever had a solid foundation in *theosophical* wisdom, I mean, in the science of the pure Lights.

(f) Book of Oriental Theosophy*

In this, the last part of his great work, Suhrawardī has just given an analytical description of how the mystics experience light or *photisms*. These photisms can be classified experientially in some fifteen categories. The author ends his analysis with some observations which complete the passage just translated. As in other passages in the same book, we have added to it indispensable additional material from the commentator Quṭb-uddīn Maḥmūd Shīrāzī.

All these are illuminations (*ishrāqāt*) which rise over the human soul when it is master of its body. Then they are reflected on the bodily habitation (the "temple"). These photisms mark a half-way stage at which some stop. Sometimes these Lights carry them, in such a way that they walk on the waters and glide through the air. It may be that they ascend to Heaven, but in a body which is their subtle body;[18] then they become united with certain of the celestial princes. But all such events are dependent on the conditions of the *Eighth Climate* with its cities, Jābalqā, Jābarṣā, and Hūrqalyā, full of wonders.

Quṭbuddīn Maḥmūd Shīrāzī: The *Eighth Climate* is the *mundus archetypus* (*'ālam al-mithāl*), the world of Images and archetypal Forms. Actually, the only universe that possesses dimensions and extent is the one that is divided into *eight* climates. *Seven* of them are the seven geographical climates with dimensions and extent which are perceptible to the senses. The

* P. 254, par. 273.

eighth climate is the one whose dimensions and extent can only be grasped by the imaginative perception. This is the world of autonomous Images and Forms (lit. "*in suspension*," that is, not mixed with any corruptible substratum, but in suspense in the way that an Image is suspended in a mirror). This is the world of the subtle bodies, which alone are able to rise to heaven, whereas material bodies, made of the substance of the Elements, are fundamentally incapable of this. This is what occurs to certain of the mystics; most of the astonishing and extraordinary things which are manifested in the case of the Prophets and the Initiates result from their reaching and entering that world, of which they know the epiphanic forms and characteristic properties. As for Jābalqā, Jābarṣā, and Hūrqalyā, these are the names of cities existing in the world of archetypal Images and the Prophet himself was heard to pronounce these names. However, a distinction must be made between Jābalqā and Jābarṣā, which are two cities belonging to the world of the *Elements* of the world of the archetypal Images, whereas Hūrqalyā, lies in the Heavens of that same world.[19]

(g) From the same work*

We have taught you that it is impossible for images to be materially imprinted upon the eye; just as it is impossible for them to be imprinted on some place in the brain. The truth is that forms seen in mirrors, just like imaginative forms, are not imprinted materially, either on the mirror or on the imagination. No, they are "bodies in suspension,"[20] not depending on a substratum (with which they would then be mixed, just as the color black, for example, is mixed with a black object). They certainly have places where they appear, epiphanic places (*maẓāhir*), but they are not materially contained in them. Certainly the mirror is the place of the apparition of forms seen in it, but the forms themselves are "in suspension" there; there they are neither like material things in a place in space, nor like an accident in its substratum. Certainly the active imagination is the place of

* P. 211, par. 225.

apparition of imaginative forms, but the forms themselves are "in *suspense*"; they are neither *in* this place, nor *in* the substratum. Now if in the case of mirrors we accept the existence of an autonomous image, even though it is only on the surface, without depth or anything back of it, and even though that of which it is the image is an accident (for example, the accidental form of Zayd, immanent in his matter), then one will admit *a fortiori* the existence of a substantial quiddity, that of the archetype (substantial, in fact, since independent of any substratum) having an accidental image (the form of Zayd immanent in his matter). Thus imperfect light is analogous to perfect light. Understand.

Quṭbuddīn Shīrāzī: Therefore, imaginative forms exist neither *in* thought, since the great cannot be imprinted in the small, nor *in* concrete reality, otherwise anyone with normally healthy senses would be able to see them. But they are not merely nonbeing, for if so one could neither represent them to oneself, nor distinguish them one from another, and different judgments of them could not be formed. Since they are something with real being and are neither *in* thought, nor *in* concrete reality, nor in the world of the Intelligences—for they are corporealized forms, not pure intelligibles—they must necessarily exist in some other region and the latter is what is called the world of the *archetypal Image* and of *imaginative perception.* It is a world intermediate between the world of the Intelligence and the world of the senses; its ontological plane is above the world of the senses and below the intelligible world; it is more immaterial than the first, less immaterial than the second. It is a world in which there exists the totality of forms and figures, dimensions and bodies, with all that is connected therewith: movements, rest, positions, configurations, etc., all of them self-subsistent "in suspense," that is to say, not being contained in a place nor depending on a substratum.

"Understand," the author says to us. Here, indeed, we have a magnificent secret, something of supreme importance. It means that the totality of the things which exist in the higher world have their *nādir* and their analogue in the lower world. All these things are known by their *nādir* and their analogue. Then, when you have learned to know, as is necessary, the reality of ephemeral lights, your knowledge helps you to know the immaterial, substantial Lights. The purpose of all this is that you should know that the imperfect, accidental light which is that of the sun of the sensory world is the *image* of the perfect substantial light, which is the sun of the world of the Intelligence, the Light of Lights. In the same way, the light of each ephemeral star is the image of an immaterial substantial light. This is an immense subject, offering many mystical experiences. Hence the author's imperative: "Understand!"

(h) From the same work*

These autonomous Images and Forms are not the Platonic Ideas, for the Ideas of Plato are of pure, immutable light, whereas among the Forms in question there are some which are dark—those which torment the reprobate; these are hideous, repulsive, the sight of them causes the soul suffering, whereas others are luminous and their sweetness is tasted by the blessed and these are beautiful, resplendent Forms.[21]

Quṭbuddīn Shīrāzī: The Sages of old, such as Plato, Socrates, Empedocles and others, not only affirmed the existence of the Platonic Ideas, which are intelligible and made of pure light, but also the existence of autonomous imaginative Forms which are not immanent in a material substratum of our world. They affirmed that these are separate substances, independent of "material matters," that they have their seat in the meditative faculty and in the soul's active Imagination, in the sense that these two faculties are the epiphanic places where these Forms appear; undoubtedly and concretely they exist, although this does not mean that they are immanent in a substratum. The Sages affirmed the existence of a twofold universe: on the one hand, a purely suprasensory universe, including the world of the Deity and the world of angelic Intelligences; on the other hand, a world of material Forms, that is, the world of the celestial Spheres and

* Pp. 230–34, pars. 246–48.

Elements and the world of apparitional forms, namely, the world of the autonomous Image. . . . These Forms and Images have no substratum in our material world, for otherwise they would necessarily be perceptible to the outer senses and would not not need places for their epiphany. They are, therefore, spiritual substances, subsisting in and by themselves in the world of imaginative perception, that is, in the spiritual universe.

Suhrawardī: I have witnessed in my soul some authentic and unquestionable experiences which prove that the universes are four in number: there is the world of dominant or archangelic Lights (*Luces victoriales*, the *Jabarūt*); there is the world of the Lights governing bodies (the Souls, that is to say, the *Malakūt*); there is a double *barzakh* and there is the world of autonomous Images and Forms, some of them dark, some luminous, the first constituting the imaginative torment of the reprobate, the second the imaginative sweetness enjoyed by the blessed. . . . This last world is the one we call the world of the *Apparentiae reales* which are independent of matter (*'ālam al-ashbāḥ al-mujarrada*); this is the universe in which the resurrection of bodies and divine apparitions are realized and where all the prophetic promises are fulfilled.

Quṭbuddīn Shīrāzī: So we have to understand that the first of these universes is that of the separated intelligible Lights which have no attachment of any kind to bodies; they are the cohorts of the divine Majesty, Angels of the highest rank (*Angeli intellectuales*). The second universe is the world of the Lights governing bodies, whether they be the *Ispahbad*[22] of a celestial Sphere (*Angeli coelestes*) or of a human body. The double *barzakh* constitutes the third universe; it is the world of bodies perceptible to the senses (because everything which has a body forms an interval, a distance, a *barzakh*).[23] It is divided into the world of the celestial Spheres with the astral bodies they enclose, and the world of the Elements with their compounds. Finally, the fourth universe is the world of the active Imagination; this is an immense world, infinite, whose creatures are in a term-for-term correspondence with those enclosed by the sensory world in the double *barzakh*—the stars and the compounds of the Elements, minerals, vegetables, animals, and man. . . .

It is to this last world that the Sages of old referred when they say that there exists a world having dimensions and extent other than the material sensible world. Infinite are its marvels, countless its cities. Amongst these are Jābalqā and Jābarṣā, two immense cities, each with a thousand gates. They are peopled by countless creatures who are not even aware that God has created terrestrial Adam and his posterity.

This world corresponds to the sensory world: its imaginative celestial Spheres (that is to say, Hūrqalyā) are in perpetual movement; its Elements (that is, Jābalqā and Jābarṣā) and their compounds receive from Hūrqalyā the influx and at the same time the illuminations of the intelligible worlds. It is there that the various kinds of autonomous archetypal Images are infinitely realized, forming a hierarchy of degrees varying according to their relative subtlety or density. The individuals peopling each degree are infinite, although the degrees themselves are finite in number. (*Same work*, p. 240: "On each of these levels species exist analogous to those in our world, but they are infinite. Some are peopled by Angels and the human Elect. Others are peopled by Angels and genii, others by demons. God alone knows the number of these levels and what they contain. The pilgrim rising from one degree to another discovers on each higher level a subtler state, a more entrancing beauty, a more intense spirituality, a more overflowing delight. The highest of these degrees borders on that of the intelligible pure entities of light and very closely resembles it.") The prophets, the Initiates, the mystical theosophists have all acknowledged the existence of this universe. The pilgrims of the spirit find there everything they need, all the marvels and wondrous works they could wish. . . .

Through this universe are realized the divine apparitional forms—sometimes majestic and dazzlingly beautiful, sometimes awesome and horrifying—under which the First Cause manifests itself. The same is true of the *apparentiae reales* under which it pleases the First Intelligence and the other archangelic Intelligences to show themselves, because for each of them there is a multitude of apparitions corresponding to the diverse forms under which it may please them to manifest themselves. The divine apparitional forms may have epiphanic places in our world; when they are manifested here, it is possible to perceive them visually. This was so in the case of Moses when God manifested Himself to him on Mount Sinai, as described in the Torah. Thus it was for the Prophet, who perceived the reality of the Angel Gabriel when the latter manifested himself in the form of the youth, Daḥya al-Kalbī. It could be said that the whole Imaginative universe is the epiphanic place of the Light of Lights and of the immaterial beings of light, each manifested in a definite form, at a definite moment, always corresponding to the correlative fitness of the receptable and of the agent.

Lastly, when it is said that the promises of prophecy are fulfilled in this universe, if this is understood as the torments suffered by the people in hell and the delights tasted by those in paradise, it is because the condition of the *subtle body* available to the soul *post mortem* corresponds to that of the material, sensory body. The subtle body also has outer senses and inner senses and the fact remains that in the one case as in the other the perceiving, feeling subject is never anything other than the soul itself.

(i) From the same work*

The suprasensory realities encountered by the prophets, the Initiates, and others appear to them sometimes in the form of lines of writing, sometimes in the hearing of a voice which may be gentle and sweet and which can also be terrifying. Sometimes they see human forms of extreme beauty who speak to them in most beautiful words and converse with them intimately about the invisible world; at other times these forms appear to them like those delicate figures proceeding from the most refined art of the painters. On occasion they are shown as if in an enclosure; at other times the forms and figures appear suspended. Everything which is perceived in dream—mountains, oceans, and

* Pp. 240–42, pars. 256–58.

continents, extraordinary voices, human personages—all these are so many figures and forms which are self-subsistent and need no substratum. The same is true of perfumes, colors, and flavors. How can the brain, or one of its cavities, contain the mountains and oceans seen in a dream, whether the dream be true or false, no matter how one conceives of, or explains, this capacity? Just as the sleeper on awakening from his dreams, or the imaginative man and the contemplative man, between the waking state and sleep, returning from their vision, leave the world of autonomous Images without having to make any movement or without having the feeling of material distance in relation to it, in the same way he who dies to this world meets the vision of the world of Light without having to make any movement because he himself is in the world of Light. . . .[24]

The celestial Spheres give out sounds which are not caused by anything existing in our sublunar world. Moreover, we have already proven that sound is something other than the undulation of air. The most that can be said on this point is that here below sound is conditioned by the undulation of air. But if a thing is the condition of another in a certain place, it does not follow that it remains a condition for its analogue. Just as anything in general can have multiple, interchangeable causes, so also its conditions can change. Just as the colors of the stars are not conditioned by that which conditions the colors in our terrestial world,[25] so it is as regards the sounds emitted by the celestial spheres. We cannot say that the tremendous terrifying sounds heard by the visionary mystics are caused by an undulation of air in the brain. For an air-wave of such force due to some disturbance in the brain is inconceivable. No, what we have here is the archetypal Image of the sound, and this autonomous Form is itself a sound [*Commentary*: Just as the archetypal Image of man is certainly a man, and that of each thing is certainly respectively that thing]. Thus, it is conceivable that there are sounds and melodies in the celestial Spheres which are not conditioned by the air nor by a vibratory disturbance. And one cannot imagine that there could be melodies more delightful than theirs, just as one cannot conceive that there could be a burning desire more ardent than the desire of the *Angeli coelestes*. Hail! then, to the company of all who have become mad and drunk with desire for the world of Light, with their passionate love for the majesty of the Light of Lights, and who, in their ecstasy, have become like the "Seven Very Firm Ones."[26] Because in their case there is a lesson for those who are capable of understanding.

Quṭbuddīn Shīrāzī: As the author mentioned in the *Book of Conversations*, all the Spirituals of the different peoples have affirmed the existence of these sonorities, not on the plane of Jābalqā and Jābarṣā, which are cities of the world of the Elements in the universe of the archetypal Forms, but on the plane of Hūrqalyā, the third city, with its many marvels, the world of the celestial Spheres of the universe of archetypal Forms.[27] To him who reaches this universe are revealed the spiritual entities of these Spheres with their beautiful forms and exquisite sonorities. Pythagoras related that his soul rose as far as the higher world. Due to the purity of his being and to the divinatory power of his heart, he heard the melodies of the Spheres and the sonorities produced by the movements of the heavenly bodies; at the same time he became aware of the discreet resonance of the voices of their angels. Afterwards he returned to his material body. As a result of what he had heard he determined the musical relationships and perfected the science of music.

II

MUḤYĪDDĪN IBN ʿARABĪ
(d. 638/1240)

The Earth Which Was Created from What Remained of the Clay of Adam

Here the indescribable
actually takes place.
Faust, Part II

The complete title of chapter VIII of Ibn ʿArabī's great work, *Kitāb al-futūḥāt al-Makkīya* (*The Book of the Spiritual Conquests of Mecca*, Cairo, 1329/1911, I, 126–31), reads as follows: "On the knowledge of the Earth which was created from what remained of the leaven of Adam's clay, and which is the Earth of True Reality, mentioning the strange things and marvels it contains." Like almost every chapter in this work, this one opens with a few verses the allusive density of which is hard to render. The *leitmotiv* is the palm tree as a symbol of the celestial Earth. On the borderline between the vegetable and the animal kingdoms, the palm tree has especially held the attention of the Islamic philosophers as being an exceptional creature. The celestial Earth being the inmost secret of man, as it were, his mystic Eve, what is hidden in the words with which the poet speaks to the palm tree that is its symbol begins, in its turn, to be divined. As the symbol of this secret earth, the palm tree, is "Adam's sister" (the word palm tree, *nakhla*, being feminine in Arabic). "O my sister! or rather, O aunt! perceptible to all, thou art the feminine Imām whose secret is nevertheless unknown to us. The sons look toward thee, O sister of their father. . . . O aunt, tell me how the fraternal secret is revealed in thee. . . . Thou art the feminine Imām and the Imām is thy brother; and those he precedes[1] are so many images drawn from himself."

All these allusions are explained up to a point in the first lines of the chapter: The secret of the creation of the palm tree made from the remainder of the clay from which Man himself was created. And, of the clay from which his own "sister" was molded, there was still an invisible remainder, the equivalent of a *sesame* seed, no more. But this very fact conveys the meaning that there is no common measure between the expanse of sensory space and that which begins at the point where the directions of sensory space come to an end. For it is exactly there that the limitless expanse of the celestial Earth will extend. This means further that one can "free oneself from space without abandoning the sense of expanse." In his turn, ʿAbd al-Karīm Jīlī (below, Art. IV) tries to make this symbol explicit: the "Earth of sesame" is Adam's sister, or rather, the daughter of his inmost secret. The lineage of the one is the lineage of the other. It endures and continues to exist, whereas everything else comes to nought. The fruit which is Adam himself sprang from a palm tree. It has no other enclosure; the grove of palm trees is nowhere else than in Adam himself. Thus they respond reciprocally and spontaneously to each other's call.[2]

Numerous references illustrating the functions of the palm tree as a symbol of the celestial Earth and of resurrection[3] need to be collated. Moreover, as is known, the Qur'ānic revelation makes no mention of the birth of Jesus at Bethlehem; on the other hand, as though to recall or transpose some tidings of the Infancy, it alludes to the miraculous birth "under the palm tree." Between the "palm tree of Mary" and the palm which is "Adam's sister" taken as a symbol of the celestial Earth, the very one under which the infant Christ is born, certain Qur'ānic commentaries allow us to discern the link.[4] We cannot go into this, no more than we can discuss here all the difficulties presented by the texts which we have attempted to translate for the first time. Nevertheless, we should call attention again to the thematic kinship between the present text dealing with "the Earth which was created from what remained of the clay of Adam," and the text to be read later (below, Art. X, 1) making explicit "in what sense the body of the faithful believer is the Earth of his paradise."

Know that when God had created Adam who was the first human organism to be constituted, and when he had established him as the origin and archetype of all human bodies, there remained a surplus of the leaven of the clay. From this surplus God created the palm tree, so that this plant (*nakhla*, palm tree, being feminine) is Adam's *sister*; for us, therefore, it is like an aunt on our father's side. In theology it is so described and is compared to the faithful believer.[5] No other plant bears within it such extraordinary secrets as are hidden in this one. Now, after the creation of the palm tree, there remained hidden a portion of the clay from which the plant had been made; what was left was the equivalent of a sesame seed. And it was in this remainder that God laid out an immense Earth. Since he arranged in it the Throne and what it contains, the Firmament,[6] the Heavens and the Earths, the worlds underground, all the paradises and hells, this means that the whole of our universe is to be found there in that Earth in its entirety, and yet the whole of it together is like a ring lost in one of our deserts[7] in comparison with the immensity of that Earth. And that same Earth has hidden in it so many marvels and strange things that their number cannot be counted and our intelligence remains dazed by them.

On that Earth God created in each soul (and corresponding to each soul[8]) universes of praise in which canticles are sung without ceasing by night and by day, for God's magnificence is manifested on that Earth and His creative power dazzles the eyes of him who contemplates it. A multitude of things exist there which are rationally impossible, that is, a multitude of things about which reason has established decisive proof that they are incompatible with real being. And yet!—all these things do indeed exist in that Earth. It is the vast prairie where the theosopher-mystics feast their eyes; they move around in it, they go and come in it as they will. In the whole of all the universes that make up that Earth, God has especially created one universe in our image (a universe corresponding to each one of us). When the mystic contemplates that universe, it is himself, his own soul, that he contemplates in it. ʿAbd Allāh ibn ʿAbbās was alluding to something like that, in a saying of his reported in a certain *ḥadīth*: "This *Kaʿba* is one dwelling among fourteen dwellings. In each of the seven Earths there is a creature like ourselves (our homologue), so that in each of the seven Earths there is an Ibn ʿAbbās who is my homologue."[9] This tradition has met with widespread assent among visionary mystics.

Let us return to the description of that Earth, with its immensity and the multitude of universes which have been constituted *from it* and *in it*. For the mystics, this Earth is where theophanies and theophanic visions take place. One of them tells us of a case which I myself know, from a personal vision: "In that Earth," he tells us, "I happened one day to penetrate into a gathering which was known as the Assembly of Mercy (*Majlis al-Raḥma*). I never saw an assembly more wonderful than that one. While I was there, there came upon me suddenly a theophanic vision; far from tearing me away from myself, it made me more firmly in my own company. This is one of the peculiar characteristics of that Earth. Indeed, when such theophanic visions come to mystics in our material world while they are present to their fleshly body they carry the ecstatic away from himself and he is annihilated before his vision; so it was in the case of the prophets, the great Initiates and all those who have experienced such ecstasies. Likewise, the world of the celestial Spheres, the Firmament (*Kursī*, the Heaven of the Fixed Stars) ablaze with constellations, the world of the Throne encircling the whole cosmos are—all of them—reft from the ecstatics when the theophanic visions come upon them; it is all destroyed as by a flash of lightning. On the other hand, when the visionary mystic has penetrated into this Earth of which I am speaking and when a theophanic vision comes to him there, his contemplative perception is not annihilated by it, it does not tear him from his act of existing; it makes possible the coexistence in him of vision and discourse."

He also says: "In this assembly I have just recalled, I went through experiences and knew secrets that I am not able to tell because of the abscondity of the things they mean and because it is not possible to reach perception and understanding of them before seeing them for oneself as they are seen by him who has direct vision of them."

In that Earth there are gardens, paradises, animals, minerals—God alone can know how many. Now, everything that is to be found on that Earth, absolutely everything, is alive and speaks, has a life analogous to that of every living being endowed with thought and speech. Endowed with thought and speech, the beings there correspond to what they are here below, with the difference that in that celestial Earth things are permanent, imperishable, unchangeable; their universe does not die. The fact is that that Earth does not allow access to any of our physical bodies made of perishable human clay; its nature is such that it will allow access only to bodies of the same quality as that of its own universe or of the world of Spirits. And so it is in their spirit and not in their material body that the mystics enter into it. They leave their fleshly habitation behind on our earthly Earth and are immaterialized.[10]

A marvelous race of forms and figures exist on that Earth, of an extraordinary nature. They keep watch over the entrances of the ways of approach lying above this world in which we are, Earth and Heaven, Paradise and Hell. Whenever one of us is searching for the way of access to that Earth, the way of the Initiates of whatever category it may be, whether men or genii, Angels or dwellers in paradise—the first condition to be fulfilled is the practice of mystical gnosis and withdrawal from the material body. Then he meets those Forms who stand and keep watch at the entrances to the ways of approach, God having especially assigned them this task. One of them hastens towards the newcomer, clothes him in a robe suitable to his rank, takes him by the hand, and walks with him over that Earth and they do in it as they will. He lingers to look at the divine works of art; every stone, every tree, every village, every single thing he comes across, he may speak with, if he wishes, as a man converses with a companion. Certainly they speak different languages, but this Earth has the gift, peculiar to it, of conferring on whomsoever enters the ability to understand all the tongues that are spoken there. When he has attained his object and thinks of returning to his dwelling place, his companion goes with him and takes him back to the place at which he entered. There she says goodbye to him; she takes off the robe in which she had clothed him and departs from him.[11] But by then he has gathered a mass of knowledge and indications and his knowledge of God has increased by something he had not previously envisioned. I do not think that understanding ever penetrates in depth with a speed comparable to that with which it proceeds when it comes about in that Earth of which I am speaking. The more so in that here among us, in our own world and in our present existence, certain manifestations come to support our assertion.

Then Ibn ʿArabī tells the tale of a strange thing that happened to an Iranian Ṣūfī, Awḥaduddīn Kirmānī (d. 624/1127)[12] during his adolescence; Kirmānī himself told Ibn ʿArabī about it (it will be noted that they met personally). The young Ṣūfī wished to come to the help of his Shaikh, who had fallen ill. On arriving at Takrīt in Mesopotamia, he asked the Shaikh's permission to go and get some remedy from the hospital in Sanjar. Moved by the grief of his young disciple, the Shaikh gave him permission. So the young man went to the *majlis* of the Amīr, but being unknown to him, he was intimidated and afraid of being rebuffed. But the Amīr greeted him with great kindness, asked what he wanted and commanded a servant to give him what he asked for. The young Ṣūfī was overwhelmed and triumphant and returned to his Shaikh, to whom he told everything that had happened. But the Shaikh smiled and said, "My child, I was inspired by my concern for you. Seeing how sorry you were for me, I let you do what you asked. But when you were gone, I was afraid that the Amīr would put you to shame by refusing to receive you. So I separated myself from my own corporeal habitation; I entered that of the Amīr and I sat down at his place. When you arrived, it was I who greeted you and behaved toward you as you saw. Then I returned to this habitation that you see. As a matter of fact, I don't need this drug and have no use for it." "So here," said Ibn ʿArabī, "you see how a person was able to manifest himself in the semblance of another man. What must it be in the case of the inhabitants of that Earth of which we were speaking?"

The following episode (pp. 128–29) is in the form of a long account by Dhū'l-Nūn Miṣrī (d. 245/869) who first tells us that the *time* of that Earth is not uniform and all of one kind. "The times of that Earth are qualitatively of different kinds." Every event, every person, has *its own* time there. One day of our earthly time may be the equivalent of a number of years. Then Dhū'l-Nūn describes at length the wonders of that Earth in words reminiscent of the traditional stories about the mountain *Qāf*, which is the psycho-cosmic mountain, like the *Var* of Yima. There he visited the land of silver, the land of white camphor, the land of saffron. He describes its wonders and beauties, the charm and gentleness of the creatures who people it, their simple customs, the minerals and precious stones, the colors which adorn it. The light which reigns there is not that of the physical sun but nevertheless night and day alternate, just as with us. However, the darkness of the nights there is never a veil; it never prevents an object from being seen. There they engage in combat which is merely a game without hatred or wounds. Sea voyages are undertaken and enlivened by shipwrecks: for water is not a hostile element. It does not endanger life. They walk on its surface until they come back to shore. There are also earthquakes on that Earth more violent even than those on our earthly earth. Dhū'l-Nūn witnessed one of them. When the tremor died down, the kindly beings surrounding him took him by the hand and consoled him regarding one of his daughters called Fāṭima. "But I left her in good health with her mother," he said. "What you say is true, but this earth never trembles while one of you is with us unless he dies (and then remains definitely among us) or one of his relatives dies. This earthquake was the sign of the death of your daughter." When Dhū'l-Nūn had left these companions (the ceremony of the return is what is described above) and returned to this earth, he did learn of the passing of his daughter. We are bound to abbreviate all these data as far as possible, the interest of which from the viewpoint of religious phenomenology depends on the principle already stated, namely: on that Earth every soul has its own universe (the palm tree, which is Adam's sister); when the soul contemplates this universe, it is contemplating itself. It is in this sense that we should interpret another vision described by Ibn ʿArabī: that of a *Kaʿba* whose proportions surpass those of the temple that lies in Mecca. Those who circumambulate it were not wearing the ritual pilgrim's clothing. It had four pillars that spoke to those who walked around them and initiated them into knowledge which they did not previously have. (See the symbol of the one visible pillar of the temple, as Holy Spirit interpreting the Mystery, in our *Creative Imagination in the Ṣūfism of Ibn ʿArabī*, p. 367, n. 44.) There again we find the same ocean, which is made of *earth*, and which nevertheless behaves like *water*. (Cf. below, Art. IX, 4, b, the passage where the First Imām, on being asked about the alchemical Work, affirms: "I call God to witness that it is nothing other than Water in the solid state . . . Earth in the fluid state.") And on this ocean is to be seen the vision of a strange vessel made of magnificent stones: two pillars rise from its wings, the rear deck of the ship between the two pillars (the author even draws a plan of it) is open to the sea but the sea does not come in. Then *thirteen cities of light* are mentioned as being situated in that Earth into which only the elect amongst the gnostics have access. (The Shīʿite interpretation spontaneously discerns the Prophet and the twelve Imāms in these cities of light.) There are many other details no less rich in symbolic possibilities. . . .

In short, everything that in our case the rational mind holds to be impossible and finds proofs to support, we find in that Earth to be not something impossible but something possible which does in fact take place.[13] "For God has power over all things (3:26 and passim)." We know that our intellect is limited, but that God has power over the *coincidentia oppositorum*: the power to cause one body to exist in two different places, the power to make the accidental subsist independently of its substance and to transfer it from one substance to another, the power to make the spiritual sense subsist thanks to the spiritual sense alone (with no exoteric support). Every event, prodigy, and sign which comes about in our world and of which the rational mind is loath to admit the *real apparition*, in that Earth we find takes place beyond a doubt as a real apparition. Every body assumed by the spiritual, whether angel or genie, every form or shape in which man looks upon himself in a dream, all these are subtle bodies belonging to that other Earth. Each of these bodies has its appropriate site there, with subtle tenuous prolongations extending to the whole of its universe. Each of these "tenuities" has a confidant who corresponds to it. When the latter sees some particular spiritual entity with his own eyes, it means he has a special affinity with such and such a definite form among forms, that exact one which the Spirit assumes, as when the Angel Gabriel assumed for the Prophet the form of the handsome adolescent Daḥya al-Kalbī. The cause of this is that God laid out this Earth in the *barzakh*, the interworld, and fixed a location there for these subtle bodies assumed by pure spiritual beings, toward which our souls themselves are transported during sleep and after death. This is why we are ourselves a part of its universe.

Lastly, that Earth opens out at one extremity onto Paradise: that end of it is known as the forecourt or esplanade. And there is another extremity which is adjacent to our earthly Earth. To give a picture which will help you to grasp how it is that that Earth can extend as far as our world, I suggest the following comparison. Suppose a man fixes his gaze on a lamp, or on the sun, or the moon, and then half shuts his eyes so that his eyelashes veil the luminous body from his gaze; then he will see something like a multitude of lines of light stretching from the luminous body to his eyes—a whole network starting from the lamp, for example, and reaching right to his own eyes. When the eyelids are slowly and gradually raised, the observer sees the network of lines of light draw back little by little and gather into the luminous body.

And so the luminous body is analogous here to the location especially reserved in that Earth for such and such a form of apparition (a subtle body clothing a spiritual entity). The observer in this case represents our own world. As for the expansion of the lines of light, this corresponds to the forms of the subtle bodies in which our souls are transported to the threshold of Paradise during sleep and after death, and which are likewise the apparitional forms assumed by the Spirits. Your intention to obtain a vision of the lines of light by covering your eyelids so that the lashes will come between your gaze and the luminous body is in this case analogous to the capacity for visionary apperception. The emission of lines of light from the luminous body when you make this experiment corresponds then to the emission of the forms (which spiritual beings assume for you) when you have attained the capacity (to see in vision such and such an apparitional form). Lastly, the retraction of the lines of light as they withdraw into the luminous body, as the interposition of the eyelids ceases, represents the return of the forms withdrawing into that Earth when your capacity to perceive them comes to an end. There is no explanation beyond this explanation. Moreover, we have already spoken at length in one of our great works[14] about the marvels in that Earth and the knowledge connected with them.

III

DĀ'ŪD QAYṢARĪ
(d. 751/1350)

Mundus Archetypus *

Know that the *mundus archetypus* (*al-ʿālam al-mithālī*, the world of the archetypal Images)[1] is a spiritual universe of luminous substance; on the one hand it has an affinity with material substance, in that it is the object of perception and possesses extent; on the other hand, it has an affinity with separate intelligible substance, in that its nature is that of pure light. It is neither a compound material body, nor a separate intelligible substance, because it is a *barzakh*, that is, an interworld, a limit, which separates the one from the other. Everything which creates an interval, a *barzakh*, between two things, must differ from these two things, or rather, it is bound to have two dimensions through each of which it symbolizes with the universe to which this dimension corresponds. One can also say, it is true, that it is a body of light equal in subtlety to the maximum of conceivable subtlety. Thus, it is a limit, an interworld separating the purely subtle separate substances and the dense and opaque material substances, though among the latter also, certain bodies are more subtle than others, as are the Heavens, for instance, compared to the other bodies.

Therefore it is not an accidental world, as a certain thinker believed, thinking—as he did—that Image-forms could be dissociated from their substantial realities and that the same was true in regard to intelligible forms. The truth is that substantial forms exist in each of the universes: the spiritual universe, the intelligible universe, the imaginative universe, and all these sub-

* Extract from the commentary on the *Fuṣūṣ al-ḥikam* of Ibn ʿArabi, ch. VII of the introduction. Bombay, 1299/1881, pp. 30 ff. and 1300/1882, pp. 25 ff. It is necessary to collate the two editions.

stantial realities assume forms which correspond to their respective universe.

When you have thoroughly understood what this is about, you will observe that the imaginative power (the *Imaginatrix*) which belongs to the Soul of the universe, and itself including everything included by the other imaginative powers (those of the *Animae coelestes*), is the substratum and epiphanic place of this interworld.[2] It is called the *mundus archetypus* because it contains the Forms of everything existing in this world, and because it is the archetype of all the Forms of the individuals and essences existing on the plane of divine knowledge. It is also called the world of the autonomous Imagination, because it is immaterial in comparison with the immanent[3] imagination. There is no suprasensory reality, no spiritual entity nor Spirit, that does not have an archetypal form corresponding to its perfections, since each of them participates in the divine Name "the Revealed" (*al-Ẓāhir*). This is the meaning of a reliable tradition, which relates that when the Prophet saw the Angel Gabriel at the *Lotus of the Limit*,[4] the Angel had six hundred wings; every morning and evening he entered the river of Life; he came out shaking his wings, and out of the scattered drops God created countless Angels.

This interworld contains the Throne (*'arsh*, the supreme Heaven), the Firmament (*Kursī*, the Heaven of the Fixed Stars), the seven Heavens and the Earths, and everything all of these contain. At that level, the consciousness of the seeker awakens; he understands of what the Prophet's *Mi'rāj* (heavenly assumption) consisted, how it was that the Prophet had the vision of Adam in the first Heaven, the vision of John and Jesus in the second Heaven, the vision of Joseph in the third, of Idrīs (Enoch-Hermes) in the fourth, of Aaron in the fifth, of Moses in the sixth, and of Abraham in the seventh. The seeker understands, on the one hand, the difference there is between what he sees in his dream and the ability of those moderately advanced in the mystical path to realize imaginatively an ascent to Heaven, and on the other hand, the difference from what is really contemplated in the spiritual world. The forms perceived in our world are *the shadows* of these archetypal Forms. That is why the gnostic, through intuitive physiognomy, recognizes the inner states of man according to his outer form. . . . In their turn, the captive[5] archetypal forms represented by our imagination are themselves only exemplifications of the spiritual world, a shadow from among the shadows which God has created as sign and proof of the existence of this spiritual world. That is why the masters of mystical vision have seen the interworld as something contiguous to the spiritual world, receiving light from it, as streams and rivers issue into the sea, and as high windows allow rays of light to enter a house.

For each of the beings existing in the world of the senses there is, respectively, a captive archetypal form perceived in the human world on the plane of the imagination, whether it be a Heaven, a star, or an Element, a mineral, a plant, or an animal, because there are a Spirit and spiritual energies for each of them, and because the Spirit participates to a certain extent in this world; otherwise, the universes would not correspond perfectly. The most that can be said is that in the mineral world the manifestation is not the same as in the animal world. God himself states: "There is no thing which does not give praise by an act of glorification proper to it, but you do not understand their hymn of praise" (17:46).[6] This is confirmed by certain of our traditions, which mention that animals *see* things which, among human beings, can be seen only by the visionary mystics. It is possible that this vision takes place in the absolute *mundus archetypus*, and it is possible that it takes place in the world of captive archetypal forms.[7] God alone knows how it is!

But as for those human beings who are incapable of raising the veil because of their blindness, the Holy Book places them "at the lowest of the lowest degrees" (95:5). As for the mystic, when he has arrived at the absolute *mundus archetypus* in the course of his pilgrimage, thanks to the exodus that leads him out of his captive imagination, he reaches the aim in everything he contemplates, and discovers reality as it is, because the archetypal Images correspond with the intelligible Forms inscribed on the *tabula secreta*, which is the manifested form of the divine world. From then on, through visionary apperception, it may be that the human being will have his eternal individuality revealed to him in its successive states, past and future, because he is then transported from the world of Shadow to the world of real and essential Lights. . . .

Finally, it is important for you to know that the *barzakh* in which the Spirits find themselves after they have left the terrestrial world is different from the *barzakh* which extends between the pure spiritual entities and the world of bodies. The fact is that the stages of the being's descent and the steps of his ascent form a cycle. Now, the stages which precede existence in the terrestrial world are degrees of descent; they are anterior; whereas those degrees which come after existence in the world are degrees of ascent; they are posterior. Besides, the Forms with which the Spirits are reunited in the second *barzakh* are the forms of their works and the result of their prior activities in this terrestrial world,[8] unlike the forms of the first *barzakh*. Hence, the latter cannot be identical with the former. Nevertheless, they have this in common: in both cases the Forms are a spiritual universe and are immaterial substances of pure Light, containing the archetypes of the forms of this world. The Shaikh (Ibn 'Arabī), in chapter 321 of *The Book of the Spiritual Conquests of Mecca*,[9] demonstrates clearly that the second *barzakh* is different from the first. He calls the latter the "mystery of the possible," whereas he calls the former the "mystery of the impossible," in the sense that what exists in the first can be manifested in our visible world, whereas it is not possible for that which is in the second to return to the visible state, except on the Day of Judgment. Very few are those to whom this second *barzakh* is revealed. The first, on the other hand, may be revealed to a good many among us and seen with our own eyes. Such people can have knowledge of future events in the world, but not the power to discover the condition of those who have left this world.

IV

ʿABD AL-KARĪM JĪLĪ
(d. 805/1403)

The text translated below is taken from the best-known work of ʿAbd al-Karīm Jīlī, the *Book of the Perfect Man* (*Kitāb al-insān al-kāmil*), Cairo, 1304/1886. There is urgent need for a critical edition which would provide a better basis for reading this text. The theme of ch. VII (II, 27–28) is that "the Imagination is the substance (*hayūlā*, matter) of all the universes."

Some preliminary and very summary remarks: one is struck, from the very beginning of the chapter, by the all-importance attributed to the imaginative power (the "Imaginatrix")—it is "the life of the Spirit of the universe, its principle, its own principle being the son of Adam." Jīlī, like Ibn ʿArabī, regards the imaginative power as the very secret of cosmogony viewed as theophany, of creation as divine self-revelation. The mystic is even said to encounter here a higher spiritual entity called the "Spirit of Imagination" and "Spirit of Paradise." But suddenly we remember the warning of the Prophet: the slumber of humans asleep in the unconsciousness of dreams that are the world of imagination. Actually, there is no contradiction or dissonance here, for what is implicit is the secret of the knowledge on which it depends whether a man remains unconscious or takes his place among the Watchers of *al-Aʿrāf*.

Since all the planes of the universe are so many theophanic acts issuing from the absolute Divine Imagination, there could be no question of reabsorbing, denying, or annihilating them without going counter to the theophanic divine Will. Such a revolt is precisely what creates the condition of the peoples of Hell, because they have not understood. But Jīlī makes it possible for us to understand, by making a distinction similar to the one already pointed out to us (see above, Art. III, n. 3). Imagination considered in its totality has a twofold principle, a twofold source: on the one hand, it is active configuration and belongs to the world of superexistence (the world of absolute Imagination, the world of *Malakūt*, the world of the Soul); on the other hand, it is the imagined image, the formed image, the perishable representation (the images held "captive" in the faculties of man in his present condition). The sleep of unconsciousness means ignorance of the true nature of sensory perceptions. It means passive subjection—as though they were material—to data (empirical, historical, and so forth) created by a power in himself of which man remains unconscious and unaware. It means complete subservience to these data, and this is why Jīlī explains (II, 59–60) that this slavery is exactly the condition of Hell which is a misinterpretation of, or rebellion against, theophany as such; because in the ignorance of what theophany is, man puts the yoke of enslaving objectivizations in its place.

By contrast, the *paradisal* condition is the overcoming of this slavery because one has become aware of the secret law of the universe as a theophany, and because one is in accord with that secret. In the case of him who attains this knowledge, "God sets him up as a judge to decide the realities of the universe." This consciousness, this awakening from the dogmatic sleep that was a slavery to the authority of outer things, is known as the reciprocal *compresence* of creator-being and creatural-being. Because he has understood the *data*, and so is no longer under their yoke, the mystic is *compresent* to the presence of the *Giver* of these data. From then on, the theophanic Imagination becomes *Imaginatio vera*, the very secret of the power creating all the universes, and that is what it means "to be a Watcher" (an *Egregoros*), one of the men of *al-Aʿrāf*. He who has attained the knowlege of the law that gives structure to this universe, and has available to him at will all that his knowledge has made real, is in *al-Aʿrāf*, the place of divine Proximity, alluded to in the Qur'ānic verse: "Dwelling place of truth, close to a powerful king" (54:55). That is why all our authors explain the mysterious term *al-Aʿrāf* by the very root from which the word comes: *maʿrifa*: knowledge of gnosis, knowledge which is spiritual realization.

There are very many traditions about *al-Aʿrāf* and an entire book would be needed to coordinate them and extract their meaning. In Shīʿism they abound (see *Safīna*, II, 182). For Shaikh Mufīd, who expresses a general opinion on this point, it is a mountain or a rampart, a place intermediate between Paradise and Hell. The Qur'ānic verses (7:44 and 46) call *al-Aʿrāf* the rampart where there exist men endowed with the power of physiognomic discernment, that is, they are capable of recognizing each one's inner essence from his physiognomy. For Shīʿite theologians, these men of *al-Aʿrāf* are the Fourteen Very-Pure (the Prophet, Fāṭima, and the twelve Imāms): only he enters Paradise who is recognized by them, but they precisely can only recognize him who has himself known them. This recognition is therefore likewise a *compresence*, for it is being known while knowing, that is, in the very act of knowing, in such a way that the inner and the outer act reciprocally. And so this *compresence* in knowing and being known depends on the theophanic function of the person of the holy Imāms. Hence the significance of the place of *al-Aʿrāf* is esotericism in general.

Al-Aʿrāf is the "height that overlooks," that from which and by which theophanic perception as such is possible, namely: the visionary apperception of the divine Being as He is epiphanized in each thing, with His Attributes of which each thing is a theophanic form.

An all-important point that follows is that our authors relate the term, *al-Aʿrāf*, as a "dominant height" or "promontory," with one of the Prophet's *ḥadīth* that governs the entire esoteric hermeneutic of the Qur'ān: each verse has an exoteric aspect (*ẓahir*, the literal text is recited), an esoteric aspect (*bāṭin*, the hidden meaning that must be understood), a definitive aspect (*ḥadd*, fixing practical conduct) and a "height of aim," which is what God aims to actualize in man and through man. This *ḥadīth* has been enriched from Imām to Imām with variations and amplifications which have become traditional (the seven esoteric meanings, the nine planes of reference, and so forth). Rūzbihān and others mention them in the beginning of their *Tafsīr*. *Al-Aʿrāf* is thus the "promontory," the height that must be attained and "realized" in order to perceive the spiritual meaning, or rather to attain it—this is just the point: to perceive, to "realize," the spiritual meaning of the Revelations, the "spiritual history" which is the invisible dimension of literal data and earthly events. The mystics, having themselves been known and recognized to the same degree that they are knowers, become in their turn "men of *al-Aʿrāf*." That is why they are the *theo-sophoi* (*al-ʿārifūn bi'llāh*), for one who knows God knows the structure of the other world.

There is yet another mystical place in the other world, close to *al-Aʿrāf*, which is mentioned in our text and it will be useful at this point to give Jīlī's own explanation (II, 59–60). This is the place known as *al-Kathīb*, the "dune" or "region of the dunes." We learn that it is a region or plane situated below *al-Aʿrāf*. The difference between the inhabitants of the *Kathīb* and those of *al-Aʿrāf* is that the former left our world before God had shown himself to them. When they emigrated to the other world, their place of sojourn was then Paradise and from there God sometimes brings them out in the direction of *al-Kathīb* in order to show himself to them there, that is to say, to show himself to each according to his faith and to the knowledge he had of God. The inhabitants of *al-Aʿrāf*, on the other hand, are Spirituals to whom God manifested himself (*tajallī*, theophany) before they left this world and who therefore already had a vision of Him here in this world of ours. For them, there is no dwelling place beyond the world except in God, "for if one arrives in a country where a friend resides, that friend cannot let him make his home anywhere but with himself."

On other pages (II, 70), in the course of a highly developed imaginative topography describing the seven Heavens and the seven Earths (see the text translated below, Art. x, § 1), Jīlī refers again to the mysterious country *Yūḥ*, the country of the "men of the Invisible," who recognize no one but the prophet Khiẓr (Khaḍir) as their overlord. The passage translated below describes the entry of the spiritual pilgrim into that country. In this case, the celestial Earth, which is the first of the earths, is called the "Earth of souls," and is described in terms that use the symbols of the North (see above, Part One, Ch. II, § 1, last part *in fine*, and § 2) and thus we here again, in Islamic gnosis, the theme of the "hyperborean Paradise" (cf. the *Var* of Yima). It is an earth which was created whiter than milk, softer than musk. When Adam was exiled from the earth, it took on the color of dust, except for a region in the extreme north, governed by Khiẓr, inhabited by the "men of the Invisible," and to which no sinner can gain access. It is the country of the "midnight sun": there the evening Prayer is not obligatory, for dawn rises before the sun sets.

1. Al-Aʿrāf, the Earth of the Watchers

Apart from Heaven's Eternity
And yet how far from Hell!
Edgar Allan Poe, *Al-Aaraf*

Know—may God bring you help!—that Imagination is the principle and source of being; it is the essence that contains the perfection of theophany (*ẓuhūr al-maʿbūd*, 'the epiphany of the Adored'). Meditate on your personal faith concerning the Divine Being. Do you not see that this faith is attached to certain attributes and Names that it includes for you? Where is the place, what is the organ of this intimate conviction in which God Most High reveals Himself to you? This place, this organ is precisely the Imagination, and exactly for that reason we affirm that the Imagination is the essence in which the perfection of theophany resides.

As soon as you have become aware of that, it becomes evident to you that the Imagination is the principle and source of the entire universe, because the Divine Being is Himself the principle and origin of all things, and because the most perfect of His epiphanies can take place only in a receptacle which is itself origin and principle. This substratum is the Imagination.

From that moment, it is certain that the Imagination is the principle and source of all the universes without exception.

Now, do you not see how the Prophet perceived what is the object of sense perception as a dream, and this dream as an imagination? "Humans are asleep," he said. "It is when they die that they awake."[1] This means that at that moment, in their true sense, the realities that were right beside them in this world are revealed, and it is then that they understand that they were asleep. This does not mean that death produces total Awakening. For unconsciousness of God hangs over the inhabitants of the interworld (the *barzakh*) as well as over the men of the Last Day, as well over the inhabitants of hell as over the inhabitants of paradise, until the Divine Being shows Himself to them in the "region of the dunes,"[2] toward which the inhabitants of paradise sometimes emerge and then contemplate God.

This unconsciousness is sleep. The principle and source of all the universes is Imagination. That is why Imagination connects all the individuals who are in these universes. Each of the communities is connected by the imagined image in whichever universe it may happen to be. The inhabitants of this world, for example, are linked together by the imagination of daily life or by that of the future life (by wanting to "ensure" one and the other). Now the one and the other involve unawareness of reciprocal *compresence* with God.[3] That is why these people are asleep, whereas one who is *compresent* with the Divine Presence is a Watcher, an Awakened One (an *Egregoros*[4]); his degree of awakening is proportionate to his reciprocal *compresence* with God.

In their turn, the inhabitants of the interworld (the *barzakh*) are also sleeping people, although their sleep is lighter than that of certain people of our world. In effect, they are quite preoccupied by anguish or enjoyment, which are both something which *is* themselves, proceeds from themselves, and something *in which* they themselves are. Now that is also sleep, because they are equally inattentive and unconscious of God. The same is true of the men of the Last Day, for although they stand before God for the "rendering of accounts," they are nonetheless *with* their "rendering of accounts," they are not *compresent* with God. And that is sleep, because it is unawareness. However their sleep is lighter than that of the inhabitants of the interworld. Thus it is the same for those who live in Paradise, and still more for those who live in Hell. The first are *with* the enjoyment that they experience; the second are *with* the anguish that they experience. And that again is to be unaware of God. It is sleep, it is not a state of wakefulness. However, the sleep of the inhabitants of Paradise is lighter than that of the men of the Last Day.

Therefore, in this way, sleep is like a law of nature for all, in the sense that each inhabitant of all the universes, while being, in a certain sense, *compresent* with the Divine Being as such, since the Divine Being is *compresent* with being in its totality—He says of Himself: "He is *with* you wherever you are (57:4)"—nevertheless, all are *compresent* with Him only in a dream, not in a state of conscious wakefulness.

That is why there is awakening and a state of wakefulness only for the inhabitants of *al-A'rāf* and for those in the "region of the dunes."[5] For they are in reciprocal *compresence* with God, and their degree of awakening is in proportion to the theophany that is manifested to them. God has shown Himself to the man who, because of a divine predisposition, obtains from God, here in this world, what is produced only later in the "region of the dunes" for the inhabitants of paradise,[6] and to him God shows Himself and he knows Him. He is therefore a Watcher (*Yaqẓān*, an *Egregoros*). And for that reason, the prince of all the Spirituals who have reached this dwelling has proclaimed that men are asleep. It was because he himself was a Watcher and knew. Therefore, now that you have understood that the inhabitants of each of the universes are under the law of sleep, declare that all the universes are so many imagined images, for dream is the world of imagination.

2. The Journey of the Stranger and the Conversation with Khiẓr

The Stranger, called by the name of Spirit,[7] journeyed until he had reached the country called the country of *Yūḥ*.[8] When he reached that heaven, he knocked on the door of the forbidden threshold.

A voice asked him, "Who are you, the lover knocking on the gate?"

He answered, "One faithful in love, separated from his own. I have been banished from your country. I have wandered far from those like you. I have been bound to the impediments of height and depth, of length and width. I have been imprisoned in the jail of Fire and Water, of Air and Earth.[9] But now that I have severed my bonds, I start to seek an escape from the prison where I had remained. . . ."

Then he found himself in the presence of a personage with white hair, who said to him, "Know that the world to which you return is the world of Mystery (*'ālam al-ghayb*, the world of the suprasensory). The men belonging[10] to it are great in number; they are sensitively helpful; they possess powerful methods; they provide plenty of scope. He who aspires to rejoin them and to present himself to them, must don their magnificent dress and be perfumed with their soft perfume."

"Where do I procure garments? Where are these perfumes sold?"

"The garments can be found in the market of sesame left over as surplus from the remainder of the clay of Adam.[11] As for the perfumes, they can be obtained on the Earth of the Imagination."

If you prefer, you may reverse this explanation: in that case borrow the clothing from the cloth of the Imagination and the perfume from the Earth of sesame. For they are unquestionably two brothers (or two sisters), both belong to the same world called the world of Mystery or world of the suprasensory.[12]

"Then I went away, first toward the Earth of Perfection, the original appearance of Beauty, called because of its aspects, 'World of Imagination.' In that very place I turned toward a personage in a sublime condition, of a high rank, and with sovereign power. He bore the name: 'Spirit of Imagination' (*rūḥ al-khayāl*) and a surname: 'Spirit of Paradise' (*rūḥ al-jinān*). When I had greeted him and stopped respectfully in front of him, he answered me with many welcoming greetings.

"I said to him, 'Oh my lord, what is this world called the sesame left over from the clay of Adam?'[13]

" 'That is the subtle world,' he said to me, 'a world forever imperishable, a place that does not pass away with the succession of nights and days. God created it from that clay; he selected this seed from out of the whole mould, then he invested it with an authority that extended to everything, to the great as to the humble. . . .[14] It is an Earth where the impossible becomes possible, where the pure figures of Imagination are contemplated with the senses.'

" 'Will I find a road leading to this extraordinary dwelling, to this strange world?'

" 'Certainly! When your active imagination will have attained all its perfection and all its plenitude, your capacity will expand till it makes possible the impossible, till it contemplates suprasensory realities of the Imagination under a sensory mode, till it understands allusive signs and deciphers the secret of the diacritical points of letters. Then you will have woven a garment from these suprasensory realities; when you have put it on, open for yourself a door giving access to the sesame.'

" 'Oh my Lord, I fulfil the conditions, for I am already here and now bound by the cable of the concluded pact. I already know, through revelation and personal discovery, that the world of pure spiritual Entities is more manifest and stronger than the world perceived by the senses, as much for intimate experience as for visionary intuition.'

"Then, after a murmur, he made a sign with his hand, and then I found myself on the Earth of sesame. . . .[15]

"When I had penetrated into this marvelous Earth and was perfumed with its strangely sweet perfumes, when I had contemplated its marvels and strangeness, things so beautiful and so rare that they have still not entered into your thought and cannot be seen either in our world or even in our imaginable world, I sought to ascend to the world of Mystery.

"At that moment I again found the Shaikh who had been my first guide, but I ascertained that practice of the divine service had made him so slim that he seemed to be a pure apparition, and that he had grown thinner than one would have thought possible. In spite of that, he had preserved all his inner strength and the same creative spiritual energy;[16] he was just as impetuous and resolute as before, just as prompt both to sit down and to stand up, his brightness was like that of the full moon.

"Having greeted him and my greeting having been returned, I said to him, 'I wish to obtain access to the men of the world of Mystery (*rijāl al-ghayb*, the Invisible Ones, the Superhuman Ones). There is no doubt that I fulfil the conditions.'

" 'Then it is the time to enter,' he said to me. 'The time to reunite has come.' With his ring he knocked on the door which remained closed hitherto and it opened very widely. I penetrated into the city of the marvelous Earth; its length and breadth are immense, its inhabitants have a knowledge of God such as is possessed by no other creature. There is no man among them who lets himself be distracted. Its soil is a pure and very white wheat flour; its Heaven is of green emerald. Its sedentary inhabitants are of a pure race and of high nobility; they recognize no other king than Khiẓr (al-Khaḍir).[17] It was precisely with him that I deposited my luggage. Entering into his presence, I kneeled down and proceeded to present my greetings. In his turn, he bid me welcome as does one friend to another. Then he invited me to be his guest, and with a smile that put me perfectly at ease, he said to me, 'Well! Now say what you have to say.'

" 'My lord,' I said, 'I would like to question you about your sublime situation since your condition is so difficult to conceive that our words become entangled when we wish to describe it, although some people blindly persist in so doing.'

" 'I am,' he said to me,[18] 'transcendent reality, and I am the tenuous thread that brings it very close.[19] I am the secret of man in his act of existing, and I am that invisible one (*al-bāṭin*, the *absconditum*, the esoteric) who is the object of worship. I am the cylinder that contains the Essences, and I am the multitude of tenuous threads projected forth as mediators. I am the Shaikh with the divine nature, and I am the guardian of the world of human nature.[20] I cause myself to be in every concept and to be manifested in every dwelling. I appear epiphanized through every form, and I make a "sign" visible in every Sūra. My condition is to be esoteric, unusual. My situation is to be the Stranger, the traveler. My permanent dwelling place is the mountain of Qāf.[21] My halting place is the *Aʿrāf*.[22] I am he who stands at the confluence of the two seas, the one who plunges into the river of the Where, the one who drinks from the source of the source.[23] I am the guide of the fish in the sea of divinity.[24] I am the secret of the embryo, and I already bear the adolescent. I am the initiator of Moses.[25] I am the First and the Last diacritical point.[26] I am the unique Pole that is the sum of all. I am the Light that scintillates. I am the full moon rising. I am the decisive word. I am the splendor of consciences. I am the desire of the seekers. Only the Perfect Man (*al-insān al-kāmil*), the ingathered Spirit, reaches and finds access to me. As for all the others, my rank is well above the dwelling place where they are established. They have no knowledge of me; they see no vestige of me. On the other hand, their dogmatic belief takes shape for them in some one of the forms of religion professed by men. They masquerade ridiculously in my name; they paint my symbol on their cheek. Then the ignorant, the inexperienced, rests his gaze there, and he imagines that indeed to be what bears the name *Khiẓr*. But how is that related to me, what have I to do with that? Or rather, what is this poor cup in relation to my jar? Unless it is said, in truth, that this is also a drop of my ocean, or an hour of my eternity, since its reality is that of a tenuous thread among my tenuities,[27] and that the way followed by those is a way among my ways. Then, in this sense, I am also this fallacious star.'

" 'What is the distinctive sign?' I asked him then, 'the symbol of one who reaches you, of one who takes up lodging in your outer sanctuary near you?'

" 'His distinctive sign,' he said to me, 'is concealed in the knowledge of the creative power, its exalted knowledge is involved in the science of the essencification of the Essences.'

"Then I questioned him on the different categories of the 'men of the Invisible' (*rijāl al-ghayb*, those of the world of Mystery).[28]

" 'There are some among them,' he said to me, 'who are Adamites, and there are some among them who are pure spiritual entities. They form six categories differing as to rank.

" 'The first category is the preeminent one; they are the Perfect Ones, the great Initiates who follow in the footsteps of the prophets[29] and who remain invisible to the creatures of this world, because they are hidden in the Mystery which is designated as the plane on which the Merciful[30] is enthroned. They are not known, they cannot be described, although they are Adamites.

" 'The second category consists of the intimates of suprasensory planes, the Spirits that inspire the hearts.[31] The spiritual Guide manifests by taking their form, in order that mortals be led by them to inner and outer perfection. They are Spirits; they are, so to speak, pure apparitional forms, in that they have the faculty of producing a visual representation of themselves. They travel, taking their departure from this visible world; they reach as far as the field of the mystery of being. Afterwards, they may pass from the hidden to the visible state. Their breath is entirely a divine service. They are the pillars of the Earth,[32] keeping watch for God over the tradition and precepts.

" 'The third category are the Angels of inspiration and impulses who, during the night visit the Initiates and converse with the Spirituals; they do not show themselves in the world of sensory perception; they are not known by ordinary men.

" 'The fourth category are the men of confidential psalms throughout their ecstasy. They are perpetually out of their world. If one ever meets them, it is always in another place than where they were supposed to be found. They manifest to other men by taking form in the world of sensory perception. When the Spirituals happen to meet them on these detours, they initiate them into the mysteries of the invisible and inform them of realities kept secret.

" 'The fifth category are the men of the wild lands; they are the privileged in the world. They are a race of Adamites, they can make themselves visible to humans, then they conceal themselves. When they are addressed, they answer. Most often, their dwellings are in the mountains and in the deserts, in streambeds or on riverbanks. Sometimes there are sedentary ones among them; then they choose among the cities some dwelling where they elect to reside; but it is not a place in which they would put their trust, any more than it satisfies the desired ambitions.

" 'The sixth category are those who resemble sudden inspirations of thought, having nothing in common with demonic suggestions. They are children whose father is mental discourse and whose mother is the active imagination. No one pays any attention to what they say; their like do not inspire ardent desire. They are between the false and the true; they are both people who have lifted the Veil and people who remain in front of the Veil. "And God is the True, he is the guide on the Way" (33:4). "Near him is the archetype of the Book" (13:39, *umm al-kitāb*, "the mother of the Book").' "

V

SHAMSUDDĪN MUḤAMMAD LĀHĪJĪ
(d. 869/1465)

Jābalqā and Jābarṣā*

In the accounts and books of traditional history, mention is made that *Jābalqā* is an immense city situated in the East, whereas *Jābarṣā* is a city just as large and spacious, situated in the West, opposite Jābalqā. The masters in the hermeneutics of symbols have made this the subject of numerous commentaries. The idea I have myself arrived at from quite independent thought can be summarized very simply as follows, under two headings:

First, Jābalqā is the *mundus archetypus* located to the East, and turned toward the spiritual entities; it is the interworld (*barzakh*) between the suprasensory world and the world visible to the senses. It contains all the archetypes of the universe, and thus of necessity is an immense city. Jābarṣā, to the West, is the world of the Image, the interworld in which the Spirits dwell when they have left the world of earthly existence.[1] That is the very place where the Forms of all completed works exist, the Forms of all moral behavior and good and bad actions, those which have been acquired in the course of earthly existence, as witnessed by the verses of the Qur'ān and our *ḥadīth*. Thus, Jābarṣā is the interworld situated in the West, and turned toward the material bodies; of necessity, it is also an immense city and faces Jābalqā. The structure of Jābalqā is more subtle and more pure, since that of Jābarṣā, being in terms of created works and moral behavior acquired in the world of earthly existence, is to a great extent made up of forms and figures enveloped in darkness.

* Extract from the Persian commentary on the "Rose Garden of the Mystery" (*Gulshan-i Rāz*), a mystical poem by Maḥmūd Shabistarī (d. 720/1320). Edition of Kayvān Samī'ī, Teheran, 1378/1958, pp. 134–36.

Most people take these two interworlds (*barzakh*) as being only one. However, it is important to recognize that the interworld where the Spirits are after they have been separated from earthly existence is different from the interworld which extends between the pure spiritual entities and the material bodies. In fact the descending degrees of being on the one hand, and the ascending degrees on the other, together form a cycle, in which the junction of the final point and the initial point can only be represented as a movement of complete revolution. The interworld preceding the sphere of earthly existence is part of the series of the descending degrees of being; with respect to earthly existence, this interworld has priority and anteriority, whereas the one succeeding earthly existence is part of the ascending degrees; with respect to earthly existence, its rank is ulterior and posterior.

Besides, the forms which again rejoin the Spirits in the second interworld are the forms of their works, the resultants of their acts, of habits acquired and behavior actualized by them in the earthly world. Now this is not the case with the archetypal Forms of the first interworld; hence, there is a very clear difference between the one and the other. On the other hand, the two interworlds have in common that they are two spiritual universes, that they have light as substance, that they are immaterial, and that they contain the autonomous Forms and Images of the universe.

Shaikh Dā'ūd Qayṣarī draws special attention to the pages of Shaikh Muḥyīddīn Ibn 'Arabī's book entitled *The Spiritual Conquests of Mecca*[2] in which the author clearly states that there is no doubt that the second interworld is different from the first. He calls the latter the mystery of the Possible (or Futurable) whereas he calls the second the mystery of the Impossible (or Irreversible). These two appellations mean that if, on the one hand, it is possible for every form or archetypal figure existing in the first interworld to be manifested in the visible world, it is, on the other hand, impossible for a Form transposed to the second world to come back to the visible world, unless it be in the *saeculum venturum*. Many are the visionary mystics, to whom the Forms of the first interworld are manifested as apparitions, and who thus have foreknowledge of events in our world. But only a very few visionaries have knowledge of the posthumous state of those who have departed from it.

Secondly, I would like to point out the following: Since the city of Jābalqā is the divine plane characterized by the "confluence of the two seas,"[3] that is, the confluence of the necessary mode of being and the possible mode of being, we can understand that in it are contained the Forms and Images of the universality of things and beings, in all their degrees: general and individual, subtle and dense, works and actions, way of being and way of doing, movement and rest. We can take it that Jābalqā includes everything that was and everything that will be, and for this reason is situated in the East, because beyond it, there is the degree of the divine Ipseity in itself, without there being any solution of continuity between the two. The suns, the moons, and the stars, which are the divine Names, eternal qualifications and hecceities arise in the East, which is divine Ipseity, from which they project their splendor. The city of Jābarsā, on the other hand, is the world of man, the place where the universality of the contents of the divine Names and all the essences of being are manifested. Everything that dawns to the East of the divine Ipseity, finally declines at the sunset of human reality and becomes hidden in the form of human existence. A poet has expressed it thus: "Should there be an Occident, here we are—become occidents of the mysteries. Should there not be an Occident, here we are—become the orients of the lights."

In short, Jābalqā and Jābarṣā are two immense cities, the one facing the other, and in truth there is no limit to the multitude of creatures which inhabit them both. And as each of the worlds has respectively its Orient and its Occident, the author of the "Rose Garden of the Mystery" declares: "Meditate conjointly the Orients and the Occidents,[4] notwithstanding that our world here below has only one of each."

Know that the world of the "deity," with respect to the world of "suzerainty"[5] is an Orient from which the primordial Emanation effuses on this world of suzerainty. And the world of suzerainty is an Orient in relation to the interworld of archetypal Images, and the world of archetypal Images is an Orient in relation to the sensory world. From each of these Orients, the divine Emanation effuses on the world which is beneath it. Each of the universes in turn, each of the degrees of being, each of the individuals, is an Orient from which rises the sun of one Name from among the divine Names. The human heart, because it recapitulates all the forms of the epiphanic function, possesses hundreds, even hundreds of thousands of Orients and still more, and all the stars which are the divine Names rise and shine through these Orients. But opposite each one there is also an Occident. How wondrous and strange the human heart, which no one can see, save the pilgrims of the spirit, who are the pure in heart.[6]

VI

ṢADRUDDĪN MUḤAMMAD SHĪRĀZĪ (MULLĀ ṢADRĀ)

(d. 1050/1640)

*Spissitudo Spiritualis**

The term *spissitudo spiritualis* (spiritual condensation or consistency) was suggested by Henry More in his *Enchiridion metaphysicum* to designate the "fourth dimension" (*quarta dimensio*), the idea of which inevitably struck him once he grasped the distinction between the concepts of space (that of the *locus supracoelestis*) and the concept of matter. The expression seemed appropriate to characterize the following pages of Mullā sadrā. It brings out a not altogether surprising affinity between the Cambridge Platonists and the Persian Platonists, to which we will return elsewhere.

Everything man pictures to himself, all that he really perceives, whether through intelligible or sensory perception, whether in this world or in the beyond, all these things are inseparable from man himself and cannot be dissociated from his essential "I." More precisely, what is essentially the object of perception is something that exists in himself, not in something else. We have already had occasion to speak of what the object of visual perception essentially is; when the sky, the earth, or anything else is perceived, by us, it is not an outer form existing in objective material data, as found in the dimensions of our world.

It is true that at the dawn of consciousness in man, the soul's perception requires the cooperation of material organs (eye, ear, and so on); it also requires that the position of objects satisfy

* Excerpt from the *Book of the Theosophy of the Throne* (*Kitāb al-ḥikmat al'arshīya*), Teheran, 1315/1897, pp. 148, 151–55, 195–98. This book has been the subject of several commentaries, notably the one by Shaikh Aḥmad Aḥsā'ī (Tabrīz, 1278/1861); see pp. 182–202, 325–34, some excerpts from which are given below (Art. IX, 4 b, c, 5).

certain relationships, because perception is still only potential in the being of man insofar as he is a feeling subject. It therefore must be placed in a suitable perspective and the conditions peculiar to the organ of perception in relation to a material object must be fulfilled. But the material object is never anything but an object perceived *by accident*; it is actually only an outer form imitating, exemplifying the form present in the soul (its archetypal Form in the *Malakūt*), which is *essentially* the object of perception. That is why, when perception has once or several times taken place in this manner, the soul is very often able to contemplate the form of a thing in its own world without requiring an outer material object as intermediary. In the *post mortem* state there remains no obstacle to prevent the soul from perceiving all that it feels and perceives without the intermediary of either external material data or of a corporeal organ belonging neither to the world of the soul nor to the true reality of the soul. . . .

Of all the realities that man sees and contemplates in the world beyond, those which delight, like houris, castles, gardens, green vegetation, and streams of running water—as well as their opposites—the horrifying kinds of which Hell is composed—none of these is extrinsic to him, to the very essence of his soul, none is distinct or separated from his own act of existing. The substantial reality is stronger, their permanence better assured, their essence more stable, than in the case of the material forms of our sensory world which are subject to incessant renewal and change. Let no one therefore believe he has the right to question the place, the *situs*, and the direction of these realities; not even to wonder whether they are on the inside or the outside of our cosmos, whether they are above the Sphere of Spheres that determines the coordinates of sensory space or whether they are included in the circles of the Heavens, or whether they are below the celestial Spheres. Such questions are meaningless once it is understood that we are concerned with another realm of existence, between which and the material world there is no relation as to *situs* or as to dimension.

Certainly, a well-known *ḥadīth* asserts that the Earth of paradise is the firmament (the eighth Heaven or Heaven of the constellations), while its "roof" is the Throne of the Merciful (the Sphere of Spheres, the empyrean). But this should not be taken as referring to the astronomical field enclosed in the space of this world, between the Heaven of the constellations and the supreme Heaven. No, we should take it as referring to that which corresponds to the esoteric plane of each Heaven, their suprasensory reality, their spiritual entity, for Paradise is interior to the suprasensory reality of Heaven.

Similarly, when it is said that Paradise is in the seventh Heaven and Hell in the lower Earth, it must be understood that it refers to something inner, something hidden under the veils of this world, for the *world beyond* is perpetual, eternal; its sweetness is unceasing, its fruition uninterrupted, its fruits never forbidden. Everything to which man aspires, everything he desires, is instantaneously present to him, or rather one should say: to picture his desire *is* itself to experience the real presence of its object. But the sweetness and delight are the expression of Paradise and Hell, good and evil, all that can reach man of what constitutes his retribution in the world beyond, have no other source than the essential "I" of man himself, formed as it is by his intentions and projects, his meditations, his innermost beliefs, his conduct. Their principle could not be in something with an existence and a *situs* different from his own act of existing. . . .

There are many differences between the bodies of this world and those of the *world beyond*. In the other world, each body is animated; it is alive thanks to essence; it is impossible to conceive of a body there as being without life, unlike in our world where there are bodies deprived of life and consciousness, and where living bodies never have more than an accidental and ephemeral life. The bodies of this world receive their souls at the end of a process that makes them fit to receive them. The souls of the *world beyond* themselves produce their bodies in accordance with their own needs. That is why in our world bodies and material realities rise progressively, according to their aptitudes and metamorphoses, to meet souls, while in that other world souls come down to meet bodies. Here below, virtuality is chronologically antecedent to an act, while the act is ontologically antecedent to virtuality. In the world beyond virtuality is ontologically, and ontically, antecedent to the act. Here, the act is nobler than virtuality because it is its fulfillment. There, virtuality is nobler than the act because it is that which produces the act.

Bodies and volumes are infinite in the other world, because they originate from the imaginations and perceptions of souls, which are both infinite. Proofs that dimensions are necessarily finite are not valid for the *other world*; they are only valid for the dimensions and material spatializations of this world. Nevertheless, there is neither crowding nor discomfort in that other world; no body is outside another, nor inside it. Every human being, blessed or damned, possesses a complete universe, vaster in itself than our world, and never forming, in relation to another man's universe, as it were, a step in the same series, because each of the blessed possesses whatever proportion of the entire series he desires. This is why the great mystic Abū Yazīd Basṭāmī declared: "Even were the Throne, with all it contains, to enter into the secret places of Abū Yazīd's heart, Abū Yazīd would not notice it." . . .

Now as to the way in which acts assume a body, and intentions assume shape on the resurrection day, you should know what has been said about the matter of their forms. Every outer form has its particular mode of apparition in the soul's dwelling. Reciprocally, every inner form, every psychic form, all behavior, every *habitus* rooted in the soul, has a certain mode of extramental existence. Do you not see that when a humid body exercises its effect on corporeal matter able to receive humidity, such matter receives it and itself becomes humid as did that body, thereafter having the same plastic flexibility as the latter? On the contrary, if it works on another matter, for example on an organ of sensory perception or of imaginative perception, even though that organ undergoes the action of humidity, this is not the same action; it does not become humid after the manner of that body, even while receiving the essence (*quiddity*) of its humidity, but in another form and of another type. In turn, the intellective faculty of man receives another form from it and perceives another mode of its existing and appearing although the quiddity in question is still the same, namely the essence (*quiddity*) of humidity and the humid.

So here we see how the same quiddity possesses three forms in three different abodes, for each of which it has an appropriate mode of existence and a definite mode of appearance. Pause to consider the difference of status shown by these three existences of one and the same quiddity, and compare the manner in which each ideal reality and each concrete quiddity can take on different configurations in their modes of existing and appearing. Then do not be surprised if anger, which is a psychic modality when it appears, by taking on form with extramental existence becomes a devouring fire; nor if knowledge, which is also a way of being of the soul, becomes a fountain called *Salsabīl* (a fountain of Paradise, Qur'ān 76: 18) when it appears as taking on a form with extramental existence, do not be surprised if that which someone has unjustly devoured of an orphan's wealth becomes, in the other world, a fire that tortures his entrails; nor if the love of this world, that is, bad passions and possessive ambitions which are maladies of the soul, become stinging scorpions, biting snakes. This should suffice to strengthen the faith of one able to understand in the promises and the threats uttered by the Prophet.

It is incumbent on anyone who has the strength to venture into higher knowledge to meditate on the psychic qualifications, the modes of being of the soul, and on the way in which these modes of being give rise to effects and external acts. He should make this knowledge a guide so that he may understand how certain modes of being and behavior imply the production, on the day of resurrection of outer effects appropriate to them. An example: the violence of anger in a man produces disturbance of the blood, redness of face, swelling of the skin. Now anger is a psychic state, something that exists in the inner world of man. As for the effects just noted, they are the modes of being of organic material bodies; the fact remains that they are the effects produced in this world by purely psychic states. Therefore why be astonished if, in another world, anger is converted into a pure fire that inflames the heart, infects the entrails, consumes the viscera, just as it is inherent to it in this world to heat the body, accelerate the pulsation of the arteries, make the limbs tremble, consume the humours, sometimes to lead to a serious illness, even to a fatal accident. Well! it is the same for all the corporeal and material forms existing in the world beyond; all of them result from habits acquired by the souls, from their good or bad behavior, from the beliefs they profess, from their healthy or corrupt intentions, from everything in them that takes root through the repetition of actions and ways of doing things in this world. That is why, if actions are the source of behavior in this world, souls are the principles of bodies in the world beyond by their modes of being.

As for the *matter* constituting bodies in the beyond through which actions take on body and intentions take shape, that matter is nothing other than the human soul itself. Just as "material matter" (*hyle*) is here the matter of which bodies and extended forms are constituted although this matter in itself does not have extent, so the human soul is the matter which, in the world beyond, constitutes the existents which there have extent and shape, although the soul in itself is a spiritual reality without extent. But here certain differences enter between the analogous functions of soul and the *hyle*.

The existence of matter (*hyle*) is purely potential existence; in itself it has no actual being except through corporeal forms. It is quite otherwise with the soul, which itself is actually existent, has substantial existence, and is endowed with the ability to perceive. It begins by being in this world the *form* of the elemental body. Then it becomes the matter of the world beyond, for the forms of the world beyond with which it is united by a mode of union *sui generis*. It is therefore on the one hand the *form* of the material realities of our world, and on the other the *matter* of the forms of the world beyond, breathed into it on "the day when the breath of the Angel will cause the trumpet to sound," when they will all come running in crowds according to their various species.

Article VI

Further, the soul is a spiritual, subtle matter (*mādda rūḥānīya laṭīfa, spissitudo spiritualis*!); it can receive forms only in a subtle suprasensory state, perceptible not to the senses of this world, but to the senses of the world beyond. On the other hand, material matter (*hyle*) is a dense, opaque matter which receives densified forms determined by sensory dimensions and sensory positions, mixtures of virtuality and of nonbeing. Further still, material matter behaves in a passive way in relation to the forms it receives; it undergoes change, alteration, movement. In contrast, the behavior of the soul in receiving forms that become rooted in it is a conservative action, an active implication. There is no incompatibility between its receptivity in regard to forms and its act of producing these same forms, since it is precisely by one and the same "reason" for its being that it simultaneously produces, and receives the forms and images produced by itself, the same holds good for its knowledge of first principles, the existence of which is not differentiated from the very existence of the Intelligence that causes them to exist.

There are yet other differences: receptivity in that world does not have the sense of a progressively acquired aptitude nor of a future potential. Finally, here forms are so many perfections as regards their matters and substrata, while there the forms, born from the soul itself, are not perfections as regards the soul insofar as they are forms *actualized* for it. There the growing perfection of the soul consists inversely in its actualization of these forms, that is, in being such that it produces these forms itself, and makes them the object of its own knowledge. There is between the two aspects a fundamental difference explained elsewhere.

VII

ʿABD AL-RAZZĀQ LĀHĪJĪ
(d. 1072/1662)

Oriental Theosophists and Peripatetic Philosophers*

Know that there was a school of philosophers in Islam, headed by Shihābuddīn Yaḥyà Suhrawardī, who was renowned under the title "Master of Oriental Theosophy" (*Shaikh al-Ishrāq*) for having created in the Islamic era the corpus of the "theosophy of the Orientals."[1] This school supports the thesis that several of the kings and princes of ancient Persia, such as Kay Khusraw[2] and his peers, were initiates of "Oriental theosophy." The Greek sages prior to Aristotle were likewise adepts of this "theosophy of the Orientals." Aristotle, on the other hand, took up an opposite position and created that aggregate of doctrines designated as the "philosophy of the Peripatetics."[3]

The difference between the theosophy of the Orientals and the philosophy of the Peripatetics can be seen from several angles. As everyone knows, the Orientals, or *Ishrāqīyūn*, affirm that wisdom can be attained only through a method of spiritual realization; they emphasize the inner effort of spiritual struggle and mystical experience. They value neither pure rational theory nor dialectics as such; one might even say that they are frankly hostile to them. The Peripatetics, on the other hand, base their philosophy on rational theory and logical reasoning, and concede no value to what cannot be reduced to rational argumentation and logical reasoning. The Orientals, or *Ishrāqīyūn*, are related to the Peripatetics as the Ṣūfīs to the scholastic theologians of Islam (the *Mutakallimūn*). This difference can be verified in the prologue of the book which was mentioned previously.[4]

* Extract from the great work in Persian entitled *Gawhar-i murad* (*The Desired Jewel*), 3d maqāla, 4th bāb, 2d faṣl, Teheran, 1313/1895, pp. 287–89.

Article VII

Briefly, the Oriental theosophists and the Ṣūfīs agree in defending in philosophy and mystical theosophy a large number of theorems which the Peripatetics and the scholastic theologians, on the grounds that they do not meet the requirements of rational theory and logical argumentation, reject. These theorems notably include the one affirming the existence of the *mundus archetypus*, the autonomous world of archetypal Images or Forms (*'ālam-i mithāl*). The Oriental theosophists and the Ṣūfīs agree in affirming the following:[5] between the intelligible world, which is the world of entirely immaterial pure Intelligences, and the sensory world, which is the world of purely material realities, there exists another universe. The beings of this intermediary universe possess shape and extent, even though they do not have "material matter." Thus the pure Intelligences are separated both from matter and extent; purely material things are clothed with both matter and extent; the beings of the *mundus archetypus* are separate from matter, but endowed with extent in the same way as the forms of imaginative consciousness. Nevertheless, the reality of the forms which are immanent in imaginative consciousness resides in that consciousness itself, not objectively or extramentally, whereas the reality of the world of archetypal Images is objective and extramental.[6]

Thus this world is intermediate between the two universes: as a result of being separated from matter, it is of the same nature as the world of pure Intelligences; as a result of possessing form and extent, it resembles the world of material things. Every being of the two universes, the intelligible and the sensory, has its archetypal Image in this intermediate universe, a self-subsistent Image with autonomous existence;—every creature and everything, including movement and rest, attitudes and physiognomies, flavors and perfumes, and other accidentals.[7] The mode of existence assumed in this intermediate world by an essentially immaterial being corresponds for this same being to a kind of descent through which it becomes able to take on extent and shape. On the other hand, the mode of existence assumed in it by a material being, for this same being corresponds to an ascent which strips it of matter and certain things inherent in matter, such as localization.[8]

This universe is also designated as the world of autonomous[9] Images and Imagination, and as the world of the *barzakh*.[10] It may happen that a being of this autonomous world of Images makes himself visible, makes his appearance in our material world, and can be perceived in it by the outer senses. Bodies which are perfectly polished and transparent bodies, such as mirrors, still water, the atmosphere, are the places of the epiphany in our material world of the beings of the world of archetypal Images. In the same way, man's Imagination is also the place of their epiphany. Forms contemplated in mirrors and those manifested in the Imagination both belong to that *mundus archetypus*, which is manifested for us in these "epiphanic places" (*maẓāhir*), that is, the mirror and the Imagination. In the same way also, the forms one sees in a dream, Angels, genii, and demons, are likewise beings belonging to this same world, who are sometimes manifest to a whole group, in such or such an epiphanic place in Air or Water.[11]

There is, moreover, a tradition dating back to the Sages of antiquity concerning the existence of a universe having extent but different from the sensory world—a universe with infinite wonders and countless cities, among them *Jābalqā* and *Jābarṣā*, two immense cities, each having a thousand gates and containing innumerable creatures. This is the universe by which the theosophists of that school (the *Ishrāqīyūn* or Orientals) explain and authenticate bodily resurrection; they affirm that Paradise, Hell, and the Earth of Resurrection have their existence in this *mundus archetypus*, the autonomous universe of the archetypal Images. This is the universe in which accidents can acquire substance, in which the acts and works of man can take on consistent form and figure.[12] Among the schools that admit bodily resurrection there is one that professes that the human *pneuma* (the subtle body) continues to exist in this world of autonomous Images during the interval which is also called a *barzakh*, and which extends from the death of the individual to the Great Resurrection. Numerous *ḥadīth* and traditions allude to this and can be quoted in support; these will be analyzed later in this book.

This world of archetypal Images differs from the world of Platonic Ideas—the one which owes its name to Plato—in this sense that the Platonic Ideas designate *universal* forms of knowledge, separate from matter and all material envelopments, self-subsistent, not subsisting only through the person of the knowing subject or through some other substratum.[13] According to Plato it is through these Ideas that the divine Being has knowledge of that which is other. Here exactly is a third way of conceiving divine knowledge insofar as it differs from two other types of knowledge: *representative* knowledge and *presential* knowledge.[14] Now, according to the Oriental theosophists, the beings of the world of archetypal Images are *particular* forms that are separate from Matter, but by no means from all material (that is, subtle) envelopes. Of course, the world of Platonic Ideas resembles this world of archetypal Images in the sense that these autonomous imaginative Forms are self-subsistent, just as the Ideas or intelligible forms are self-subsistent. In sum, the thesis of the autonomous world of archetypal Images is peculiar to the Oriental theosophists (*Ishrāqīyūn*) and to the Ṣūfīs, and to support this thesis they refer to mystical experience. . . .

The author then recalls a number of objections which the Peripatetics and scholastic theologians brought against the *Ishrāqīyūn.* It is not possible here to dwell on these technical details. Among other things, the Peripatetics of Islam persisted in objecting that every extent implies divisibility, and that every divisibility implies matter, and consequently that it is impossible for extended forms to exist without matter. Unfortunately the idea of divisibility seemed to be limited for them to that of anatomical divisibility, and their concept of matter to that of the composite, dense, and corruptible matter of the sublunar world. With the "Oriental theosophists" the idea of the *mundus archetypus* presupposes the idea of "*absolute* matter," that is, *absolved* from the determinations that are peculiar to the state of matter in the terrestrial world. This very idea of a primordial "immaterial" matter is the key to the cosmogony of Ibn ʿArabī (*nafas al-Raḥmān*, the Breath of the Merciful); without it, the *spissitudo spiritualis*, namely, the subtle condensation of the pre-material matter of the beings of the *mundus archetypus*, is inconceivable. In this sense, there is no form without matter. We will meet with this idea throughout the following passages. The excerpts from Mullā Ṣadrā, translated above, can serve as a prelude to them.

VIII

MUḤSIN FAYẒ KĀSHĀNĪ
(d. 1091/1680)

A World in Which Spirits Are Corporealized and in Which Bodies Are Spiritualized*

Because the power to govern bodies has been entrusted to Spirits, and because it is impossible for a direct connection to be established between spirits and bodies on account of their heterogeneous essence, God created the world of the archetypal Images as an intermediary (*barzakh*) linking the world of Spirits and the world of bodies. Hence the connection and articulation of each of the two worlds with the other is assured. The emission and reception of the influx of spiritual entities then becomes conceivable; spirits are able to exercise their regency over bodies and come to their assistance.

This archetypal world is a spiritual universe. On the one hand, it symbolizes with material substance in that it can be an object of perception, is endowed with extent, and can manifest in time and in space. On the other hand, it symbolizes with pure intelligible substance, in that it is formed of pure light and is independent of space and time. Thus, it is neither a composite material body, nor a pure intelligible substance completely separate from matter. One might rather describe it as a universe having duality of dimensions through each of which it symbolizes with the universe to which that dimension corresponds.[2] There is no existent thing, whether in the intelligible world or in the sensory world, whose image is not recorded in this intermediate universe. This universe, in the macrocosm, is homologous to the active Imagination in the human microcosm. Indeed,

* Extract from *Kalimāt maknūna* (*Sayings Kept Secret*), ch. xxx,[1] lith. Teheran, 12/16/1801, pp. 68–70; Bombay, 1296/1878, pp. 69–72. The work is in Arabic and Persian.

it comprises an aspect the perception of which is dependent upon the faculties having their seat in the brain, this being technically called the contiguous imagination (contiguous to the archetypal world, while remaining immanent in man). But it also comprises an aspect not subject to this condition, and which is called the Autonomous Imagination (the world of the *Malakūt*).[3]

It is through this world, and through its characteristic property, that spiritual entities are corporealized, are embodied, when they are manifested in the epiphanic forms which are the Images with which they symbolize. This is what is referred to in the verse telling how Gabriel "took on a body (was typified) before Maryam in the form of a human being of perfect beauty" (19:16). The story told about the Samaritan alludes to the same thing: "I saw what they did not see; I took a handful of earth from under the feet of the Messenger" (20:96), that is, from under the feet of the Archangel Gabriel.[4] The same reference is also contained in the tradition which relates that the Prophet saw the Archangel Gabriel in the guise of the adolescent Daḥya al-Kalbī and heard him read a discourse clothed in words and letters.

This is the intermediate world to which those who are spiritualized (the "pneumatic ones") are carried off in their spiritual assumptions when they shed their elemental physical forms and when their Spirits put on their epiphanic spiritual form. It is in the intermediate world that perfect Souls put on the apparitional forms in which they are perceived in a place other than the one where they actually are; or else appear to him to whom they wish to appear in a form different from that in which they are perceived by the senses during their earthly sojourn. That very thing can come to pass after their transfer to the other world, for then the psycho-spiritual energy is further increased by the fact that the obstacle of the body has been removed.

In short, this is the world of archetypal Images through and in which *Spirits are corporealized and bodies spiritualized.* Through and in this world, ways of being and moral behaviour are personalized, and supersensory realities are manifested in the forms and figures with which they symbolize.[5] And further, the appearance of figures in mirrors or in any reflecting substance, for instance clear water, likewise takes place in this intermediate world, since all figures reflected by mirrors also belong to this world.[6] Again, all forms and figures immanent in our active Imagination are seen in this intermediate world, whether in dreams or in the waking state, because these forms and figures are contiguous to this archetypal world; they receive its light in the way that a ray of light penetrates into a dwelling place through skylight and lattices.

So, this is an immense world, so vast that it contains not only the Forms of the immaterial substances above it, but also the material realities below it. It is the intermediary, the medium through which the connection is effected. The senses and sensory perceptions rise toward it, as the supersensory[7] realities descend toward it. From the place it occupies it continues to gather in the fruits of each thing. It is through this world that the truth is confirmed of the accounts of the Prophet's assumption to Heaven which mention that, in the manner of an eyewitness, he had a vision of the Angels and prophets.[8] It is in this intermediate world that the Holy Imāms are present when they appear before a dying person, as related in so many traditional accounts. This is the world in which the interrogation of the tomb takes place, with its delights and its torments; and it is in this intermediate world also that the faithful believer can visit those near to him after their death.[9] Likewise, this intermediate world accounts for the possibility of scenes alluded to in certain traditions: where the Spirits recognize one another *post mortem*, just as corporeal beings recognize one another, ask questions of one another, and so forth.

It would seem that the "descent of Jesus" (at the time of the *parousia* of the hidden Imām) belongs to this category of events. In the words of Shaikh Ṣadūq:[10] "The descent of Jesus to the Earth is his return to this world after being carried away from this world," because God himself proclaims: "It is I who receive you, who carry you off toward myself, and deliver you from those who deny you . . . until the Resurrection day."[11] (3:48) In the same way, our traditions deriving from the Holy Imāms teach us: "At the time of the *parousia* of the *Mahdī* (the 'Guide'), God will cause to come back a certain number of persons who died before; that is, a certain number from among the Initiates and adepts of the Imām, his 'Shī'ites,' pure believers with pure faith, so that they may gather with him the fruit of his triumph and his invincible help and taste the joy of the epiphany of his reign. God will likewise cause a certain number of the enemies of the Imām to return, pure infidels with pure impiety, so that they may stand accused and receive the punishment they have deserved. . . ." All of this refers to the return which accompanies the *parousia* and to which the faith of our Imāmite coreligionists is particularly attached.[12] And this is the spiritual meaning of certain verses relating to the resurrection, when interpreted according to the teaching of our Imāms.

IX

THE SHAIKHĪ SCHOOL: SHAIKH AḤMAD AḤSĀ'Ī
(d. 1241/1826)

1. Physiology of the Resurrection Body*

. . . In short, what the lexicographers, philologists, and specialists in exegesis of the Qur'ān teach us is that the "flesh" (*jasad*) designates the body, the "volume" (*jism*) of the living, manifest, and visible being. It is true that the term frequently occurs also in the technical language of the alchemists, and in this case designates metallic substance, that of the seven metals: gold, silver, copper, iron, lead, tin, and mercury.[2] What seems most likely to me is that originally, or as time went on, the word *jasad* in the Arabic language was taken to mean the body (*jism*) of the living being insofar as the spirit (*rūḥ*) is absent from it. But elsewhere, the term is used for something different. Thus the *Qāmūs* mentions its use to designate saffron (*jasad* and *jisād*), and even to designate that which is animated by the *pneuma*, the spirit (*rūḥ*), as when speaking of the "body of Zayd."

However, it could be said that in the last case the term is indeed used to designate that which is animated by the *spirit*, but only when regarding it as a composite resulting from a physical organism and from a spirit; the word would then apply precisely to that which is different from the spirit and not to the spirit nor to the composite as such. Perhaps, then, the alchemists' particular use of the word would enter into this category, either on the grounds that metals are different from "spirits" or because the alchemists consider some metals as deficient, namely, lead, tin, and copper—others as intermediary, namely, silver and

* Extract from the *Kitāb Sharḥ al-Ziyāra*, Tabrīz, 1276/1859, pp. 369–70.[1]

mercury—and one only as complete and finished, namely, gold. This gradation has to be understood in relation to the Elixir which, as regards the first six, perfects them, or else makes them tend to perfect the others, as it does in the case of gold. In this sense the metals are represented as inanimate bodies without the spirit (*ajsād*), the spirit being for them the Elixir.

It may also be that if the astronomers, on the contrary, use the word *jism* (not *jasad*), in the proper sense, it is because the celestial Spheres are in a subtle state comparable to that of the Spirits, or else because astronomers regard them from the point of view of their eternal interdependence with the Souls by which they are moved, according to the doctrine of the specialists in celestial physics. The terminology used by Muslims among themselves accords with this usage, since their explanations, like those of the astronomers, deal with the astral masses (*ajrām*) as such, without further definition.

As for the word *jism*, when used without further definition, it designates that which forms *volume*, in the sense of volume that can be divided according to the three dimensions. It follows then: either that 1) it refers to an indeterminate and simple body, without, so to speak, any composition. Sometimes it is referred to as *body* (*jism*) considered in itself, as that of which its substance is made. Sometimes it is referred to as *matter* (*hayūlā*, *hyle*), when regarded from the point of view of its capacity to receive the forms of the species; or else, 2) it may refer to the *mathematical solid* body (*jism ta'līmī*), that is to say, the body when dimension as such is the primary consideration. This term is derived from the fact that the Ancients used to teach their children geometry in terms of the body insofar as it includes lines and surfaces, nothing further; or else it may refer to the *physical body* (*ṭabī'ī*), so designated because the discussion is confined to considering it from the point of view of *physis*.

In the traditions concerning the holy Imāms, and in invocations addressed to them, sometimes *jasad* (their *fleshly* body) is spoken of, sometimes their *jism* (*body*, undefined). Frequently also, both of these terms are used, and on occasion the second term (*jism*) is substituted for the first. The Imāms themselves, in conversation with the pupils, must surely have been guided by some considerations which they alone saw as a whole. In any case, the result, for those who are fairly familiar with the vocabulary of the holy Imāms, is that the word *ajsād* (plural of *jasad*, material, fleshly body) is obviously used by them as the antithesis of "Spirit," whereas the word *jism* (body, undefined, plural *ajsām*) has a much more general meaning in their terminology. Occasionally, even the terms "figures," "real appearances," "apparitional forms" (*ashbāḥ*), are used by them as equivalent to "material body," and the term "Spirits" as equivalent to "bodies" undefined (*ajsām*).

Now you should be informed that the human being possesses two *jasad* and two *jism*. The first *jasad* (*jasad A*, that is, the elemental terrestrial *body of flesh*) is the one which is made up of elements that are a prey to time. This *jasad*, this *flesh*, is like a garment that a man puts on and later casts off again; this body in itself has neither enjoyment nor suffering; it is subject neither to fidelity nor to rebellion.

Do you not see how it may happen to Zayd, for instance, to be consumed by disease; he wastes away to the point where one cannot believe there is one *raṭl*[3] of flesh left on him. Yet he is certainly Zayd; he retains his identity. Spontaneously and without doubt you recognize him as still Zayd the rebel; not one particle of his rebellion has disappeared. If what disappeared as the result of his wasting away had been capable of producing the disappearance of his rebellion, then the latter would have almost entirely disappeared, because in that case it would have lost both its support and its source. The same could be said about Zayd the faithful. Not one particle of his fidelity will have disappeared, since his fidelity has no connection whatever with that part of him which has disappeared, neither the connection of an effect with its cause, nor that of a derivative with its source —no interdependence exists of any kind whatsoever. If that which the sickness has caused to disappear in Zayd had really been a part of him, its disappearance would have been accompanied by the disappearance of the good and evil proper to Zayd's person. Inversely, if he puts on weight, Zayd remains the same Zayd; just as in the previous case when there was no decrease, so here there is no increase, so far as his essence and qualities are concerned, nor any increase of fidelity or rebellion.

In short, this *jasad, this body of flesh consisting of terrestrial Elements*, is not a part of Zayd. It is homologous to the opacity that exists in silica and potash. When these are fused together, liquified, they turn into glass. The glass is certainly the same silica and the same potash that were completely dense and opaque. But after the fusion, the opacity disappeared. This means that the opacity is not a property of the earth itself. The earth itself is subtle and transparent; its opacity is caused by the clash between the Elements. When water is still and pure, you see everything in its depths. But if you stir it up, you can no longer distinguish anything in it so long as it is in movement, because of the collision between its parts and the rarefaction of the element air. What then happens when the four elemental Natures come into collision! This *jasad*, this body of flesh made of terrestrial elements, is comparable to the density that makes silica and potash opaque, although this is not a part of their essence, of their ipseity.

Another comparison: a garment, for example, is an assembly of woven threads. As for the colors, these are accidentals, which are no part of it; it may be dyed in various shades, then lose them; it remains the same garment. This is probably what the First Imām, ʿAlī, had in mind when he said in answer to the Arab who was questioning him about the sensitive animal soul: "When it is separated," he said, "it returns whence it came, just as a mixture is dissolved, and not in the way that autonomous elements in juxtaposition are separated one from another. Its form is destroyed; action and being are abolished from it, so that the composition of the mixture is itself destroyed, since it is evident that the cessation of form and being entails the disappearance of the composition itself."

As for the second *jasad* (*jasad B*, the *caro spiritualis* of the Elements of the spiritual world), this body survives, for the "clay" from which it was constituted survives "in the tomb," when the Earth has devoured the elementary terrestrial body of flesh (*jasad A*), and when every part of the latter has dissolved into its source: the fiery parts going back to Fire, the airy parts to Air, the watery parts to Water, the earthy parts to Earth; whereas the "body of celestial flesh" survives and retains its perfect "shape," as the Imām Ja'far Ṣādiq says. On the other hand, the answer we heard read a moment ago, given by the First Imām to an Arab, referred precisely to the first *jasad*, to the corruptible body of flesh made from terrestrial elements. But the body of spiritual flesh (*jasad B*) is, on the contrary, the one referred to in the saying of the Imām Ja'far, when he states that the "clay" of which it is made survives "in the tomb" and retains its shape intact and perfect. This last expression means: retaining the shape which corresponds to its own conformation, that is, that the elements of the head, the neck, the chest, and so forth remain respectively each in their own place. This is the symbolic explanation (*ta'wīl*) of the verse "No one among us but has his appointed place (37:164)."

This body (*jasad B*) is the reality of the human being which, without increase or decrease, survives "in the tomb" after the body of flesh made of terrestrial elements, that is to say, the opaque density and accidentals, have been separated from it and dissolved. When these accidentals, the totality of which is named the elementary body of flesh (*jasad 'unṣurī, jasad A*), have thus been separated from the human being, the fleshly eyes, the organs of optical perception, no longer see him. When it is thus decomposed and destroyed, there is finally nothing of it to be found, so that some people affirm that the human being is annihilated. Not at all! Not so! But if we say that there is a body that survives "in the tomb," that body is nonetheless *invisible* to earthly beings, to the people of this world, on account of the opacity that darkens their fleshly eyes and prevents them from *seeing* what is not of the same kind as themselves. This is why the Imām Ja'far again compares this invisible body to the gold dust in the goldsmith's crucible. This, likewise, the eyes do not see. But the goldsmith, having washed it with water and purified it of the earth with which it was mixed, causes it to become visible.

The same applies to the body of "spiritual flesh" (*jasad B*) that survives "in the tomb." When God wishes to bring his creatures back to life[4] he causes a rain coming from the ocean situated below the Throne to spread out over the Earth, the water of this rain being colder than snow. . . . This is alluded to in a verse in the Qur'ān ("and His Throne rested on the Waters," 11:9). Then the face of the Earth becomes blended into a single ocean. The waves dash against one another under the vehemence of the winds. A universal refining process takes place. The members of the spiritual body (*jasad B*) of each individual join together to form an organism in perfect "shape," that is to say conforming to the structure the body had in this world; the elements of the neck are welded to the elements of the head, then to those of the bust and so forth. Elements of this other Earth (the celestial Earth) mingle with it. And in this way the spiritual body comes to birth "in the tomb" like the mushroom in its humus. When the breath of Seraphiel[5] causes the trumpet to vibrate, the Spirits take flight. Each Spirit flies swiftly toward its spiritual flesh (*jasad B*); it bursts the tomb, just as the bed of humus yields to the thrust of the mushroom. "And lo! behold them standing upright gazing forth (39:69)." This spiritual body coming back to life is the body which belongs to the Earth, *Hūrqalyā*. This is the body in which humans are resurrected, and with which they enter into Paradise or into Hell.

Someone will perhaps reply: "The obvious meaning of your words is in any case that this body of flesh we see here today is not resurrected. Now, such a doctrine contradicts the teaching followed by those who profess Islam in accordance with the verse from the Book: 'God will raise up all who are in the graves (22:7).' "[6]

To that I answer: what I profess is precisely what the *Muslimūn* profess. For do they not say that the "bodies" in which they will be resurrected are indeed the same bodies that existed in the present earthly life, with the difference, however, that they are entirely purified from accidents and all tarnish? Are the *Muslimūn* not all agreed in professing that these bodies will not be resurrected in their opacity and density, but will have to undergo purification and will only be resuscitated when perfectly pure, though retaining their identity? This is exactly what I say and intend to say. For the opacity of the present body is destroyed, which means that it returns to its source; for its part this elementary flesh has no connection with the Spirit, nor with fidelity or infidelity, nor with pleasure or suffering; by itself, it does not even possess the capacity to feel the one or the other. Indeed, in regard to the human being it is, as it were, a garment thrown over him. The opacity is exactly this fleshly body made of terrestrial elements (*jasad A*), which is destroyed beyond recall.

So understand what I wish to say, for this is the way in which those traditions are to be understood which state that the bodies of the holy Imāms[7] have now been "taken up to Heaven." Certainly if the body of the Imām Ḥusayn had been exhumed soon after his burial it would still have been visible; but now no human eye would be able to see it. He is now "attendant on the Throne, contemplating his pilgrims, etc." The spiritual meaning of these traditions should therefore be understood as referring to the final separation from the terrestrial elemental bodies that constitute the carnal state, a state associated for a moment with the archetypal spiritual bodies. As soon as the latter separate from this carnal coating, they become imperceptible to the sight of ordinary humans. I have dealt with that already in certain passages of the present book, to which I would ask you to refer.

As for the two *jism* (that is *jism A*, or astral subtle body, and *jism B*, the supracelestial archetypal body), the first (*jism A*) is the body in which the Spirit departs from its body of terrestrial flesh (i.e., *jasad A*). The "astral subtle body" (*jism A*) remains with the Spirit, whereas the Spirit is separated from its "subtle body of spiritual flesh" (*jasad B*) at the moment when death intervenes between them. The astral body is with the Spirit in the earthly Paradise (*Jannat al-dunyā*), situated in the West; with this astral body it enters the abode of Peace (*Dar al-Salām*), visits its habitation and place of origin. The spirit of the infidel is also accompanied by this astral body when it enters the terrestrial Hell (*Nār al-dunyā*) at the rising of the sun, whereas at sunset it takes refuge with this body in the valley of Barhūt,[8] and wanders with it, during the night, in the valley of Sulphur.

So that is the state in which the two groups remain until the first blast of the Trumpet vibrates.[9] Then the Spirits themselves are annihilated during the interval between the "two blasts of the Trumpet." All movement of the celestial Spheres and everything, animal and vegetable, possessing spirit and soul is halted. This cosmic pause lasts "four hundred years." Thereupon the Spirits are resuscitated, each in its second *jism* (that is, *jism B*, the supracelestial archetypal body). That is possible because these bodies (*jism B*) have been completely purified and have lost all their opacity, that is, the opacity they had had from the first *jism* (*jism A* or astral body), exactly as we explained with regard to what occurs to the fleshly body (of Earthly elements, *jasad A*, and the body of spiritual flesh, *jasad B*), word for word.[10] The Spirits are therefore resuscitated, each respectively in its second *jism* (*jism B*, or archetypal body). This celestial body is, indeed, the one that formerly existed in the earthly life —none other; if it were otherwise, reward and punishment of the Spirits would have disappeared along with the first body. However, the *jism* that exists during life on earth, and which is at the same time this body that we see, includes subtle and dense elements. The density that made it opaque will have been purified and destroyed. This density is what we call the first *jasad* (*jasad A*, the elemental body of perishable flesh). The subtle element, however, survives "in the tomb"; this is what we designate as the second *jasad* (*jasad B*, the body of spiritual flesh).

It is in the astral body (*jism A*) that the spirit makes its appearance in the *barzakh* (the intermediate world). This astral body is the vehicle (*markab*, *okhēma*) and habitation of the Spirit until the "first sounding" of the Trumpet. At that moment it receives a last purification, and the density which we call the first *jism* (*jism A*, or astral body) also departs from it. Only the subtle element of this *jism* remains in the world of seminal reasons[11] in three "treasuries," while the density vanishes from three other "treasuries." These six "treasuries" are arranged in the treasury of the orifices (of Seraphiel's cosmic Trumpet, which is the matrix) of this Spirit. When the archangel Seraphiel sounds the "Trumpet of Resurrection" (i.e., "the second blast" of the Trumpet), the Spirit descends toward the tomb. All its treasures blend together, it penetrates into the subtle *jasad* (*jasad B*, *caro spiritualis*); they are then "reassembled," that is, resuscitated.[12]

But know that if you were able to weigh this spiritual body in the course of this present life, and if, after being weighed, it were to undergo a purification that would entirely separate it from the elemental body of perishable flesh, so that nothing would subsist save this permanent spiritual body (*jasad B*) that belongs to the world of Hūrqalyā; and supposing further that you were able then to weigh it again, you would find that it would not have diminished by even so much as the weight of a sesame seed in comparison with the result of the first weighing. The fact is that the density that constituted the elemental fleshly body (*jasad A*) is an accident. Now accidents in no way modify the "weight" we are concerned with here; they neither increase it when they come about, nor decrease it by departing from it. In this sense it would be a mistake to picture to oneself the "resurrection body," the organ of beatitude or damnation, as something other than the body that exists in the present life, in spite of there having been a change and complete purification. Or, one should say rather that it is indeed this body, and yet it is also something other than it from the fact of having been purified, broken down, refashioned.

According to Abū Manṣūr ʿAlī Ṭabarsī,[13] commenting on the verse from the Qur'ān: "Each time their skin shall be consumed, we shall replace it by another skin, so that they may taste the chastisement (4:59)"—the Imām Jaʿfar Ṣādiq answered someone in his entourage who was asking him about the meaning of this verse: "Be careful! they are indeed the same skins and yet each time it is something else." "Give me a comparison with something in this world." "Very well, do you not see that if a man takes a brick, breaks it in pieces, then puts it back into its mold, the brick will be the same and yet it will be another brick?"

And in the *Tafsīr* of ʿAlī ibn Ibrāhīm[14] it tells how they asked the Imām: "How can one conceive of a skin being replaced by another one?" "Suppose," replied the Imām, "you take a brick, break it up and reduce it to dust, and then reshape it in the mold, will this brick be the same as the first one? In fact, the first will have been changed into another one, although the original, the archetype, is identical."

In this way the Imām makes it clear that the skin replacing the first skin is another one, while remaining "their skin." The differentiation is a difference in mode of being and qualification. Similarly, in respect to what we are considering here: the body, the object which is visible during this present life, is indeed what will be the "resurrection body," but after having undergone that alchemy we have several times described. . . .

2. On the Esoteric Meaning of the Tomb*

The essential nature of the tomb is that it is the resting place of the dead, the first of the stages toward the *saeculum venturum*. In its visible aspect and exoteric meaning, it is the abode of the material body from which life has departed. This is the ordinary opinion. But understood esoterically (*ta'wīl*), the tomb signifies the nature of the person, his life, his inmost desire. God said to his Prophet: "God makes himself heard by whomsoever he wishes, but thou canst not make thyself heard by those who are *in their tomb* (35:21)." And again: "Dead, not living, knowing not when they will be raised (16:21–22)."

Expressions such as "The Spirit will return to man (in the tomb)" are expressions that correspond to the apparent or exoteric meaning. In reality, what is in question are events that take place not in the lower temporal world, that of the thing-object, but on the higher plane of the degrees of time, that is to say in Hūrqalyā. And if I say "on the highest plane"—"at the highest degree of time," it is because Hūrqalyā is an intermediary.[16]

* Extract from the *Risālat al-qaṭīfīya*, published in the collection of the works of Shaikh Aḥmad Aḥsā'ī, *Jawāmiʿ al-kalim*, Tabrīz, 1273–76/1856–59, 2 vols. in folio; Vol. I, Pt. 2, 3d risāla, p. 136.[15]

Sometimes it serves to designate the higher degree of time (*zamān*), sometimes it is used to designate the lower plane or degree of the *Aevum* (*dahr*, eternity).

Thus, this double use of the term is justified by homogeneity and genuine correspondence. During his sleep, a man can be the seat of violent movements, although his material body (*jasad*) remains motionless. The explanation of such movements lies in the proximity of the subtle body (*jism*) to the material body. For while a man is sleeping, his Spirit "sings" in freedom in the high branches of the great tree, which is the autonomous world of Forms and Images (*'ālam al-mithāl*, *mundus archetypus*). This full-grown tree has its roots in the soil of the "subtle bodies," and there are as many individuations of these subtle bodies as there are material bodies.

When we speak of "that which returns" (as in the phrase above), we refer to the Spirit subsisting in the autonomous *mundus archetypus*. When we speak of "that toward which the return takes place," we refer to the spiritual body (*jasad B*) with which the supracelestial archetypal body (*jism B*) will be reunited.[17] As for "punishment in the tomb,"[18] this has to do with what we mentioned concerning the "return of the Spirit," because the totality of the world of the *barzakh* (the intermediate world), all that reaches it and is changed in it, refers to the same (that is to say, to the esoteric meaning of the "tomb"). The appearance of the holy Imāms at the moment of death or "in the tomb," whether to believer or to unbeliever, is also an event taking place in the world of Hūrqalyā. It is to this that the following verses from the Qur'ān allude: "If we had caused an Angel to descend, the affair would have been finished, they would have had no respite (6:8)." "The day when they behold the Angels coming, it will not be good tidings for the guilty (25:24)."

These verses and some others, together with certain of our traditions, signify that the Angels are not perceptible to anyone in the world of material bodies, unless the Angel takes on the appearance of a material body. As when the Angel Gabriel takes on the aspect of the adolescent Daḥya Kalbī in order to appear to the Prophet, or again, when he comes down to Abraham accompanied by Kerubiel and Michael on the occasion of the philoxenia, or again, to Lot, in order to chastise his people. For every soul is in direct contact with those beings and those realities of the intermediate world that correspond to its own spiritual state. . . .

3. The Heavens and Elements of Hūrqalyā*

. . . As for the world Hūrqalyā, its meaning relates to an *other world*. What this word designates is the world of the *barzakh* or the *interworld*. In fact, there is the lower, or terrestrial world; this is the world of material bodies made up of Elements, the world visible to the senses. Then there is the world of Souls, which is the world of *Malakūt*. The world of the *barzakh*, which is the world intermediate between the visible material world (*'ālam al-mulk*) and the world of the *Malakūt*, is another universe. It is a material world that is *other*. To put it differently, the world of bodies composed of Elements constitutes what we call the visible, material world. The world of *Hūrqalyā* is a material world (the world of matter in the subtle state), which is *other*.

As for its position, it is situated in the *eighth climate*.[20] Its lower plane borders on the convex surface of the Sphere of Spheres, the surface that defines the directions of space. It is not itself in a dimension or direction of our space, since there is nothing *beyond* the convexity of the supreme celestial Sphere that defines orientations; or rather, it has no spatial beyond. Nevertheless, the lower plane of the world of Hūrqalyā corresponds, by its position, to the highest degree of the supreme Sphere, that which is called the "crystalline sphere." The form or image at which you look in a mirror belongs to this lower plane of the world or Hūrqalyā.

The language from which this term comes is the Syriac Language (*sūryānīya*), that is, the language in use today among

* Extract from the answer given to Mullā Muhammad Ḥusayn Anārī Kirmānī in *Jawāmi' al-kalim*, Vol. I, Pt. 3, 9th risāla, pp. 153–54.[19]

the Sabeans, those whom we now call the *Ṣubbāh* (more exactly, the Mandeans), most of whom, and they are many, have settled in and around Baṣra.[21]

Now, when we speak of the universe of Hūrqalyā, its Heavens and Elements, you should know the following: the world of the *barzakh*, intermediate between the present world and the *saeculum venturum*, is the *mundus archetypus*, the autonomous world of Forms and Images; it is the world intermediate between the world of the *Malakūt* and the visible, material world. The term Hūrqalyā is used to designate the Heavens of this intermediate world, together with all the heavenly bodies they contain. When we speak of Jābalqā and Jābarṣā, we mean the lower regions of this intermediate world.[22] Jābalqā is a city to the East, that is, in the direction of the beginning. Jābarṣā is a city to the West, that is, in the direction of the return and ending. The Elements of this intermediate world are what constitute the second and imperishable *jasad* (*jasad B*, the spiritual body), that is, the body whose "clay" survives invisibly "in the tomb,"[23] retaining its same perfect "shape." In the eastern part of this universe there is the "earthly Hell." In its western part, there is the "earthly Paradise," Adam's Paradise. There it is that the Spirits of faithful believers take refuge, and these are the "two gardens covered with greenery" alluded to in the Qur'ān (55:64). As for the proofs that testify to the existence of this universe, there are, on the one hand, those known to theology. There are the many traditions referring to the existence of the intermediate world of the *barzakh*. There are verses from the Qur'ān like the following: "Behind them a *barzakh* until the day when they will be raised up (23:202)." And lastly, there are the many traditional accounts referring to the existence of the cities of the intermediate world. In commenting on the *Book of the Theosophy of the Throne* (*Kitāb al-ḥikma al-ʿarshīya*) by Mullā Ṣadrā Shīrāzī,[24] on cosmogony and eschatology, I myself have repeated, as elsewhere in my books, many *ḥadith* that leave no room for doubt. Equally, philosophical understanding gives further evidence of the existence of this universe. Indeed, the world of the *Malakūt* is made up of substances and beings separate from matter, while our visible, physical world is made up of material realities. There necessarily has to be an intermediary between the two worlds, a *barzakh*, that is, a world whose state is neither the absolutely subtle state of separate substances, nor the opaque density of the material things of our world. In the absence of such a universe, there would be a leap, a hiatus in the gradation of being. Proofs guaranteeing the existence of such a state after death and preceding the Great Resurrection are so numerous that they cannot be counted. Among the philosophers, none reject these proofs, although each one expresses himself in his own way and pursues his own line. My correspondent remarks that among other statements that remain obscure for him in my answer (i.e., *in the Risāla al-Khāqānīya*)[25] are some that demonstrate that the elementary body of material flosh (*jasad A*) is destroyed and "does not return." It seems to him that this contradicts the literal meaning of the Qur'ānic verse and the traditional statements referring to it.[26]

I shall answer him as follows: know that the "material body" (*jasad*) which is in the human being is in reality made up of two bodies.[27] One of them, the first one (*jasad A*) is annihilated and will not "return." The subtle body (*jism*) is also in reality made up of a double body, the first (*jism A*, the astral body) likewise does not "return." On the other hand, the second material body (*jasad B*, the *caro spiritualis*, made from the Elements of Hūrqalyā), and also the second subtle body (*jism B*, the supracelestial, archetypal body) will both "return." This is the doctrine I have expounded in the text of my intended answer.

What I mean to say is the following: the human being has descended from the suprasensory world (*'ālam al-ghayb*, the world of Mystery) from those archetypes or treasuries to which the following verse of the Book refers: "Nothing exists but that its treasury is in our hands (15:21)." Thus the human being descends into this world, the sojourn of effort and struggle, and amasses something of his own in view of the *Futurum Resurrection*. But as he descends from step to step, passing gradually from one plane of being to another in the course of his descent, at each step he acquires a certain mixture with the accidents corresponding to that step or plane. Just so, in the time of the Prophet, when the Angel Gabriel descended to this world, he took on the form and appearance of the beautiful adolescent Daḥya al-Kalbī. But when he "went back up to Heaven" this form did not accompany him on his return. And so it was each time he came down to one of the earlier Prophets: he showed himself to the Prophet in the form of a very beautiful human being, resembling some contemporary of that Prophet. Well, it is just the same when the human being "descends" with his subtle body, which is his archetypal body (*jism B*, *jism aṣlī*) and the support of his Soul (cf. the *okhēma symphyēs* of Proclus, above, p. 92). He passes through the autonomous world of Forms and Images (*'ālam al-mithāl*); there the astral body (*jism A*) becomes attached to him. The latter will not "return" when the Great Resurrection takes place, because it is not a part of the essential reality of man. It can be compared to the filth that is deposited on your clothing and which goes away "without return" when you clean it.

When, at the end of his descent, the human being has reached this lower world, then the elemental, material body the body of flesh (*jasad A*), composed of the Elements of our sublunary world, becomes attached to him. In relation to the reality of the human being, it is an accident; it is not a constituent of his essence. This body of flesh belongs to the filth of this world of ours. At the moment of the *exitus* from this world, the earth devours this body of flesh as soon as it is placed in the tomb. But, as against this, that other body (*jasad B*, composed of the Elements of Hūrqalyā) survives invisibly "in the tomb" until the Resurrection Day, when the Spirit (the "I"-spirit) returns to it, penetrates it, and enters its Paradise or its Hell with it. This spiritual body is what "returns," while the material body of flesh, composed of sublunary Elements, that is, the totality of accidents and stains that belong to this world below, all of that neither belonged to the man nor was with him, but was just something that adhered to him due to the fact of his existence in this world. And so all of that goes back to its origin "without return." It is the same when mud and filth stain your cotton robe: as soon as you have washed it, the mud and filth will go away "without return." Will you then say, or will some one else think of saying, that something is missing from the robe because of what has departed from it? No, what has departed from it was precisely not a *part* of it.

Thus when *post mortem* the Spirit has entered the world of the *barzakh*, it exists there in its archetypal body (*jism B*), to which a body originating in this *barzakh* (*jism A*, the astral body) provisionally adheres. In fact, the latter is not a part of it, but is a temporary accident. On the Resurrection Day man in his wholeness returns and leaves behind him that which was no part of him, which was not *himself*. Compare this: Break your seal; see how the form of it departs. Refashion it, now you see the first seal, returned to its original form, identical to itself. Nevertheless, the first form has not returned and never will. This is the esoteric meaning of the verse: "Each time their skin is consumed, We will replace it with another skin (4:59)." Although the skin substituted may be identical to the first, it is called *other* because the first form has departed from it and has been replaced by another form. This is what is emphasized in the commentary on this verse by the Imām Ja'far Ṣādiq. "It is the *same* and yet it is an other."[28]

Compare this further with the clay brick which you pulverize and then put back into its mold. It is certainly the same and yet it is other. And it is the same in the case of the material elementary body (*jasad A*) and of the astral body (*jism A*) regarding which we say that neither the one nor the other "returns." By the one and the other we designate the accidentals that adhere to the human being due to the fact of his descent by successive steps. And yet this same apparent, visible, sensible, palpable body is *also* the one which is not annihilated and from which nothing essential departs.[29] Or rather, it survives invisibly until the Resurrection Day, that is, until it returns and the Spirit enters into it to make its Paradise or its Hell. Certainly it has to be broken and has to be refashioned. Thus it will be pulverized, purified of all that was not a part of it. Afterwards it will be shaped, for unless it is purified of all the accidents that are not *itself*, it would not be fit for survival. The very fact of existing in this world implies its mixture with accidents, and here is exactly the obstacle to its survival.

My correspondent asks further what I mean to say when I state that between the two "blasts" of Seraphiel's Trumpet, the Spirit is attracted, reabsorbed, into whichever orifices of the Trumpet are its matrix; he asks me what I mean by the "six Treasuries" and what proof there is of all this?

I say to him: the proof has already been given that the Spirit is the real man, he to whom one speaks, he who assumes. The visible organism of his material body is to him an abode in which he finds himself imprisoned, but into which he has been made to descend, because it is for him an instrument thanks to which he attains exoteric and esoteric knowledge. So when it was resolved to send him down to this world, the nature of being necessitated the intermediary of the sensitive, vital Soul bestowed by the celestial Sphere, in order that there should be no hiatus in the gradation of being and in the Emanation. When the time comes to go back to its original world, the intermediary, that is to say, the vital Soul emanated by the celestial Spheres, returns to the Souls that move the Spheres, as it were, by reversion to a mixture, just as a drop of water returns to the sea.

But the "I"-spirit survives, it stays awake, it does not succumb to sleep. As Imām Jaʿfar says: "When it returns, it returns to the state in which it began." It is not a return to a mixture, but a return to a state of juxtaposition because it survives. When the wind of the first blast vibrates in the Trumpet, the "flashing sound," it is then reabsorbed, each thing returning to its source. It returns, and this is a return from juxtaposition. Because it was sent down from the "six Treasuries,"[30] it returns to them, its own cessation leads to their separation; its archetypal Image returns to the Treasury from which it descended. In the same way, its *materia prima*,[31] its nature, its soul, its *pneuma*, its intellect, return each to the Treasury from which respectively they descended. Those are the Treasuries alluded to, as we said, in the verse in the Qur'ān: "Nothing exists but that its Treasury is in our Hands (15:21)." Those are the Treasuries which in each case form a whole, which is the respective matrix of each "I"-spirit, symbolically designated as the orifice or the "hole" which corresponds to that spirit on Seraphiel's Trumpet.

As for the proofs of what we have stated, they are contained not in one *ḥadīth* alone, nor in tens of *ḥadīths*, but in a multitude of traditions. However, their demonstrative value in discussion can only be understood by meditating on many of them. Or rather, it is a matter of letting oneself be guided by a higher wisdom, and the proof furnished by the latter can only be recognized as demonstrative thanks to special divine help, bestowed by God on hearts that have attained full maturity, for "he to whom wisdom has been given has received much good (2:272)."

4. Alchemy and the Resurrection Body

(a)*

Know that what returns to Paradise, in this case the earthly Paradise,[33] is what is reaped by the Angel of Death, and that this is man's essential reality, man in the true sense (*insān ḥaqīqī*). The source and principle of his being is, in fact, composed of five things: the intellect, the soul, the essential nature, the *materia prima*, the Image or archetypal Form.[34] The intellect is in the soul. The soul, with everything it infolds, is in the incorruptible nature. All these three together are in the *materia prima*, again with all that is implied therein. When the Image or archetypal Form is conjoined with the latter, then the original essential body, (*jism aṣli, jism B*) is realized,[35] that is, the body which is hidden in the material, visible envelope, in the elemental body (*jasad A*) formed from the four sublunar Elements: fire, air, water, and earth.

The elemental material body (*jasad A*), the body of perishable flesh, is the one that remains in the earth; its visible aspect is destroyed there. This is the organic body that undergoes the

* Extract from the epistle addressed to Fatḥ-ʿAli Shāh Qājār, Shah of Persia (1797–1834) in *Jawāmīʿ al-kalim*, Vol. I, Pt. 1, 5th risāla, pp. 122–24.[32]

phenomenon of growth by assimilating the subtle elements of food. I have just said that its visible aspect, its "outerness," is destroyed in the earth. But the fact is that its hidden invisible element, its "innerness," survives; this is the spiritual body (*jasad B*, *caro spiritualis*), which is not formed from the sublunar Elements, but from the four Elements of the world of Hūrqalyā, which are seventy times nobler and more precious than the Elements of the terrestrial world.[36] This spiritual body rests in the quiet state referred to in a verse from the Qur'ān. Indeed, when the faithful adept has given an account of himself "in the tomb,"[37] he hollows out a channel for himself between the "tomb" and the Paradise in the West through which repose and sustenance come to him. It is said: "For him who is of the number of those brought nigh there shall be repose, sustenance, and a sojourn in Paradise (56:87–88)." What is subject to this repose is precisely the spiritual body (*jasad B*), the body formed from the Elements of the world of Hūrqalyā, and hidden within the elemental, material body (*jasad A*), the apparent visible body, formed from the ordinary Elements of this world.

As for the body that remains with the Spirit (the "I"-Spirit) at the time of the *exitus*, this is the essential body, the body in the true sense (*the jism ḥaqīqī*, *jism B*),[38] which is composed of the *materia prima* and of the Image or archetypal Form (*mithāl*). It is the support of the incorruptible nature, the Soul and the intellect. It is the essential reality of man, of man in the true sense. This essential body is of the same nature as the essential body of the universe: for the microcosm it is homologous to the supreme sphere, the sphere that governs and defines spatial orientations. Its capacity to experience enjoyment of food, drink, touch, amorous delights, is seventy times greater than the capacity of the elemental, material body.[39] The "I"-Spirit is never separated from this essential body, which itself is never separated from the Spirit[40] except at the time of the cosmic pause marking the interval between the two blasts of Seraphiel's Trumpet.

When Seraphiel causes the Trumpet to vibrate with the "fiery blast,"[41] which is the "breath of universal reabsorption," every Spirit is drawn in, reabsorbed in the particular "hole" in the Trumpet which is its matrix. The matrix is made up of six "Treasuries." As soon as it is drawn in, the "I"-Spirit meets its own Image, or archetypal Form,[42] in the first Treasury; in the second of these, it finds its *materia prima*; in the third, its incorruptible nature; in the fourth, its Soul; in the fifth, the *pneuma*; in the sixth, the intellect. When these Treasuries are disassociated, the "I"-Spirit is abolished and its power to work also is abolished. It is in this sense alone that it can be said to be "annihilated" (namely, until the second "blast" of Seraphiel's Trumpet). But no mixture fusing the component parts takes place, for such mixture applies only to the vegetable and animal souls: to the vegetable soul because it is composed of the sublunar Elements—fire, air, water, earth. When these elemental parts are disassociated, they "return" to that from which they came, there to be mixed with it, not put together with it, each as an autonomous thing. The igneous parts return to the elemental fire, are mixed and blend with it. In the same way, each part returns to its place of origin—air, water, earth—there to be mixed and blend with it.[43] The same applies to the animal Soul, which had its source in the movements of the celestial Spheres. When it is separated it returns whence it arose, and is mixed, not added to it, because it is merely a combination of energies resulting from the energies of the celestial Spheres and proportionate to the movements of the latter. . . .[44]

Therefore, these two souls, vegetable and vital, return *post mortem* to their source and blend with it. However, this is true only of their outer part, their "exoteric" part (*ẓāhir*); for the inner, "esoteric" part (*bāṭin*) of the vegetable soul survives "in the tomb"; this inner part is the *Elements of Hūrqalyā* and is that body (*jasad B*) which rests in "quietness and sojourns in Paradise."[45] As to the esoteric part of the vital soul, it is made up of the "natures" of the Souls which move the *Heavens of Hūrqalyā* and goes to the "earthly Paradise," as we have already said.[46] To conclude: the spirit is never separated from its original essential body (*jism B*); it never leaves it—never, that is to say, "dies" except during the interval between the two blasts of the Trumpet; the first, which is the "flaming sound" or the in-breath of universal reabsorption, and the second, which is the breath of the Resurrection.[47]

Now, as to this other question: "Should one understand the Spirit by itself as being the Spirit with an Image or archetypal Form, or with a subtle body?" The answer should be: "That which enters the 'Earthly Paradise' is the Spirit (the 'I'-Spirit) with its original essential body (*jism aṣlī, jism B*),[48] because in the Spirit there is the intellect, the intellect is in the soul, and the latter is in the incorruptible nature. The essential body is the *materia prima* which is their support, and the Image or archetypal Form conjoined to the latter. This is why the capacity to feel and enjoy is, as we have said, seventy times greater in this essential body than in the material body; because its enjoyment is both sensory and spiritual. It is a spiritual/sensory faculty. As to what survives invisibly 'in the tomb' (that is to say in Hūrqalyā) this is the Spiritual body (*jasad B*), which is made from the Elements of Hūrqalyā, whereas the body made from the four ordinary Elements (*jasad A*, the body of material flesh) is annihilated."

A number of symbols need to be pondered here. We will mention one or two. Glass, for example; it is produced from silica and potash, both of these, dense and opaque, are homologous to the elemental material body (*jasad A*), the body of perishable flesh with which we are all familiar. When subjected to fusion, their impurity and dirt go away; we are left with clear glass; the interior is visible through the exterior, the exterior is visible through the interior.[49] This, then, is homologous to the spiritual body (*jasad B*), the *caro spiritualis*; the body which survives "in the tomb," that is, in Hūrqalyā, and to which "respite and sojourn in Paradise" are given, whereas the opaque density of the silica and potash was homologous to the material elemental body (*jasad A*). Consider how, from silica and potash, dense and opaque, there issued a body in a transparent subtle state. The latter is unquestionably the same mineral substance, and yet it is not. It is something other.

Now, supposing this glass in its turn is subjected to fusion:

let a certain appropriate chemical be projected onto it and thoroughly penetrate the whole mass; the glass becomes very fine and brilliant glass. If the Elixir of whiteness, the "philosopher's chemical" be projected onto this fine glass, it then becomes a crystal which flames in sunlight (lens glass), because it causes the sun's rays on striking its surface, to converge. It is certainly still glass, and yet it is something other than glass; while remaining glass, it is, however, glass to which something has happened, something which has so completely purified it that now it ranks much higher than the first glass. This incandescent glass is homologous to the astral body (*jism A*) which accompanied the Spirit at the time of the *exitus*, when the latter departs from its elemental material body. It is the body with which the Spirit enters the Western Paradise, the Paradise of Adam. Well then! if this sparkling crystal is melted once again and the white Elixir is again projected onto it, lo and behold! it becomes diamond (*almās*). It is still glass, and yet no—it is something other—but not so, it is certainly itself but itself after undergoing all these trials.

It was a mineral substance, dense and opaque; it was melted and became transparent glass and then became a much finer glass. And when this latter had been subjected for the first time to fusion and projection of the white Elixir, it became incandescent crystal. It was fused a second time and the Elixir was projected on it; it became diamond. Place it on the anvil, strike it with a hammer, it will dent the anvil and the hammer but it will not break. Strike it with a piece of lead and it will break into cubiform fragments and if each cube in turn is struck with the lead it will in its turn break into cubiform fragments. That is the true sign that it really is diamond, but if it has become diamond it is also a sign that the diamond was hidden in the essential depths of the mineral substance, because, in fact, the composition of the latter is the result of two well-known principles, mercury and sulphur, according to what is established in physics. And this diamond, separated from the crystal, this crystal, separated from glass, this glass separated from its mineral opacity, is homologous to the "Resurrection Body" of the faithful believer in the Paradise of the future *Aeon* (that is to say, *jism B*, the essential archetypal body, the *corpus supra coeleste*, the "diamond body").[50]

Another symbol: tin. At first it is homologous to the elemental body of flesh (*jasad A*) which we know in our terrestrial world. When the white Elixir is projected on it, it becomes pure silver; it is then homologous to the subtle Spiritual body (*jasad B*, *caro spiritualis*), which survives invisibly in Hūrqalyā. But when the red Elixir is projected on it, it becomes pure gold, and it is then homologous to the astral body (*jism A*) originating in the heavens of Hūrqalyā, which leaves the elemental body of flesh (*jasad A*) and accompanies the Spirit in its *exitus*, that is to say, the subtle body which returns to Adam's Paradise *post mortem* and tastes the delight thereof. If the red Elixir is projected a second time, this gold itself becomes an Elixir; it is homologous to the original, essential body (*jism B*, *corpus supra coeleste*), the one which enters the paradise of the future *Aeon*. The fact that this gold has become Elixir is the sign and the proof that it was hidden in the essential depths of tin, because in fact its composition is the result of the two well-known principles. Then this Elixir, freed from the gold, the gold freed from silver, the silver freed from tin, is homologous to the future *Aeon*. Many symbols of this still exist, which are well known to those who possess inner sight. . . .

In the following table we can recapitulate the correspondances analysed by Shaikh Aḥmad Aḥsā'ī between the physiology of the "resurrection body" and the phases of the alchemical Work:

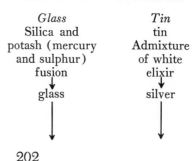

The human body	Alchemical homologues	
	Glass	*Tin*
Jasad A: The elemental, material body, the body of perishable flesh, composed of the sublunar Elements	Silica and potash (mercury and sulphur) fusion ↓	tin Admixture of white elixir ↓
Jasad B: Incorruptible Spiritual body, *caro spiritualis*, composed of the Elements of	glass ↓	silver ↓

Hūrqalyā. It survives invisibly *post-mortem* "in the tomb," that is, in Hūrqalyā. It will be reunited with the Spirit at the time of the Great Resurrection	↓ fine glass	↓
Jism A: The astral body, composed of the celestial matter of the *Heavens* of Hūrqalyā; put on by the Spirit at the time of its descent to this world; accompanies it at the time of the *exitus*, enters the terrestrial Paradise (or the *infernum*) with it; disappears at the time of the Great Resurrection and the final union of *jasad B* and *jism B* in the *corpus resurrectionis*	↓ first admixture of the white elixir ↓ flaming crystal	first admixture of the red elixir ↓ gold
Jism B: The essential, original body, the archetypal body, imperishable and inseparable from the Spirit (*okhēma symphyes*), the supracelestial body made of six "treasures"; joined with *jasad B*, forms the wholeness of the resurrection body ("body of diamond") in the *Aeon* to come.	↓ second admixture of white elixir ↓ diamond	↓ second admixture of red elixir ↓ elixir = *lapis philosophorum*

(b)*

This commentary is as original as it is important. Shaikh Aḥmad Aḥsā'ī here makes clear his standpoint in regard to Mullā

* Extract from the commentary by Shaikh Aḥmād Aḥsā'ī on the *Theosophy of the Throne* by Mullā Ṣadrā (Ṣadruddin Shirāzī), Tabrīz, 1278/1861, pp. 165–66.[51]

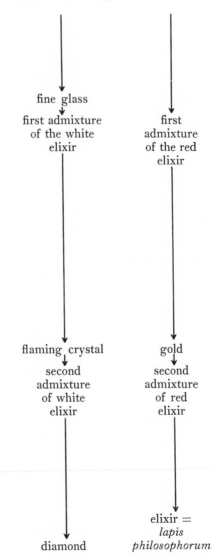

> Ṣadrā's philosophy (see above, Art. VI). He neither adheres to it nor systematically refutes it. It is impartial criticism, helping better to situate the Shaikhī school in the general perspective of Shī'ite thought. In his book, Mullā Ṣadrā poses all the problems relating as a whole to the posthumous becoming of the human being, in the twofold aspect of "return" or "reversion" of Spirits to their original world (*ma'ād*) and the resurrection of bodies. He remarks that the second aspect is not situated on the same plane—the intelligibly evident—as the first. His thought, being theosophical thought, employs rational argument as well as texts from the religious tradition. The conjunction of these is made possible by the practice of the *ta'wil* (the exegesis of the spiritual meaning), whose alchemical operation is shown to be an application (to hide the apparent, to manifest the hidden). This is exactly the operation that Shaikh Aḥmad Aḥsā'ī stresses, as in the above passage, showing correspondence between the *operatio secreta artis* and the physiology of the resurrection body. This correspondance even postulates an anthropology in which the theme of the "Reversion," determining future metamorphoses is antithetical to the idea of reversibility, which in general predominates in our historical points of view.

Philosophical understanding, guided by the very thing which proves that spirits are imperishable and return to their original world, finds therein the evidence for the resurrection of bodies; for resurrection of bodies and reversion of Spirits taken together have one and the same cause. He who has meditated before the "Philosophers' mirror" has been able to see it with his own eyes. When I speak of the "Philosophers' mirror," I mean the *operatio secreta artis*,[52] that is, the operation of the Elixir, for the Philosophers have used it as a mirror in which everything existing is reflected in the same way as the return and resurrection of Spirits.

As the Philosophers understand it, the demonstration can be expressed as follows: The material existence of all that exists in the world emanates from the divine Work, as light emanates from a lamp. Everyone knows that this Operation is life, consciousness, discrimination, power of choice. The closer something is to the Principle, the more powerful are these four things in it; the further something is from the Principle, the weaker these four things become in it. In the same way, the light of the lamp is constant as to radiation, dryness, and heat; the nearer something is to the lamp, the more powerful in it are these three things; the further away it is, the weaker they become, until finally the light vanishes and simultaneously these three things vanish.

The act of existing can be seen in an analogous way in every thing: the further something is from the Principle, the weaker become the four realities composing its existence, which is the divine Operation, until the extinction of the latter finally brings about the extinction of the said realities. For the life which is in the Spirit—consciousness, discrimination, power of choice—all of this exists, indeed, in the body and even in mineral substance, but to an infinitely lesser degree than in the Spirit. To say that bodies "become tired" is to say that they also are alive, conscious, have discrimination and power of choice, in proportion to their degree of participation in being. Hence this Qur'ānic verse: "He said to the Heavens and the Earth: come, willingly or in spite of yourselves. They said: 'we come willingly.'" Or again: "nothing is that does not proclaim his praise, but you do not understand their hymn."[53] Ample commentary on this has been given in the present book.

For, in the last analysis, spirits are *light-being* in the fluid state (*nūr wujūdī dhā'ib*). Bodies are also light-being, but in the solid state. The difference between them is the same as the difference between water and snow. This is why the evidence tending to the affirmation of the "return" of Spirits is itself the evidence tending to affirm the resurrection of bodies. . . .

The alchemical Work testifies to the validity of this affirmation. The fact is that bodies that have reached maturity and completeness through this operation are in the liquid-solid state. This is what the First Imām, ʿAlī ibn Abī-Ṭālib, declares, according to the report of his biographer Ibn Shahr-Āshūb, and of Abū'l-ʿAbbās in his book bringing to light the secret concerning the science of the Elixir.[54] Someone therefore asked the Imām about alchemy, when he was delivering a discourse: "It is the sister of prophecy," he exclaimed; "for there is an immunity which keeps prophecy from being desecrated, which is that ordinary people do no more than discuss its literal outer meaning. I call God to witness that it is none other than water in the solid state, immobilized air, compact fire, fluid earth.[55] For earth in the fluid state is water in the solid state. In the same sense bodies also are Spirits. . . .

"Bodies, as we have already said, are things which have come down from 'archetypal Treasuries' to this terrestrial world, as it is said in the verse: 'Nothing exists but its Treasury is with Us and We send it not down but in a known measure (15:21).' Given that each thing returns to its origin and principle, if bodies were an exception, whether in the sense of survival in this world or of annihilation, they would not 'return' to their origin and principle. But this would contradict what is implied in the law of universal return to the principle, universal resurrection, a well-founded thesis on which philosophers and religious traditions agree. Hence, philosophical understanding discovers the proofs of the resurrection of bodies in the manner described above. . . ."

(c)*

Mullā Ṣadrā Shīrāzī:[56] The soul is spiritual "matter" (*mādda rūḥānīya*), a subtle organism that can only receive Forms which are themselves in the subtle and suprasensory state, such that they are not perceptible to the physical senses, but only to the organs of psycho-spiritual perception (the suprasensory senses). As against this, "material matter" (*hayūlā*) is a dense, opaque matter capable of receiving Forms whose state is equally dense and opaque, determined by spatial dimensions and positions, mixed with virtualities and negativities.

Shaikh Aḥmad Aḥsā'ī: It is correct to say that the soul is a subtle organism unable to receive any but Forms in a subtle, suprasensory state. It is equally correct to say that it cannot be perceived by our physical senses, because the latter are soiled and paralyzed by the infirmities inherent in the elemental natures of which the fleshly body is composed. As against this, to say that Paradise, with its castles, houris, and the delights it con-

* Extract from the same work, pp. 331–32.

tains are no more than "intentions," that is, consist only of pure psychic Forms, imaginative Forms of the *Malakūt* (the world of the *Animae coelestes*), is something I cannot accept. For from that point one would be forced to negate resurrection, as the author (Mullā Ṣadrā) appeared to be doing in certain passages referred to earlier in this book, at least judging from what the literal sense of his words appears to convey. We have noted that, in comparison with the doctrine of the holy Imāms, what he says does not sound like the words of one professing belief in bodily resurrection.[57]

The fact is: to say that Matter, *hyle*, as such is dense and dark is not correct. No matter can be seen as necessarily dense and dark. Matter has other states. The celestial Spheres, for instance, are not perceptible to our physical senses; not even the Earth, that is, the Earth untrodden by the feet of the sons of Adam (i.e., the celestial Earth, the Paradise from which Adam was exiled and whither the Spirit returns in its subtle body), for that Earth is in the subtle state, it cannot be perceived by the eyes of this world, the eyes of flesh.

Furthermore, those who live in Paradise are all bodies determined by dimensions and positions: but the fact of being such a body by no means excludes survival or perpetuity as such. Certainly these spiritual bodies include no negativity, no density, no opacity, since these are concomitants of alteration and substitution, replacing what disappears by something weaker. But these exactly are what are excluded from these bodies in the world beyond our world. Therein even bodies are in perpetual upward movement; if some change and replacement takes place in them, it can only be thanks to some force and renewal coming from above.

As for dimensions and positions, these are inherent in places and in bodies. They are not incompatible as such with the state of those who live in Paradise. The latter are similar to those who dwell on Earth, except that they have no density, no opacity, no tendency to weaken, no tendency toward decay and annihilation. Their state is that of experiencing no replacement in their bodies which is not a strengthening, no change which is not an increase in power, a renewal, a betterment. But why deny the material reality of such experience (provided the matter thereof does not descend to being the dense, dark matter of this world below)? Those who live in Paradise in their spiritual flesh (*jasad B*), in their essential original body (*jism B*), in their "I"-spirit, are certainly the same persons who were in this world below. One change alone has taken place in them: accidents foreign to them, making them prey to destruction, have disappeared, darkness in them has been dispelled and has vanished.

Yes, when these bodies, such as you see them in our world, have been completely purified of accidents foreign to them, the way of being of those who were below rejoin the way of being of those who are above. Then the spiritual bodies perceive of and by themselves the spiritual realities of the *Jabarūt* as well as the pure suprasensory forms of the *Malakūt*.[58] Reciprocally, when Spirits whose existence is connected with these bodies in order to govern them are completely purified from the disturbance that rebellion mixed with their being, and from the unconsciousness that condemned them to forgetfulness, then, of and by themselves, they perceive their spiritual bodies and all the realities related thereto. In fact, for their bodies to be spiritualized, to become spirits, they only have to will it; on the other hand, for their spirits to be embodied, to become bodies, they likewise have only to wish for it.[59]

There is a symbol of this situation in this very world, and those who know will understand to what we refer. The natural Philosophers, those who practice the secret science (i.e., the Alchemists) always described their work as follows: first they dissolve the Stone, then they coagulate it with a portion of its spirit.[60] Next they dissolve the resultant, and once more coagulate it with a part of its spirit. Again they dissolve, again they coagulate, and so forth. When they have treated the Stone, according to their established rule, three times with the white Elixir, then nine times with the red, the Stone will have become spiritual-living-mineral substance (*lapis vivus*).[61]

This means that in itself it remains a body, but as regards its work it has become *spirit*—a spirit able to "bring to life" metals which are *dead*, for the spirit of definitive survival has been blown into it. After the first part of the operation it is already capable of bringing to life a mass one thousand times its own weight, by fusing it with its own substance. Its thirst having been quenched a second time (i.e., after the second admixture of the Elixir), it is able to bring to life a mass two thousand times its own weight. If it were to be saturated a thousand times, its own weight would be able to bring to life a weight a million times greater, and so on to infinity. It is said that a certain Philosopher projected the Elixir three hundred times onto the Stone, and thereby vivified the equivalent of three hundred thousand times its original weight.

The quantitative increase is proportionate to the qualitative increase. If, for instance, the Stone's mass having been subjected once to the red Elixir, six dissolutions followed by six coagulations are performed upon it, the unit of its original weight is multiplied forty-nine times, each unit of which is able to vivify respectively a weight equivalent to two thousand times its own. Thus, prior to this operation, we had a unit of weight capable of vivifying one thousand times its equivalent; this unit is now multiplied by forty-nine, and each of these units in turn multiplies the Gold-making power of the original unit, which in relation to it represents an increase of approximately a hundred thousand units of weight, to the nearest two thousand units (i.e., ninety thousand exactly).

Such an operation would be inconceivable if it had to be carried out on inert material bodies; on the other hand, it is perfectly intelligible as soon as Spirits are in question. This is why the Philosophers affirm: it is certainly a *body*, but its virtue and operation are *spiritual*. So be sure you understand the sign, the marvel here described. For this kind of corporeality is exactly the marvel that characterizes the spiritual body of those who live in Paradise. Certainly they are bodies with all the attributes, conditions, and operations that belong to bodies; and yet they carry out all the actions proper to pure Intelligences and Spirits, and are able to perceive directly for themselves what Souls and Intelligences (i.e., *Angeli coelestes* and *Angeli intellectuales*) are able to perceive. Likewise, and reciprocally, the Intelligences perceive for themselves directly the objects perceived by the Souls and these bodies. Likewise, also, they perceive the Souls. And this is the meaning of what we stated above: the way of being of those who were below is joined with the way of being of those who are above.

5. The Active Imagination and the Resurrection Body*

Mullā Ṣadrā Shīrāzī: Just as dimensional forms, plastic shapes, and figures are produced by an active subject in proportion to the suitability of a given matter and the participation of their receptacle, so it may also be that they result from a pure foundation, the active subject's way of picturing them; the latter's activity is then the sufficient reason, without needing the help of a receptacle, nor of its *situs*, nor even of the suitability of a previously given matter.

The existence of the celestial Spheres and constellations falls exactly into this category, since their existence is founded on acts of contemplation and representations of the archangelic Principles;[62] it results from their active "dimensions," as from divine knowledge of the most perfect order, without presupposing any receptacle or aptitude of preexisting matter. Now the production of autonomous imaginative Forms falls into the same category, subsisting without any material substratum and by the single will emanating from the imaginative consciousness. The latter, as you know, is independent of this world and of the material forms perceived by the senses. One cannot say either that they subsist through the organ of the brain, nor in the astral mass of the Spheres, as certain people have believed, or even in a universe of archetypal Images which could be conceived as subsisting otherwise than through the soul itself.

Shaikh Aḥmad Aḥsā'ī: In speaking thus about imaginative Forms, Mullā Ṣadrā intends to point out that in all the Forms that owe their existence to the pure activity of their agent, with-

* Further extracts from the above work (commentary on the *Theosophy of the Throne*), pp. 175–76, 179–80, 186–87.

out any need to presuppose a receptacle, or any suitable matter, we must include the imaginative Forms that are produced solely by the will, intention, and inclination of the imaginative consciousness. They do not need a material substratum in order to exist. They are conditioned neither by material causes nor by any kind of receptivity. Actually imaginative Forms subsist by the light of the imaginative power, for since the active Imagination is itself a psycho-spiritual power belonging to the world of the *Malakūt*, all the forms arising from it are of the same nature as itself; these forms are independent of external, sensory realities.

Imaginative power is like a mirror; a thing only has to be in front of it for the mirror to manifest the form of this thing. If the thing belongs to the world of the *Malakūt*, it is revealed there directly; if it belongs to the visible, material world, the faculties of sensory perception have first to extract the form and project it onto the *sensus communis*,[63] which transmits it to the imagination. Everyone translates what is transmitted to him into his own language, that is, he makes it into something of the same nature as his own person. Thus, if it is something that escapes the sensory perception, the Imagination takes from it its subtle "celestial" Form (*malakūtīya*); it may be led thereto by a word overheard or by some knowledge previously acquired or by some other means.

That is why I personally should say that the imaginative Forms are not merely creations of the Imagination but that they are a creation of the creator of the Imagination,[64] who, in creating something, places it in the substratum that corresponds to it. If it is a light, he places it in something that has a certain opacity, because a light could not subsist in something like elemental, absolutely pure, diaphanous air. If it is a Form, he places it in a smooth and polished receptacle, like a mirror or still water. If a light and a form belong to a world other than the material, visible world, he places them in their own world, proper to them. The imaginative Forms are not part of the world of visible objects; he makes them apparent in a mirror which is of exactly the same nature as their world. In his Book, God himself says: "Whether ye hide your word or publish it abroad, God has full knowledge of the secrets of all hearts. How should He who created not know that which he created (67:13–14)."

The imaginative Forms belong precisely to what is secretly contained in the heart, and of which God has told us that if he knows it, it is because he made it. Here again: "Nothing is which does not have its Treasury with Us, and we send them down only in strict measure (15:21)." The imaginative Forms are also things that He brings down from the Treasuries in a definite measure into a substratum that is proper to Forms. True, Mullā Ṣadrā affirms that they are not "in a substratum," that is, in a corporeal substratum. This is because he considers that all the thinkers who maintain that the Forms have a substratum mean that the Imaginative exists only in and through the brain. However, they do not all mean that the psycho-spiritual faculties are immanent in the body; they mean that they are attached to it, but in order to govern it.

This having been set forth clearly, it is evident that the imaginative Forms belong to the world of the *Malakūt*, as does the imaginative power itself. They subsist through the mirror which is the imaginative consciousness. Their "matter" is the illumination (*ishrāq*) that projects the Form itself of the thing imagined. Their "form" is the very conformation of the mirror constituted by the Imagination. The mirror includes greatness, purity, whiteness, or else their opposites. We have previously had occasion to recall that in the second Heaven, the Heaven of Mercury, three Angels, Maymūn, Sha'mūn and Zaytūn, have the function of causing the epiphany of the imaginative Forms to appear; each of these Angels has a multitude of angels at his service, whose number, according to practitioners of the theurgic art, is known to God alone. One can take for granted that the creator and producer of the imaginative Forms is God himself; however, according to the law of His creative work, acting through intermediate causes, He has created the imaginative Power in the shape of a mirror that makes the forms appear on receiving a kind of imprint of them. . . .

Mullā Ṣadrā Shīrāzī (pp. 179–80): The imaginative power

in man—I mean the degree or imaginative level of his spiritual "I"—is a substance existing independently, as regards its essence and its operation, of the material body which is the object of sensory perception and of the tangible habitation. As we already said, at the moment when the bodily mold is annihilated, it survives—obliteration and dissolution have no effect on it; at the moment of death, it can be touched by the bewilderment and bitterness of death because of its immersion in the material body, but *post mortem* it continues to see itself as a human being with dimensions and shape corresponding to those that were its own in this world, just as it can picture to itself its body inert and buried.

Shaikh Aḥmad Aḥsā'ī: The power of imagination is without doubt consubstantial with the soul, is an organ comparable in that respect to what the hand is for the body. The soul perceives sensory objects through its organ alone, since the soul belongs to the world of the *Malakūt*. In fact, with respect to the soul, the Imagination is like the Soul of the Heaven of Venus in relation to the Soul of the Heaven of the constellations (the Heaven of the fixed stars, the Zodiac). "It is independent of the material body," says Mullā Ṣadrā. Now we would like to recapitulate briefly all the inferences of this statement, in accordance with our doctrine. We have said that Zayd has two *jasad* and two *jism*.[65] We would like to complete what we have already said about it, and add in conclusion the following clarifications.

The first *jasad* (*jasad A*): Let it be understood that this is the visible body, the material fleshly body, composed of the four Elements of our world; the plants also have a body in their fashion. After death, this body is gradually annihilated in the tomb; each of its elemental components, in dissolving, returns to its origin, where it blends with it and is lost in it; the earthly parts return to the Earth, where they intermingle; the fluid, aerial, igneous parts each blend with their respective element.

The second *jasad* (*jasad B*) is hidden in the first; it also is composed of Elements, not the Elements of our world, but of the world of Hūrqalyā from which it came down. All its separate parts and the connections between them endure "in the tomb," because it keeps its "shape" so well that all its parts remain perfectly articulated. This body that preserves its perfect shape "in the tomb" is that imperishable "clay" of which the Imām Jaʿfar Ṣādiq was thinking when he declared: "The clay of which it was composed continues to exist in its perfect shape in the tomb." What we have to understand by the lasting perfection of this "shape" is that the parts that make up the head, corresponding to the "headstone" of the tomb, remain joined to the elements of the neck, which remain linked with the elements of the bust, which remain connected to the parts of the belly, the latter to the legs, even if a marine monster or some wild beast has devoured the body of material flesh (*jasad A*) or if it has been mutilated, and its parts scattered in different places, or even wrongly reassembled.

When the elements of this invisible body (*jasad B*) have become disassociated and freed from the material flesh composed of lower Elements, their entire structure remains unchanged "in the tomb."[66] And what is more, even if the material body is not buried in the tomb, they retain this structure. For when we talk about this other body, what we should understand by the "tomb" (it is not the cemetery) is the original place, the womb[67] from which the "clay" was extracted and mixed by the Angel with the twofold fluid issued from father and mother. Being incorruptible, this "clay" will coagulate the water flowing down from the ocean of Ṣād (situated below the Throne) when the time comes for the breath of the great Awakening to vibrate in the second blast of the Trumpet. It is this body, this spiritual flesh, that the Spirit will assume on the day of the great Resurrection.

Perhaps, you will say, as others have already, that the apparent meaning of my exposition is to rule out the possibility that the first *jasad* (*jasad A*, the elemental body of corruptible flesh) can "return," and that one must concur with the thesis denying and rejecting bodily resurrection.[68] In that case, I would point out that when speaking of the second *jasad* (*jasad B*, the body of resurrection) this is also that very body that is visible and tangible today. But, precisely, in order for it to be the "resurrection body," it must have been broken, pulverized, and reshaped in a *form* that excludes all corruption and decrepitude, whereas the present earthly *form* is dissolved forever. This outer form, gone forever, and described as a composite of the sublunar Elements, is the one to which the Amīr of the believers (the First Imām) alluded in the *ḥadīth* relating to souls, mentioned above, wherein he declared concerning the vegetable soul in man: "When it is separated, it returns to its origin, there to blend and be lost, not to survive there autonomously." In short, by the first elemental *jasad* (*jasad A*) we mean the earthly accidents. For when the second *jasad* (*jasad B*, the spiritual flesh made of the Elements of Hūrqalyā, the resurrection body) came down into this world, accidents issuing from the Elements adhered to it, just as when you have worn a garment for some time, the dirt adheres to it but is not a part of it. All you have to do is to wash it and these accidents will go away, and the garment will lose nothing of what made it what it is. Therefore ponder and understand the doctrine of your Imāms and spiritual guides.

As for the first *jism* (*jism A*, the astral body made of the influx from the Heavens of Hūrqalyā), we said that it is with this body that the "I"-spirit departs from the elemental, material body (*jasad A*) when the Angel of Death seizes it. The archetypal body (*jism B*) continues to exist with this actual body, the latter being the accumulator of its energies in the intermediate world or *barzakh* (until the first blast of the Trumpet, that is, until the great cosmic pause). When Seraphiel's breath causes the Trumpet to vibrate for the first time, the Spirit casts off the *jism A* and disappears. Actually, this body is also an accident, like the first *jasad* (*jasad A*, the elemental material body), but in its case an accident of the intermediate world or *barzakh*; it also is a form which the Imām Jaʿfar, as we mentioned previously, compares to a brick that is broken; when reduced to dust, its first shape has gone forever; but replaced in the mold, it emerges identical to itself in one respect, but different in another. As God says in his Book: "Each time their skin will be consumed we will replace it by another, so that they may taste the chastisement." In all fairness, they cannot be given a skin other than their own: that would be chastisement for a non-existent fault, or being obliged to suffer the chastisement for the fault of another. No, it really is the first skin. Yet, since it has been consumed, its first form, which was an accident, has gone forever. Therefore, when it returns, it is true to say that it is different if one considers the change, substitution, and renewal of the *form*; whereas, if one considers its *matter*, it remains the same skin.[69]

This is why we can sum it up as follows: the first *jasad* (*jasad A*) is the form belonging to the lower Elements. The first *jism* (*jism A*) is the form belonging to the intermediate world or *barzakh*; the latter is the prototype of the former. When you break your seal and reshape another seal, similar to the first, from the same matter, the soul has lost nothing essential, for it is certainly itself; but it has shed one accident and assumed another accident. The first accident would here correspond to *jasad A* (the material body) in this present life, whereas the second accident would be homologous to *jism A*, the astral body in the intermediate world, or *barzakh*. The "I"-soul is different from the elemental *jasad A*, which is annihilated after death; it is different also from the imperishable *jasad B* (the elemental body of Hūrqalyā, the body of spiritual flesh), and it is different lastly from the *jism A* (the astral body, which will not reappear from the moment of the return of the *jasad B* at the great Resurrection). As for *jism B* (the essential or archetypal original body), it is forever identical to itself. To go into this in detail would take a long time; suffice it to recall one essential thing which will lead you to the knowledge of many other things.

So we shall still add the following: When the "I"-spirit, that which the Angel of Death gathers up and carries away, has finally shed its astral body (*jism A*),[70] it also will disappear, but only during the interval (the "cosmic pause") between the two "blasts of the Trumpet." When we speak of its disappearance, what we in fact mean is that when the Angel of Death gathers up the "I"-spirit from its material body (*jasad A*), this spirit "goes away" though keeping its original preterrestrial structure (*jism B*) intact, and that it survives in the *barzakh* in the waking state and in full consciousness.

As the Imām Ja'far said, when commenting on this descriptive verse (79:13), "It will sound but once, since all are in the waking state."

This first sounding of Seraphiel's trumpet is the one referred to as the "fiery blast"; it is an intake of breath and draws up the spirits in order to reabsorb them in Seraphiel's Trumpet. Each "I"-spirit goes back into its own matrix, symbolically represented as one of the "holes" perforated in the length of the Trumpet; this is the place from which it was originally extracted, the place from which it came out in order to go down toward the bodies at the time of its preceding existence. The matrix itself comprises six dwellings or habitations: into the first of these the Image or archetypal Form of the "I"-spirit is breathed; its subtle consubstantial matter into the second; into the third, its luminous nature corresponding to the igneous Element; into the fourth, its soul corresponding to the fluid Element; into the fifth, its own *pneuma*, corresponding to the aerial Element; into the sixth, its consubstantial intellect. When we speak of its disappearance, we refer to this separation and disintegration of the six constitutive principles (of its essential body, *jism B*). The "I"-spirit then no longer possesses consciousness or feeling. During this pause, the six constitutive principles are not dissolved in mixture, for each retains its specific reality; they remain as though side by side in their respective autonomy.

When the divine Will intends to renew Creation and to cause the seeds from the preceding existence to germinate, Seraphiel is commanded to blow into the Trumpet the breath of the great Awakening. As opposed to the "blazing sound," this is a propulsive breath. Entering the sixth dwelling, it propells the intellect towards the *pneuma* in the fifth dwelling; next it propells intellect and *pneuma* together toward the soul in the fourth dwelling; then it propels all three together, intellect, *pneuma*, and soul, towards the luminous nature in the third dwelling; then it propels all four together towards the subtle consubstantial matter in the second dwelling; finally it propels all five toward the Image or archetypal Form in the first dwelling. Then the "I"-spirit finds again its composition and structure, its consciousness and capacity to feel.

On the other hand, before the vibration of the breath of the great Awakening, the water of the sea of Ṣād, situated below the Throne, comes down and rains over the surface of the Earth. Then *Jasad B*, the spiritual body made of the Elements of Hūrqalyā, serves as a "vehicle" for the new form, the "second accident" referred to above. Its structure being completed, its "I"-spirit enters it. This is what is meant when the "headstone of the tomb's bursting" is symbolically mentioned. For then the individual arises in his imperishable Form, shaking the terrestrial dust from his head. "As you were made in the beginning, that you will again become (7:28)," as it is said. So here we have very briefly all the points we wish to cover in speaking of the fourfold bodily organism of the human being: a twofold *jasad* or elemental body, the one *accidental* (*jasad A*, the elemental body of perishable flesh), the other *essential* (*jasad B*, the body made of the Elements of Hūrqalyā, the imperishable spiritual flesh); and a twofold *jism*, the one *accidental* (*jism A*, the astral body) the other *essential* (*jism B*, the archetypal body inseparable from the "I"-spirit).

In these pages, which were written in response to the passage in which Mullā Ṣadrā affirms that the imaginative power survives, Shaikh Aḥmad Aḥsā'ī has summed up the entire physiology of the body of resurrection, without which Mullā Ṣadrā's affirmation would have no support. Doubtless, a very important point is the one in which *form* is described as an accident that goes away without returning, whereas *matter*, its permanent element in its different states, is "that which returns"; and this precisely because new form means *metamorphosis*, the transmutation of matter "returning" to the state of incorruptible spiritual matter. The terminology peculiar to Shaikh Aḥmad must evidently be taken into account. Mullā Ṣadrā's successors —for example, Hādī Sabzavārī in the last century (d. 1878)— have sometimes missed his point, as evidenced by certain criticisms that fall wide of the mark. In any case, the page translated below is the best illustration of what Shaikh Aḥmad Aḥsā'ī means; it is also the best transition to a subsequent extract, from one of the great works written by one of his eminent successors at the head of the Shaikhī school.*

As for Form, if contrary to the opinion of Mullā Ṣadrā, I say that it is an accident and is not "that which returns," it is because form is a conformation of matter. What "returns" in reality is matter in a certain form, but this form is precisely the work of the individual person. Even if the matter undergoes metamorphosis, exchanges one species for another in terms of the forms corresponding to the person's acts, nevertheless that which returns, which "comes to life again," is precisely that which assumes Form, and not, as Mullā Ṣadrā thinks, Form itself. For example, the outer appearance of Zayd was initially created in a human form, solely because of the affirmative answer he gave in preeternity to the question "*Am I not your Lord?* (7:171)."[71] If he fulfills the pact into which he entered and works accordingly, then his "esoteric nature," the inner man, is also created in human form, thanks to his action. He truly dies and comes to life again as a human being, because then his consubstantial matter, through his work, is homogeneous in the true meaning to the matter of human reality.

On the other hand, if he betrays his pact and complacently follows evil passions, his consubstantial matter will assume a form to match it, the form of a beast, even though he will continue externally to assume the form of a human being which will be like a veil before God, and a test for those who remain faithful to the pact. So says this verse: "The hour will come which I wish to keep hidden, so that every soul may gather the fruits of its effort (20:15–16)." When he dies and his outer human form disappears "in the tomb" and goes to the Throne (that is, withdraws into Hūrqalyā), then at once the form of an animal manifests in him, since it is the very form of his work, his consubstantial matter now being available for this form that matches it. He will be brought back to life as an animal, because his personal work will have made this matter of his into something homogeneous to the matter of an animal. Matter is, in fact,

* Extract from pp. 186–87 follows.

the substance that is made available for and by what he has done, and is shaped by the very form of his work.

In the world of seminal reasons Zayd had apparently answered "yes" to the question asked on the day of the preeternal Covenant, while secretly his choice fell on his own passion.[72] He apparently chose rightly when he answered in the affirmative the question that was put to him. But though his choice was sufficient to commit him to the effort, nevertheless his secret state of mind outweighed the formulated answer. For this answer was certainly on his lips, but his secret tendency contradicted it. After he descended into this world, and the effort he had to make was shown to him a second time, everything was dissipated in doubt and confusion. His case was confirmed by the following verse: "They could not consent, for they had previously denied (7:99)."

Thus, the secret thought contradicting the answer which was then formulated, was the matrix of the work later carried on by evil passion. That is why this secret thought is surely the "clay" from which Zayd was created by his own works, and he can but rise again with it. For at the very moment when his secret thought was contradicting his answer, his "clay," that is, the consubstantial matter of his being, was molded by this thought in the likeness of an animal, being henceforth the only matter available for the germination of his own seminal reason. So when he descended to this world, when he had settled down there in accordance with his choice, and when he had consummated his choice by repetition and by applying his effort to what he had already undertaken in the world of seminal reasons, what had existed in his secret thoughts was revealed in the light of day and he manifested the works of his animal nature.

That is also why he is resurrected in the animal state, since all his consubstantial matter had been molded by his works, which were homogeneous to the substantial nature of an animal. For in truth Form is the configuration of matter; therefore it is the configuration of the thing "which returns," it is not the thing itself. That is why the Imām Jaʿfar compares it with the brick of potter's clay which is broken, and again replaced in the mold. It is indeed the same brick, and yet it is another brick: the matter is the same, but the form is different. . . . Each individual, when resurrected, assumes the form which, thanks to his works, has lodged in his most secret part (p. 227).

X

SHAIKH ḤĀJJ MUḤAMMAD KARĪM KHĀN KIRMĀNĪ, SECOND SUCCESSOR OF SHAIKH AḤMAD AḤSĀ'Ī
(d. 1288/1870)

1. In What Sense the Body of the Faithful Believer is the Earth of His Paradise *

Inasmuch as in this world there are certain accidents that are not inherent in the human body and are not an integral part of that body, you should understand that such accidents do not have to rise again with a man. The only body which is raised from the dead is the human body in its individual, archetypal state; this is the body to which everything known as "reward" or "punishment" occurs. This body persists through all the successive states from earliest infancy until the moment of death. Or rather, it is already there in the seed of the human being and in all the successive stages: embryonic, moment of birth, first breath, and so forth. It is a body which has length, breadth, depth, color, shape, and structure, just like the other bodies, except that it has the advantage, as an archetype, of retaining its identity, whereas all the accidents of this earthly world are ephemeral, appear and disappear. This body is the resurrection body, the one referred to when it is said that it enters Paradise or Hell.[2]

But here a subtle theme comes in, which requires explanation. The structure of the archetypal body of man depends on his works and on the feeling he professes about the world and about God. When the inmost faith he professes is genuine, when his behavior is virtuous and pure, in harmony with the very pure

* Extract from the *Irshād al-ʿawāmm* (*Spiritual Directives for the Use of the Faithful*), Kirman, 1354/1935, Vol. I, Pt. 2, pp. 48–49, 66–68, 271, 277, 282–86. This work is entirely in Persian.[1]

religion of the Messenger of the end of time, then the form of his primordial spiritual body is truly the human form.[3] For, in fact, the human form corresponds to the Divine Will as a light does to its source. You see, for example, how the light of the sun corresponds to the conformation of the sun, moonlight to the conformation of the moon, and lamplight to the conformation of the lamp. Therefore the light of the Divine Will necessarily corresponds to the form of that Will. This is why man, who is the light of the Divine Will, takes on that very form.

Now the Divine Will is God's well-beloved—the object of his love; its nature and mode of being thus correspond to love and divine desire. Or rather, this Will is what Divine Love itself *is*. The two shades of meaning expressed by the Arabic terms for will (*mashī'a*) and desire (*irāda*) are combined in Persian in a single word expressing the idea of *wish* as both will and desire (*khwāhish*). The Divine Will is God's wish and God's wish is none other than His Love, for God cannot will anything other, wish anything other than His Love. In combination, therefore, Divine Will and Divine Desire take on the form of Divine Love. But the human form, on the other hand, being the light of the Divine Will, assumes the very form of the Will. And this is why the human form is the God's beloved, the object of the Divine Love.

Thus we understand that God ordains for man only what is the object of His Love and forbids him only what He abhors. That is why all the Prophet's prescriptions are in harmony with Divine Love. Divine Love is the very form of the Divine Will which is the wish of God, His fondest desire. It follows that the prophetic religion is in harmony with the form of the Divine Will. Thus the conformation of the inmost being of him who acts in accordance with this religion assumes the very form of the Divine Will, which is the object of Divine Love, or rather *is* that love itself. Hence such a man will be God's well-beloved, and that is exactly what God commanded his Prophet to teach men: "If you love God, follow me so that God may love you (3:29)." Thus, following the Prophet is what makes God love man. And following the Prophet means to model your own way of being and acting on the example of the Magnanimous One (*buzurgvār*); it means to model the form of your own being in the likeness of his. . . . He who shapes his outer body and his inner being on the model of the Prophet, such a one is surely the friend and beloved of God, since he who makes himself absolutely similar to the friend of someone, also becomes the friend of the latter. And the Prophet is God's beloved, because he assumes the form of God's wish, the form of His Will and His Desire. . . .

(Pp. 66–68) The paradise of the faithful believer is his own body.[4] His virtuous works, after the manner previously described, are its trees, fresh running water, castles, and houris.[5] The Gehenna of the unbeliever is likewise nothing but his own body; his hateful works are its fiery furnaces, monsters, serpents, dogs, dragons, and so on. Perhaps you will think that under the guise of spiritual interpretation I am transposing everything into pure allegory? Perhaps you are wondering how the human body of a believer, a minute human body, could be a paradise, when the faithful believer is promised a paradise a thousand times the size of this world? And how the body of the ungodly man could be his Gehenna, when Hell is immense and described as containing abysses and fiery mountains? God forbid that a philosopher should talk without rhyme or reason! So pay attention, in order to understand the reality and true meaning of the theme we are discussing here.

You have already been given to understand that the faithful believer possesses a certain body, which includes something accidental. Everything that in this terrestrial world can be seen by the organs of physical perception is accidental, mere coloring and appearance passing through successive states that appear and disappear without in any way being an integral part of the essential or archetypal body. This body which you are now seeing, with its minute material dimensions, is the accidental body; in no way is it an integral part of the essential body. As for the essential or archetypal body, for instance that of Zayd, it is fashioned according to the extent of his knowledge, to his capacity to understand, to his spiritual consciousness, to his moral conduct; for the more developed his spiritual consciousness, the nobler his moral conduct, the subtler also will be his essential body. Now, the subtler this body becomes, the greater also is its magnitude. It is in this sense that the size of the paradise of the faithful adepts is measured by their knowledge, their spiritual consciousness, and their moral conduct. The more "gnostic," faithful, and perfect they are, the vaster appears their paradise, and the more their body grows. The volume of the paradise of one faithful adept may be seven times the volume of this terrestrial world; in the case of another it can be ten times greater, and for still another a million times. Each of them creates for himself a dwelling place in proportion to the capacity of his spiritual energy.[6]

That is why the essential or archetypal body of the faithful adepts is the very Earth of their Paradise, just as the essential body of the impious man is the very Earth of his Gehenna. The narrowness of the place, its sordid filth, its dense gloom, the suffering he endures there, are in proportion to his impiety and his dissociation from the One.[7] Try to understand what I mean. This is a very subtle theme: nobody can escape from himself, get out of himself; nobody becomes someone other than himself; nothing becomes something other than itself.

Don't tell yourself that the state which I have just described is not exactly the one made known to us by divine Revelation. I call God as witness! Paradise abounds in houris, castles, green plants, and fresh running water, unlimited—just as described in the Revealed Book—but not as they are depicted by your fantasy.[8] We are not the community of our fancy; we are the community of the Prophet, we follow the Book of the Tradition. Are you not aware that when you hear the word *tree* in the Qur'ān, you picture to yourself trees exactly like the trees of this world? Now, there is a verse that declares: "Their fruits are below" (69:23), which means that the top of the trees of Paradise are below. His Holiness the Amīr of the Believers, our First Imām, observes by way of commentary: "The trees of Paradise are the inverse of the trees of this world. The trees of

Paradise have their root above and their branches below."[9] When you hear the words "fresh running water" you imagine a stream like the streams of this world, whereas it is said that the *Tasnīm* (cf. 83:27) enters the abodes of the inhabitants of Paradise from above. Therefore it behooves me to deal with these questions in conformity with the Revealed Book and our Tradition, not according to your fantasy.

Therefore I declare that the essential or archetypal body of the faithful adept is itself his Paradise. He himself is inside his own Paradise, in this world already as in the *Aevum* to come. The archetypal body of the impious man is itself his Gehenna; he dwells in his own Hell, in this world as well as in the world to come. Have you not heard it said that the "clay" out of which the faithful believer is made belongs to the Earth of Paradise, whereas the "clay" of the impious man belongs to the Earth of Gehenna? So that the Earth of Paradise *is* Paradise, and the Earth of Gehenna *is* Gehenna. As regards Paradise or Hell, to each one can be given only what he is capable of receiving, and which is of the same nature as the "clay" of which he is made. No one is qualified to taste reward or punishment that surpasses the extent of his fitness. From the First Day, each one has been given the Last Day. If, in the preterrestrial world, the world of seminal reasons, he was a faithful adept, he was then and there worthy of reward, and he was given a proportionate share of the Earth of Paradise. If, on the other hand, he deserved punishment, he was given a proportionate share of the Earth of Gehenna. No faithful believer becomes more of a believer in this world than he himself decided in the preterrestrial world. No impious one becomes more impious than he decided in the preterrestrial world. To each one is done and given according to his faith or his faithlessness. Ponder on what I am saying so as to make no mistake, since this is a subtle question.[10]

Having said this, we must still mention that Paradise comprises eight degrees, and that Gehenna comprises seven. Many faithful believers are in the first degree of Paradise; many of them are in the second degree, and so on up to the eighth. Inversely, many impious are in the first circle of Hell; as well as in the second and the seventh. The reason for this is that the Lord of the worlds incorporated eight "handfuls of Heaven" into the archetypal body of the believer, eight "handfuls" of primordial matter belonging to the Heavens of his universe, as we explained previously. His body contains one handful of the subtle matter of the first Heaven (that of the moon), and his spirit (*rūḥ*, vital *pneuma*) was made from this "handful of Heaven"; one handful of the subtle matter of the second Heaven (that of Mercury) and his meditative power was made from this "handful of Heaven;" his imaginative power was made from a handful of the third Heaven (that of Venus); one handful of the fourth Heaven (that of the Sun) constituted his "consubstantial matter:" one handful of the fifth Heaven (that of Mars) constituted his representative faculty; a handful of the sixth Heaven (that of Jupiter) constituted his cognitive power; one handful of the seventh Heaven (that of Saturn) constituted his individual intellect; one handful of the eighth Heaven (the Heaven of the Fixed Stars, *Kursī*, the *Firmament*) constituted his soul. And finally, his body contains a handful of the subtle matter of the Throne (*ʿarsh*, the Empyrean); from this is formed his essential and fundamental reality.[11]

Consequently, when the believer obeys his vital spirit, and nothing above that has been manifested in him, then that believer is on the first level of paradise. When he obeys his meditative power, he is on the second level of paradise and so on: whichever level in himself he obeys, which manifests in him and determines his spiritual rank, is also his rank in Paradise, on the level corresponding to him. He belongs to the spiritual family that is situated on this level. Every higher level, compared to the lower level, is so vast that if one were to compare the lower level with the higher level the latter would seem like the circle of the horizon arising at the boundary of the immense desert. This is so to such an extent that the lowest level of all is still seventy times[12] higher than our terrestrial world.

In the same way, the body of the impious man comprises seven "handfuls of earth," seven handfuls of the matter of the circles of Sijjīn.[13] The first belongs to the Earth of death, the second to the Earth of innate tendencies, the third to the Earth of nature, the fourth to the Earth of lust, the fifth to the Earth of fury, the sixth to the Earth of aberration, the seventh to the Earth of abomination. Therefore, in the event that the source of the negative attitude of the impious man is the first "handful of earth" of his being and the second is not manifested in it, then he dwells in the first circle of Gehenna. If the source is the second handful, and the third does not appear in it, then he dwells in the second circle of Hell. And so forth: as the descent proceeds, each circle becomes narrower and narrower, more and more wretched, compared to the preceding one. Thus, each one continues according to his fundamental nature, until he returns to his origin. . . .

(P. 271) Know that a creature has two faces or dimensions; the one is its divine face or dimension, the other is the face or dimension of its own selfhood. By divine face or dimension what must be understood is not that creatures are God, but have a face or dimension *toward* God which is Light, Good, Perfection, because each creature is a trace born of the Divine Will and, since the Divine Will is Light, Good and Perfection, the trace naturally resembles that which imprinted it. The other face or dimension of the creature is its face toward itself, and this dimension is darkness, evil, deficiency. All creatures are made with these two faces or dimensions. However, the nearer the creatures are to the primordial Will, the more abundant is their light and the more rarefied their darkness. On the other hand, the farther away they are from that primordial Will, the denser becomes their darkness and the weaker their light. On the one hand, therefore, everything is light on the plane coinciding with the greatest proximity to the primordial Will; there, the proportion of darkness is but that of a speck of dust, its effect is exhausted; it is but a drop of water lost in the ocean. On the other hand, all is darkness on the plane most distant from the primordial Will; there, only one atom of light remains [Fig. 3].

The light and darkness can be represented in the form of two intersecting triangles, as suggested by the above diagram.

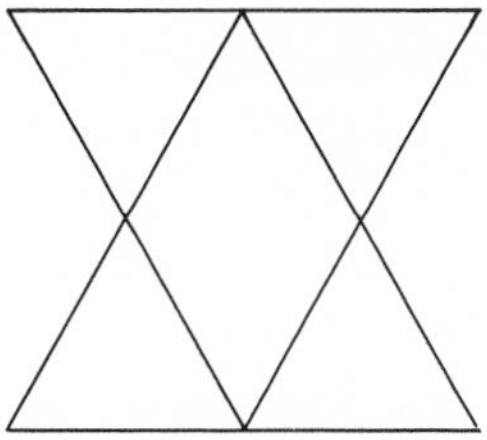

Figure 3.

The upper triangle is the triangle of light; the base of this triangle (at the top of the diagram) is the light which is very close to the primordial Will; at one point it is touched by one of the apexes of the triangle of darkness. The base of the lower triangle —which is this triangle of darkness—is at the maximum distance from the primordial Will; it is touched at one point by the apex of the triangle of light. Therefore, everything is light very close to the primordial Will; there is just a trace of an atom of darkness. But, with the downward movement, the light gradually diminishes while the darkness increases, until, at the end, the darkness prevails; there remains only a trace of an atom of light. On the other hand, with the upward movement the darkness wanes, while the light waxes, until it reaches the point nearest to the primordial Will . . . half-way between the two limits, light and darkness are equal. From this it can be understood that in case a "handful of matter" is taken upwards from the center, and if a creature is formed out of this matter, light will prevail in this creature over darkness. But if the "handful of matter" is taken downwards from the center, and a creature is molded out of it then, on the contrary, darkness will prevail in this creature and light will be overcome.[14]

(P. 277) Work fulfilled is itself the reward, and the reward is itself the accomplished task. However, it must be added that in this world works and actions are visible to the eyes of your body as outer appearances, whereas in the other world these same actions are seen in other forms (their *apparentiae reales*). Some are seen in the shape of castles, others in the shape of houris, of plants, trees, or streams of living water, others in the form of birds, camels, or horses, in the manner and sense which we went into previously. All of them, in fact, are attributes and qualities of the man himself; they are the outer manifestations of his inner being. For all of them are there in the other world, where they surround him and become his reward. . . . Earlier we described the process by which works and actions are thus shaped, and take the form, now of minerals, now of vegetables, now of animals, now of houris and attendants in Paradise, or, on the contrary, become his companions in Gehenna. . . .[15]

(Pp. 282–86) When it is said that Paradise is in Heaven and Gehenna is in the Earth, that is because the human being has two dimensions: a dimension of light and a dimension of darkness. His dimension of light is the Heaven of his being; his dimension of darkness is the Earth of his being. Every faithful act a man does is done through his dimension of light. Then he is wholly luminous, celestial, subtle. Conversely, his betrayals and denials come from his dimension of darkness; he is then wholly dark, earthly, dense, and opaque. If then it is said that Paradise is in Heaven, it is because it is the dimension of light and of good, the dimension of approach to the Divine: conversely, Hell is in the Earth, because it is the dimension of Darkness and of evil, the dimension of utmost remoteness from the Divine.

Now, Paradise includes eight degrees; Hell contains seven. Each of these stages contain several enclosures; however, there is one degree of Paradise that does not include a plurality of enclosures. All the abodes of the other world together number twenty-nine: fifteen are primary, fourteen derived from these.

In analysis of this theme, we will say that for the human being there are fifteen degrees or planes; eight of them belong to the dimension of light, which is called *ʿIllīyūn*; seven others are in the dimension of darkness which is called *Sijjīn*. One of the eight degrees or planes which are in the dimension of light is the abode of that handful of heaven in man belonging to the eighth Heaven (*Kursī*, the *Firmament*), from which the heart of man was created. The second is the abode of that handful of heaven which, in man, belongs to the Heaven of Saturn, from which man's intellective power was made. The third is the abode of that handful of heaven in man which belongs to the Heaven of Jupiter, from which his cognitive power was made. The fourth is the abode of the handful of heaven belonging to the Heaven of Mars, from which his representative faculty was made. The fifth is the abode of the handful of heaven in man belonging to the Heaven of the Sun, out of which his subtle consubstantial matter was made. The sixth is that of the handful of heaven belonging to the Heaven of Venus, from which man's imaginative power was constituted. The seventh is the handful of heaven which belongs to the Heaven of Mercury, and from it his meditative power was constituted. And finally, the eighth is the handful of heaven which belongs to the Heaven of the Moon, and from it his spirit (*rūḥ*, *pneuma*) was created. These are the eight degrees which are the Abodes of Light of man; these Abodes are his luminous and divine dimension; they form the inner Heaven, they are Heaven in man.

With the exception of the first "handful of heaven" (the one issuing from the eighth Heaven or *Kursī*), the above are matched by the seven "handfuls of earth" which in man originate respectively in one of the seven Earths. One handful originates in the first Earth: from it the outer appearance of the physical body of the human being was constituted. Another one originates in the second Earth, and out of it were created man's innate dispositions. And so forth: the third Earth, from a handful of which the physical temperament of man was made; the fourth Earth, from a handful of which lust was made; the fifth Earth, from a handful of which frenzy was created; the sixth Earth, from a handful of which going astray was created, which consists in running away from the divine Being; the seventh Earth, from a handful of which evil in man was created. Such are the seven categories of Earths, which match the seven categories of

Heavens. As for the eighth Heaven, it has no equivalent among the Earths, because there are seven Earths, no more, just as there are seven Heavens; actually, the Heaven which is called *Kursī* (Firmament) is not an integral part of the Heavens; it is one of the thresholds of the Mystery, of the Invisible. Just as the Throne (*'arsh*, the Empyrean) is also one of the thresholds of the Mystery, and is not an integral part of the celestial Spheres.

Thus, the universe of the seven Heavens and the universe of the seven Earths have their mutual correspondences in man. Of course, when we talk about these "handfuls of Heaven," we do not mean that a material section has been removed from each Heaven. What we wish to convey is the degree of man's participation in the Soul of each of the Heavens which are in him (the share allotted to him of this psycho-spiritual organ of each Heaven). The esoteric, psycho-spiritual reality of the totality of the Heavens is situated in the thinking Soul of the world. Now, the human being is the irradiation of that Soul; his whole being exemplifies its archetype. That is why his being likewise possesses a "handful" of that esoteric reality of each Heaven.[16]

Men differ profoundly in regard to their respective spiritual dwelling place. They are by no means all on the same low or high level. When we say that there is in man a handful of the psycho-spiritual substance of each Heaven, this refers only to the Perfect Man. In the same way, if a man's being contains a handful of each of the Earths, it refers to a man who has reached the degree of total, perfect evil. As for the average man, one of them may possess a handful of only one Heaven; another a handful of two or three Heavens, or four or five, or even six or seven, if he belongs to the people of Light and Goodness. On the other hand, if he belongs to the people of Darkness and Evil, it may be that his being contains a handful of only one Earth, or again it may contain handfuls from several Earths.

Thus, when there is a "handful of Heaven" in man and when thanks to it, his moral conduct is excellent, while his life in its various aspects actualizes faithful service of the divine, then all his actions and works will be gathered together on the

Resurrection Day, in different forms, but all of them on the level and degree to which this "handful of Heaven" corresponds. If, for example, this handful belongs to the first Heaven, all his works will be of the nature of the first Heaven. If it issues from the second Heaven, they will be of the same nature as the second Heaven. And so forth. For him who holds one handful from one Heaven, his works will be all on that one level. The work of one who has two handfuls from two Heavens will be of two levels. And so forth, so that the work of the man whose being is made up of all "seven handfuls" will be of seven degrees. It goes without saying that the works that spring from a "handful" from the second Heaven are more subtle than those that spring from a "handful" from the first Heaven. And so forth, the result being that those that spring from a handful of the seventh Heaven are the subtlest of all. Do you not see that the intellect (*nous*) is subtler in state than the soul, and how much subtler is what you produce through your intellect than what you produce through your soul,[17] just as what you produce through your soul is far more subtle in state than your physical nature. And such is the case proportionately for each "handful of Heaven" in relation to the works that spring from it.

Thus, the "Heavens of your being" are ones I have just described (the eight "abodes of light" of your being). The Paradise of each one of us is absolutely proper to him. It consists of the man's works and actions, which in the other world will appear to him in the form of houris, castles, and verdant trees. *That is why the Paradise of each of us is in the Heaven of his being*; it is absolutely his own, for no one else has a share in it. As God expresses it in his Book: "In that very place is prepared that which the souls desire and which delights the eyes (43:71)." There is a degree of Paradise that corresponds to the respective capacity and conduct of each man. To one is given a place in the first Heaven; to another, in the second Heaven. And so forth: finally, to some is given a place in the seventh Heaven.

The eight thresholds of Paradise in their turn form eight degrees. Everyone enters by a threshold, in terms of his spiritual rank and the work he has accomplished. In the words of Ḥaẓrat

Amīr, the First Imām: "Paradise has eight thresholds. The Prophets and their Imāms enter by one of these thresholds. The Imāms of Muḥammad's family[18] enter by another threshold. All our Shī'ites (adepts) and those who are our friends enter by five other thresholds. Ordinary Muslims, those who have borne witness to *non deus nisi Deus* and have not fostered in their hearts one atom of hatred against us who are members of the sacred Family,[19] enter through the last threshold."

To sum up, from whatever Heaven the "clay" of each one of us has been taken, to whatever Heaven his spirit belongs, this is the very Heaven to which he will return. His actions and his works are gathered together in this Heaven, and it is there that they are made manifest to him in their form of the world beyond, their resurrection form. All his activities are gathered around him, they become his Paradise. That is why the works of the just man continue to rise until they have reached their Heaven, because they issue from this same Heaven; that is their origin and their true reality; inversely, evil acts descend into the Earth until they reach their own Earth, the circle of Hell which is their place of origin and return. . . . The degrees of Paradise, as we have said, are eight in number. However, the eighth is the one that belongs to the Prophet and to the Twelve Imāms. It is the "Paradise of the Permanent Abode" (53:15) or the "Garden of Eden" (18:30, et al.) which is situated in that eighth Heaven called the *Lotus of the Boundary* (53:14). As the eighth Heaven is the rank of the most sacred Soul of the world,[20] whose verdant offspring, as I have explained previously, is the soul of man, and as the Soul of the world is the "place" of knowledge, this soul has many branches. It is the Tree, and the lotus, which is called *Lotus of the Boundary*. In that very place there is the "Paradise of the Permanent Abode," the one which belongs to the Prophets. The "roof" of this paradise is the Throne (*'arsh*), as a *ḥadīth* says: "the roof of Paradise is the Throne of the Merciful."

Now, that degree has no opposite, because, ontologically, the Prophet and the Imāms have no opposites. Ontologically, opposites appear only on the level of our existence, that is, of the

Shīʿites and the True Faithful. That is why the Antagonist, in the true and ontological sense, is the adversary of the Shīʿites, or adepts of the holy Imāms. But they, that is, the Prophets and the Imāms, have neither opposite nor adversary in the true and essential meaning of the word, because the adversaries themselves rank below them. Ontologically, they rank on the universal level, where all is made whole, and that which makes a whole cannot include an opposite. To include an opposite is characteristic of all that is partial. That is why this degree of Paradise has nothing counterbalancing it on the side of Gehenna. On the contrary, the other seven degrees—those relating to the True Faithful and Muslims in general—do have opposites on the side of Gehenna to counterbalance them, as we pointed out a few pages back.

Certain authors place these eight degrees of Paradise in the following order: the gardens of Paradise (18:107), which are in the eighth Heaven; the lofty gardens (69:22); the gardens of bliss (10:9 etc.); the gardens of Eden (18:25 etc.), which have no opposite on the side of Gehenna; the gardens of the secure place (44:51); the gardens of eternity (50:33); the gardens of the refuge (32:19); the gardens of the abode of peace (6:127). As regards the degrees or circles of Hell, the same authors rank them thus: Gehenna (3:196 etc.); the flaming fire (70:15); the consuming fire (104:4–5); the brazier (67:5 etc.); the devastating fire (74:26–27); the furnace (79:39 etc.); the abyss (101:6). Other authors, on the contrary, claim that the furnace is the highest degree, while Gehenna is the lowest, but I know no *ḥadīth* to support this classification, although all of these names appear in the Book and in the Tradition.[21]

In short, just as in Perfect Man there are seven "handfuls of heaven," issuing respectively from each of the Heavens, so in the "perfectly evil man" there are seven "handfuls of earth," originating in each of the seven Earths, whereas for the common run of humanity the proportion varies according to the differences in degree.

The seven degrees of Paradise have seven degrees of radiation, that is, to each of the degrees corresponds a radiation proper to it, in the same way as the solar radiation corresponds to the nature of the sun. These seven radiations form seven enclosures for the seven Paradises. But the eighth Paradise has no enclosure, since it is universal, the one which makes whole. Now, the nature of that which makes whole is not the same as that which has only a partial function and a partial radiation. Everything that issues from the radiation of the faithful in the true sense and is "fit for Paradise" has its abode in these enclosures, and not in the original Paradise itself, because radiation is not of the same degree as the source of light. . . .[22]

2. A World in Ascent, Not in Evolution*

We are translating below two more pages of the great work of Muḥammad Karīm Khān Kirmānī, in the first place because they gave rise to a valuable commentary on the part of the present head of the Shaikhī school, which is given at the end of these selected passages; and in the second place because, in condensation, these two pages recall a few essential themes.

Above all, the idea of a world whose "history" has a vertical axis and is not seen in the horizontal perspective of an indefinite evolution. The history of this world, "in the Gothic style," is not that of an *irreversible* evolution, but of a progressive *reversion*. Our concept of "historical causality" no longer applies. This vertical orientation toward the celestial pole represented by Hūrqalyā is determined by the idea of a *descent*, followed by a *reascent*: the first is the fall of the intelligence (*Ennoia*) down to the terrestrial world, and this is the cycle of cosmo-genesis. The second is the ascent from our world, which began with the cycle of prophecy inaugurated by Adam. The traditional gnostic thesis introduces the further idea (echoed by Franz von Baader, as we recalled above) that even the Biblical history of Adam only begins on the day after a catastrophe whose magnitude we can perhaps no longer conceive.

Shīʿite consciousness superimposes the perspective of Imāmology on that of Prophetology: the *parousia* of the hidden *Imām*, as the definitive theophany, the advent of pure spiritual religion. For the Shīʿite adept, to attain personal consciousness of this *parousia* is to enter into Hūrqalyā, and that means into the world where the Imām becomes visible to the inner perception, where eschatology breaks through *into the present*. Hence

* Extract from the same work, Vol. II, Pt. 3, pp. 274–75.

the theme of the last pages translated below: *Hūrqalyā and the Shīʿite faith.*

Know that when God had created Intelligence (*Ennoia*) on the first of the Days, he said to it: "Now go down." And Intelligence went down until it reached our world. The final stage of its descent coincided with the time of Adam. Then the call resounded in the world through the mouth of Ḥaẓrat Adam and through the mouths of all those who summon men to God: "Now turn around and go up again." At the time of the Descent, those who spoke for God were cosmic expressions in the language of cosmo-genesis. At the time of the Ascent they were inspired expressions in the language of prophecy. The world undertakes its ascent, its gradual return, thanks to the prophetic language of the Messengers. If it should happen that past times are revealed to you, you will see them under your feet, vertically, not beside you, horizontally.

The adventure of our world is the adventure of someone who has to be brought up from the bottom of a well. Moment by moment he reaches a certain level in the well; from level to level he comes to the upper level.[23] At each moment the level he has passed is under his feet. Whoever knows how to look with the organ of inner sight will thus see past times beneath his feet more and more opaque, dense, and dark; whereas, day after day, he continues to ascend time, drawing nearer to the primordial Will and becoming more luminous, more subtle.

Let us imagine a being coming down from Heaven and entering the Sphere of elemental air; descending further, he enters the Sphere of atmospheric vapor; descending still further, he will enter in succession the Sphere of the clouds, then the water of the ocean, and then the bowels of the Earth. Should one then say to him: "Now, climb up again," up he goes, emerging from the darkness of the Earth, entering the Sphere of water, passing through its density, and then traversing the Spheres of the clouds and the vapor one after another. Emerging from the last of these Spheres, he enters into the air in the pure state. His eyes gaze on everything around him; he breathes deeply; he is freed from the restrictions that stifled him; he gives himself up to relaxation in immense tranquility; at last he breathes freely.

And so, this is exactly the spiritual history of our world. For this world had descended into the midst of the Earth, when it was told, at the time of Adam: "Now, go up again." This is the climb it is engaged in making; it is not yet freed from the heaviness and roughness, the darkness and mist. It has not yet come out into the pure air. For these places we are in are the abode of darkness. And it is in darkness that one must seek a religion, behave in a certain way, profess some belief. But as soon as men have emerged from these mists and entered into pure air, they gaze at the Sun, the face of the Friend, the Imām; then they contemplate its lights uncovered and unveiled, without needing to dissemble. For the laws are no longer laws; religion is no longer religion; institutions are no longer institutions.[24]

What is needed, therefore, is for us ourselves to reach the spiritual level where the Friend, the Imām, becomes visible. The Imām cannot go there before us. If the Imām were to arrive before we were able to recognize him, it would be of no benefit to us. The following verse expresses it: "The Friend is nearer to me than myself. But what is stranger still is that I am far from him." Thus, if the Imām came before we ourselves were there, that is, before there was a change in our way of being, we would not even see him; we would reap no advantage from it; it would even be the contrary of wisdom. On the other hand, when our spiritual capacity has changed and we have been transformed, it means that we have come up higher. For, as we have said, we must get out of the well; we must rise in order to reach that place where it is possible to see the Imām. And the name of that place, in the language of the theosophists (*ahl-i ḥikmat*) is *Hūrqalyā.*

When our world, the world which we *are*, rises until it reaches the level of *Hūrqalyā*, it sees in that very place the splendor of its Imām. The Truth is revealed. Darkness is dissipated. Conditions are changed. Do not think that this spiritual reality is far away. It is drawing near, for the signs of achievement and crisis have already become apparent. From the world of *Hūrqalyā* a breeze is blowing, and the perfume of that world has reached the senses of the Soul of the True Faithful. If you are capable of feeling, you yourself will perceive, in the pages of this book and its contents, a perfume emanating from the flowers of the world of *Hūrqalyā*. But be careful! There are a great many people whose nature is weak and deformed, who are inflamed by these perfumes and then become dizzy. On the other hand, a large number of those who by nature fully merit the name of man take delight in these fragrant scents which become the food of their soul. So the evidence is there, God willing! *Hūrqalyā* is near.

XI

SHAIKH ABU'L-QĀSIM KHĀN IBRĀHĪMĪ (SARKĀR ĀGHĀ), FIFTH SUCCESSOR OF SHAIKH AHMAD AḤSĀ'Ī

(b. 1314/1896)

The Celestial Earth of Hūrqalyā and the Shī'ite Faith*

We should at this point give a brief outline of the question of Hūrqalyā, of the description of that universe and its situation among the planes of being. We would like to bring to an end all the difficulties of those of our brothers who, having been attracted to theosophical gnosis, have perhaps not paid sufficient attention to this point. . . .

In order to summarize the nature of this universe, here is what the explicit assertions of our traditions, together with the explanations furnished by our great Shaikhs, have made it possible for me to understand and to set forth in my turn very briefly. Roughly, the word *Hūrqalyā* refers to the *mundus archetypus*, the world of Images (*'ālam al-mithāl*), the world of autonomous Figures and Forms (*'ālam al-ṣuwar*). Although, strictly speaking, the Heavens of this universe are what we designate as *Hūrqalyā*, whereas its Earth is referred to by the names *Jābalqā* and *Jābarṣā*, philosophers sometimes refer to this universe as a whole, with its different planes and degrees as *Hūrqalyā*.

It is also called the "eighth climate," referring to the fact that the philosophers and learned men of former times divided the Earth into seven climates. The term "eighth climate" is self-explanatory, since the universe of Hūrqalyā is above all these climates, and is not included within their visible boundaries. Of course, the division of the earth into seven climates taught by

* Extract from *Tanzīh al-awliyā*, Kirman, 1367/1947, 58th Question, pp. 702–26. The work is entirely in Persian.[1]

the ancient sages can be traced to a number of other sources. This division was known to the ancient prophets, and its source is authentic, since we find the terminology used frequently in the traditions of our holy Imāms. The mention of the seven climates recurs repeatedly in the sayings of the First Imām, Ḥaẓrat Amīr. Likewise, the Sixth Imām, Ḥaẓrat Ja'far Ṣādiq, explicitly states in a *ḥadīth* that the world is divided into seven climates. Personally, I would say it is absolutely correct to have called Hūrqalyā the eighth climate, since it is *beyond* our world; but it must not be forgotten that it is also invisibly *in our world* itself.

Briefly, it is evident, not only from the Book of God, but also from the reported sayings of the holy Imāms, that the divine creation is by no means limited to the world in which we are traveling and of which we perceive the visible appearance. There are many worlds. The first verse of the Book declares: "*Glory be to God, the Lord of the Worlds*" (1:1). And elsewhere: "Blessed be he who caused the Qur'ān to descend upon his servant, so that he might be a prophet for *the Worlds*" (25:1). Therefore there is really no doubt that there is a multitude of universes.

Another verse states: "To God belong creation and the creative Imperative" (7:52). So we must distinguish between two things: a world of creation which is the creatural universe, and a world of the Imperative which is the creative Universe. If one meditates on these two universes in detail, each reveals a multitude of other universes, but our purpose here can be no more than to give a general outline concerning them. The creative universe, that of the Imperative, is the primordial divine Will. The meaning of this thesis is made explicit in the traditions which the holy Imāms have left us, but again we cannot go into further detail here. By his Will and his Imperative (KN= *Esto*!), the "Lord of the Worlds" has existentialized the totality of the universes and the totality of beings. Hence true reality, the essences of all things, are comprised in the divine Will, but still in a state of generality and possibility, not of concrete determination and individuation. These essences of things remain on the lower plane of the "world of the Imperative," which constitutes its Earth; this plane can nevertheless rightly be referred to as the "world of the Imperative." The ultimate term of the Imperative is designated as a *materia prima*, which is pure passivity. Sometimes it is called "virgin Earth" and sometimes the "sempiternal world." Sometimes it is called "sea of the *Ṣād*," sometimes the "dwelling place of the *Nūn*," or again, the "world of the heart." There are other names for it, each referring to a corresponding aspect, but there is no time to mention all of them here; those who are interested will find the explanation of each in its place.

So this sempiternal world, the world of essences and prime origin of beings is on this level; it is in continuity with the whole "world of the Imperative" and itself is part of the worlds of Mystery, the unrevealed universes. After this world there is the creatural world, taken as a whole. The creatural world also comprises several planes and degrees. Each degree, within its own limits, forms an autonomous universe, and to all these planes and degrees, taken as a whole, we give the name "creatural universe," "world of creation."

The first of these universes is the world of the Intelligence (*Ennoia*). It is repeatedly mentioned in the traditions, for instance, in the following: "The first thing that God created was the Intelligence." There are many variants of this tradition, which we refrain from quoting here for brevity's sake.[2] The world of the Intelligence is the world of "consubstantial matters," which means that the inalienable consubstantial matter of every being issues from this world of Intelligence.[3] This, furthermore, is the definition we find in the traditions of our Imāms. There it is said that the Intelligence encloses, comprehends all things, and is the cause of all existing things. This all-embracing comprehension and this causativity define everything having to do with the "consubstantial matter" of each being. Indeed, all existing creatural things are so many forms and attributes of the Intelligence. The latter possesses perfect understanding of the whole of its own forms; one can say that it is their consubstantial matter, because it embraces and encloses them. Similarly, clay contains and embraces the totality of vases, bowls, and other objects manufactured from clay. This is what the *ḥadīth* states when it says that the Lord created Intelligence and saw to it that it should include as many heads as are included in the totality of creatures. "Whatever creature Thou lookest upon, that creature is a head among heads, that is, a form among forms."

Thus we understand that the Intelligence includes a multitude of forms, and that creatures are so many forms of the Intelligence. Considered from this point of view, all of God's creatures possess Intelligence, knowledge, and consciousness. All of them fulfill a doxological and liturgical function. "Everything in the Heavens and on the Earth glorifies God" (62:1 and 64:1). Now the principle of this hymnology and this divine service is in the Intelligence[4] for, as it is said, "Intelligence is that through which the divine service is carried out" or again, "Intelligence is the most faithful of the most faithful of beings with respect to God." That is why, if a being performs this act of glorification, it is because this Intelligence in him is fulfilling its divine service.

So, in short, all creatures are forms of the Intelligence; they are so many "heads" created by God for this Intelligence. That is why all these forms owe their stability and consistency to Intelligence, and are inseparable from it. Indeed, "matter" does not exist without "form," nor form without matter; they come to be simultaneously; neither one can precede or follow the other; their existence is synchronical. Yet each of them has its respective rank and position, which it is important to remember. If we say that "matter" ranks before or is "above," while "form" ranks after or is "below," it is because form in this case is taken to mean the "boundaries" and "demarcations" of matter. From this point of view, we can say that matter is first, while form is second, since matter must *be* in order for these delimitations to take place in it. It is therefore advisable to be careful in regard to this "above" and "below."

Indeed, it can be said that the "dwelling place" of forms is "below," that is, on the lower plane of the dwelling place of the Intelligence. And this *place* is what, in philosophical terminology, we call the *world of the Souls*, or the world of immaterial substances.[5] It is also called the world of Forms and Figures, the world of the *Aeon*, and it is adjacent to the world of the Intelligence. The traditional terminology of the holy Imāms gives the name *Malakūt* to this dwelling place, which is the world of the Soul, whereas the world of the Intelligence is called *Jabarūt*, and the world of the creative Imperative is called *Lāhūt* (Deity).

This world is also called the world of the sacrosanct Soul, as it is the world from which the souls of human beings have been extracted. The soul is "sacrosanct" because it remains inviolate and immune from the impurities and vicissitudes of the world in which we are now. It is also called the world of seminal reasons[6] and the world of the shades. One explanation of this world of seminal reasons in which the souls of humans were created has already been given in this book. That is the very place to which the Prophet was sent in order to make his call to the souls heard. It was in that very place that the question and the answer were exchanged with each and every soul, and where from each and every one was received the commitment of faith and fidelity to the initiatic pact. It was in that dwelling place that whoever wished became a believer, and whoever wished became an infidel.[7] Finally, this is the world we call the world of resurrection and reassembly, because this is the place to which human beings go back at the time of their Return, each one returning to the place from which he was created, no higher.

Thus this "dwelling place" has many names. Each philosopher uses a name corresponding to his point of view. Testimonies concerning these different planes or degrees abound in our traditions also, but this is not the place to discuss them. After all, those who practice theosophy know what we mean; as for the others, they would understand neither a general account nor a detailed exposé; if anything, a detailed exposé at this point would only make the problem more difficult.

So, this world which is the *world of Forms* is called the world of the sacrosanct Soul. You must often have met with the expression universal Soul, Soul of the world, in the works of the philosophers. Their meaning corresponds to what we ourselves understand as the world of the Intelligence and as the world of the Soul taken together, for they are considering "matter" and "form" simultaneously. In saying *soul* they are referring to the rank of the form; when saying *universal* they are referring to conceptual reality and to the universality of the Intelligence. This merits our close attention, because these developments will not be explained so simply elsewhere. Although I am not a "philosopher" by profession, at least I am the son of a philosopher, and the sons of philosophers perhaps understand the terminology of their fathers better than others.

In any case, everything that has just been said was more in the nature of a parenthesis, for the rank or dwelling place of God's prophets is above the rank or dwelling place of human souls. This does not mean that they belong to the world of pure Intelligence, for the number of the nativities in that world is limited to the *Fourteen* most sacred souls.[8] No, the dwelling place of the prophets is the abode called the world of the Spirit and the Spirit of the *Malakūt*. This world of the Spirit is an intermediary (a *barzakh*) between the world of the Intelligence and the world of the Soul, because it possesses neither the substantiality of the Intelligence nor the plasticity and individuality of the soul. A *barzakh* is an intermediary between two worlds. It would be difficult, indeed superfluous, to go deeply into the idea at this point. Our purpose is limited to explaining that there is an intermediary, a *barzakh*, between the world of the Intelligence and the world of the Soul, because such is the divinely ordained structure and because it is a philosophical constant that God's universe contains no hiatus. The worlds are connected with one another; they form a continuous whole. Whenever one is considering two universes, there must be a *barzakh* between them. A verse in the Qur'ān states: "He has separated the two confluent seas. Between them there is a *barzakh*; the one does not overflow into the other" (55:19–20).

What can be said in broad outline about the world of the Soul is that it is the world of those Forms which are the primary Forms of the world of the Intelligence. These are sacrosanct Forms, that is, protected from the impurities and blemishes of our world, and they exist in an autonomous state. From this point of view, therefore, it is fitting to speak of the world of sacrosanct Souls, for they are wholly exempt from the accidents and opacity of our world, and have no connection with the opaque and accidental matters and forms of our world. This, in relation to this world of ours, is called the "higher world." Ḥaẓrat Amīr, the First Imām, in describing this world of the Soul, speaks of "Forms stripped of all matter, free from everything other than what is potential, and purely virtual." He quotes a variant of the same *ḥadīth*: "Forms transcending all matter." And these two lessons contain an equally authentic meaning.

These statements signify that the Forms in question are indeed Forms stripped of all earthly, accidental, and corruptible matter, or else are Forms transcending such matter. In accordance with this *ḥadīth*, as with the explicit meaning of the other traditions received from the holy Imāms, it is quite evident that one must take "matter" to mean corruptible and accidental matter, in the state in which we find it in our earthly world. This by no means implies that these Souls are "Forms without matter," since it is out of the question for a Form to exist without matter. Matter and Form are the two factors constituting the substantiality of each being and each thing; they cannot be dissociated from one another. If one of them were missing, then the thing itself would cease to exist, would become pure nonbeing. The expression "matter" as used in the above *ḥadīth* refers to accidental matters, subject to the conditions of time and of becoming. And the purpose of this same *ḥadīth* is to affirm that the sacrosanct Souls in no wise owe their origin to these accidental, earthly, and corruptible matters, and that they have autonomous existence.

So the theologian philosopher Mullā Ṣadrā (Ṣadruddīn Shīrāzī) is quite mistaken in thinking that human souls can from the beginning be associated with these corporeal matters, subject to the conditions of time and becoming. His system presupposes a series of transformations: the mineral itself becomes vegetable, which in turn passes to the animal state; the animal finally becomes a human being. This system is contrary to the teaching of the Book of God and the traditions of our Imāms.

The same could be said of those literal and superficial theologians who are incapable of seeing in the word *Man* anything other than an expression designating material bodies composed of physical elements. They claim that it is these same accidental and corruptible, dense and opaque bodies that "return" to the other world, on the pretext that the *Return* has to be understood as a "bodily resurrection."

They make a serious error, simply by forgetting that the reality of what makes a body, its corporeity, is not limited to that of the accidental and corruptible bodies of our earthly world. What God's Book and the prophets indicate is the existence of primordial or archetypal human bodies. They *originate* in their own world, the world of the Soul; as for their *matter*, it comes from the world of the Intelligence. Ḥaẓrat Amīr, the First Imām, in the *ḥadīth* which tells of his interview with Kumayl on the condition of human souls, declares that "the *matter* of these souls consists of the energies they receive from the Intelligence and which are *substantialized* in them." He declares further in the same *ḥadīth* that the human soul by no means owes its origin to visible physical bodies. It is neither the "sap" nor the subtle element of the body of flesh. It can be compared neither to the perfume given out by a flower, nor to the essence extracted from a rose. Far from it! These souls are Forms subsisting independently of all corruptible physical matter, and existing in their own world in an autonomous state.

As for the manner in which souls make their entrance into this world, it should be compared to the manner in which the image of the human person makes its entrance, its appearance, in the mirror which reflects it, or else with the light of the sun that falls from on high on this mirror or on the surface of calm water. Neither the matter nor the form of the image you see in the mirror originates in the mineral substance of the mirror. No, this image possesses, separately and in itself, its own matter and its own form, which are in no way part of the mirror and in no way derive from its mineral substance, for they neither blend with it nor alter it. This Image has autonomous existence; it was created separately. If the mirror is there, the image is projected on it and mirrored in it, looks at itself in it. If the mirror is not there, the Image nonetheless subsists in itself and for itself; it subsists in its own world, with its own matter and its own form. Doubtless it will be said that it is "a part of this world." But to say that it is dead "to" and "for" this world in no way means that it is dead "to" and "for" its own world. Quite the contrary; there it is indeed, living and close to the divine, which guarantees its subsistence. The phenomenon of death took place in this world, not in the world beyond.

True, the individuality *post mortem* has no longer any form (*maẓhar*) in which to manifest in our world unless God wishes it to have an epiphanic form a second time in this world, to live and be visible here a second time. Such a case is possible, and such an event has occurred. For instance, there are the accounts of those raised from the dead by Jesus, or the resurrection of the prophet ʿUzayr (Esdras) mentioned in the Qur'ān (9:30), the traditions concerning the resurrection of Shem, son of Noah, and still others attributed to the intercession of the holy Imāms.

Briefly, these are the themes which should be expanded for a thorough discussion of the question we have just opened. However, our contribution must be limited to stressing certain aspects of the cosmology that includes the totality of these universes, by way of an introduction that will enable us to understand the *whereabouts* of the world of Hūrqalyā.

To sum up: 1) The first of the universes is the world of the creative Imperative, which is the sempiternal world and the world of pure essences. 2) Then there is the world of the Intelligence, which is the Abode of "consubstantial matters" granted respectively to the being of every being. 3) Next the world of the Spirit, which is the intermediary, the *barzakh*, between the world of the Intelligence and the world of the Soul. 4) This same world of the Soul, which is the world of the Forms of beings. 5) And finally, after the world of the Soul, our world, which is the temporal, sensory, and visible world. The last is the world in which we are at present, you and I, and it is the plane on which all the universes finally converge. The eternal higher Forms, those of the world of the Soul, have at last reached their end on this plane; they have been hidden there in the earthly dust of this world, although virtually they have already departed from it. For this world is the tomb of the higher universes. All the beings who inhabit these other universes have been buried here in the earth. In accordance with the order of the Lord of the worlds, they must shake this dust from their heads and emerge, freed from their tomb; it behooves each of them to achieve his Exodus, to regain his Abode, to return *home*.

Our purpose in this book is only to comment on the state of this other world to the extent needed to characterize the world subject to time. This world of ours is the place in which the Souls and eternal higher Forms become dependent on corporeal, accidental, and perishable matters, and are henceforth connected with them and bound to them. However, these temporal matters of our world, in their totality, are nonetheless an accident with respect to these eternal Forms. Their relation and connection with these Forms are not lasting but temporary. At any moment they may become dissociated and separate from each other. The forms return to their own eternal world, while the corporeal matters remain in their world. That is why, although the Soul is the first thing created by God, every Soul which comes into this world must finally die. That is, be dissociated and separated from the accidental matters that are foreign to it. The Lord of the worlds declares it: "Every soul will taste death" (3:182), "thou shalt die and they shall die"(29:31). Every form, during a definite period, remains "on the surface" of this accidental matter. This duration is what is called *time*, the limit of this Form. Nights and days, hours and minutes, are simply means of determining the *measure* of time; but these measurements are not *time* itself. In itself, time is the limit of the persistence of the eternal Form "on the surface" of the accidental matter of this world.[9]

If this question has been fully understood, I can now attempt to explain the way in which these eternal Forms belonging to the world of the Soul come "onto the surface" of the accidental matters of the perishable world. They "come" there in the same way that the light of the sun "comes" onto this Earth or "into" mirrors, or in the same way that a man's reflection, his silhouette, and his image "enter," come "into" mirrors. Actually, these eternal Forms in themselves never at any time "come down" from their own world, any more than a man himself enters the mirror in which his image appears, any more than the astral mass of the sun descends onto the Earth from the sky. That is why the eternal human soul itself, which was created in the world of seminal reasons, and with which, in its own world, the Lord of the worlds exchanged question and answer—when the human being, having been given the power of speech, uttered his profession of Faith to the Lord of the Worlds and the soul was thus promoted to being a "speaking soul"—this soul, I say, does not itself come "in person" and materially into this world of accidental and temporal matters. Its silhouette, its image, its projected shadow is what "comes into this world," as the comparisons already given have suggested to you. In every case the divine arrangement is constant. The visible, the outer, the exoteric, is the façade of the invisible, the inner, the esoteric, and in all divine creation there is no deviation from this rule.[10]

The more attentive you are to the implications of the theme, the better you will understand our intention. Whether we speak in terms of reflection, silhouette, image, or shadow—and we take all these technical terms either from the Book of God or from the traditions of our Imāms—or whether we speak about light, we always take these terms as they refer to the operation of the human soul. Each essence, each substance, has a mode of operation which is proper to it; it also goes without saying that this essence and substance call for a certain perfection and qualification. Because, in fact, everything is created by a divine Will; it *is* that Will. Now the divine Will calls for perfection; so all such wills which created things *are* essentially call for perfection.

Now the perfection of each thing consists in surpassing itself, in overflowing its own limits, or "transgressing" itself, in order to spread, to penetrate into other places, just as the fiery glow of a lamp is the superabundance of its being and of its perfection. Its perfection is its light; its light is the action brought about by its burning, for burning is the generator of light. Therefore each thing has its particular manner of being perfect and of operating. Finally, the weakness and the intensity of the perfect quality of each thing depend on its greater or lesser proximity to the divine Being, which is the principle and center of all perfections. The closer it is, the greater its perfection and the more powerful its capacity to penetrate, to expand, and to blend with everything else. The further it is from this center and from the supreme archetypes, the lesser its perfection, the weaker its operation becomes, and correspondingly its capacity to penetrate, to spread, to mingle, and to produce any action whatsoever.

Philosophers will have no difficulty in understanding our thought. But perhaps, for the sake of beginners, it will be useful if we illustrate it by a further comparison. For example, let us take the invisible Fire; this is an eternal substance, one of the higher Forms. At the very moment when it reaches the surface of temporal matter and when, having become its partner, this smoking mass begins to glow, at that moment the characteristic way of being of Fire is manifested. For immediately it "transgresses" the limits of this accidental, smoking mass; it begins to spread and to extend as far as it has the force to act and to spread. And whatsoever fire it may be, whatsoever the matter on which it feeds—vegetable oil, naphtha, brushwood—whatsoever the matter through which its brilliancy may appear, be it metal or astral matter such as the moon and the stars, or incandescent solar matter, in each case it gives out light in proportion to the rank and degree of these "matters." But it does not itself remain without moving in the place where it has "caught fire"; it extends beyond it, "breaks out" of it, and communicates to others its perfection and its activity. Such is the way of being peculiar to Fire, which is one of the eternal Forms.

However, some of these eternal Forms do not possess perfection and operative power to such a degree. For example, the color black, or white, or red, or some other color. For all these colors are eternal Forms; they "descend" from the secret "Treasuries" of the higher universes; these colors are not temporal matter; they are Forms which manifest, are epiphanized, on the surface of temporal matter. However, after they have thus manifested on the surface of matter, they remain fixed and motionless at the same point; they do not spread, they do not penetrate, nor do they have any further effect, because in themselves they are weak and deficient. A given color proper to a given matter cannot escape from the boundaries of that matter, nor "break out" of it, unless, some perfecting agent having intervened to complete this Form, it then appears to be endowed with expansive force. For example, it may happen that light falls on some color or another—for instance, on glass which is red in color—and heightens the red of this glass; if the glass is moved, it takes the color with it. This is possible, of course, but it does not mean that the color red has spread and been conveyed from one point to another. It remains fixed on the surface of that same red matter.

The examples just brought may to some extent clarify the theme with which we are at present concerned. In the midst of the eternal Forms belonging to the *Malakūt*, the human soul ranks among the most magnificent, sublime, and perfect of these Forms; it is the attestation to the divine Being attesting for itself to the other Forms, which are imperfect and lower in rank. As Ḥaẓrat Amīr, the First Imām, has said, the human Form is God's most magnificent surety for His creatures. It bears witness to the divine Being because it is the fullness of everything proceeding from Him, and it is the perfector of the other Forms; it possesses the maximum of operated activity and of operating activity, as well as perfection; and it is the seat of multiple energies.

In short, our present theme is that the Souls and eternal Forms—each within their own limits—are invested with a specific perfection and operative power. Thus, the divine, total, and eternal Soul is invested with absolute and universal operative power, since all the operations effected by the individual eternal souls are an effect of the operation of the divine Soul. And this absolute operation is what is called in theosophical terminology, *a world*, a world situated at once above our world of temporal and accidental matters, and beneath the world of the sacrosanct Soul. Or to be more exact, it is a *barzakh*, that is, an interval, or intermediary, between these two universes, a *between-two-ness*, a median reality between two realities: an *interworld*. It is not an autonomous world—since it is not substantial, but subsists thanks to the sacrosanct Soul—just as the activity of the person of Zayd does not subsist as a thing in itself, but exists thanks to the person of Zayd, or as the light of the lamp does not subsist independently, but thanks to the lamp itself.

Therefore it is a world which cannot be considered as being a part of our material universe, being clearly independent of the accidental matters of our universe and having a right of origin and a mode of subsistence peculiar to it, which do not derive from this material universe. The most that can be said is that with respect to it the matters of our world fulfill the function of a vehicle, of apparitional form, and of places in which to manifest. It has its own permanent existence above all these material realities. As in the case of the reflection manifested in a mirror: the image is other than the mirror, is distinct from the matter and form of the mirror. If the mirror is there, the image appears in it, if the mirror is not there, your silhouette and your image continue nonetheless to subsist through your person, without having anything to do with the mirror. It is exactly the same in the case of the world of the *barzakh*, the interworld. This world has its own independent existence; if the temporal and accidental matters of our world are there, the reflection of its image appears in them; if they are not there it continues to exist in its own "place" and to subsist, thanks to the Soul. It simply means that it no longer has a form in which it can appear in the earthly material world. To recapitulate, there is the world of the *barzakh*, a world which exists and is permanent; it is invisibly, suprasensibly within our world, and corresponds to it insofar as all the universes taken as a whole *symbolize with* one another.

In the *barzakh*, in this interworld, there are in a perfectly concrete state, Heavens and Earths, Elements, continents, seas, the natural kingdoms—humans, animals, plants, minerals—all corresponding to those we see in our earthly world. We have to be guided by the fact that if we see beings and things in our world it is exactly because everything we see here below "came down" from this other universe. God says so in his Book: "Nothing is which does not have its Treasury with Us and we send them down only in strict measure (15:21)." The divine Treasuries are exactly those higher universes of which we are speaking.

The first of these Treasuries is the world of the divine Imperative, the world where to be is eternally in the imperative: "Be! and it is (2:111)." Every being proceeds from this existence-giving Imperative. The second Treasury is the world of the Intelligence, which is the world of the *materia consubstantialis*, for the *materia prima* of beings and things was created first, and afterwards their form.[11] The third Treasury is the world of the Soul, the place in which the Forms of beings and things are "situated." It has already been explained how the enlightenment of the absolute Soul, the total Soul, rises over the world and how the temporal world comes into existence thanks to the dawning of this light. This *aurora consurgens* (*ishrāq*) and operant power of the Soul, considered apart and separate from the soul, is precisely what constitutes the world of the *barzakh*, the interworld. Sometimes we even refer to this also as the world of the Soul, on account of its perfect likeness in regard to the world of the *Aevum*. Lastly we talk of it as the "Soul in projection," meaning that it is the projected picture of the world of the Soul and the activity of that world. Indeed, it reproduces it so perfectly that the very name of that world has been given to it and this world itself is called the "Soul in projection." The shadow, image, and apparition of all that the divine Being has created in the eternal Soul, exists in the world of the *barzakh*, the only difference being that which stems from the fact that the *barzakh* lacks independence and autonomy. The *barzakh*, the interworld, subsists only thanks to the Soul of the world, the eternal, celestial Soul.

So we understand how it is that the *barzakh* or interworld

undoubtedly exists: all things exist in it synchronically; beyond and above our earthly world in the invisible, suprasensible part of our world, it constitutes a "world-beyond." Whenever Forms from this world-beyond (*ṣuwar-i barzakhī*)—eternal Forms in the constitutive reality of their essence—happen to manifest on the surface of the accidental matter of our world, you and I are able to see them. But such of those eternal Forms as do not appear on the surface of this matter remain invisible and hidden from your eyes and from mine. It is possible, of course, that apart from you and me, someone whose eyes are open and who has better sight than ourselves may see the Forms of this other world. In fact, there is no need for all the Forms of the other world to be manifested continuously and appear at every moment on the surface of accidental, corporeal matters. What is more, it can also happen that their accidental mirror may be broken; the reality of the persons and images nonetheless continues to subsist in their own matter and in their other-worldly form, their reality not being connected with the reality of temporal and temporary mirrors. In the same way, if your photograph is torn to pieces, the picture on the paper vanishes, but as long as you live your image is everywhere where you are, and does not depend on this paper in particular. None of the forms of this other world is effaced from the record of the being, so long as the eternal duration, the *Aevum*, of the world of the *barzakh* continues. You and I, perhaps, do not possess the "eye of the world-beyond" (*chashm-i barzakhī*) which would make it possible to see them; but this is by no means either a sign or a proof of their nonexistence.

For example, Ḥaẓrat Amīr, the First Imām, happened to stop at Wādī al-Salām, and converse for a while with certain persons. "With whom were you talking?" he was asked. "With a group of Spirits from among the faithful adepts," he answered. Moreover, we see how often the following question is asked in our traditional narratives (*akhbār*): "*Where* are the spirits of the faithful believers *post mortem*?" And the answer is always the same: "They are in bodies which are in the likeness of their material bodies." They do exist; they have not disintegrated;

we simply do not see them. This is how the genii and the angels exist; while belonging to the other universe they pass through our world. You and I do not see them; but what is written in the Qur'ān duly testifies to their existence. By right of origin they are inhabitants of that world of the *barzakh*, the other world which we call the *mundus archetypus*, the world of the archetypal Images. They pass through our world, and we do not see them with our bodily eyes, but the Prophet and the Imām, who saw them, are sure and reliable informants, and inform us of their existence. The Angel Gabriel "came down" and appeared to all the prophets, one after the other. The prophet of Islam reports that he appeared to him at one time in the form of the beautiful adolescent Daḥya al-Kalbī, at another time in a different form. The same can be said in regard to the existence of the genii, who are reported to have shown themselves on many occasions to some persons or to have made their voice heard by them. We refer those who are interested in this subject to the book *Madīnat al-maʿājiz*.

In the same way, by virtue of the divine declarations and the declarations of the Prophet and of truthful informants, we affirm that in this other universe, in the world of archetypal Images, there exist animals, plants, Elements, oceans, continents, cities, even Paradise and Hell. The "two gardens covered with verdure," to which the Qur'ānic text alludes (55:64) are situated precisely in this *mundus archetypus*, not yet in the world of the *futurum resurrectionis*. In that very same world of the archetypal Images is the paradise where Adam was created, and from which God sent him forth to fulfill a mission in this world below. It is still not the primordial Paradise of the future Resurrection; from that Paradise no one can be "cast out," and the faithful believers will be there *in aeternum*.

It would require many pages to go into detail, and this is not the place for it. We shall restrict ourselves to discussing some of the degrees or levels of this world of the *barzakh* or world of the archetypal Images. Shaikh Aḥmad Aḥsā'ī and the author of the *Spiritual Directory*[12] sometimes speak about the world of Hūrqalyā, in order to remind men of the necessity to rise up spiritually; they tell them of their need to raise themselves up to this world, that there alone can they contemplate the light of their Imām, only there understand how their Imām acts in the highest degree and manifests himself; in short, it is there that they discover high Knowledge. When they speak in this manner of the world of Hūrqalyā what our Shaikhs have in view is, indeed, this same universe about which we are speaking here, and concerning which so many of our traditional accounts, for example the *ḥadīth* of Mufaḍḍal and others, teach us the manifestations and modalities, by showing us how human beings will be brought together there with the genii and Angels, see them and speak with them.

As for the word Hūrqalyā, whatever its etymology, it designates that *other world*, some of whose characteristics we have described in the course of the present book. Let us add, for greater clarity, that the Earth of Hūrqalyā is situated on the lower level of the *mundus archetypus*,[13] on the boundary between our terrestrial world and the world of material realities. We still need to mention certain of the Qur'ānic verses and traditional accounts about the modalities peculiar to this universe, for as we know, our Shaikhs make no pronouncements on their own authority.

In the Sūra of the Cave it is said: "They will question you about Alexander. . . . He walked until he reached the setting Sun; and he saw it setting in muddy water, near which he found a people who had settled there. We said to him: 'O Alexander! will you punish them or treat them with kindness?'—and he walked until he reached the rising Sun; and he saw it rise on a people to whom we had given no veil to protect themselves from it. . . . And he walked until he reached a place between the two embankments, before which he found a people who hardly understood a word. They said to him: 'O Alexander! Gog and Magog are spreading corruption over the Earth.' "

Here we must refer you to many traditional accounts commenting on these and other verses; traditions which, by allusion, describe these universes, the peoples who inhabit them, the living religions existing there, how these peoples live, what divine services they practice, what knowledge is theirs, and what are their beliefs, what the degree of their faith and devotion to the Very-Pure Imāms, who are the guarantors of God for them as for all the universes as a whole;[14] finally they describe how most of these people are companions and assistants of the hidden Imām who will work with their help to bring about the final consummation of the terrestrial world.[15] One would need also to speak about their food and drink, describe the customs and ceremonial courtesies they observe among themselves, the veneration they display for their Sages; we could also quote some descriptions of their duties, and their buildings, houses, and castles.[16]

Moreover, we have traditions that inform us about the topography of that universe, its continents, oceans, and mountains, the permanent buildings, the tents which are pitched there, and the peoples who dwell in it. We owe traditions of this kind to Salmān Pārsī, Abū Dharr, Jābir, and several other companions of Ḥaẓrat Amīr, the First Imām; they have already inspired long commentaries. From them we also learn that so far as they themselves are concerned, these people do not recognize any divine testimony other than that of the Very-Pure Imāms, and reject with loathing this or that deceptive pretender. Indeed, if we desired to extract all this information from the Qur'ānic *tafsīr* and collected traditions and bring it together in some *corpus*, we would have to write an immense volume. But God be praised! This is a theme which is not denied by the learned among the *Muslimūn*; we are rejecting neither the traditions nor the verses of the Book. We are trying to understand their meaning. It is true that this traditional information contains obscurities and difficulties, the key to which is preciously guarded by those who are learned in *this* knowledge. It is not necessary for us to know all the details, but it is important that we give our assent, both inner and outer, to what they have said about it. We will quote two or three of these *ḥadīth*.

We read in the *Kitāb al-mubīn*, according to the *Biḥār al-anwār*,[17] this *ḥadīth* which comes to us from the First Imām, 'Alī ibn Abī-Ṭālib, through the intermediary of Ḥaẓrat Abū

ʿAbd Allāh (Jaʿfar Ṣādiq, the Sixth Imām), from the august father of the latter (Muḥammad Bāqir, the Fifth Imām), and from ʿAli ibn al-Ḥusayn (the Fourth Imām): "The Lord possesses a city beyond the West which is called *Jābalqā*. Seventy thousand peoples dwell in this city of *Jābalqā*. Not one among them but symbolizes with some community here below. Not for one instant have they weakened in their pact with God. Whatever they do or say, they never fail to execrate the first usurpers, to dissociate themselves from them, and to affirm their devotion and passionate love for the members of the Family (*ahl-i bayt*) of God's Messenger."

From the Second Imām, Ḥasan ibn ʿAlī, the following saying is reported: "God possesses two cities, one to the West, the other to the East, at whose summit there rises an iron fortress. Encircling both of these cities there is a surrounding wall containing one million golden gates. Seven million languages are spoken there, each different from the other. I know all of these languages, just as I know everything within these two cities and everything contained in the space between them. They know no other guarantor of God than my brother Ḥusayn and myself."[18]

Lastly, I would like to mention the *ḥadīth* which my own master[19] relates in his short work answering Mīrzā Ṣādiq Khān Pīrniyā, in which several of the characteristics of this universe and its cities are described. This *ḥadīth* is somewhat lengthy, but I wish to quote it here precisely because of the detailed descriptions of these universes, which may contain some useful teaching for our brothers.

The following is told about Muhammad ibn Muslim.[20] He said: "I was questioning Abū ʿAbd Allāh (namely, the Sixth Imām, Jaʿfar Ṣādiq) about the heritage of higher knowledge. To what does it amount? Is it the understanding as a whole of everything that belongs to this knowledge, or else is it the exegesis explaining in detail everything that we have been talking about?" He said to me: "In truth, God possesses two cities, one in the East, the other in the West. They are inhabited by people who know not *Iblīs* (Satan); they do not even know that he has been created. At every moment We[21] meet them, and then they ask us for what they need. For example, they question us about how to pray; then we initiate them. They ask us about the one amongst us who will raise us from the dead (the *Qā'im*, the hidden Imām) and they inquire when his epiphany will take place. Their devotion is ardent and their diligence passionate. The wall surrounding their cities is pierced by gates; between each gate there is a distance of one hundred parasangs (*farsakh*). They celebrate magnificent liturgies and devotions. Their invocation and their spiritual effort are so intense, that if you saw them, you would have but a poor opinion of your own behavior. Some of them pray for a whole month without raising their heads from their prostrate position. Their nourishment is hymnology; their clothing is verdant youth; their faces have the brilliance of the morning light. When they see one of Us, they greet him with a kiss; they gather around him and cut out the earth which retains his footprint in order to keep it as a kind of relic. When they intone the Prayer, the hum of their psalmody is heard above the roar of the most violent wind. Among them there is a whole group who have not laid down their arms since they began to await the advent of the one among Us who will be the Resurrector (the *Qā'im*), and they call on God to reveal Him to them; one of them is a thousand years old.

"When you see them, you will find in them only gentleness, modesty, and the search for what brings them near to God. Whenever We are not near them, they fear that we are offended with them. They give all their attentive care in the moments when we come near them; they never show the slightest fatigue or lukewarmness. They read the Book of God as we have taught them to read it, and indeed certain of our teachings, if they were revealed to the people hereabouts (i.e., non-Shī'ites, exotericists, literalists), would be rejected and condemned as so many blasphemies.[22] They question us about all the difficulties which the Qur'ān holds for them, when they do not understand. Then, as soon as We have made it clear, their hearts expand because of what they have learned from Us. They ask God to grant Us eternal life, and that there may never be a time when they would no longer find Us. They know that God has done them an immense favor through the teaching into which We have initiated them.

"It is they who are destined to arise in the company of the Imām, on the day of the *Parousia*, and go at the head of the knights in armor. They ask God to place them among those who give battle for his Religion in Truth. Among them there are mature men and young boys. When one of the latter meets his elder, he sits down modestly before him and awaits a sign before getting up. They have a Path, which they know better than anyone, leading to the place corresponding to the Imām's intent. When the Imām gives them an order they work on it without respite, until the Imām himself orders them to do something else. If they were to invade the space between the East and the West, the creatures therein would be destroyed in an hour. They are invulnerable; fire does not touch them. They have swords which are forged from another iron than the material iron of the world.[23] If one of them were to strike one of our mountains with his sword, he would pierce it and shatter it into pieces.[24] It is with companions armed with blades such as these that the Imām confronts India and Daylam, the Kurds and the Byzantines, the Berbers and the Persians, and everything enclosed between Jābalqā and Jābarṣā, the two cities lying between the Far East and the Far West. But they attack the people of another religion only to call them to God, to true Islam, to the *tawḥīd*, to acknowledgment of the *prophetic* message of Muḥammad and the *initiatic* function of the members of his House. Those who answer the call are safe and sound, and are given one from among them as their prince. Those who reject the call are left for dead, so that between Jābalqā and Jābarṣā, and beneath the whole mountain of Qāf, there is no one left who is not a true and pure believer."

There are so many *ḥadīths* of this kind that we must forgo offering them here in detail. Our purpose, in quoting the preceding ones, was to illustrate the thesis that above this world, which is that of the senses, and below the world of the sacrosanct Soul universes exist which, considered as a whole, are referred to by the name world of the *barzakh* and world of the Return, in the traditional terminology of our Imāms. On the lower plane of this totality of universes, the level adjacent to our material universe, there is the universe which is called the *mundus archetypus*, or world of archetypal Images. In the theosophical terminology of the Ancients, this is the very same universe they called *Hūrqalyā*, namely, the other world. That world is the exact Image of this world—without any difference—as shown by the explicit descriptions given in our traditions and the proofs which the theosophists, especially our own Shaikhs, have established, which proofs are supported by Qur'ānic verses and our traditions. Indeed, they have shown that those universes resemble and correspond to this universe of ours, which is the world of sensory phenomena. However, there is a difference, in that our sensory universe is the universe of ephemeral accidentals; in it the deterioration of forms and matters increases from day to day, from hour to hour; or rather, every minute some change for the worse takes place.

On the other hand, no deterioration takes place in those higher and eternal universes, where matters and forms possess an essential reality and where nothing is accidental. Since matter and form possess an essential reality there, they remain forever united; they cannot be dissolved or disassociated. There is neither past time nor future time there, nor is there morning or evening after the manner of our world. By that very fact death is unknown there. Every being, every thing, continues to exist there in its eternal form. Paradise and the people of Paradise are eternal, alive forever, just as the people of Hell endure forever in their Gehenna. All continue to exist in the identity of their form; in this eternal universe a faithful adept can never become an unbeliever, nor can an unbeliever be transformed into a faithful adept; in this sense they are no longer subject to the obligations of the Law, to the bondage of works, to the acquiring of merits. Thus, everything there is different from our world, where black can become white, white can become green, and so on.

Nevertheless, in the interworlds that precede the higher universes, that is, in the worlds of the *barzakh*, the worlds of *Hūr-*

qalyā, the situation is intermediate. It is quite unlike the situation in our world of sensory phenomena, where forms and matters deteriorate and vanish rapidly and at every instant. Nor is the situation stable and permanent, like that of the higher universes, which are lasting and perdurable. It is a between-the-two, precisely an interworld. This is doubtless a difficult thing to perceive and understand for one who does not possess the organ of perception and understanding. The unlimited duration of these universes of the *barzakh* contains gradations which are likewise unlimited, and which are not like the measurements of this world of ours. In our traditions, the duration of these worlds is often interpreted in terms of millennia. We learn from the traditions that in these worlds the faithful adept sees his posterity increase to a thousand children; according to some the number is even greater. In fact, these symbolic expressions are intended to suggest a kind of magnitude which is not our ordinary measurement. The days and the years are different from our earthly accidental days and years, which follow one another and replace one another. We lack the means of comparison.[25] All of that will be made manifest in the days of the *parousia*, that is, in the days of the Epiphany of the Imām, when the Earth dwellers will arise and be transported to the heights where they will become Hūrqalyāvīs, that is, inhabitants of the Earth of Hūrqalyā. Then, the knowledge of this other world and the nature of its people will be revealed. The Imām will reign over them for 50,000 years.[26] Many things of this kind concerning the characteristics of this other world can be read in numerous traditions that describe the circumstances of the Imām's Epiphany. We cannot go into detail here.

How we are to understand this "being transported to the heights," our metamorphosis into Hūrqalyāvīs, or inhabitants of Hūrqalyā, is precisely what Shaikh Muḥammad Karīm Khān Kirmānī alludes to in his "spiritual directory."[27] It has nothing whatsoever to do with intentionally abandoning this world, of changing at present the status and conditions of the organic body composed of terrestrial elements. No, we reach it *in this very world* through which we are at present plodding, in just the same way as some of the Prophet's Companions reached it. We are all familiar with the *ḥadīth* in which Zayd ibn Ḥāritha relates that one day in the mosque he declared in the presence of the Prophet: "Now I *see* Paradise and its inhabitants, Gehenna and its people; my ears hear their groans." And the Prophet confirms his sincerity with these words: "Remain in your certainty."

For the sake of brevity, I have not quoted this *ḥadīth verbatim* here, but we have a number of traditions that can guide us on this theme. The following, for example: His Holiness the Imām Ḥasan ʿAskarī (the Eleventh Imām)[28] was held prisoner in the paupers' caravanserai, which was the special dwelling place of the destitute and the beggars. One of the Companions came to him to pay his respects. Sadly and indignantly he said to the Imām: "You, the guarantor of God on this Earth, held prisoner in the caravanserai of the beggars!" But His Holiness the Imām, replied with a gesture: "Look!" At that very instant the faithful devotee saw gardens, flower beds and streams of fresh water all around him. In rapt amazement he heard the Holy Imām say to him: "Wherever We are, it is like that. No, *we are not in* the beggars' caravanserai." Again, in the treatise from which I quoted just now,[29] my own master, after repeating this same ḥadīth, declares: "As Shaikh Aḥmad Aḥsā'ī has so clearly indicated, the Imām *while* visible and manifesting in this world, was in *Hūrqalyā.* What the *ḥadīth* gives us to understand is not that the Imām did not possess an earthly body, but that he had the spiritual strength to make this world invisible, and to make himself present to the higher world." And this was what he expressed when he said: "We are not in the caravanserai of the beggars."

As for the Very-Pure Imāms and His Holiness the Imām of our time[30]—may God hasten the joy of his coming—whose rank surpasses every other conceivable rank, they remain eternally in the higher universes, both during the life they spent on earth and also in their existence after death. What is more, they are the divine testimony, the guarantors of God, for the peoples of these higher universes, who recognize no other guarantor of

God than them. What this teaches us is that it is the business of the rest of the community, its earthly members, to attain this point of view, this spiritual level. This is exactly what it means to "rise," to be transported to the heights. It has nothing to do with "flying away" and arriving somewhere in Heaven. Nor does it mean that the physical *exitus* of death is necessary to take you out of this earthly elemental world we perceive with our senses and help you reach this other world. No, what is meant is to die in spirit, to die a voluntary death. It means to get *there* while remaining *in this world*. Of course, there is no objection to interpreting this inner experience and the knowledge of it as a death. But this death is in no way incompatible with the continuation of earthly life, and many traditions allude to this very thing. The following for example: "Know how to die before you are dead; know how to settle your accounts before you are called upon to give an account." The significance of this death is to absent oneself from this terrestrial world, by becoming present to the other world, *futurum resurrectionis*. But this is in no way incompatible with continuing life on earth.

This was precisely the permanent inner state of the Holy Imāms; and such also is the state experienced by their perfect Friends, the "perfect Shī'ites";[31] each in terms of his spiritual rank, either as a lasting and permanent experience, or as a state that makes itself felt in exceptional moments. The fact is that their manner of being is to be available to the Imām; the Imām arouses in them whatever inner state he may desire. Their heart remains at his disposal. And the approach to the day of the *parousia*, to the Epiphany of the Imām, consists in exactly that. The approach implies that this availability continues to grow, until it becomes that of the majority of humans. For this will mean that the eyes of humans are opening at last to the world of Hūrqalyā, and are seeing there the light and royal splendor of their Imām existing in that very place.

For that is exactly what the Epiphany of the Imām means. Is there a single Shī'ite who would agree that the Imām of this time—may God hasten the joy of his coming—is at present deprived of his universal initiatic priesthood, of the royal charisma that influences all the atoms of the visible world? that he is deprived of the sacred prerogative of the divine caliphate, even though others have taken it over? Far from it. We Shīʿites, all of us, are well aware that today the Imām is already the Imām, with all the prerogatives of the Imāmate. You and I do not see this royal splendor, this sovereign dignity, this supernatural power with our physical eyes. But the Epiphany of the Imām takes place for us *at the very instant when our eyes open to the world of* Hūrqalyā, and when we look upon the epiphany of the royal majesty of the Imām in the whole of the universes together.

When the venerated Shaikh Aḥmad Aḥsā'ī, and all our Shaikhs with him, repeat that already now the Imām is visible to them and contemplated by them in Hūrqalyā, the hidden meaning of such a statement is that for those who belong to the world of Hūrqalyā the Imām is recognized as being already invested with the Imāmate, with sovereign dignity and royal splendor. Yes, they recognize him and pledge him their allegiance. But the fact is that in this world, he cannot be perceived by the senses of people like ourselves, and we do not see him. This does not mean that the Imām is not here, in our world. Of course he is here. His presence in this world is like the presence of Joseph among his brothers. Joseph was there, beside them, and in spite of that they did not recognize him. And until Joseph made himself known, his brothers did not recognize him, so our traditions tell us. The same applies in this case. So long as the Imām does not make himself known, we do not recognize him. We remain ignorant and unconscious. But he can only make himself known at the very moment when we are capable of recognizing him, at the very moment when we have attained the capacity for this spiritual consciousness with its prerequisites, that is, when we have opened the eye which is capable of knowing the Imām (*chashm-i Imām-shinās*, lit. the "Imām-gnostic eye") and awakened the senses belonging to men of Hūrqalyā (lit. "our organs of Hūrqalyāvī perception"). Then indeed, at that very instant, we shall see that the whole visible realm is the realm of the Imāmate and of the prophetic message, and that sovereign dignity, royal charisma, and epiphany belong to the Imām.

And it is by living this state experimentally that we see and understand how it is that the sun of the most sacred existence of the Imām *rises in the West*,[32] in other words, where and when the present world has finished setting. One must never forget the *true* meaning, which is the *spiritual* meaning. It must be understood that our world in itself has no "Orient" or "Occident," any more than the sun "rises" or "sets"; its revolution in its orbit is our own revolution around ourselves. Every time we turn away from this world and go forward spiritually toward the other world, the earthly world sinks toward its setting, while the light of the other world rises in the East. What should be understood here by "Orient" and "Occident," is the Orient and Occident, unaffected by the cardinal points of sensory space, and not the metaphorical Orient and Occident of our geography. Thus, a sun "which rises in the West" heralds the hour of the "setting," the definitive decline of this world. And the light which rises is the most sacred existence of the Imām. One should pay close attention to the spiritual significance of such statements. I am no specialist in the hermeneutics of symbols, but I understand and interpret according to their spiritual meaning the words of God, the Prophet, and the Holy Imāms, whose eminence is such that it does not allow anything to be asserted or intended unless it compels recognition of the spiritual sense.

In conclusion, Hūrqalyā is the *mundus archetypus*, the world of archetypal Images, of autonomous Forms. If you can turn your eyes away from the elementary, temporary, perpetually changing realities, and have eyes for nothing but their very Form, their pure Figure, their archetypal Image, which subsists with and by its own matter and its own form, after the manner of the image of Zayd in the mirror, then, at that very instant and as far as you are able, you will have contemplated the world of Hūrqalyā. You will be raised above this world of sensory phenomena; you will have perceived and contemplated the eternal Image, the pure Form and light of your Imām, which is like a primordial Image covering over the entire horizon of this world and everything included between Jābalqā and Jābarṣā. Then you will understand how it is that he alone governs and decides, and how everything and everybody can do no more than carry out his order. You will see all activities and all operations as they are governed by this Image, and as dependent always and forever on the Imām. If the archer happens to shoot an arrow and kills his unfortunate mount, you will understand that it is the Imām who shot the arrow and who sacrificed the mount.

Of course, for anyone who has not been initiated to gnosis, it will be extremely difficult to perceive these hidden meanings. I can say no more about it here by way of elucidation, since my purpose was only to open up a brief survey of the world of Hūrqalyā.

NOTES

PART ONE

SPIRITUAL BODY AND CELESTIAL EARTH

CHAPTER I

THE MAZDEAN *IMAGO TERRAE*

1. "I was walking in the open air on a beautiful spring morning. The wheat was growing green, the birds were singing, the dew was sparkling, the smoke rising; a transfiguring light lay over everything; this was only a tiny fragment of Earth . . . and yet the idea seemed to me not only so beautiful, but also so true and so obvious that she was an Angel—an Angel so sumptuous, so fresh, so like a flower and at the same time so firm and so composed, who was moving through the sky . . . that I asked myself how it was possible that men should have blinded themselves to the point of seeing the Earth as nothing but a dried-up mass and to the point where they go looking for Angels above them, or somewhere in the emptiness of the Sky, and find them nowhere. Yet here is a concept which will be considered extravagant. The Earth is a sphere, and if there is more to it than that, then the place to look is in the natural history archives." *Uber die Seelenfrage*, pp. 170–71. (For full bibliographical data on references, see the List of Works Cited.)
2. *Sīrōza*, 28th day.
3. Concerning the word *spenta*, see H. W. Bailey, "Iranian Studies III," particularly p. 292. J. Hertel (*Die awestischen Herrschafts-und Siegesfeuer*), in accordance with his general method of interpreting the Avesta, regards it as the qualification of a being in which an effusion or effluence of celestial Light is immanent. It should be made clear that this Light is an Energy and that the *spenta* being is precisely one which activates and communicates this Energy; see H. S. Nyberg, *Die Religionen des alten Iran*, German tr. H. H. Schaeder, p. 442. See also Nyberg, *Hilfsbuch des Pehlevi*, II, Glossary, p. 5, s.v. *afzōnīkīh* (*afzōn*: superabundance, exuberant force), where the word is related to the technical lexicon of Ibn ʿArabī, which is common to our emanatist theosophers, whether Avicennan or Suhrawardian.
4. *Garōtmān*, the highest degree of Paradise.
5. Yasht XIX, 16–18; cf. Yasht, XIII, 83–84.

6. It is said that Ohrmazd created the Amahraspands (cf. *Bundahishn*, I, in H. S. Nyberg, "Questions de cosmogonie et de cosmologie mazdéennes," *Journal asiatique*, CCXIV : 2 [1929], 218–19, henceforth referred to as "Questions," I), but he is also the seventh (or the first) among them. It is said that Ohrmazd divided among them the task of creation (ibid., p. 231), but it is also said that all seven together produced the Creation by a liturgical act, that is, by celebrating the "celestial Liturgy" (ibid., p. 237), and that each of the Seven Powers of the Heptad of Light produced its own Creation; see *Shāyast lā-shāyast*, XV, 4 (*Pahlavi Texts*, tr. E. W. West, I, 373), in which Ohrmazd himself declares to his prophet: "*Each of us* has produced his own Creation." The creation of the Archangels is also regarded as an evocation or emanation producing their being "like one torch being lighted from another torch." The first is evoked directly by Ohrmazd; each of the other six is revealed, comes *to be*, through the intermediary of the one that precedes it (*Āyātkār-i-žhāmāspīk*, ed. G. Messina, book III, lines 3–7). Ohrmazd can test them by asking them: "Who has created us?" And Arta Vahishta, the fairest among them, thereupon replies: "It is thou" (see J. Darmesteter, *Le Zend-Avesta*, II, 311); it is true that the meaning of the test is above all a primordial *choice* decided against the Antagonist. And another passage describes the council of the Archangels discussing among themselves in order to choose which of them might be their lord (*Āyātkār-i-žhāmāspīk*, III, 8–9).
7. Discussed above, n. 6; see, among other references, *Shāyast lā-shāyast*, XV, 4; the case occurs so frequently that a list of references cannot be given here.
8. See Nyberg, *Religionen*, pp. 207, 226, where Nyberg speaks of a "henotheism"; I prefer the term "kathenotheism," as used by Betty Heimann, *Indian and Western Philosophy, a Study in Contrasts*, p. 35.
9. See *De somniis*, I, 157, and E. Zeller, *Die Philosophie der Griechen*, III, pt. 2, p. 379, n. 4; cf. H. A. Wolfson, *Philo*, I, 377 ff.
10. See Louis H. Gray, *The Foundations of the Iranian Religions*, pp. 18 ff. (following the great *Bundahishn*, XXVI, 4; Darmesteter, *Zend-Avesta*, II, 306). Concerning the traces of a real iconography, see J. Bidez and F. Cumont, *Les Mages hellénisés*, II, 284, n. 3; L. I. Ringbom, *Graltempel und Paradies*, p. 416.
11. *Bundahishn*, in Nyberg, "Questions," I, 220–21.
12. *Mēnōkē-Yazishn*; see n. 6 above.

13. A sentence such as this is worth pondering: "From the terrestrial light (*gētīk rōshnīh*), Ohrmazd created truthfulness (*rāstgōbishnīh*)" ("Questions," I, 216–17). This sentence alone would suffice to show that one should not translate Mazdean concepts, as is too often done, by equivalents that only evoke the idea of an abstract moralism; for example, when one is content to translate *asha*, *arta*, by "justice." Hertel used to translate it "*das Licht-des-Heils*." The sentence recalled at the beginning of this note can lead to this same meaning by a path independent of the theories of Hertel. The *ashavan* are not merely the "just"; cf. Nyberg, *Religionen*, pp. 133, 368.
14. Cf. *Shāyast lā-shāyast*, the whole of ch. XV.
15. The Angel-Gods of Proclus are the hermeneuts of the hidden deity; their theurgic role as demiurges is one aspect of this essential mediation; there are celestial Angels of creation, generation, and salvation. Their multitude is grouped in choirs that escort the Archangel or the God who leads them and whose Energy they diffuse in those parts of the cosmos which are dependent on his hierurgy and providence. See F. Cumont, "Les Anges du paganisme," pp. 171 ff. When they show themselves to men, "their admirable beauty and the brilliance of their light bring them nearer to the divine splendor." But to say that "man always organizes Heaven in the image of Earth" would be a quite superficial judgment (ibid., p. 164). For what if it were the other way around? Could it not be that man, at least in his sacred rituals, sought to organize the Earth by projecting an *Imago* which is precisely the image of his Paradise? (Cf. with what Mircea Eliade [*The Myth of the Eternal Return*, p. 91] has admirably characterized as "nostalgia for paradise.") Needless to say, a phenomenology of the *Imago* goes beyond the questions arising within the limits of historicism.
16. She is on the same angelological plane as Daēna; she is the *Imago Terrae* as it can be perceived by the soul, the soul exactly conforming to Daēnā, the daughter of Spenta Armaiti. See further § 4, below.
17. Concerning the etymology of the word *Fravarti* (or *Fravashi*), see H. W. Bailey, *Zoroastrian Problems in the Ninth-Century Books*, pp. 107–10.
18. Cf. the Yasht dedicated to them: XIII, 1–2, 9, 12–13, 22, 28–29. Resembling the Valkyries who, lances in hand, make long journeys on horseback, they keep watch unceasingly from the high ramparts of Heaven; see *Bundahishn*, VI, 3, and *Zāt-Spram*, V, 2 (*Pahlavi Texts*, I, 25, 167).
19. Cf. Yasna XXIII, 2; XXVI, 2; Yasht XIII, 80, 82, 85;

Mēnōkē-Xrat, XLIX, 23 ("Questions," I, 204–205); regarding this cosmology in the "Gothic style" emphasizing the archetypal dimension, see our study "Cyclical Time in Mazdaism and Ismailism," p. 168. One quite fails to catch the concept in simply comparing the Fravartis to the "souls of the ancestors"; in fact, such a comparison does not take into account either the Fravartis of the Celestials, of the Yazatas, or those human Fravartis of the Creation of Light whose incarnation is yet to come and who are, nevertheless, invoked in the liturgies.

20. A concept already admitted in the earliest Christian writings; cf. the passage from the "Testament of the Lord," quoted in J. H. Moulton, "It Is His Angel," p. 518: "Cujusvis enim animae simulacrum seu typus coram Deo ante constitutionem mundi stat." Compare the great *Bundahishn*, III: of the five energies created for the redemption of man (body, soul, spirit, individuality, and guardian spirit), the guardian spirit (*fravahr*) is the one who stands in the presence of Ohrmazd the Lord (Nyberg, "Questions," I, 232–33).
21. Ibid., p. 237.
22. Cf. Yasht XI, 21–22, honoring the "body" (*kehrpa*) of each of the archangelic Powers.
23. Cf. Nyberg, *Hilfsbuch*, Glossary, pp. 251–52, s.v. *zām* and *zāmik*.
24. Cf. C. G. Jung, *Psychology and Alchemy*, pars. 393 ff.
25. See our study "Le 'Livre du Glorieux' de Jābir ibn Ḥayyān," pp. 76 ff.
26. Cf. our "Prolégomènes" I and II to the (*Opera metaphysica et mystica*, I, LI ff.; II, 34, n. 75); cf. below, Ch. II, §§ 3, 4, and the texts translated in Part Two.
27. Ibid. and our book: *En Islam izanien*, II.
28. See the table recapitulating all the projected translations, prepared by Bailey, *Zoroastrian Problems*, pp. 75–77.
29. Concerning the conjunction of these two aspects in one and the same "person-archetype," see "Cyclical Time," pp. 140 ff.
30. This Light of Glory, which is preeminently the attribute of the Amahraspands and Īzads, is above all manifested among terrestrial beings in the form of the royal *Xvarnah* (*Kavaēm Xvarnah*, which is also *Farr-i Yazdān*, the divine Light of Glory whose image remains so living for the Ishrāqīyūn theosophers, the disciples of Suhrawardī). The three forms of the *Xvarnah*, that of priests, laborers, and warriors—three forms corresponding to the three sacral forms of fire—are all combined in the royal *Xvarnah* (see Darmesteter, *Zend-Avesta*, II, 615 ff., introduction to Yasht XIX).

31. This identification of the *Xvarnah* with the soul, the consequences of which are considerable, has been stressed by H. H. Schaeder in the footnotes to his translation of a passage of the great *Bundahishn* in respect to anthropogony; see R. Reitzenstein and H. H. Schaeder, *Studien zum antiken Synkretismus aus Iran und Griechenland*, p. 230, n. 1.
32. Cf. our translation of *Pand Nāmak i Zartusht*, pp. 144–45 (unhappily, published five years after we submitted it, without our having the opportunity to revise either the manuscript or the proofs. While we were grateful to our Zoroastrian friends for publishing it, we have to apologize for the many typographical errors, inevitable but catastrophic).
33. Cf. *Bundahishn*, XI (*Pahlavi Texts*, I, 32 ff.); F. Spiegel, *Avesta, die heiligen Schriften der Parsen*, III, 53; F. Justi, *Der Bundehesh*, p. 214.
34. Cf. Vendidād XIX, 129 ff.; Vispered XI, 1; Ringbom, *Graltempel*, pp. 279 ff.
35. Cf. *Dātistān-i-Dīnīk*, XXXVI, 3–6 (*Pahlavi Texts*, II, 78–79). Darmesteter (*Zend-Avesta*, II, 547, n. 265) also interprets the names of the six heroes: to the west, he "who teaches the way to the light"; to the east, he "who teaches the way to the sun"; to the south, he "who magnifies the Glory" and "who spreads the Glory"; to the north, he "who prays his wish" and "who has the wished-for benefit."
36. Thanks to a mythical animal now preserved in a secret place until the *Frashkart*, when he must be sacrificed and his body used to make the potion of immortality.
37. We mention in this connection the presence in Mazdaism of an ecumenical feeling of the "invisible Church." Since Zarathustra, with his revelation, was sent only to Xvaniratha, all those in the other keshvars who are believers cannot be so as direct adepts of Zarathustra; they are so in an intermediate way, that is to say, in the same way as the first adherents to the pure primitive faith (*Pōryōtkēshān*); having been created by Ohrmazd, they have preserved this purity, living according to the Mazdean religion without knowing it and forming an "invisible community" together with the Zoroastrian believers (cf. Spiegel, *Avesta*, III, 239, n. 1). This is why the *Afrīn Gāhanbār* (in Darmesteter, *Zend-Avesta*, III, 180) mentions "the good beings of the seven keshvars, those who believe in the good and pure Daēnā of the *Pōryōtkēshān*"; their Fravartis are also mentioned (Yasht XIII, 17).
38. See Yāqūt, *Muʿjam al-buldān*, I, 25; cf. the use of this method

of representation in the case of Bīrūnī, *Kitāb al-tafhīm*, ed. Humāyī, p. 196.

39. The method suggests many connections with other projections of mental Images. The very name "Xvaniratha" evokes the image of a wheel, a central wheel surrounded by six others, the whole world having, in its turn, the form of a wheel. The six boundaries between the keshvars can be imagined as starting from Xvaniratha (like spokes from the hub). The entire earth surrounding the central keshvar is thus divided into six sections corresponding to six arcs of a circle on the periphery of the world (cf. Fig. 1). In its turn, through a new division, the terrestrial circle can be placed in correspondence with the celestial circle, which is divided into twelve regions, the six keshvars being thus placed in direct relation with the signs of the Zodiac. This same method of figuration of the *medium mundi* is also found in the West (in a ninth-century manuscript). These figures from Iranian or Christian sources are analogous to the one known in Buddhism as *bhabacakra* (the wheel of life and death). For all of this, see Ringbom, *Graltempel*, pp. 279–85, and H. Leisegang, *La Gnose*, J. Gouillard, p. 22; pl. II, p. 16. Of course, the complex of intentions differs from one to the other, but to the extent that the Buddhist diagram (in which the "six fields between the spokes of the wheel represent the six forms of existence of all beings") was also used as a plan of terrestrial divisions, the method of representing the Earth with seven keshvars can be considered as a construction analogous to a *mandala*; for the instrument of meditation to be perfect it is sufficient, in addition, to inscribe in it the figures and names of the six Saoshyants-Bodhisattvas mentioned above (cf. the arrangement of the seven archangels in certain Russian icons).
40. Louis Massignon, in a very valuable treatise, was the first to have brought out some suggestive homologies (cartography, the art of gardening, methods of writing); see "Comment ramener à une base commune l'étude textuelle de deux cultures: l'arabe et la gréco-latine," pp. 137 ff.
41. Enclosed gardens, sometimes immense, the memory of which has remained alive in the Iranian imagination (for a description of them in some classical texts, see Ringbom, *Graltempel*, p. 272, n. 22; cf. pp. 53 ff.). The paradise-garden symbolizes the Earth, just as much as it makes the Earth a symbol. Thus, the Iranian garden, at least as it was and as it remains in its archetype, consists of those quincunxes of trees massed around the central body of water, like the keshvars around the original central keshvar. Their height decreases progressively from the

horizon, which they outline; gathering together and themselves collecting toward the center, they likewise concentrate recollected thought in the mirror of contemplation, which then is silently exalted in the mental vision of the Image, which has finally been rediscovered (see Massignon, p. 137).

42. This was not possible in the diagram of Ptolemy mentioned above; see Bīrūnī, *Tafhīm*, p. 191.
43. Cf. E. Benveniste, "L'Erān-vēž et l'origine légendaire des Iraniens," pp. 265–74.
44. Nyberg, *Religionen*, pp. 396–403.
45. See very especially Mircea Eliade, *Patterns in Comparative religion*, pp. 380–82, and *Images and Symbols*, pp. 27–56 (the chapter entitled "Symbolism of the Center").
46. We might mention in passing that the historians, surprised by these "Events in Ērān-Vēj," have created many problems for themselves. Ohrmazd, the "supreme God" of the Aryans, is certainly a "priest" (Yasht I, 12), but how does he come to be the priest of a goddess and to address prayers to her? What is more, we are reminded (see below, § 4) that another "feminine Angel" of the Avesta, Ashi Vanuhi, is similarly honored by Ohrmazd. It is these traces, together with a new interpretation of a *Gāthā* or Psalm employed as a wedding liturgy (Yasna LIII), which have justifiably led Nyberg to develop the hypothesis that the primitive Zoroastrian community of the *Gāthās* probably lived under a matriarchal system (*Religionen*, pp. 252 ff., 271–72). However, as we have recalled, the canonical Avesta forms a whole, and could have been recited from beginning to end without the pious being struck by the contradictions that might emerge from an analysis of historical "stratifications." To speak of "syncretism" is to oversimplify the question somewhat; we suggested earlier (n. 8, above) the expression "kathenotheism" to describe the intimate process of a lived devotion that is insensitive to these "contradictions." Furthermore, we should never lose sight of the eschatological role of Ardvī Sūrā (parallel to the primordial role of Spenta Armaiti, whose helper she is) in preserving the *Xvarnah* of Zarathustra in the waters of a mystical lake, with a view to the conception of the final Savior who will be brought into the world by the Virgin-Mother Vispa-Taurvairi (see § 4, below). All these Figures give substance to the idea of a feminine Divinity whose presence is precisely in accord with the characteristic features of Mazdean religious feeling. We also wish to point out that Joseph Campbell, editor of the posthumous works of Heinrich Zimmer, recently indicated how one could discover,

in the Zoroastrian dualist reform, the resurgence in Iran of religious factors that belong to the pre-Aryan matriarchal world (*Philosophies of India*, pp. 185–86, n. 6).

47. See Vendidād II, 21 ff.; cf. *Dātistān-i-dīnīk*, XXXVII, 126 ff. According to other traditions (*Mēnōke-Xrat*, XXVII, 27–28; LXII, 15–19) this Var is a place built in Ērān-Vēj, but under the Earth, hence secreting its own light, without any need of sun, moon, or stars. There it was that from among all creatures the most beautiful and exquisite were borne and are preserved. This concept has been rightly compared with the Mandean concept of Mshunia Kushta (Hastings, *Encyclopedia of Religion and Ethics*, II, 702–708; Brandt, *Die mandäische Religion*, p. 154), a mysterious and invisible earth, where live human beings who are perfectly beautiful, good, and happy, by which, after the final catastrophes, the transfigured world will be repopulated, and where, *post mortem*, the meeting with the celestial Image or *alter ego* takes place. The comparison with Mandeism is all the more interesting in that we shall see, below, other later Iranian traditions dealing with the mysterious Earth of Hūrqalyā (*Ishrāqīya* and *Shaikhī* traditions). Now, between the eighteenth and nineteenth centuries, when Shaikh Aḥmad Aḥsā'ī (founder of the Shaikhī school) was questioned about this unusual word designating the celestial Earth where the seed of the Resurrection Bodies is preserved, he answered: "It is a word used by the Sabeans (that is, the Mandeans) of Baṣra." See below, Part Two, Art. IX, § 3.

48. This caused astonishment, as if it were a peculiarity or a contradiction, because of the fact that Zamyāt is no longer named in it! We hope here to suggest a different relationship between the *Imago* and the angelophany, the manner in which the Angel reveals itself in the hierurgical relations experienced by the soul to whom it "shows itself."

49. *Sīrōza*, 28th day.

50. *Bundahishn*, VIII (*Pahlavi Texts*, I, 29–30).

51. *Bundahishn*, XII (loc. cit., pp. 34 ff.).

52. Yasht X, 50; XII, 23.

53. *Bundahishn*, VIII, 4.

54. In order to complete this, we should mention Mount Terak (Taera), the central peak of the mythical Elbruz (Alburz) and center of the world, around which the heavenly bodies revolve (ibid., V, 3–4; XII, 4; Yasna XLI, 24; Yasht XV, 7; XIX, 6).

55. Yasht V, 3 is dedicated in its entirety to Ardvī Sūrā and describes her hierophanies with such exact features that it has

been supposed that they correspond to statues or figures of the goddess "drawn by four white horses (13) . . . having the form of a beautiful young girl, very strong and tall, her girdle fastened high, pure, of noble illustrious blood, dazzling (64, 78, 126). . . . Her head is crowned with a golden diadem, containing one hundred eight-pointed stars (128). . . . Her garments are made of beaver skin . . . it is gold drowned in silver (129)." See also, e.g., Yasht X, 88; XII, 24; VIII, 6; Yasna LXIV, 14.

56. Yasht V, 96; see n. 46, above, and below, § 4—the eschatological role of Ardvī Sūrā preserving, in the Waters of which she is the goddess, the *Xvarnah* through which the mystical conception of the final Savior will be accomplished.

57. *Bundahishn*, IX, 6; XVIII, 1–4; XXIV, 27; cf. Ringbom, *Graltempel*, p. 293 (the pomegranate tree?).

58. *Bundahishn*, XXVII, 4; it is the "head of the plants" (XXIV, 18).

59. Yasht XII, 17. This is the tree in which dwells the bird Sīn, the *Sīmurgh* (Sīn-murgh); cf. Darmesteter, *Zend-Avesta*, II, 495, n. 26 (the *Sīmurgh* which later, in the twelfth century, will become the central symbol of a great mystical poem in Persian by ʿAṭṭār).

60. Ringbom, *Graltempel*, pp. 292 ff., 406 ff., 448.

61. *Bundahishn*, XII, 6 (Aūsīndōm); XIII, 3–5.

62. Cf. Darmesteter, *Zend-Avesta*, II, 633, n. 98. The ray of the dawn *Oshbām* is "that ray of light which comes the moment when the light of the sun is visible, without its body being yet visible, up to the moment when the sun itself appears (daybreak). Its function is to give intelligence to man" (ibid., p. 316). Regarding these two words as having a common root (*ush*, ear, understanding, and also dawn; cf. Latin *aures*, *aurora*), see E. E. Herzfeld, *Archäologische Mitteilungen aus Iran*, II, 90 (cf. Hertel, *Die awestischen Herrschafts- und Siegesfeuer*, p. 17). As shown by Yasht XIX, 66, in the later tradition, the active Imagination seems to have projected and grasped this hierophany in the mountain rising from the lake known today as Hāmūn (on the Irano-Afghan frontier), which is identified with Lake Kansaoya (Kansu, Kayānsēh), and this mountain would then be called Mount Kūh-i Khwājah (Mountain of the Lord). Herzfeld (p. 99) has given a fine description of the mysterious block of basalt that emerges from the plain of Seistan at the light of dawn. This mountain is likewise identified with the *Mons Victorialis* mentioned in the fragment of the "Book of Seth" contained in the *Opus imperfectum in Matthaeum* (cf. G. Messina, *I Magi a Betlemme e una predi-*

zione di Zoroastro, pp. 65–67, 83). Since the water of this lake preserves the *Xvarnah* of Zarathustra in expectation of the virginal conception of the Savior to come (see above, nn. 46, 56), we can understand all the better how Christian exegesis, by having the Kings-Magi come from the *Mons Victorialis*, has valorized the Zoroastrian prophecy. This same mountain is also linked with the memory of King Gondophares, whose image is introduced into Christian hagiography by the Gnostic book the *Acts of Thomas*; this book brings to mind the celebrated "Song of the Pearl," or "Hymn of the Soul," the prefiguration of the Quest of Parsifal. From there it was only a step to identify Kūh-i Khwājah, the *Mons Victorialis*, with Mount Salvat. But, unfortunately, this hardly suffices to verify the hypothesis of a "Pārsīwāl-Nāma," a "Book of Parsifal" in Persian!

63. *Sīrōza*, § 26; Darmesteter, *Zend-Avesta*, II, 316; cf. *Dātistān-i-dīnīk*, XXX, 2.
64. *Sīrōza*, § 39; Darmesteter, II, 321 ff. Here we might mention other figures of "feminine Angels," in connection with eschatological annunciations of dawn: *Pārendi*, especially associated with Daēnā and Ashi Vanuhi (see below, § 4, and Gray, *The Foundations of the Iranian Religions*, pp. 155–56); *Bāmyā* (beaming, radiant), who drives the chariot of Mithra and the third night after death appears to the sacred soul when Mithra climbs the mountain; in Manicheism, she becomes the "Friend of the Light" (ibid., p. 139); *Ushah*, who bears the very name of dawn (ibid., p. 164); *Ushahina*, the special Angel of the hours between midnight and the moment when the stars become invisible (ibid., p. 165).
65. *Bundahishn*, XII, 7; *Dātistān-i-dīnīk*, XXI, 1 ff.; XXXIV, 1–4.
66. *Dātistān-i-dīnīk*, XXXIV, 3.
67. As E. Herzfeld, *Zoroaster and His World*, I, 352, has rather too hastily concluded.
68. This mode of perception is a constant. Thus, the mother of Zarathustra, before his birth, sees in a dream the *Xvarnah* "in person" in the form of a fifteen-year-old adolescent (cf. the beginning of *Zarātusht-Nāma*, a Persian text edited and translated by F. Rosenberg, *Le Livre de Zoroastre*; this book is a long poem composed in Iran by a Zoroastrian in the twelfth century). On the plane of speculative philosophy, this would correspond to the cosmology of Avicenna, which in a way is a phenomenology of angelic consciousness, understanding each Heaven as the "thought" of an Angel. Unfortunately, we cannot here stress this essential correspondence.
69. We have already called attention above (n. 31) to the extreme

importance of a passage in the great *Bundahishn* in which the *Xvarnah* is identified with the soul itself.

70. We call your special attention to an article by Pierre Deffontaines entitled "The Religious Factor in Human Geography: Its Force and Its Limits," pp. 34 ff. On the other hand, when nowadays there is no question of the "earth" being anything but "a support for culture" or a "social function," we can measure the downfall that has befallen the phenomenon of the Earth as it appears to the socialized consciousness.

71. This manuscript is now the property of the Evkaf Museum in Istanbul. It is an imposing volume (31 × 20 cm.) of some thousand pages containing an anthology of the Persian poets, at the beginning of which stands the work of Niẓāmī. It was studied and its plates published by Mehmet Ağa-Oğlu "The Landscape Miniatures of an Anthology Manuscript of the Year 1398 A.D." Of the twelve paintings, eleven are inserted in the portion of the book containing the poetic novels of Niẓāmī. What strikes one is that these paintings have no connection with Niẓāmī's text itself, nor with the customary manner of handling the subject in miniatures of post-Islamic Persian literature, including the themes borrowed from the works of Niẓāmī. The high mountains in the full-page reproduction, the leaping waters of Ardvī Sūrā, the cypresses (this is Zarathustra's sacred tree, perhaps the Gaokerena), the fantastic colors which transfigure the landscape and illuminate it with the Image of *Xvarnah*, and finally—this is a unique example—the fact that there is not a single personage in the composition (the *visionary* soul is precisely the Presence that peoples and inhabits the landscape): all these characteristics and procedures take us far from Niẓāmī and classical Persian miniature. In commenting on the data of the problem, Mehmet Ağa-Oğlu had an inkling of the truth when he referred to certain passages of the *Bundahishn* (to which we have referred in this book); if we take into account certain evidence testifying to the continuance of Zoroastrian communities in the province of Kirmān up to the present, and in Fārs up to the sixteenth century, the idea dawns that the paintings of our anthology could have been made by a Zoroastrian artist. The author of the article quite naturally was led to pick up the motif of the "landscape of *Xvarnah*." We recall the ardor with which J. Strzygowski formerly put into words and defended this motif (*Xvarnah Landschaft*), his intuition of which was doubtless inspired; but to the pure historians it appeared as a deduction *a priori*, all the more irritating because its validity was being discussed on a

plane (perhaps unknown to the author) to which it was in fact foreign. Even if the motif became widespread, as is the way with myths, this already shows that its field of application in reality is not one in which the "facts" are systematized in such a way that they can and should be explained "historically" by the method of causal reduction and material identification. Its significance is more connected with the phenomenology which we have attempted to bring out here. Where the material and causal connections between "facts" are not subject to analyses, there can be a connection between *visions*, which are also *facts*, but different in nature (we have already referred [above, n. 10] to a recent work by L. I. Ringbom, *Graltempel und Paradies*, aiming at a new set of values for the same motif, especially p. 113, n. 43, and pp. 306, 338).

72. Cf. *Bundahishn*, XXVII, the entire long strophe 24.

73. Concerning the liturgical symbolism of this "celestial" botany, see J. J. Modi, *The Religious Ceremonies and Customs of the Parsees*, pp. 373–77 (especially the diagram depicting the way in which the flowers are arranged in groups of eight, and the manner in which they are displaced and exchanged so as to symbolize the exchanges between the terrestrial world and the heavenly world).

74. See *Zarātusht-Nāma* (above, n. 68), p. 22. Cf. *Zāt-Spram*, XXI, 1 (*Pahlavi Texts*, V, 154).

75. Here we wish to point out a small error, which is important from the point of view of iconography. In describing the beauty of the Archangel and his great height (nine times that of Zoroaster), the *Zāt-Spram* (XXI, 8) mentions (if we may believe what we have read in E. W. West) that the hair of the Archangel was rolled up "like the tail of a scorpion." We fail to understand exactly what the learned translator understood when he states (*Pahlavi Texts*, V, 156, n. 8, repeated by Rosenberg, *Zarātusht-Nāma*, p. 27, n. 4) that this is a "sign of duality" since the scorpion (*kajdom*) is obviously an evil creature of Ahriman. But how could such a sign exist on the person of the Amahraspand? The reality is simpler. This is a classical metaphor in Persian lyrical poetry to designate the ringlets and waves (*ẓulf*) of the hair (according to Dr. Muḥ. Moʿīn).

76. Represented by the "garment perfumed with musk" (prefiguration of the body of light of the heavenly Earth) which Zarathustra donned when he emerged from the purifying waters of the river Dāitī (mental anticipation of eschatology, *Zarātusht-Nāma*, XXI), and it is precisely at this moment that the first

theophany occurs; cf. below, the body of the Earth of Hūrqalyā (*jism Hūrqalyī*). It is perfectly understandable that the ecstasies of Zarathustra created the same problems in Zoroastrianism as the heavenly ascension (*Miʿrāj*) of the prophet Muḥammad did in Islam. Was the latter to be understood as an ascension *in corpore* (as by the orthodox)? As a spiritual rapture (the philosophers' view)? Or as in the subtle body (the *Shaikhīs*)? See our study *Avicenna and the Visionary Recital*, IV, n. 26. Now, the Archangel, before leading Zarathustra (*Zarātusht-Nāma*, XXII, p. 28), says to him: "Close your eyes for a moment," and when Zarathustra opens them, he is "in Paradise" (the converse of the man Adam asleep to eternity and awakened to the Earth).

77. Vendidād XXII, 19. Let us also remember that the "temptation" of Zarathustra by Ahriman takes place in Ērān-Vēj, on the bank of the same river, when Ahriman "attempts" to entice Zarathustra from his prophetic vocation (Vendidād XIX, 1 ff.). Ahriman is defeated, crushed by the liturgical incantation (as pointed out above, n. 6, Creation also is a liturgical act).
78. Sometimes it is Mount Savalān, a high peak in Azerbaijan (4850 m.), sometimes the mountain of the dawns (above, n. 62) in Seistān.
79. In the *Zāt-Spram*, XXII (*Pahlavi Texts*, V, 159–62), the place and the heavenly witnesses of the theophany in the case of each separate conversation with the Seven is given in detail: e.g., the mystical conversation with the Archangel Vohuman "took place" on the mountains of Hūkairya and Ushidarena.
80. *De antro nympharum*, 6, cited in A.V.W. Jackson, *Zoroaster, the Prophet of Ancient Iran*; Bidez and Cumont, *Les Mages hellénisés*, II, 29 (according to the testimony of Euboulos in which the initiative of Zarathustra is connected with the foundation of the mysteries of Mithra).
81. See the text in Jackson, *Zoroaster*, p. 236, and *Les Mages hellénisés*, II, 28, 142 ff. Mīrkhwānd, a Persian historian of the fifteenth century, again passes on the memory of this ecstatic ascent to the summit of the psycho-cosmic mountain in Ērān-Vēj. In this account Zarathustra is supposed to have said: "This book [the Avesta] came down towards me from the roof of the house which is on the summit of that mountain" (Jackson, p. 34, n. 7).
82. See our study "Cyclical Time in Mazdaism and Ismailism," pp. 136 ff., on Daēnā-Sophia-Aeon as an archetype-Person; cf. in Proclus, Αἰών as hypostasis and the Αἰῶνες (*The Elements of*

Theology, ed. and tr. E. R. Dodds, pp. 228–29); see also R. Reitzenstein, in *Historische Zeitschrift*, CXXVI (1922), 32, n. 1, and p. 51.

83. The etymology of the name Armaiti (Aramati) is perhaps insoluble. However, it may be possible to come close to its meaning indirectly; for more details, see n. 92, below.
84. See the *Pand Nāmak i Zartusht* (above, n. 32), pp. 144–45, strophe 2.
85. See the text of the great *Bundahishn* in Nyberg, "Questions," I, 237 (cf. this choice of the scene of the *Gāthā* of the Great Decision, Yasna XXX). Shahrastānī, too, attributes the idea of this free decision, prior to existence in the world of material bodies, to a sect which he calls the "Gayōmartians."
86. On this concept (*Spendarmatīh*, *Spendarmatīkīh*) essential for us here, see *Dēnkart*, IX, chs. 53, 27; 54, 2; 60, 4; and 69, 14–15 and 47–48 (*Pahlavi Texts*, IV); these are highly interesting passages, which demand much more attention than we can give them here.
87. Cf. W. Bousset, *Die Religion des Judentums im späthellenistischen Zeitalter*, ed. H. Gressmann, p. 520; elsewhere, however (*Zeitschrift für Kirchengeschichte*, XLI (1922), 174), Gressmann objects to Bousset's view (*Hauptprobleme der Gnosis*, p. 336) that it is preferable to identify Sophia with Daēnā (the first comparison in no way excludes this—quite the contrary, as we shall see later) on the pretext that Spenta Armaiti, unlike Daēnā, has no real demonic antagonist; this merely proves that the distinguished scholar here had lost sight of the Archdemon Taromati.
88. Cf. the curious passage in a Pahlavi Rivāyat, translated by Darmesteter (*Zend-Avesta*, I, 128, n. 5): "One day Zoroaster was standing in front of Ohrmazd, and the Amahraspands were gathered around their chief, but Spendarmat was near him with her hand around his neck, and Zoroaster asked him: 'Who is that creature standing near you, who seems so dear to you? Your eyes never leave her, nor do hers leave you. You never let go of her hand, nor she of yours.' And Ohrmazd answered: 'That is Spendarmat, my daughter, the mistress of my house (Paradise), and the mother of creatures.'" This quality of Spendarmat as "mistress of the house" (*kadbānū*) has been retained even in the cosmo-angelology of Suhrawardī; cf. below, Ch. II, § 1.
89. Yasna XVI, 10; cf. Darmesteter, *Zend-Avesta*, I, 144, n. 17. On Sophia as a "garden" and as "Earth," cf. also J. Pascher, *Der*

Königsweg zu Wiedergeburt und Vergottung bei Philon v. Alexandreia, pp. 58 ff.

90. Cf. *Le Livre de Zoroastre* (*Zarātusht-Nāma*, n. 68, above), XXXII, p. 37 (this conversation should be interpreted in the context of the exchanges which Zoroaster had with each of the Seven; unfortunately, the translation we quote from could be improved upon). Also to be noted is what can be deduced from the mention of Daēnā as "spiritual Lord" (*ratu*) of the "Ohrmazdian" women (Yasna XIII, 1); all the latter are associated with Spenta Armaiti in the liturgical "intention" addressed to her. Now, according to the Pahlavi commentary on Vendidād XI, 5, they are identical with the Angel Artāi-Fravart, who, in her "person," typifies the Fravartis as a whole (see Darmesteter, *Zend-Avesta*, I, 123); concerning the role of Artāi-Fravart at the time of the supernatural birth of Zoroaster, cf. *Zāt-Spram*, XVI, 2 (*Pahlavi Texts*, V, 145).
91. *Dēnkart*, IX, ch. 43, 2.
92. Without reopening an unresolved etymological problem, we can approach the significance of the name and person of Spenta Armaiti by cross reference. With E. Herzfeld (though we are far from sharing all of his views) we can compare *Armaiti* (Aramati, Armati) and *Tushnāmaiti* (Tushnāmati, thinking-in-silence; in Yasht XIII, 139, this is the proper name of a woman; cf. Herzfeld, *Zoroaster and His World*, I, 341). We have further to take into account that the direct antagonist of Spenta Armaiti is the Archdemon Taromati (but then we must guard against the fatal tendency of giving only colorless equivalents to Mazdean concepts, secularized by innocuous moralism or quite abstract legalism; Taromati is not merely "thinking outside the rule," nor is Aramati "thinking according to the rule"). We can also note in Yasht XIII, 29 and 73, the association of the words *tushnishad* (living in silence) and *armēshad* (living in quiet), for which Herzfeld (*Zoroaster*, pp. 353–54) gives as Greek equivalents σιγῇ and ἡμέρᾳ ἔχειν. Even if the etymology is uncertain, the representation is definite—all the more so, since *tushnāmatish vahishtā* is substituted for *ārmatish vahishtā* (ibid. and Yasna XLIII, 15), for then the Pahlavi expression *bavandak-mēnishnīh* (perfect thought) is really the exact equivalent of *Spenta Armaiti* (see Nyberg, *Hilfsbuch*, Glossary, p. 33, s.v.), and Plutarch's translation of it as *Sophia* (*Isis and Osiris*, 46) is completely justified. See Spiegel, *Avesta*, III, x, and cf. Nyberg, *Religionen*, pp. 109 ff.
93. Cf. references to the texts, above, n. 86.

94. *Dātistān-i-Dīnīk*, XCIV, 2. There are variants: for instance, the trilogy *Vohuman* (Thought), *Xarat* (Wisdom), *Spannāk-Mēnūk* (Holy Spirit); cf. our translation of the *Pand Nāmak i Zartusht*, § 26, pp. 150–51 (cf. also West, *Pahlavi Texts*, II, 270, n. 3). *Dēnkart*, IX, ch. 60, 5, seems to give preference to the liturgical sense of the trilogy as putting the Spendarmatīkīh into practice. Nyberg had already drawn a like conclusion from the Avesta (the entire series "Manah, Wort und Tat" is connected with the terminology referring to the mysteries; cf. *Religionen*, pp. 163–66). It would be useful to compare our text with a passage from the *Taṣawwurāt*, a treatise on Ismāʿīlī theosophy attributed to Naṣīruddīn Ṭūsī: "His *thought* becomes an Angel proceeding from the spiritual world; his *word* becomes a spirit proceeding from this Angel; his *action* becomes a body proceeding from this spirit." (Cf. our "Cyclical Time in Mazdaism and Ismailism," p. 167.)
95. Cf. Gray, *Foundations*, p. 49, and *En Islam iranien* II, 121 ff.
96. This already becomes apparent and is imprinted, unconsciously and somewhat clumsily, on the physical features of the child Zarathustra: the shoulders are those of Ardvī Sūrā, the torso and loins are those of Ashi Vanuhi, and the breast resembles that of Spenta Armaiti (*Dēnkart*, IX, ch. 24, 3).
97. This designation of Daēnā, here fulfilling the role of the Fravarti "who has remained in the celestial world," would have to be developed in a manner which I am unable to undertake here (cf. Bailey, *Zoroastrian Problems*, p. 115), all the more so as she continues to be represented in this manner even in the late Mazdean tradition in Persian (*ravān-i rāh*; cf. *Saddar Bundehesh*, in *The Persian Rivayats of Hormazyar Framarz*, p. 511).
98. See the references cited above, n. 87, and our "Cyclical Time," pp. 122 ff.
99. Ecclesiasticus 51:13 ff. Cf. *Odes of Salomon*, 38 (M. R. James and H. E. Ryle, *Old Testament Apocryphal Books: The Psalms and Odes of Salomon*), where Wisdom, the heavenly betrothed, is opposed to the fallen Sophia, Achamoth.
100. Gressmann, in *Zeitschrift für Kirchengeschichte*, XLI (1922), 158–59; R. Reitzenstein, *Das iranische Erlösungsmysterium*, pp. 240 ff.
101. Cf. Gray, *Foundations*, pp. 70 ff.; actually (since Bartholomae) a distinction in fact was made between two words: on the one hand the "I" the innermost part of the personality, the heavenly essence of man, and, on the other, "religion." The penetrating

analysis of Mr. Nyberg (*Religionen*, pp. 114 ff.) makes it possible to bring back together into one, not two words, but precisely two *meanings* of the same word. However, contrary to the learned author, I do not for a moment believe that the first meaning is the fruit of philosophical speculation, out of place here (after all, no one can decide this except according to his own particular idea of philosophy). For if we are told (p. 114), as regards the meaning of "to see" (*schauen*), "It has nothing to do with vision in the ordinary sense. The word means solely *religious vision* and the organ through which man experiences the divine, thus a *visionary sense*, an *inner eye*, a ray of light issuing from the innermost depth of man, a ray which, being itself divine, is united with the light," then somebody might object that here we are right in the midst of philosophical speculation! Far from raising an objection, we are delighted with the explanation and we return to the first and condemned meaning, on condition that the "I" be given a depth of meaning other than that of rational psychology or current experimental psychology.

102. Thus the word *Dīn* (the Pahlavi form of the Avestan Daēnā) has finally come to mean "religion." However, the "subliminal" religious consciousness is necessarily different from the complex attached in the West today to the word "religion" (the "*personal*" figure of Dīn continues to exist). That is why it is important in translation to retain the proper name, even in its Avestan form (as we have already done in our translation of the *Pand Nāmak*).

103. Cf. *Odes of Salomon*, 33, in which the Virgin Sophia proclaims: "I am your Judge," or again (in Syriac) "your Faith (your Religion, your Truth)"; cf. Gressmann, *loc. cit.*

104. The *locus classicus* of the account of the Apparition in the Avesta is Yasht XXII (= *Hādhōkht Nask*); for parallel passages in Pahlavi and Parsi-Persian literature, as well as in Manicheism, see J. D. Cursetji Pavry, *The Zoroastrian Doctrine of a Future Life*, pp. 39–48. In the Persian version of the *Saddar Bundehesh* (ch. 99) there is an allusion to the growth of the soul, the weakness of which is here protected by the Angel Serōsh (Sraosha) during the three days after death preceding the episode at the Chinvat Bridge. The development of the three successive stages (the infant, the seven-year-old, the fifteen-year-old, which is the archetypal age of the Immortals) presupposes an organ of immortality, a spiritual organ, a seed which has been acquired during life and which blossoms at

death. Thus Mazdaism really does contain the idea of a mystical physiology, already alluded to in this book; consequently, it will be well to give close attention to the Shaikhī texts which will be studied later on (see below, Ch. II, § 4), and translated in Part Two, Arts. IX and X. Note, in the same treatise (ch. 46), the saving intervention of Ardvī Sūrā at the Chinvat Bridge, which is to be connected with the parallelism indicated between Spenta Armaiti and Ardvī Sūrā at the end of this paragraph. Moreover, the common characteristics which mental iconography has attributed to Daēnā, to Ardvī Sūrā, and to the Virgin of Light of Manicheism and the Coptic gnostic documents have already been pointed out (cf. Kramers, *The Daēnā in the Gāthās*, pp. 236–37, and ibid., p. 225). The Mazdean and Manichean representation of the descent of Daēnā-Sophia to the meeting with the soul has also prompted comparisons with the theme of the "descent of Amithaba" in Pure Land Buddhism.

105. Cf. n. 82 above. We would like to call attention to the following: in the *Saddar Bundehesh* (ch. 99) the radiant Apparition answers the astonished soul: "I am your own good Action." The "imagery" is none the less quite concrete: "She puts her arm around his neck, and both enter into Paradise, filled with an immense gladness and an immense quietude." This feature and many other similar ones should save us from confusing Figures like this with what are ordinarily called "allegory" or "personification." These terms refer to a process of abstraction which differs *toto caelo* from the mode of perception that is peculiar to angelology. The holy action (or faithfulness, or knowledge, or any other Mazdean virtue) is perceived by the *Imago* which *from the beginning* causes the mental *apparition* of the heavenly person to be virtually present to the soul. This is something quite different from the *appearance* of a person imposed upon us by allegorical personification. That is why, for example, it is stated in the great *Bundahishn* (Nyberg, "Questions," I, 235): "From Arshisvang [= Ashi Vanuhi] proceeds the splendor of the piety which gives access to Paradise" (and not the opposite). If the Apparition can answer: "I am your Action," that is because the *Xvarnah* is the divine principle (existing prior to the body) which confers on a being the capacity for autonomous action (*xvēshkārīh*, *αὐτοπραγία*), an activity responsible for a task which is absolutely its own (cf. Reitzenstein and Schaeder, *Studien*, pp. 230–31). Thus the Action is revealed at its source, and here Daēnā is indeed shown in the

double aspect of *Xvarnah*, which is both Glory and Destiny, and which she herself *is*. We can say that the valorization of Mazdaism has greatly suffered because of the lack of phenomenology in its interpretations.

106. Here again (as in Yasht XIX; see above nn. 48, 67), if all of Yasht XVI, devoted to Daēnā, extols Chisti, we should not speak of inconsistency, but grasp the reason for the transparency of one mirror-image to the other. Concerning Chisti, see Gray, *Foundations*, pp. 140–42; Nyberg, *Religionen*, pp. 81 ff.; Hertel, *Die awestischen Herrschafts*, p. 69 (*Chisti*: active illumination; *Chistā*: irradiated illumination).
107. Yasht X, 126. Rashnu, the most beneficent, very tall and slender, walks at the right of Mithra's chariot; on his left, bearing the offerings, Chisti, very straight, clothed in white garments, the *paredros* of Daēnā.
108. Cf. also Yasht XVI, 15—Hvogvi (wife of Zarathustra) praying that her thought, her words, and her action may conform to the wish of Daēnā.
109. Yasht XVII, 16.
110. Yasht XIII, 107.
111. Yasht XVII, 60–61 (cf. Yasht V, 17–19); see n. 46, above.
112. Yasht XVII, 17–24 (Darmesteter, *Zend-Avesta*, II, 604): "The good, the great Ashi, cantor of the gods, harmless to the just, rose up on her chariot, and pronounced the following words: 'Who art thou, thou who invokes me? Thou whose voice is sweeter to my ear than any of those who have invoked me the most?' " Answering, Zarathustra recalls the episode of his triumphal nativity; then follows the invitation of the "Angel-Nike."
113. See Gray, *Foundations*, pp. 63–66. Elsewhere we have shown how this complicated representation persists even in the archangelical triad of Ismaelian theosophy; see our *Étude préliminaire pour le "Livre réunissant les deux sagesses" de Nāṣir-e Khosraw*, pp. 91 ff.
114. *Dēnkart*, IX, ch. 43, 6.
115. Cf. the text of the great *Bundahishn*, appended to the *Sīrōza*, in Darmesteter, *Zend-Avesta*, II, 318.
116. She is most often shown as the angel of "Righteousness." This may be so, but such a translation merely illustrates this "laicization" which reduces Mazdean concepts to the abstractions of rational and rationalist morals, commonplace enough to fit anywhere at all except in the context of an absolutely specific Mazdean vision of the world. A Western man easily distin-

guishes between a simple act of "virtue" and an act of "Christian virtue." But there is also a "Mazdean virtue" which needs to be understood from this particular point of view. We should come back tirelessly to such an exemplary sentence as the one which was recalled earlier (above, n. 13): "From the terrestrial light, Ohrmazd created truthfulness" (cf. n. 105, above). On the other hand, Yasht XVIII (like Yasht XIX), dedicated to the Angel Arshtāt, extols *Xvarnah.* The aspect which for us is "moral" is only one aspect, even a secondary aspect, of the polymorphism proper to Mazdean concepts. That is why Hertel (*Die awestischen Herrschafts*, pp. 60–64) seems to us to be at least searching in the right direction (Ashi, Arshti: "irradiation" as *nomen actionis*, and "radiatrix" as *nomen agentis*; Arshtāt: "the state of the irradiated being, uninterrupted radiance or totality of what is irradiated"). This may remind us of the idea of *Nūr qāhir* (victorial, triumphal Light) in the philosophy of Suhrawardī.

117. Arshtāt is she who activates and gives permanency to the energy of the *Xvarnah*; she is *savagaethā* (Yasht XI, 16, 21), i.e., according to Hertel (pp. 68–69), "transmuting living beings into celestial fire," *sava* being the term meaning the "heaven of light," insofar as it is the abode of the igneous elements constituting a human being separated by death from his mortal elements. Ohrmazdian creatures derive their capacity for this metamorphosis from the fact that Ohrmazd emitted them into being (cf. Yasht XIX, 10) through that *Xvarnah* which constitutes the core of their own being (their "Glory and Destiny"). But we have seen earlier that Ashi Vanuhi is its possessor and dispenser (she confers and she *is* that Light of Glory); its efficiency depends on her (she it is who "causes to grow").
118. Cf. Vispered II, 2, and its interpretation by Hertel (p. 69); from which Yasna, XVI, 6 ff. (Hertel, p. 65).
119. Cf. the great *Bundahishn*, XXVI, 36, 38; Gray, *Foundations*, pp. 136–37, 172.
120. Of course, in this case the number forty does not determine a measure of physical time; it symbolizes the totality and completeness of the event which is, on the contrary, the measure of "time" (and not the other way round). Likewise, every forty years, in the paradise of the *archetypes* of Yima (above, n. 47, and the comparison is significant), from every human (or androgynous) couple there issues another; Salāmān has to meditate for forty days in the Sarapeion in order for Absāl to appear before him (cf. our study *Avicenna and the Visionary Recital*,

ch. V, § 20); note also the importance of "periods of forty" in Ṣūfī spiritual practice.

121. Cf. the passages of the great *Bundahishn* and the *Zāt-Spram* transcribed and translated by Schaeder in Reitzenstein and Schaeder, *Studien*, pp. 214–43, a distinct improvement on the previous translation by Christensen who, especially in the all-important passage from ch. XIV of the great *Bandahishn* (p. 230, n. 2), failed to recognize the Aramaic ideogram (*gaddeh*) representing the *Xvarnah*.
122. Cf. our translation of the *Pand Nāmak i Zartusht*, p. 145.
123. Thus, this is one of the prototypes of the *xvēdhvaghdas* (marriage between close relatives). Whatever may be the sacred mythical meaning of this custom venerated by the ancient Persians, we wish exactly on this point to note that for the great poet Farīduddīn ʿAṭṭār (d. 618/1221), it was the inspiration of one of his most mystical paradoxes: "Of this mother who begot me, I have in turn become the spouse. If I am called Mazdean, it is because I have made love with my mother." The famous Ṣūfī Shaikh Ṣafīuddīn Ardabīlī (*Ṣafwat al-Ṣafā'*, p. 176) commented on this couplet as follows: The human soul was engendered from the mysterious womb of the Spirits (*Arwāh*, the Fravartis); for the mystic, to return to his origin is to be born again in the heavenly pleroma which gave him birth. This birth is at the same time the aspect and the fruit of his being conjoined with the mother-source of his being, whose spouse and child he becomes at one and the same time. Here we have once again one of these little-studied cases in which the Persian mystic typifies in symbols the characteristics and images deriving from pre-Islamic Iran.
124. *Dātistān-i-Dīnīk*, II, 10–13; IV, 6; cf. LXIV, 3–7: From infinite Light Ohrmazd produced the form of a priest whose name was that of Ohrmazd, whose brilliance was that of fire, and who was as incombustible as the inner part of light; and in the form of this priest he created that essence which is called Man. Cf. Nyberg, *Religionen*, pp. 30–31, 301–304, 391–92.
125. See above, n. 62; *Bundahishn*, XXXII, 8; cf. Darmesteter, *Zend-Avesta*, II, 521, n. 112.
126. Yasht XIII, 141; cf. Nyberg, *Religionen*, pp. 305–306. The Pahlavi (tradition based on Yasht XIII, 128 *in fine*) has knowledge of a series of three Saoshyants (Hushētar, Hushētarmāh, and Sōshyans = Saoshyant), each of whom brings one of the last millenaries (the tenth, eleventh, and twelfth) to a close.

The two Saoshyants preceding the last Saoshyant are also born supernaturally of a maiden who is said to have penetrated into the waters of Lake Kansaoya. Thus there is a whole feminine eschatological series corresponding to the masculine series. Cf. Yasht XIX, 89 (Darmesteter, *Zend-Avesta*, II, 638, n. 125), concerning the thirty immortal heroes (fifteen men and fifteen women) plunged in mystical sleep until the arrival of the Saoshyant, who will then arise to aid him in his work. As another illustration of the archetype that here determines the feminine eschatological series, we should perhaps mention the legend according to which a hero of recent times, Bahrām Varjavānd, comes from the "City of the Maidens" (*shahr-i dukhtarān*) in the direction of Tibet (*Persian Rivayats*, p. 434); could this be an allusion to that kingdom of Amazons to the north of India referred to in Chinese chronicles? (Cf. J. J. Bachofen, *Das Mutterrecht*, I, 521 ff.)

127. Cf. the text of the great *Bundahishn* (Darmesteter, *Zend-Avesta*, II, 316).
128. By an epilogue that corresponds to the descent of the heavenly Jerusalem, symbol of the celestial Sophia, at the end of the Apocalypse. The Abode of Hymns (the *Garōtmān*, highest degree of Heaven) *descends* to the sphere of the stars (the lower degree of Heaven; see above, § 3), while the transfigured Earth is itself carried up to the sphere of the stars. Everything then becomes *Garōtmān*; there is no longer anything but the Abode of Hymns (cf. *Dēnkart* IX, ch. 28, 3; see also below, Part Two, Art. XI, n. 27).

CHAPTER II
THE MYSTICAL EARTH OF HŪRQALYĀ

1. See below, Part Two, Introduction and Art. I, for information on the inspiring figure and principal work of the Shaikh al-Ishrāq; also *En Islam iranien*, II.
2. See our edition of the *Book of Oriental Theosophy* (*Ḥikmat al-Ishrāq*), § 209, pp. 199–200 (see n. 1 to Art. I, below), and in the lithograph of Teheran, 1315/1897, p. 439, the commentaries of Ṣadruddīn Shīrāzī (Mullā Ṣadrā).
3. For details impossible to give here, see our book *En Islam iranien*, I, 51, 100; and III, 197, 198.
4. See the general information concerning Shaikhism, *ibid.*, IV, 205–302.

5. A western bibliography on the "sacrality" of the person of Fāṭima is almost nonexistent. Only Louis Massignon has given it careful thought; see, notably, his two studies *La Mubāhala de Medine et l'hyperdulie de Fāṭima* and "La Notion du vœu et la dévotion musulmane à Fāṭima."
6. For what follows, see Shaikh Ḥājj Muḥammad. Karīm Khān Kirmānī, *Irshād al-ʿawāmm*, III, 194–95.
7. The title *Ḥaẓrat* (literally, "Presence") has no exact equivalent in our language. It is used in addressing high personages of this world or the other; it conveys the ideas of excellence, majesty, and sanctity. It is, therefore, better to retain it and give the reader a chance to become familiar with its usage.
8. For further details, see our study cited above, n. 3.
9. For what follows, see *Irshād al-ʿawāmm* (above, n. 6), III, 110–17.
10. See his *Risāla-yi Sulṭānīya*, pp. 164–67.
11. To Muḥ. Moʿīn we owe a note drawing attention to the word *varj* (= *farr*, *khurrah*, *xvarnah*) and its compounds, and to the fact that its use conforms perfectly to the etymology of Persian authors; see the long account in his edition of the dictionary *Burhān-i qāṭiʿ*, IV, 2265–67.
12. We have dealt with this in detail in our book, *L'Homme de lumière dans le soufisme iranien.*
13. See Ṭabarī, *Chronique*, tr. H. Zotenberg, I, 33–36; cf. Yāqūt, *Muʿjam al-buldān*, III, 32 (*Jābars* and *Jābalqo*!); VIII, 15 ff. (Qāf = *Alburz*); Moʿīn, *Burhān-i qāṭiʿ*, s.v. See the texts translated below, Part Two, Arts. I, V, IX, XI.
14. Undifferentiation generally symbolizes the androgyne; here, the historian, who is not a symbolist and who besides is Muslim, presents these beings as all of the masculine sex; cf. the fragment of the *Gospel According to the Egyptians*, which points out that the reign of death will last until masculine and feminine form but one (M. R. James, *The Apocryphal New Testament*, p. 11; and *The Gospel According to Thomas*, log. 22, 114).
15. See our *Avicenna and the Visionary Recital*, pp. 113 ff.
16. See *The Encyclopedia of Islam*, s.v. Ḳāf; compare the emerald rock (*ṣakhra*) with the Great Rock (the mystic Sinai) mentioned in Suhrawardī's "Recital of the Occidental Exile," in Corbin, ed., *Œuvres philosophiques*. See our *En Islam iranien* II, 258 ff.
17. See above, n. 13, and Ch. I, § 3, the "visionary geography."
18. See *En Islam iranien*, II, 283.
19. Cf. the text of Shaikh Sarkār Āghā translated below, Part Two, Art. XI.

20. As to what follows, see *Avicenna and the Visionary Recital*, § 13, and the notes and commentaries on the "Recital of Ḥayy ibn Yaqẓān," in which the mountain of Qāf, as it traditionally is among the Spirituals, is already the cosmic montain, and cf. *L'Homme de lumière*, Ch. III, § 3.
21. Fritz Meier has devoted a study in depth to this world of the archetype-Images and to the function of the Imagination as the required organ of perception in a very great Iranian mystic of the eighth/fourteenth century, Mīr Sayyid ʿAlī Hamadānī; see "Die Welt der Urbilder bei ʿAlī Hamadānī († 1385)," especially pp. 143 ff., where the schema of the world is in striking harmony with that of Mazdaism: two absolute worlds, that of absolute Light and that of absolute Darkness; the interworld of "mixture," the world of "clarity." The *mundus archetypus* is situated at the lower level of the first.
22. In the southeast of Iran, a little more than a thousand kilometers from Teheran; Kirmān is the usual residence of Shaikh Sarkār Āghā (see below, Part Two, Introduction and Art. XI); there the Shaikhī community has its school of theology, a college, and a small press. As will be noted below, the Shaikhī school has produced a considerable number of works, a large part of which are still in manuscript and unedited.
23. See the Suhrawardī texts quoted below, Part Two, Art. I.
24. See ibid. "All the charisma, all thaumaturgical actions, the meetings of celestial princely angels mentioned in the biographies of mystics, all that refers to the laws of the *eighth climate*, in which Jābalqā, Jābarṣā, and Hūrqalyā are found to be rich in marvels." Our language of today, even philosophical, is so unfit to describe this world of the Imagination as a perfectly *real* world that a satisfactory term is lacking here. We must avoid all confusion with simple "fantasy"; "imaginable" too particularly indicates possibility. We need some such adjective as *imaginal* to qualify everything related to this intermediate universe (dimensions, figures, landscapes, and so on). Then we would have *Imaginalia* (as *original*, not as mere "effigies" of sensory things), just as we have *Divinalia*. And *imaginal* is no more to be confused with *imaginary* than *original* with *originary*. We have already entered into these problems in our book *Creative Imagination in the Ṣūfism of Ibn ʿArabī*.
25. See Dā'ūd Qayṣarī, commentary on the *Fuṣūṣ al-Ḥikam* of Ibn ʿArabī. The text is translated in Part Two, Art. III, below.
26. The *mundus archetypus* is one of the *loci* of the studies of our philosophers from Suhrawardī to Mullā Ṣadrā Shīrāzī and

Hādī Sabzavārī (see below, Part Two). This demands much research; cf. the anonymous treatise in Arabic published by A. Badawī, *Ideae platonicae*.

27. See Shaikh Aḥmad Aḥsa'ī, *Jawāmiʿ al-Kalim*, p. 153 (artificial pagination; an error of arranging the pages in this lithograph gives this place to a treatise which is really the ninth *risāla* of the third part of the Works). See the text translated below, Part Two, Art. IX, § 3.
28. That is why Suhrawardī created the Persian expression *Nā-Kujā-Ābād* (a region which is not *in* a *Where*); the *Where* is hereafter involved *in* the soul.
29. See *Jawāmiʿ*, I, 2d part, p. 136.
30. See ibid., p. 153, where it is confirmed that Hūrqalyā is homologous with the Heavens of our physical universe, while Jābalqā in the Orient and Jābarṣā in the Occident are, in this intermediate world, homologues of our elemental earthly climate. The meaning of other traditions should be more deeply investigated: that, for example, which locates the hell of the earthly world at the east of this world of the *barzakh*, while the earthly paradise is at the west (see "Western Paradise" in the Buddhism of the Pure Earth), the double garden covered with greenery, mentioned in the Qur'ān (55:64).
31. See *Tanzīh al-awliyā'*, p. 709. The translation of this entire chapter will be found in Part Two, Art. XI, below.
32. In the sense in which Suhrawardī uses this word both in his *Book of Oriental Theosophy* and in his "Recital of the Occidental Exile" (in Corbin, ed., *Œuvres philosophiques*), the affinity of which with the "Song of the Pearl" in the *Acts of Thomas* bears witness to its gnostic filiation.
33. *Tanzīh al-awliyā'*, p. 711.
34. See ibid., pp. 713–15.
35. See *Kitāb al-futūḥāt al-Makkīya*, Vol. I, ch. VIII, pp. 126 ff. The translation of this text will be found in Part Two, Art. II, below.
36. Ibid., p. 127, the striking text that describes the ceremonial of penetration into the Earth of Truth, where even the *impossible* is accomplished (see below, Part Two, Art. II). Ibn ʿArabī was right in saying that even what has *rationally* been demonstrated to be impossible in our world nevertheless exists in this Earth of True Reality, first, the coincidence of Representation and of the Unrepresentable, of what signifies and the signified, of the exoteric and the esoteric—in short, everything that makes this Earth of Truth an "absolute affirmation."

37. Muḥsin Fayẓ Kāshānī, *Kalimāt maknūna*, ch. XXX, lith., Teheran, p. 69 (translated below, Part Two, Art. VIII).
38. *Book of Elucidations* (*Talwīḥāt*), § 55, translated below, Part Two, Art. I.
39. *Nūr sha'sha'ānī*, Form of Translucent Light, both resplendent and delicate; the term characterizes, especially in the Ismā'īlī lexicon, the beings of the spiritual and angelic world.
40. See the *Book of Conversations* (*Muṭāraḥāt*), § 208, translated below, Part Two, Art. I.
41. *Book of Elucidations* (*Talwīḥāt*), § 108; see the translation of the text and commentaries below, Part Two, Art. I.
42. See the commentaries of Shahrazūrī and Ibn Kammūna, below, Part Two, Art. I.
43. It has been dealt with in the preceding chapter, § 3.
44. As the exemplary case which each Spiritual is called on to reproduce, see *Avicenna and the Visionary Recital*, ch. IV, § 14.
45. One can only allude here to the extremely complex data of lived experience. The "cities swallowed up" represent the failure of the sensory faculties (compare the abandonment of Absalom by his army in the Avicennan recital of Salāmān and Absāl). The being Hermes calls to his aid is the Angel whom the Suhrawardian pilgrim meets ("Recital of the Occidental Exile," Wing of Gabriel), or the youthful sage who guides the Avicennan pilgrim, a central figure of the same archetype, or the one who leads Ibn 'Arabī into the mystical Ka'ba (see our *Creative Imagination in the Ṣūfism of Ibn 'Arabī*, ch. VI). Let us remember the "suprasensory personal guide" in the school of Najmuddīn Kubrā. Sometimes the circumstances of this reunion are described as "fission of the moon" (*shaqq al-qamar*, an allusion to the Qur'ān 34:1), because the active intelligence proceeds from the Angel of the Heaven of the Moon, or rather is the latter's "esoteric" (there exists, on this point, an entire treatise of a Spiritual of the fifteenth century, 'Alī Turkah Iṣfahānī; see *En Islam iranien*, III, 275–355). Each Spiritual becoming in his turn the "seal of the prophetic mission"; sometimes, as is here the case, the circumstances are interpreted as the "bursting forth of the column of dawn." That is evidently reminiscent of Manicheism, whose meaning for Ishrāqī eschatology Shahrazūrī was able to valorize, as the irruption of the "*Oriental* presence." On the mutation of the Manichean image of "column of praise" into "column of dawn," see below, Part Two, Art. I, n. 4. Suhrawardī himself says again: "The experience of the authentic raptures in the world of Hūrqalyā depends

on the magnificent prince *Hūrakhsh*, the most sublime of those who have assumed a body, the Most Venerated, who is the supreme *Face* of God, in the terminology of Oriental theosophy" (*Muṭāraḥāt*, § 215, translated below, Part Two, Art. I). Hūrakhsh denotes the Angel of the Sun, whose "exoteric" is the flaming mass of the star, his theurgy in the corporealized world. Suhrawardī addresses one of his psalms to him; on the etymology, see Muḥ. Moʿīn, *The Philosophy of Illumination and the Ancient Iranian Culture*, pp. 22–24. According to a Pahlavi commentary on Yasht VI, 2 (Darmesteter, *Zend-Avesta*, II, 404, n. 2), "*hvare raokhshnē*" would seem to denote more especially the rising or ascending sun from which the Angels receive the *Xvarnah* and distribute it on Earth. Indeed (here as in the episode of Hermes), it is through the rising light (*nūr shāriq*) that the soul divests itself of its material tunic and puts on the auroral robe (*libās al-shurūq*), becomes itself auroral substance, rising Sun (*Muṭāraḥāt*, § 223). Compare with the musk-perfumed robe that Zarathustra puts on and the one put on by Ibn ʿArabī's mystic when he penetrates into Hūrqalyā (translated from the text, below, Part Two, Art. II). If one keeps in mind what has been said here (ch. I, § 3) concerning the blaze of the *Xvarnah in Ērān-Vēj*, on the summit of the mountain of dawns, in the visionary landscape of the Avestan liturgies, one will understand how, by making this sacred Light the agent of ecstasy, Suhrawardī represented his own mystical experience in the terms of a tradition that has been barely studied, nor even recognized, until now.

46. See our edition of the *Oriental Theosophy* (*Ḥikmat al-ishrāq*), § 225 (translated below, Part Two, Art. I).
47. See the commentary of Quṭbuddīn Shīrāzī, p. 538 (translated below, Part Two, Art. I).
48. Ibid., p. 258, §§ 240–42; see the translation of the entire context below, Part Two, Art. I.
49. Ibid., p. 242. Hence the cardinal importance of the affirmation of Iranian Avicennism (as opposed to Averroism) of the existence of the *Animae coelestes*—that is, the Angels who move the Heavens and are distinct from the pure Intelligences or Cherubim whom they contemplate; they represent the world of pure or absolute Imagination, free of the sensory perceptions that cause the paralysis or the imaginative absurdities of the imagination in *Animae humanae*. This world of the *Animae coelestes* is the one which is terminologically designated as the *Malakūt*.

50. See *Tanzīh al-awliyā'*, p. 725. (translated below, Part Two, Art. xi).
51. See the admirable episode mentioned by Shaikh Sarkār Āghā (ibid., p. 723), concerning the Imām Ḥasan ʿAskarī (eleventh Imām of the Twelver Shīʿites, tenth century). The Imām is being held prisoner in the caravanserai of the beggars; nevertheless, with a simple gesture he appears before his visitor as he ordinarily *appears*. "Wherever we are, it is like that. We are not *in* the caravanserai of the beggars." (See the context in the translation below, Part Two, Art. xi.) In his real person, the Imām is in Hūrqalyā, while remaining visible (materially) on this Earth. In the same way, our commentaries on the *ḥadīth* (traditions) as often as not become irrelevant if we apply to them our criteria of historical criticism. The "spiritual fact" whose theme is to be found in the *ḥadīth* attests to its authenticity.
52. See the very fine text of Shaikh Muḥ. Karīm Khān Kirmānī, second successor to Shaikh Aḥmad Aḥsā'ī, translated below, Part Two, Art. x, 2.
53. We should meditate upon the following: the concise sentence in Peter's Sermon on Transfiguration: *Talem eum vidi qualem capere potui* (*Acts of Peter*, XX); the conversation of the Angel Christ with John during the passion of Jesus; the latter's steps left no footmarks on the soil (*Acts of John*). See our study "Divine Epiphany and Spiritual Rebirth in Ismailian Gnosis," § 1: Metamorphoses des visions théophaniques.
54. See *Kitāb sharḥ al-ziyāra*, II, 369. This very important passage is completely translated below, Part Two, Art. ix, 1.
55. See principally the following works of Shaikh Aḥmad: *Jawāmiʿ*, I, 136, 153; *Risāla khāqānīya* (ibid., I, 122); *Sharḥ al-ziyāra*, II, 369; his commentary on the *Ḥikma al- arshīya* of Ṣadrā Shīrāzī, pp. 179 ff. The translation of these texts will be found below in Part Two, Art. ix. This is one of the points on which the Shaikhīs and the "orthodox" have come up against each other; actually, the latter do not possess the capacity, nor have they ever made the effort, to understand the terms of the problem. A friend has called to my attention that there is a striking consonance between the idea of the "fourfold body" and the doctrine of Rudolf Steiner. As a matter of fact, a rapid comparison of a few texts should suffice to draw one's attention to it, despite certain "functional" differences. It would be worthwhile coming back to it.
56. See Proclus, *The Elements of Theology*, ed. and tr. E. R.

Dodds, prop. 205 and commentary, p. 304. Cf. the important work of J. J. Poortman, *Okhēma, Geschiedenis en zin van het hylisch pluralisme.*

57. *Corpus hermeticum*, XIII, 3.
58. See Dodds, *Elements of Theology*, Appendix II, pp. 313 ff. (the Astral Body in Neoplatonism).
59. Ibid., pp. 316–17; see that Heraclitus of Pontus, the Platonist, already makes the soul an *ouranion soma* of luminous substance (ibid., p. 316, n. 3, but why the need to interpret this idea as a survival of so-called "primitive thought"?).
60. Ibid., pp. 319–20. Representatives of the first tradition: Eratosthenes, Ptolemy the Platonist, Iamblicus, Heracles; representatives of the second: Plotinus, Porphyry.
61. We can compare the passage of the *Risāla khāqānīya*, I, 122, in which it is stated that the *jism aṣlī* (= *insān ḥaqīqī*) is homologous with the *jism al-kullī* or ninth Sphere, with prop. 205 of Proclus (Dodds, p. 181), in which it is said that each individual soul is related to its individual "vehicle" (*okhēma*) as the divine Soul (below which it is ranked ontologically) to the divine body. By an analogy of relationships we can compare this with the relationship of the *okhēmata*, which are also related to each other in the same way as the souls.
62. Dodds, *Elements of Theology*, p. 321.
63. Thus, the only "death," and a very momentary death, which can occur to the *jism aṣlī* is the sleep during the interval between the two "soundings" of the trumpet (this sleep can be compared to that of the Seven Sleepers in the cavern, Sūra 18; see the *Risāla Khāqānīya*, loc. cit.). In this manner, the general eschatology of the Qur'ān (implying that *every* being must of necessity die) is safeguarded. As a philosopher, Ṣadrā Shīrāzī (on whom Shaikh Aḥmad comments with a sympathy not excluding criticism) allows himself more liberty with the eschatological Qur'ānic data. In the passages translated below (Part Two, Art. IX) we shall see that the "first sounding" is designated as a "fulgurant blast" or a "blast which reabsorbs"; the second is called the "blast which propels."
64. M. Maeterlinck, "Le Vieux qui ne veut pas mourir" (in *Le Cadran stellaire*).
65. See Dodds, *Elements of Theology*, p. 320.
66. We should also take note that the Neoplatonists thought of the *okhēma symphyes* as spherical (in the shape of an egg, according to Olympiodorus), whence the opinion, accepted by Origen, that man returns to life with a spherical body (see Dodds,

Elements of Theology, p. 308). This is a strange, even shocking, picture, if one were to take it in the literal, geometrical meaning, since it goes against every imaginable form corresponding to the canon of perfect human stature. Here the Shaikh's teaching can be our guide. The *jasad hūrqalyī*, the body that is the paradigm of the human body, is preserved in its "tomb" (that is, in the Earth of Hūrqalyā) "in a spherical shape" (*mustadīr*), but here the *nomen agentis* indicates "that which draws a perfect circle by closing itself on itself"—that is, a complete whole, a system which is closed and sufficient to itself. The symbolical reference to spherical shape does not allude to geometrical figuration but to the perfection of the structure, which is wholly preserved and invisibly *circumscribed*, to its imperishable *form*. The spherical shape means that even if the perishable elementary body (*jasad A*) is mutilated, scattered, the Earth of Hūrqalyā preserves the archetypal body in its perfection and in the integrity of its structure; see the commentary on the *Ḥikma al-ʿarshīya* of Shīrāzī, p. 179; *Sharḥ al-ziyāra*, II, 370 (see the passages translated below, Part Two, Art. IX).

67. Besides the works of Shaikh Aḥmad previously cited, we must at least mention here some of the works on alchemy written by his successors: Shaikh Muḥammad Karīm Khān Kirmānī, among others, has composed a trilogy: *Iṣlāḥ al-ajsād* (on the rectification or purification of bodies); *Iṣlāḥ al-arwāḥ* (on the rectification of spirits); and *Iṣlāḥ al-nufūs* (on the rectification of souls). We might also mention a basic theoretical exposition: *Mir'āt al-ḥikma* (*The Mirror of Wisdom*). Then there is another great treatise on the physical, psychic, and esoteric meaning of the color red (*Risāla-yi yāqūtīya*), after the manner of Goethe, which is the basis of an Iranian theory on colors (*Farbenlehre*). Until now all these works have existed only in manuscript form.

68. Commentary on the *Ḥikma al-ʿarshīya*, p. 179 (below, Part Two, Art. IX, 5).

69. See C. G. Jung, *Psychology and Alchemy*, pars. 393 ff. (in the method of the alchemical Work, "imaginations" are by no means schemas without substance, or "fantasies," but something like a *corpus subtile*); idem, "Paracelsus as a Spiritual Phenomenon," pars. 173 ff.; (*imaginatio-meditatio* as the psychic factor in alchemy).

70. Commentary on the *Ḥikma al-ʿarshīya*, p. 165 (see below, Part Two, Art. IX, 4).

71. Ibid., p. 331, in which it is demonstrated that life, consciousness, will, which are in the spirit, also exist—but in a lesser degree—in minerals, which likewise live, toil, and choose. If the truth be told, what is called *hyle* (*materia*) is by no means opaque and dense in itself; mixture is what creates denseness and decay (cf. the Mazdean idea of *gumechishn*). The celestial Spheres themselves are also material, but of a very subtle matter not perceptible to the senses. The Earth of the Paradise of Adam (which belongs to the celestial Earth of Hūrqalyā), which the sons of Adam today are no longer permitted to tread, is not perceptible to the senses, but only to pure Imagination; so it is with the creatures who populate it and who have an extent, a *situs*, without that excluding the perpetuity and the perenniality of their being.
72. Ibid., pp. 165, 166, containing a commentary on the remark of the First Imām of Shīʿism (ʿAlī ibn ʿAlī-Ṭālib) in which he proclaims that "alchemy is the sister of prophecy"; like the revelation of the Prophet, it protects esotericism (*bāṭin*) with an exoteric envelope (*ẓāhir*), so that ordinary mortals can speak of it and know it only from the exoteric point of view. "I call God to witness! It is nothing but solid Water, incompressible Air, impenetrable Fire, fluid Earth."
73. Literally, it is its "nadir"; see *Risāla khāqānīya* in *Jawāmiʿ*, I, 123–24 (below, Part Two, Art. IX, 4). Thus we come precisely to the representation of the "Diamond Body," and here again the expression issuing from the heart of Shīʿite Islam concords unexpectedly with a concept of Vajrayana Buddhism.
74. Ibid., p. 124.
75. *Ḥikma al-ʿarshīya*, p. 332.
76. See Jung, *Psychology and Alchemy*, par. 426, n. 2; *Avicenna and the Visionary Recital*, I, ch. IV, n. 26.
77. Commentary on the *Ḥikma al-ʿarshīya*, p. 332.
78. Ibid., p. 119.
79. See the important work in Persian of Shaikh Ḥājj Muḥammad Karīm Khān Kirmānī, *Irshād al-ʿawāmm* (above, n. 6), some pages from which are translated below, Part Two, Art. X.
80. Ibid., II, 277. Compare also the extract from Mullā Ṣadrā Shīrāzī, Part Two, Art. VI, below (*Spissitudo spiritualis*).
81. Ibid. Here one could insert an exhaustive comparative study of spirituality. What we alluded to above as "docetism" (nn. 42 ff.) would be seen in quite another light than in the framework of historical theological polemics. Between Hūrqalyā and Sambhogakāya homologies can be foreseen that it is impossible

to go into here. Perhaps even Avicennan cosmology, seen as a phenomenology of angelic consciousness, would reveal to us this world of "absolute affirmation," since each Archangel, each celestial Soul, and each Heaven realizes, hypostasizes the consciousness of another Archangel. See our book *Avicenna and the Visionary Recital*, pp. 46 ff.

82. Swedenborg, *De Coelo et ejus mirabilibus*, 156.
83. Ibid., 175.
84. Ibid., 363: from this it becomes clear in what sense the alchemical Operation prefigures the condition of the Paradisiacs. It makes manifest what was hidden, occult (esoteric, *bāṭin*) under the *ẓāhir*, which then becomes transparent. Now it is said: the Angel has the vision, the *real apparition* of what he meditates; his esoteric part is spontaneously manifested in an external form. This is why the alchemical Operation, as a psychic event, takes place in the Earth of Hūrqalyā.
85. *Irshād al-ʿawāmm*, II, 66–67.
86. Commentary on the *Ḥikma al-ʿarshīya*, pp. 187, 227. The process leading to this equation between the archetype "I" as an essential body and the Paradise which is its celestial Earth is extremely complex. I would like to add further the following, in order to emphasize the thematic articulation of a few pages, the translation of which will be found in Part Two, Art. x, below. "I am not speaking in metaphors," says Shaikh Karīm Khān, "in announcing that the celestial Earth of the believer is his body itself." Man is composed of a dimension of Light and a dimension of Darkness. The first is constituted by the Heaven of his being, which is formed of eight Heavens or celestial Earths. The second is constituted by the obscure Earth of his being, comprising seven Earths. A "handful" of each of these Heavens and these Earths can enter into the formation of his "essential body." The presence of the eight Heavens in man applies only to the Perfect Man. As for ordinary men, some have received a handful of one of the celestial Earths, the others two or three, and so on. At their resurrection, their acts thus appear in different forms, but they correspond to the degree of the celestial Earth of which they have received a "handful" (see that with Proclus, the souls have been "sown" among the stars). If this handful is from the first Heaven, for example, the totality of their acts will be epiphanized in form homologous to the first Heaven, and so forth. This is why, since the celestial Earth of each man is absolutely his own and since this celestial Earth is his own acts epiphanized in the form of palaces,

gardens, houris, and the like, one can truthfully say that the Paradise, the celestial Earth of each man, is "in the Heaven of his being" and is absolutely his own, for no one else has a share in it. Thus we see the outline of the circle (individuation) appear. Each action of Light comes from a Heaven of the soul's dimension of Light; one can say, therefore, that "the clay of each of the faithful has been taken from the Earth of his Paradise." In their turn, these acts go back to this same Heaven and are epiphanized there. His essential body originates in the Heaven of his being (his celestial Earth), and by its action, which "returns" to its own Heaven, produces its own celestial Earth. Hence one can truthfully say that the celestial Earth of the faithful gnostic in his own "essential original body" (ὄχημα συμφυής of Proclus); see *Irshād al-ʿawāmm*, II, 282–84.

87. See above, Ch. I, n. 47 *in fine*, and *Jawāmiʿ*, I, 153. Actually, the word was already known to Suhrawardī in the twelfth century.
88. Text quoted by E. S. Drower, *The Mandaeans of Iraq and Iran*, p. 55 (cf. above, Ch. I, nn. 105–106); see ibid. (according to *Das Johannesbuch der Mandäer*, ed. M. Lidzbarski, p. 126), the story of the maiden awakened from her sleep and warned by "her sister in *Mshunia Kushta*."
89. E. S. Drower, "Hibil Ziwa and the Parthian Prince," pp. 152–156.
90. "Hymn of the Soul," 76 ff.; see above, Ch. I, n. 62 *in fine*, and H. Leisegang, *La Gnose*, tr. J. Gouillard, p. 249.
91. *The Gospel According to Thomas*, p. 45, log. 84. Cf. above, Ch. I, n. 20.
92. These words were reported by Bernard Gavoty in *Journal musical français*, December 25, 1952, p. 8, according to the personal testimony of the composer's son, Dr. Franz Strauss, who was at his father's bedside and took down these "golden words."

PART TWO

SELECTIONS FROM TRADITIONAL TEXTS

ARTICLE I
SHIHĀBUDDĪN YAḤYA SUHRAWARDĪ

1. Concerning all the Suhrawardī texts given here, we refer once and for all to the critical edition we ourselves made of the following works: (1) *Opera metaphysica et mystica, I*; (2) *Œuvres philosophiques et mystiques de Sohrawardī* (*Opera metaphysica et mystica, II*). Each volume is preceded by *Prolégomènes* (I and II) in French.
2. This is followed by a lengthy conversation about initiation into "presential knowledge" as opposed to re-presentative knowledge through the intermediary of a form or *species*. The first is presence of oneself to oneself, *aurorante* illumination, *cognitio matutina*. The dialogue is not without its humor. In it Aristotle expresses himself as a Platonist and speaks highly of Plato, ending with praise of the great Ṣūfī masters. " 'Among the Islamic philosophers,' I asked him, 'is there one who approaches Plato in rank?' 'No,' he answered, 'not by one-thousandth of a degree.' Then I recapitulated the names of those I knew and decided to take no further interest in them. My thoughts returned to Abū Yazīd Basṭāmī and to Abū Sahl Tustarī. It seemed to me that Aristotle was delighted with them. He told me that these were philosophers and Sages in the true meaning of the words. They have not become bogged down in purely descriptive knowledge, which is merely representation through an intermediary form. They have progressed as far as that knowledge which is Presence, union, direct vision." It must not be forgotten that when our authors were reading the *Theology* said to be by Aristotle, they thought that they were reading Aristotle, when they were actually reading Plotinus. Therefore, Suhrawardī will make a distinction between his case and that of the Peripatetics of Islam; as for Mullā Ṣadrā, whose judgment is that of a good Shī'ite accustomed to esotericism, if Aristotle criticized the Platonic doctrines, then according to him this was a purely exoteric attitude.
3. This is an important allusion: it is in Jābarṣā—that is, in the world of Hūrqalyā—that the conversation takes place which

initiates into the knowledge of self as an *aurorante* Presence, *cognitio matutina* ("he who knows himself, knows his Lord"); this means that such knowledge marks the entrance into that celestial Earth which is the Earth of Visions and Earth of Resurrection, the Earth of which the body of resurrection is made, as the fruition of everything which has been attained in the course of this earthly life by knowledge and way of being (see the Shaikhī texts, below, Art. IX).

4. *'Amūd al-Ṣubḥ*, spelled with *ṣād*, "column of dawn." In fact, the word should be spelled with *sīn*, "column of praise," one of the basic images of Manichean eschatology. Actually, some manuscripts do give this spelling. On the one hand, there are two very good reasons for the orthographic mutation: the expression *'Amūd al-Ṣubḥ* (with *ṣād*) ordinarily indicates the "light of dawn," and its "bursting forth" supplied our Spirituals with a theme of meditation very close to the one which is suggested by the Qur'ānic verse 54:1, the "bursting forth of the moon" (*shaqq al-qamar*). On the other hand, although the ascent of the "column of praise" here corresponds perfectly to the ecstasy of Hermes, the expression "bursting forth" (*shaqq*) retained by the author and his commentators makes it obligatory to preserve the image of the column of dawn. Besides, the "column of praise" is a "column of light." In any case, our authors were so aware of being in the presence of a Manichean idea that Shahrazūrī, in commenting on the corresponding passage of the *Oriental Theosophy* (our edition, p. 233), seized the occasion to explain the individual eschatology of Manicheism with all the more sympathy in that he interprets it as being accomplished in the world of Hūrqalyā. On the Manichean idea, see especially Henri-Charles Puech, report in the *Annuaire du Collège de France*, 59th year, 1959, p. 269. Prayer, as an "exhalation of light," is imagined as being a "column of praise" made, accordingly, out of luminous elements, "the channel through which pass first the souls, the fragments of the living Soul, the prayers, and the hymns which accompany them."
5. An allusion to the verses of the Qur'ān 6:131 and 28:59.
6. In n. 4, above, we called attention to the orthographic mutation of the word *ṣubḥ*. On the theme of the bursting forth of the Moon (Qur'ān 54:1), see above, Part One, Ch. II, n. 45.
7. The contrast between the two commentators is striking. Ibn Kammūna toils and hesitates; Shahrazūrī is a disciple completely sure of what he is interpreting.
8. See Georges Vajda, "Les Notes d'Avicenne sur la 'Théologie

d'Aristote,' " p. 351. The reference is to the *marginalia* of Avicenna. These notes are all the more precious since they throw some light on his own project of "Oriental Philosophy," the drafts for which are now lost.

9. *Hūrakhsh*, spiritual entity, the Angel of the Sun; see Part One, Ch. II, n. 45. Concerning the various etymologies suggested, see Muḥ. Moʿīn, *Burhān-i qāṭi*, IV, 2390. With reference to this Mazdean solar Archangel, we are reminded that certain texts of Islamic gnosis interpret the fourth heaven (Heaven of the Sun) as the Heaven of Christ; in Jewish gnosis, it is interpreted as the Heaven of the Archangel Michael.
10. Regarding this idea of "witness of contemplation" (*shāhid*) on which we cannot expand in this book, see our book *En Islam iranien*: III, 65 ff.
11. Concerning this word, see our *Prolégomène II* to the *Œuvres de Sohrawardī* (*ḥikma ilāhīya=theo-sophia*, the *ḥakīm muta'allih* and the *theosis*).
12. This passage has been repeated verbatim by Mīr Dāmād; see *En Islam iranien*, IV, 9–53.
13. With regard to the sequence of the following themes: Angel of the Sun, rising sun, *Xvarnah*, ecstasy of Hermes at dawn, auroral light, and auroral robe, see n. 9, above, and Part One, Ch. II, n. 45.
14. So attention is called to the fact that here again a basic representation of Suhrawardī's *Oriental Theosophy* (donning the auroral robe as the introduction into the world of Hūrqalyā) is expressed in terms of the investiture of the *Xvarnah*—that is, in terms of Mazdean tradition. In Part One of this book (Ch. I) we saw that the idea of this Light of Glory predominates in all expressions of Iranian thought. It serves also to support homologations of the Zoroastrian Saoshyant with the hidden Imām.
15. That is, of Hūrakhsh, the Angel-Prince of the Sun (see n. 9, above); this allusion again underscores the solar character of the royal *Xvarnah*.
16. Hence the case of Kay Khusraw, the ecstatic King (who disappeared mysteriously from this world, "taken up" like Elijah, Enoch, Jesus) typifying with Zarathustra, in Suhrawardī's view, the mystical charisma of ancient pre-Islamic Iran.
17. That is, intermediate between the greater Orient, world of pure Intelligences, and the lesser Orient, or world of the Soul (see Part One, Ch. II, § 2); its location is that of *al-Aʿrāf*, or the "Earth of sesame" created from what was left over from the

clay of Adam (see below, Arts. II and IV). According to our text, these events are psycho-spiritual *facts*; they do not come to pass in the world perceptible and verifiable by the senses; their narration deals not with outer empirical data but with events taking place in Hūrqalyā, the *mundus archetypus*, where the light of dawn rises, and which is entered only by him who has put on the robe of this light (cf. the robe donned by Zoroaster in order to come into the presence of the Immortal Saints, and that donned by the initiate in the account of Ibn ʿArabī, below, Art. II).

18. The two commentators stress that it is not with the material body. Here we might call to mind the *photisms* experienced by Najmuddīn Kubrā; see our book "*L'Homme de lumière dans le soufisme iranien.*"
19. It is of the utmost importance to distinguish between the *Elements* and the *Heavens* of the world of subtle bodies in order to understand not only the foundations of imaginative perception (itself operating on a twofold plane) but, in addition, all that the Shaikhī texts suggest about the physiology of the "resurrection body" (see below, Art. IX).
20. *Ṣayāṣī* (with two *ṣād*'s) *muʿallaqa*: literally, citadels, fortresses; the word is used metaphorically to designate bodies—in this case, bodies which are "subtle" but all the more substantial in that they do not depend upon a substratum, upon a matter foreign to themselves, and for that reason are said to be "in suspense." The ever-recurring example of the mirror, which bears witness to the presence of the suprasensory world in our very perceptions, would call for an *excursus* into a kind of esoteric verification of the laws of optics (this applies also to the hermeneutics of the spiritual senses).
21. For the meaning and the being of these forms whose "matter" is the soul itself, see the text of Mullā Ṣadrā Shīrāzī (below, Art. VI); this is also the way in which Shahrazūrī interpreted Manichean eschatology (above, n. 4). Referring to the distinction of a double *barzakh* (corresponding elsewhere to preexistence and to *post mortem* becoming), see below, Arts. II, III, and V.
22. This expression, which the *Ishrāqīyūn* have borrowed from pre-Islamic Iranian chivalry (*sipah-bud* today is the title of a commander-in-chief); in this case, the image is equivalent to the *hegemonikon* of the Stoics.
23. We are reminded that in the case of Suhrawardī this word *barzakh* technically refers to everything that is body and extent

and, consequently, forms an interval, a distance. In this sense, the world of autonomous Images and subtle bodies is also a *barzakh*, since it is provided with extent. But it is also the world through which resurrection comes to pass; in that case, *barzakh* means the interval between the *exitus* and the great Resurrection. This is the sense in which our authors most frequently take it.

24. In support of this we would at least like to mention two exceptionally interesting documents: the *Diarium spirituale* of Rūzbihān (n. 10, above) and the personal testimony of Najmuddīn Kubrā (n. 18, above).
25. This brings to mind the symbolical color connected with each heavenly body.
26. "Seven Very Firm Ones" (*sabʿ shidād*) is the *Qurʾānic* term for the Heavens of the seven planets (78:12).
27. In n. 19, above, we have already called attention to the importance of the distinction between the Elements and the Heavens of the *mundus archetypus*.

Article II
MUḤYĪDDĪN IBN ʿARABĪ

1. It need hardly be pointed out that, in describing Adam as the "Imām of mankind," the word *Imām* has as full a significance as in Shīʿite theology: the guide, the one who goes before, the leader, the one whose example is followed by all those who come after—that is, the archetype. Suhrawardī, in his *Book of Oriental Theosophy* (§ 173 in our edition), also mentions the special nature of the palm tree; his commentator takes the opportunity to quote a saying of the Prophet which we find echoed here: "Honor your *aunt* the palm tree, for *she* was created out of the remainder of Adam's clay."
2. ʿAbd al-Karīm Jīlī, *Kitāb al-insān al-kāmil*, II, 28 (see below, Art. IV).
3. The passages translated here would call, in context, for a complete study of the symbolism of the palm tree; see J. J. Herzog, *Real-encyklopädie für protestantische Theologie und Kirche*, 3d edn., VI, 305 (*Phoenix dactylifera*), and XVIII, 388–90 (*Sinnbilder*). C. G. Jung, in his article "The Philosophical Tree," collected extremely interesting texts regarding the symbolism of the tree in general. The palm tree as a symbol of the celestial Earth of Light is the antithesis of the mandrake as the symbol of the dark, demonic Earth, also created out of

Adam's clay. Hildegarde of Bingen writes: "*Mandragora . . . de terra illa, de qua Adam creatus est, dilatata est . . . sed tamen herba haec et propter similitudinem hominis, suggestio diaboli huic plus quam aliis herebis adest et insidiatur*" (*Physica*, I, 56, cited in Hugo Rahner, "*Die seelenheilende Blume.* Moly und Mandragore in antiker und christlicher Symbolik," p. 224).

4. Here the context calls for a comparative study of the Qur'ānic commentaries (*tafsīr*) on Sūra 19:23 ff., grouped by families. (1) Sunnite *tafsīr*: Fakhruddīn Razī, *Mafātīḥ al-ghayb*, V, 784: the palm tree which had not been fertilized is an exemplification of Maryam. (2) Ṣūfī *tafsīr*: *Tafsīr* attributed to Ibn ʿArabī: the palm tree is "the palm tree of your soul springing up toward the Heaven of the Spirit through your union with the Holy Spirit" (II, 4). The same idea of Maryam exemplifying the mystic in the *tafsīr* of Rūzbihān of Shīrāz, *ʿArā'is al-bayān*, II, 8. (3) Shīʿite *tafsīr*: for the Ismāʿīlīs, the whole of the Sūra is interpreted in terms of their esoteric prophetology. The palm tree typifies gnosis as spiritual food (*Mizāj al-tasnīm*, ed. R. Strothmann, p. 189). For the Twelve Shīʿites: Ṭabarsī, *Majmaʿ al-bayān*, II, ad loc.: Maryam's palm tree is connected with the heavenly palm tree referred to in Imām Jaʿfar's *ḥadīth* quoted in n. 5, below. *Tafsīr al-ṣāfī*, Muḥsan Fayẓ, p. 299: Maryam leaves her family and withdraws to the East (19:16), that is, toward the Earth of the Imāms. See also Muḥ. Bāqir Majlisī, *Biḥār al-anwār*, V, 319 ff. (*Safīna*, II, 582). We would very quickly rediscover the sources of the theme of Fāṭima as supracelestial Earth (above, Ch. II, § 1) and the typological correspondences between Maryam, mother of Jesus, and Fāṭima, mother of the Holy Imāms. Let this note suffice to suggest to the reader, by one small example, the amplitude of research to be done in Islamic theology.
5. The tradition of the palm tree created out of Adam's clay is recorded in the great encyclopedia of Shīʿite traditions by Majlisī, *Biḥār al-anwār*, XIV, 840 (*Safīna*, II, 581); it figures as a lengthy answer given by the sixth Imām, Jaʿfar Ṣādiq, to someone who asked him about the origin of the palm tree. The answer includes further details illustrating the significance of the palm tree as a symbol of the celestial Earth. When God banished Adam from Paradise he ordered him to take the palm tree (down) with him. Adam planted it in Mecca. All the palm trees "directly descended" from it belong to the species *ʿajwa* (the unusually exquisite and substantial Medina dates). All other palm trees, in the Eastern and Western parts of the Earth, came from the pits of these dates.

6. The Throne (*ʿarsh*) and the Firmament (*kursī*): concerning these classical terms in hierocosmology, see again the teaching of the Imām Jaʿfar, *Biḥār*, XIV, 98: the *kursī* is the outer threshold of the Invisible; the *ʿarsh* is its inner threshold. In the celestial physics of the philosophers, the *ʿarsh* is the Sphere of Spheres, or ninth Sphere; the *kursī* is the eighth Heaven, or Heaven of the constellations.
7. Dhūl-Nūn Miṣrī again uses this image, word for word, in the account of him given by Ibn ʿArabī (p. 128, lines 15–16), to compare the dimension of the heavens according to our astronomy with the extent of the "Earth of white camphor," which is one of the earths of the celestial Earth: "If our heavens were to be placed in it, they would be in regard to it as a ring lost in a desert."
8. This whole text from Ibn ʿArabī is reproduced and developed in Majlisī's Shīʿite encyclopedia, XIV, 87.
9. Concerning ʿAbd Allāh ibn ʿAbbās, see Māmaqānī, *Tanqīḥ al-maqāl*, no. 6921. For the fourteen dwelling places, see the passage translated below, Art. X, 1.
10. Cf. the passage from Muḥsin Fayẓ translated below, Art., VIII.
11. See our *Creative Imagination in the Ṣūfism of Ibn ʿArabī*, p. 350, n. 10 (hereafter cited as *Ṣūfism of Ibn ʿArabī*).
12. For the date of the death of Awḥadī Kirmānī, see M. A. Tabrīzī, *Rayḥānat al-adab*, I, 123, n. 291.
13. Cf. lines 12, 108–109 of the last scene in Goethe's *Faust: Part II* here used as an epigraph: *Das Unbeschreibliche, Hier ist's getan*—what is undescribable here takes place in fact.
14. See the last allusion in ch. III (Noah) of the *Fuṣūṣ al-ḥikam* (ed. A. E. Affifi, I, 74; II, 43). Ibn ʿArabī states that he has written about the Heaven of *Yūḥ* in his book on the *Tanazzulāt mawṣilīya* (unedited MS; *Yūḥ* is the name of the Angel governing the fourth heaven, the Heaven of the Sun; see also Art. IV, below).

ARTICLE III
DĀ'ŪD QAYṢARĪ

1. On the situation of this *mundus archetypus* in the hierarchy of the levels of being, or *Ḥaḍarāt*, see our *Ṣūfism of Ibn ʿArabī*, pp. 225 ff., 360 ff.
2. In the following passages this will also be expressed in other allusive forms: as a world contained in the horizon of the Soul of the world, or "topographically" as a world beginning at "the

convex surface of the Sphere of Spheres," the threshold of which is the celestial pole, the rock of emerald. Among the philosophers, the subtle and original matter of the supreme Heaven emanates from the first Intelligence through the act of contemplation of its virtual negativity; the matter of the Heaven of each Intelligence marks the "distance" between itself and the Soul issued from it.

3. Concerning this distinction, see our *Ṣūfism of Ibn ʿArabī*, pp. 219, 358–59. In short (see below, Arts. VII and VIII): the separated imaginative world (*munfaṣil*) is the absolute *mundus archetypus*, the world of autonomous Images, subsisting in themselves. It is the *Malakūt*, the world of the Soul existing *apart* from the human faculties which have their seat in the brain. Then again, the world of the Images of our active imagination is a world of Images that are imminent to this imagination and "captive" in it. Nevertheless, it is an imaginative world which is adjacent (*muttaṣil*) to *Malakūt*, in continuity with it; hence the *noetic value* of Images and imaginative perception as a "window" or "lattice" (see our text) through which the light of the *Malakūt* penetrates into us.
4. An allusion to the vision of the Prophet mentioned in Sūra 53 (The Star), v. 14.
5. See above, n. 3: the forms present or "captive" in our imagination exemplify the forms of the world of the absolute Imagination, not engaged in a substratum of "material matter," as they appear to the souls of the *Malakūt*. Dā'ūd Qayṣarī also says (p. 28): "The visible world is the epiphany (*maẓhar*) of the world of the *Malakūt*, that is, of the absolute archetypal world."
6. See the context of the "prayer of the heliotrope" of Proclus in our *Ṣūfism of Ibn ʿArabī*, pp. 105–11.
7. See above, nn. 3, 5.
8. Cf. the text of Mullā Ṣadrā Shīrāzī, translated below, Art. VI.
9. See the Cairo edition, III, 78. Shamsuddīn Lāhījī will lay great stress on this distinction, which is based on the cycle of the forms of being.

Article IV
ʿABD AL-KARĪM JĪLĪ

1. For the context of this sentence of the Prophet, see our *Ṣūfism of Ibn ʿArabī*, pp. 239–41.

2. That is, *al-Kathīb*; as to this place in the other world, see our Introduction to Part Two above, *in fine.*
3. To designate this state of *compresence*, we must say *consens* (from *consum*, as *praesens* comes from *praesum*); see our *Ṣūfism of Ibn ʿArabī*, p. 374, n. 27. The idea referred to is that of a call, a reciprocal exigency like that of the lord (*rabb*) and the one of whom he is lord (*marbūb*), without which he would not be this lord; a reciprocal co-naturalization of "that which is shown" and "the one to whom it is shown," of the Giver of gifts and the one to whom and for whom they are given. To be a Watcher is to be "in the present" of this *compresence*, not to be *present with* something or someone *other.*
4. The Watcher, Awakened, is the *Muntabih*, the *Yaqẓān*—precisely the word that appears in the name of the hero of one of the mystical novels of Avicenna, *Ḥayy Ibn Yaqẓān*, and which is the literal equivalent of the Greek *Egregoros.* See our book *Avicenna and the Visionary Recital.* The concept of *Egregoros* has been "reactivated" in our day by Etienne Souriau in his book *L'Ombre de Dieu.*
5. See the Introduction, above.
6. Ibid.
7. In this theme of the Stranger we rediscover a characteristic Gnostic theme, the fundamental note of the "Recital of the Occidental Exile" of Suhrawardī (in Corbin, ed., *Œuvres philosophiques*), as well as of the "Song of the Pearl" of the *Acts of Thomas.* For other statements by Jīlī clarifying his concept of Spirit, cf. the books cited in our *Ṣūfism of Ibn ʿArabī*, pp. 249 and 369 f., nn. 59, 60.
8. On the country of *Yūḥ*, see above, Art. II, n. 14.
9. That is, imprisoned in the world of the Elements, of sensory space, which must be left behind to reach the nonsensory extension of the world of *Yūḥ*—an attainment assuming, as in all similar passages of our authors, that one can leave space without leaving extension.
10. On the "men of mystery," the Invisible Ones, forming the final theme of the present chapter, see below, n. 28.
11. On the sesame "left over from the clay of Adam," see above, Art. II, the text by Ibn ʿArabī.
12. This phrase seems to have been inserted by the author himself in the thread of the recital, which continues immediately afterwards in the first person. Note the reciprocity, especially emphasized, between the two ideas: Earth of Imagination and Earth of sesame.

13. See above, Art. II, the text by Ibn ʿArabī.
14. Here a new occurrence is slipped in by the author, which we prefer to report in a note for better clarity: "That is what we are interpreting in the present book; to that we are opening this door."
15. Here there is a poem of fifteen couplets, continuing the theme already developed by Ibn ʿArabī: the Earth of sesame, of which the palm tree is the symbol, is the sister of Adam—that is, of man—or rather, the daughter of his mystery (see above, preface to Art. II).
16. On the *himma*, the *enthymesis*, creative power of the heart, see our *Ṣūfism of Ibn ʿArabī*, p. 222 ff.
17. On the prophet Khiẓr (Khaḍir), see ibid., pp. 53 ff., and above, Introduction: his sovereignty over the "Earth of souls" (the "hyperborean paradise"), which is the very same as that referred to here.
18. In order to understand here the mysterious and paradoxical statements of Khiẓr about himself, it is appropriate to recall that a fraction of Twelver Shīʿite Ṣūfism identified him with the hidden Imām (the twelfth Imām). Certain of these statements recall and even reproduce some of those that figure in certain sermons attributed to the first Imām: the full moon, the decisive word, the *pole* to which the entire hierarchy of the Invisible Ones is attached. These among other things reveal the affinites of Shīʿite Imāmology with a Gnostic Christology. The *coincidentia oppositorum* (*Deus absconditus* : *Deus revelatus; lāhūt* : *nāsūt*; esoteric : exoteric) is resolved in the person of the Imām who is not an Incarnation (hypostatic union) but a theophany (see the Shaikhī texts cited below: the theophanic person of the Imām is perceived "in Hūrqalyā," not in the empirical data of ordinary evidence).
19. The *raqīqa* is the subtle intermediary (the tenuous thread) that joins two things, like the unfolding of the link that binds God to man; see Sprenger, *Dictionary*, 582, cited in H. S. Nyberg, *Kleinere Schriften des Ibn al-ʿArabī*, p. 72, n. 2 (cf. above, the text of Art. II *in fine*).
20. *Lāhūt* and *nāsūt*: divinity and humanity, classic terms of Shīʿite Imāmology (see above, n. 18).
21. On the mountain of Qāf, see above, Part One, Ch. II, § 2.
22. On *al-Aʿrāf*, see the preface to the present article and § 1, above. Here the secret of *al-Aʿrāf* is revealed as the dwelling place of Khezr and therefore as the interworld (*barzakh*) connecting the divine (*lāhūt*) and the human (*nāsūt*).

23. Here we have a whole series of references alluding to Sūra 18 (The Cave—that is, the Sūra of the Seven Sleepers): 18:59–60 (the confluence of the two seas); 18:64 (Khiẓr is in this). The symbols are linked here like a progression of chords; if one says *al-Aʿrāf* or *Hūrqalyā*, it is the confluence of the two seas—that is, of *lāhūt* and *nāsūt*; that is why Khiẓr is found with the *rijāl al-ghayb*, the "men of the Invisible Ones," the "men of *al-Aʿrāf*" (the Imāms and their people); that is why from one shore he plunges into the river *Where* (the *nāsūt*, the dimensions of sensory space), and from the other he quenches his thirst at the source (the *lāhūt*), the most frequent theme in the iconography of Khiẓr.
24. See Sūra 18:60 (and the "Recital of the Occidental Exile" of Suhrawardī (in Corbin, ed., *Œuvres philosophiques*); the symbol of the fish typifies the pilgrims who have found their way to the lake that the mystical Sinai overhangs).
25. See the entire episode of Sūra 18, in which Khiẓr appears as the one who initiates Moses and who therefore is invested with a charisma superior to that of the prophets (an idea held especially in certain Imāmite Ṣūfī circles).
26. An allusion to the secrets of the "philosophical alphabet"; on this point Shīʿite Imāmology has even affected a literal transposition of a well-known episode in the Childhood Gospels, the young Imām Muḥ. Bāqir (the Fifth Imām) being substituted for Jesus. See our study "De la Gnose antique à la gnose ismaelienne," p. 121.
27. On this idea, see above, n. 19, and cf. our *Ṣūfism of Ibn ʿArabī*, pp. 195 ff.: "the God created in the faiths."
28. This is one of the most important themes of the esoteric theosophy of Ṣūfism. What Jīlī says here about it is so much more difficult to determine and to translate because it tends simultaneously toward a phenomenology of the presence of these Invisible Ones for the adepts (their apparitional forms) and to a description of their way of being in themselves, all in symbolic allusions valid on one plane and another. As a short indication of the hierarchy of these initiates (*awliyā'*), let us simply recall this *ḥadīth*: "God has on Earth three hundred *eyes* or *persons* whose heart is conformed to the heart of Adam (the 300 *nuqabā'*); forty whose heart is conformed to the heart of Moses (the 40 *nujabā'*); seven whose heart is conformed to the heart of Abraham (the 7 *abdāl*); five whose heart is conformed to the heart of Gabriel; three whose heart is conformed to the heart of Michael; *one* whose heart is conformed to the heart of Chamuel [the *pole*; in Shīʿite terms, the hidden Imām]." For

the context, see *En Islam iranien*, III, and IV, 261. But there are many variations; instead of the group of *five*, the group of *four awtād* (below, n. 32), and the six categories of Jīlī do not necessarily have to be put in exact correspondence with those enumerated above.

29. On the relationship between *nubūwa* and *walāya*, the cycle of prophecy and the cycle of Initiation, see *En Islam iranien*, I, 220, 239.
30. Allusion to Qur'ānic verse 7:52.
31. Literally, the "vases," receptacles (*al-awānī*). The great mystic Ḥakīm Tirmidhī, in his *Ithbāt al-ʿilal*, recalls a *ḥadīth* where it is said: "There are for God certain *vases* on earth, yes! hearts [of the spirituals]." (Brought to our attention by M. Osman Yahya.)
32. The *Awtād al-arḍ*. If the expression of Jīlī is to be taken here in a strict sense, it refers to the four *awtād* arranged around the *pole*. Just as the hierarchy described above (n. 28) corresponds to an astronomical symbolism, so the idea of the four *awtād* ("pillars") presumes the homologation of the spiritual cosmos to a vision of Heaven as a tent resting on four "posts," the *pole* at the center representing the support of the whole. In any case, what is said here about the situation of the four *awtād* corresponds well to what Khiẓr, their *pole*, previously gave about himself. See our book, *L'Homme de lumière dans le soufisme iranien*, ch. III, §§ 2, 3.

Article V
SHAMSUDDĪN MUḤAMMAD LĀHĪJĪ

1. Thus it was in Jābarṣā that Suhrawardī says he had his conversation with the apparition of the *Magister primus*, Aristotle. See above, Art. I, b.
2. Here the author has in view the pages of Dā'ūd Qayṣarī cited above, Art. III, n. 9.
3. Allusion to the Qur'ānic verse 18:59. As we have seen previously (above, Art. IV, n. 23), this "confluence of the two seas" is where Khiẓr is to be found, the sovereign of the land of *Yūḥ*, of the "Earth of the Souls," of the Watchers of *al-Aʿrāf*, in the place between: between *lāhūt* and *nāsūt*.
4. An allusion to Qur'ānic verses 7:136 and 70:40.
5. Regarding this distinction between the plane of the deity and the plane of the Names or divine personalizations which for each creature are respectively the divine Lord or "suzerain"

(*rabb*) of this creature, to whom the divinity manifests himself in the form of this Name, see *Ṣūfism of Ibn 'Arabī*, pp. 121 ff.

6. Thus we see how the traditional meaning of Jābalqā and Jābarṣā bears fruit for Lāhījī in a very personal experience, which shaped an idea of the Orient which ultimately is that of Suhrawardī. Each universe, each individual, has its Jābalqā and its Jābarṣā, its Orient and its Occident, its dimension of light and its dimension of darkness. To pass through this, according to the expression of the poet quoted in the above text, is to become "oneself an orient of lights."

Article VII
'ABD AL-RAZZĀQ LĀHĪJĪ

1. Regarding this designation, see the Introduction to Part Two of this volume and the texts of Suhrawardī translated above, Art. I. In his lexicon, Jurjānī gives "Platonists" as an equivalent of the term *Ishrāqīyūn.*
2. See above, Art. I, n. 16.
3. It must not be forgotten, however, that Suhrawardī, as well as Mullā Ṣadrā, puts the responsibility for this opposition not so much on Aristotle (presumed author of the celebrated *Theology*, with whom Suhrawardī conversed "in Jābarṣā") as on the Peripatetics themselves.
4. That is, the prologue of the *Book of Oriental Theosophy* (*Ḥikmat al-ishrāq*; see above, Art. I).
5. Concerning the Ṣūfīs, see the passages translated in Arts. II–V and the reference to 'Alī Hamadānī in Part One, Ch. II, n. 21.
6. Regarding this distinction, see above, Art. III, n. 3.
7. However, Suhrawardī states explicitly that the archetypal Image exists only for a complete being; for instance, there is not one image for musk and another for the perfume of musk.
8. See the theme of "condescendence" in our *Ṣūfism of Ibn 'Arabī*, pp. 156 ff.
9. See the passages referred to in Art. III, n. 3, above.
10. The meaning of the word *barzakh* (which in Greek has produced the form παρασάγγης), interval, something between, *interworld*, has been made sufficiently plain in all the passages which have been translated in this book, so that there is no need to stress it again.
11. It has already been pointed out that our authors couple the theory of visionary apperceptions (including the perception of

the spiritual meaning of revelations) with the theory of mirrors and an esoteric interpretation of laws of optics (*De perspectiva*).

12. Refer here especially to the excerpts from Mullā Ṣadrā translated above, Art. VI.
13. The *Ishrāqīyūn* have always been careful to uphold this distinction, which has motivated more than one controversy. The problem is complicated by the fact that the same word (*mithāl*, plural *muthul*) is always used. The Platonic Ideas interpreted in angelological terms cannot, of course, be either universals or simply ideas in the divine mind. On the other hand, the Form or Image of Light—for example, Perfect Nature or celestial *Alter Ego*—is perfectly individualized; it is neither logical universal nor concrete sensory. In any case, it is through the "regional ontology" of the *mundus archetypus* that the Platonism of the *Ishrāqīyūn* became an essential organ of their Islamic eschatology.
14. The first (*'ilm ḥuṣūlī*) presupposes a *species*, the creation of a form which represents the object for the knowing subject. The second (*'ilm ḥuḍūrī*) is a direct intuitive knowledge, the type of knowledge that the subject has of himself; see above, Art. I, b, and the notes thereto.

Article VIII
MUḤSIN FAYẒ KĀSHĀNĪ

1. The chapter is entitled "In which the existence of the *mundus archetypus* or interworld (*barzakh*) is made clear, and its qualitative and quantitative aspects."
2. These lines are in literal agreement with a passage in the text of Dā'ūd Qayṣarī translated above, Art. III.
3. Regarding this distinction, see above, Art. III, n. 3, and the text of Lāhījī, Art. VII.
4. The Samaritan, in fact, saw the Angel whom the others did not see (as the Prophet saw the Angel, whereas the Companions saw only the young Daḥya al-Kalbī). That is why the Samaritan, knowing that the Earth over which the Angel had passed could give life to inanimate things, gathered a handful of that earth and threw it into the molten metal of the golden calf.
5. Concerning this theme, see above, Art. VI (Mullā Ṣadrā), and cf. the text translated below, Art. IX, 1.
6. For this theory of the mirrors, see above, Art. VII, n. 11.

7. See above, Art. VII, n. 8. That is why, if a philosophy denies the world of Hūrqalyā, it can no longer perceive the events of spiritual history on their own plane of reality. Rational consciousness is faced with this dilemma: either the abstract truths of reason, or the empirical facts of history (whether from the viewpoint of contingency or determinism). And all the rest is degraded to the level of myth or allegory.
8. See Part One, Ch. II, § 3: the *Miʿrāj* of the Prophet has become the archetype of mystical experience for all Ṣūfīs. Here again, lacking Hūrqalyā as the Earth of Visions and the idea of the "spiritual body" it postulates, one is once more faced with this dilemma: either to see the *Miʿrāj* as a philosophical allegory, or to understand it in a literalist, ordinary, and absurd manner as an assumption *in corpore.*
9. This means that one does not in fact pay this visit "in the cemetery" but, consciously or not, "in Hūrqalyā" (see the words of Maeterlinck quoted above, p. 96, and the passage translated below, Art. IX, 2). Hence the significance of the *ziyārat* (ziyāra), "religious visitation, pilgrimage," especially in Shīʿism. Certainly, it is good to make a physical pilgrimage to the sanctuaries which shelter the tombs of the Holy Imāms. But, in fact, this spatial movement is a *rite* intended to sustain the mental pilgrimage into the invisible, "into Hūrqalyā." That is why the *ziyārat* (for which so many prayers have been composed in Shīʿism) are practiced privately, and frequently where one happens to be, in the privacy of one's own oratory. (See below, Art. IX, the passages concerning the "body of spiritual flesh," which is preserved intact "in Hūrqalyā.")
10. Shaikh Ṣadūq (Ibn Bābūyah) of Qumm (140 km. southwest of Teheran), one of the most eminent Shīʿite theologians of the tenth century (d. 381/991), author of 189 works, of which only a few have reached us.
11. It is known that Qur'ānic Christology is determinedly docetist (3:48, 4:156). So, although the text of Muḥsin Fayẓ here says *baʿd mawtihi*, one should read *baʿd rafʿihi*, in keeping with all the Shīʿite traditions on this point (*Safīna*, II, 192; Muh. Bāqir Majlisī, *Biḥār al-Anwār*, V, 348–52), as with Muḥsin's own commentary on the Qur'ān (*Kitāb Tafsīr al-Ṣāfī*, pp. 89 f.) and the others (see Mullā Fatḥ Allāh *ad* III:48). Jesus was "carried away" to Heaven like Khiẓr-Elijah, Idrīs-Enoch, and kept apart until the Resurrection. It is precisely thanks to the world of Hūrqalyā that the Christology of this Islamic prophetology is docetist, yet without turning the person of Christ, so to

speak, into a phantasm. Later on, the reader will see (Art. XI) the deep meaning which the idea of the hidden Imām acquires: it is men who have made themselves incapable of seeing him and have hidden him from themselves. In the same way his enemies, in denying Jesus his prophetic message, have obscured him from themselves: he whom they believed they had put to death was no longer there (4:156), and he is never there when one interprets events by historical materialism, under the guise of theology, instead of grasping the spiritual history "in Hūrqalyā."

12. Imāmites—that is, Twelver Shī'ites or adepts of the twelve Imāms. In Shī'ite eschatology, the theme of the "return" is that of the "Companions of the Imām," who put an end to historical time; previously (Part One, Ch. II, § 1) we called attention to the correspondence with the Zoroastrian motif of the "Companions of the Saoshyant."

Article IX
SHAIKH AḤMAT AḤSĀ'Ī

1. This great work on 460 pages in folio is without doubt the most important of Shaikh Aḥmad Aḥsā'ī's writings; cf. the *Fihrist* or bibliography of Shaikhite works by Shaikh Sarkār Āghā, pp. 15–16 (hereafter: *Fihrist*). The general *ziyāra* (see above, Art. VIII, n. 9) addressing the Fourteen Very-Pure commemorates all the qualifications of the Imāms; the commentary thus becomes a summary of Shī'ite theosophy. The arrangement of the texts here translated will make it possible to understand step by step the idea of the twofold *jasad* and the twofold *jism*; in what sense the *jasad B* is preserved; how the four bodies are respectively constituted; the type of meditation which substantiates the subtle body and which is homologous to the alchemical operation; and last, the function of the active Imagination in regard to that operation. The reader is referred to Part One of the present book, Ch. II, § 4. Shaikh Aḥmad, it will be noted, makes his thought more explicit with each stage of his exposé.
2. Regarding the complexity of the terminology, cf. Paul Kraus, *Studien zu Jābir ibn Ḥayyān*, II, 19 ff.; Muḥ. Khān Kirmānī, *Risāla-yi Naṣīrīya*, pp. 56 ff. The distinction between *jasad* and *jism* is correlative to the distinction between the "Heavens" and the "Elements" of Hūrqalyā.

3. Measure of weight equivalent to 2,564 grams.
4. Regarding the events heralding the dawn of the Resurrection, that is, the new cosmic cycle, see the following texts.
5. Sometimes changed to *Sorayel* or *Souriel.*
6. Here Shaikh Aḥmad clearly wishes to forestall the objection of the orthodox literalists; but, as we have already pointed out, the latter have never understood or really wished to understand the problem as it was posed by the Shaikhīs.
7. This description still refers to the pleroma of the Twelve; see Part One, Ch. II, § 1.
8. Concerning the valley of Barhūt, see *Safīna*, I, 74.
9. Concerning the meaning of the "two blasts of the Trumpet," see below, § 4.
10. In other words, the relationship of the body of perishable flesh (*jasad A*) with the body of spiritual flesh (the subtle body, *jasad B*) is analogous to the relationship of the astral body (*jism A*) with the supracelestial archetypal body (*jism B*). The purification in readiness for the Resurrection consists in the elimination of *Elements A* (those of the physical world, *jasad A*) and of the astral elements (those of Hūrqalyā, *jism A*). The *corpus resurrectionis* in its integrity is *jism B* plus *jasad B.* This analogy explains the terminology of the holy Imāms previously pointed out by the author: the term *ashbāḥ* (subtle body) used for *asjād* (that is to say, *jasad B*) and the word "Spirit" substituted for the word "body" (that is to say, *jism B*).
11. The *ʿālam al-dharr*; cf. the *logoi spermatikoi.* The Qur'ānic announcement that "every being must die" is carried out by the first blast of the Trumpet. But it is no more than a cosmic pause, a momentary reabsorption. The spirit departs from its astral body as it departed from its body of perishable flesh and, at the second blast of the Trumpet, rediscovers its body of spiritual flesh.
12. Regarding the series of symbols describing eschatology and renewal, see again below, § 4.
13. Ṭabarsī, the eminent Shīʿite theologian of the fifth/eleventh century; regarding the book (*Iḥtijāj*) in which the saying of the Imām is recorded, see Shaikh Āghā Buzurg, *Dharīʿa*, I, 281, Art. 1472.
14. ʿAlī ibn Ibrāhīm of Qumm (fourth/tenth century), the author of one of the most ancient Shīʿite commentaries on the Qur'ān (Māmaqānī, *Tanqīḥ*, no. 8102).
15. Regarding this treatise of Shaikh Aḥmad, see *Fihrist*, p. 15.

The work referred to as *Jawāmiʿ al-Kalim*, 2 vols. in folio, is a large collection of writings by the Shaikh.

16. This is the traditional idea of Hūrqalyā, already met with in the present book. However, we should note in this case the further detail that "between the times"—between "physical time" and "eternal time"—is the time of the Soul or of the *Malakūt* (what Simnānī calls *zamān anfusī*, endogenous time).
17. See above, n. 10.
18. Regarding this notion of the eschatological episode in Islam in general, see A. J. Wensinck, *The Muslim Creed*, pp. 163 ff.
19. Regarding this treatise in which Shaikh Aḥmad answers four questions concerning Hūrqalyā, see *Fihrist*, p. 34.
20. See above, Art. I, and Part One, Ch. II, § 2 (the *quarta dimensio*, above, Art. VI).
21. Up to now we have been unable to confirm this reference. In fact, we have already pointed out that everything our authors say about Hūrqalyā exactly corresponds in Mandean cosmology to the world of the Doubles or celestial Images, *Mshunia Kushta.* But Suhrawardī, in the twelfth century, was already familiar with the term, as we have seen.
22. Namely, the world of the "Elements" in the universe of Hūrqalyā. See also above, Art. V.
23. The "tomb" which is not "in the cemetery" but in Hūrqalyā; see above, § 2, and Art. VIII, n. 9.
24. See the extracts from this commentary, below, §§ 4, 5.
25. That is, the epistle addressed to Fatḥ-ʿAlī Shāh Qājār, from which an extract is translated below, § 4.
26. This refers to the unending source of misunderstanding of the Shaikhs (above, n. 6)—i.e., confusion between arithmetical unity and ontological unity, inability or refusal to conceive the idea of a *caro spiritualis* implicit in the idea of resurrection, as in Imāmology.
27. See the other texts translated here, §§ 1 and 4.
28. See above, § 1, last part.
29. The spiritual body, the reality of the *caro spiritualis* (*jasad B*, composed of the Elements of the universe of Hūrqalyā), is hidden in the dense, opaque, corruptible body of flesh. It loses nothing of what it is when the latter disappears. *Jasad B*, the body of the Earth of Hūrqalyā, together with *jism B*, form the supracelestial body, the *corpus resurrectionis.*
30. Regarding this symbol, see below, §§ 4, 5.
31. *Habā'*, *ʿamā'*; cf. our *Ṣūfism of Ibn ʿArabī*, pp. 185 ff.
32. Refers to the *Risāla al-Khāqānīya* (cf. *Fihrist*, p. 31), in which

Shaikh Aḥmad answers five questions put by Fatḥ-ʿAlī Shāh; the text given here is taken from the answer to the first question.

33. Refers to the paradise described herein under the various names of the celestial Earth; our authors make a distinction between this and the paradise of the *Aeon* to come, the "absolute Paradise."
34. Five things to which the Spirit itself (*Rūḥ*) is added as a sixth; cf. below.
35. This is Proclus' *okhēma symphyes*; cf. the previous passages from Shaikh Aḥmad.
36. The number 70 is not a cipher representing a quantitative relationship, but is a form or multiple of the *numerous septenarius* (cf. Kraus, *Studien zu Jābir ibn Ḥayyān*, II, 221). It is the symbol of a qualitative differentiation, expressed here as ten cycles of seven (ten *octaves*); *jasad B* does not belong to the "carbon cycle."
37. Still, that is to say, "in Hūrqalyā" until reunited with *jism B*; see above, n. 23.
38. It should not, however, be forgotten that it has been said and will be said again that the Spirit departs with its *jism A* (the astral body of the Heavens of Hūrqalyā), which it will abandon "when the Trumpet sounds." But, *a fortiori*, it leaves with its *jism B*, the archetypal body from which it cannot be dissociated.
39. Regarding the qualitative sense of the number 70, see above, n. 36.
40. In passing, let us note that Shaikh Aḥmad always uses the word *rūḥ*, spirit, in the feminine. It can be of either gender in Arabic. In Aramaic, the word is feminine ("my mother the Holy Spirit" in the Gospel of the Hebrews in the Gnostic Apocrypha), and this is not a mere grammatical coincidence.
41. Whereas the first blast of the Trumpet is the "flaming breath" or Breath of Universal Reabsorption, the second, being the Breath of Resurrection, is a breath of propulsion, inaugurating the reintegration of all things, the *apokatastasis* which figures in many other cosmogonies; in Ismailian gnosis, the great Ressurrection inaugurates the "Cycle of Epiphany" (*dawr al-kashf*).
42. Cf. with what has been said above about the archetypal Image, Part One, Ch. I, § 4; Ch. II, § 4 *in fine*.
43. Thus a comparison could be made, both of the "six Treasuries" and also of the rejunction of the elemental parts with the Ele-

ment from which they sprang, with the anthropology of the Mazdean Book of Genesis, the *Bundahishn.*

44. A rather long passage has here been omitted concerning the process by which the vital soul comes to be adjoined to the embryonic organism.
45. An allusion to the Qur'ān, 56:87–88.
46. Here then we have further information concerning the physiology of the resurrection body: the esoteric or suprasensory part of the vegetable soul, coming from the Elements of Hūrqalyā, is the *jasad B*, the *caro spiritualis*; the esoteric part of the vital or animal soul, emanated from the Souls which move the Heavens of Hūrqalyā, is the *jism A*, the astral body which goes with the Spirit at the moment of the *exitus*, but which is separated from it at the Resurrection, when the Spirit dons its "spiritual flesh," its *jasad B*.
47. The interval of the cosmic pause is ciphered as 400 years. Here again, as in the case of the number 70 (above, n. 36), this has nothing to do with quantitative time, but is a "figure" symbolizing the endogenous time of the total maturation of the resurrection: the *tetrad* multiplied by a hundred (cf. the symbolic value of the "figure" forty, above, Part One, Ch. I, n. 120). For this symbol, cf. also C. G. Jung's *Alchemical Studies*, Index, s.v. quaternity; see also below, § 5.
48. Cf. the remark above, n. 40.
49. The definition of the alchemical operation is exactly that of spiritual hermeneutics: to hide the apparent and manifest what is hidden. Hence, it is not exactly a chapter in the "pre-history of science."
50. It would be important to compare these data, translated here for the first time, with the homologations studied by Jung in *Psychology and Alchemy* and *Mysterium Coniunctionis*, and by Mircea Eliade, *The Forge and the Crucible.*
51. Concerning this important work of Shaikh Aḥmad, see *Fihrist*, p. 32. A few pages from Mullā Ṣadrā's own work are included in the present book (above, Art. VI).
52. *Mir' āt al-ḥukama' : speculum philosophorum*, the word "philosopher" being understood in the sense in which Olympiodorus and Stephen of Alexandria take it. The terms *operatio secreta artis*, traditional in Latin alchemy, are the exact equivalent of the Arabic *'amal al-ṣinā'a al-maktūm.*
53. See our *Ṣūfism of Ibn 'Arabī*, pp. 108 ff.
54. Ibn Shahr-Āshūb was a famous Iranian Shī'ite theologian who lived in the Māzandarān (southern shore of the Caspian Sea);

he died in 588/1192. The extract from the homily attributed here to the first Imām serves only to illustrate the original connection between the alchemical idea and Shīʿite esotericism (the Imām and the Stone): the similarity between the prophetic message and the alchemical Work emphasizes it further. It is known that Jābir ibn Ḥayyān proclaimed himself to be a disciple of Jaʿfar Ṣādiq, the Sixth Imām (see the work of Paul Kraus cited above, n. 2).

55. *Coincidentia oppositorum*, possibly referring also to anterior states of matter, to cycles of cosmic alchemy (homologous to the cycles of prophecy), of which the posthumous development of the four bodies constituting man would itself be only one phase.

56. In the traditional manner, Shaikh Aḥmad quotes *lemmata* at some length from the writings of Mullā Ṣadrā and inserts his own commentary, which is why our translation of this and the following passages appears to be a dialogue.

57. Shaikh Aḥmad's reservation is interesting. It underscores the fact we have already pointed out that the view of Shaikhite philosophy differed equally from that of the philosophers and from that of the theologians of literalist orthodoxy in relating the fact of resurrection to the *spiritual body.*

58. The two terms have appeared here so frequently that there is no need to go into them again. However, let us just note that in our day terms such as *noosphere* and *psychosphere* have been invented and excite all the more admiration on the part of those who adopt them in that they have no idea that the traditional theosophers of old already had something of the sort in mind!

59. Cf. the passage from Muḥsin Fayẓ translated above, Art. VIII.

60. The classical precept of alchemy: *solve et coagula.*

61. *Maʿdan ḥayawānī rūḥānī* = *lapis vivus spiritualis.* Cf. C. G. Jung, *Psychology and Alchemy*, par. 426.

62. Allusion to the Avicennian theory of the procession of the Intelligences producing, by their acts of contemplation, their Heavens and the Souls moving them, a cosmology described by us elsewhere as a "phenomenology of angelic consciousness."

63. *Koine aisthesis*, or *synaisthesis*; cf. our book *Avicenna and the Visionary Recital*, Index, s.v.

64. Cf. this theme in our *Ṣūfism of Ibn ʿArabī*, pp. 180 ff. This exactly guarantees the noetic value of the forms of the imaginative consciousness: the God imagined therein is the very God *imagining* himself through this organ; hence the reciprocity,

the undeniable correlation of the two situations: *knowing* being and being *known*, known, that is to say, in the very act of knowing, and vice versa.

65. In the following lines, Shaikh Aḥmad gives us a complete recapitulation of the physiology of the resurrection body, starting from the four bodies of man, with which we have become acquainted in the preceding texts. What it is important to notice, apropos the passages from Mullā Ṣadrā, is the emphasis on the preeminent, transcendent part played by the active Imagination, the latter being so nearly consubstantial with the spiritual *anima*, the "I"-spirit, that, contrary to the common opinion of the Philosophers, physical death does not touch it. Thanks to it the "Form of Resurrection" is the work of the Person. This "subtle matter" has to be given its human form, whereas many give it only an animal form. So the Imagination here performs the alchemical work, the mediant action, active meditation, *imaginatio vera* (see the passages from Mullā Ṣadrā, above, Art. VI). Here we find the transition toward the text that will be given below, Art. X, 1.
66. These reflections developing, it will be recalled, a proposition of the Imām Jaʿfar confirm that we have to take the terms *istidāra*, *mustadīr*, not in the sense of rotundity, sphericity, but as what we suggest by the expression "perfect shape," signifying the constant perfection and harmony of structure (*tartīb*, *tarattub*); cf. above, Part One, Ch. II, § 4, n. 66.
67. We have been given to understand here many times that the "tomb" is not "in the cemetery" (see above, n. 23) but "in Hūrqalyā," where it is symbolized for each being by one of the "holes" perforated in Seraphiel's cosmic Trumpet.
68. This is the everlasting objection, as we have said, of the literalist "orthodox" in opposition to the Shaikhīs. And because they have not so much as glimpsed the metaphysical import of the idea of *metamorphosis*, they have equally failed to grasp the essential link between the *physics of resurrection* and the *ethics of resurrection*, whereas the Shaikhīs are continually and strongly stressing it (cf. above, n. 65).
69. As regards *form*, it follows that it is true that numerically it makes two, and this is exactly why there are two *jasad*, the one made up of sublunar Elements, the other of the Elements of Hūrqalyā.
70. Namely, the astral body that accompanies the "I"-spirit at the moment of the *exitus* and remains conjoined with it until the "first blast of the Trumpet" inaugurates the great cosmic pause.

71. We have already had occasion to recall how this primordial question and answer make their effects felt on all the planes of all the universes. Beginning from the pleroma of the *lāhūt*, the order of succession of the responses typifies the order of succession of the Fourteen Very-Pure and of their Heavens (see above, Part One, Ch. II, § 1). It could be said that this Qur'ānic verse, used as a key to the Shī'ite metaphysics, in which the preexistence of souls is a premise, also determines its "personalism." And the same remark applies to the Mazdean idea of the "preexistential choice" of the Fravartis.
72. The soul's preexistential choice may also call to mind here the Platonic myth of *Gorgias*.

Article X
SHAIKH ḤĀJJ MUḤAMMAD KARĪM KHĀN KIRMĀNĪ

1. On this work, to which we have already referred (Part One, Ch. II, § 1), see *Fihrist*, pp. 184 ff. This important work in four volumes was composed at the request of a few pious *mu'min* (in the Shī'ite meaning of the word, that is, adepts of the Holy Imāms). It does not claim to be a technical work; nonetheless, it does contain the essential points of the doctrine, very clearly set forth. It has been reedited several times and is current reading in Shaikhī circles. It has been somewhat enlarged in the work of Shaikh Sarkār Āghā, a chapter of which we translate in Art. XI, below.
2. Here, no doubt in order to simplify the exposition, the schema of the four bodies, as it was given to us in the previous passages of Shaikh Aḥmad Ahsā'ī, has been abridged. Here the essential archetypal body, or "Hūrqalyan body," combines the functions of what was presented as *jasad B* and *jism B*, whereas the material or accidental body combines the functions of *jasad A* and *jism A*.
3. Cf. the last passage from Shaikh Aḥmad quoted above, Art. IX, 5.
4. This is the old Iranian word *tan*, whence in Pahlavi *tan i pasen*, the word which, in Mazdean eschatology, designates the "body to come" or resurrection body, which is born at the moment of the final consummation. We have already referred above (Ch. I, n. 104) to the Mazdean idea of a "subtle physiology."
5. Here one should remember the theme of the *spissitudo spiritualis* (see above, Art. VI, the text of Mullā Ṣadrā *in fine*).

6. Regarding the notion of *himma*, see our *Ṣūfism of Ibn ʿArabī*, pp. 222 ff.
7. As a rule, *shirk* is translated as the act of *associating* other gods with the One; actually the term "dissociation" is just as appropriate. The *tawḥīd*, as an act of unification, effects an integration. Consequently *shirk* involves a disintegration of being; and that, as we saw earlier, is what *Hell* is.
8. What is in question here is not the active Imagination with the paramount function previously ascribed to it, but "fantasy." Regarding this all-important distinction, see again our *Ṣūfism of Ibn ʿArabī*, pp. 216 ff.
9. Concerning the symbol of the *arbor inversa*, see the documents studied by C. G. Jung in "The Philosophical Tree," pars. 410 ff.
10. See above, Art. IX, nn. 71, 72.
11. This concept thus justifies astral symbolism as a characterological procedure. The Ismāʿīlīs also regard the astronomical Heavens as homologous to the Heavens of the esoteric world. Thus, the Heavens and the heavenly bodies are merely the physical aspects of psycho-spiritual organs (see the passage from Mullā Ṣadrā, above, Art. VI. That is why in this case they represent factors or states of anthropogenesis).
12. Regarding the qualitative significance of the number 70, see above, Art. IX, n. 36. A comparison could be made here with the Ten Heavens and Eight Earths of Manicheism; cf. also with what follows below.
13. *Sijjīn*, the *Infernum*, Qur'ān 83:7–8; *Safīna* I, 603; on the Seven Earths, see *Safīna* I, 19, 661.
14. The diagram reproduced here is an exact copy of the original. The area indicated by the central diamond thus corresponds to the state designated in Mazdean cosmology as "mixture" (*gumechisn*).
15. Cf. the text of Mullā Ṣadrā (Art. VI, above) and Swedenborg, *De Coelo et ejus mirabilibus*, 156: "The things outside the Angels assume an appearance corresponding to those which are within them."
16. On the "esoteric" of each Heaven (*bāṭin al-falak*), see Mullā Ṣadrā (above, Art. VI), and see *En Islam izanien*, III, 225.
17. Of course, here we should not take "soul" in the Cartesian sense of the word, but as *spissitudo spiritualis*.
18. The remark of the Imām alludes to verse 4:71 in the Qur'ān, which we are translating here as required by Shīʿite hermeneutics; see *Safīna*, II, 18 (quoting a *Tafsīr* attributed to the Fifth Imām).

19. An allusion to verse 33:33 which, in Shīʿite hermeneutics, sacralizes the Prophet's family. Professing Islam, being a *Muslim*, still does not confer the quality of a *mu'mim*, True Faithful; the latter implies devotion to and love for the Fourteen Very-Pure.
20. *Nafs-i qudsī-yi kullī: sacrosancta Anima generalis.*
21. It goes without saying that all these expressions should be understood in the psycho-spiritual sense suggested from the very beginning of this book by such terms as the "Heavens of your being," the "Hells of your being," in the same way as Simnānī, when he interiorizes the science of prophecy, speaks of the "seven prophets of your being." (See our book cited above, n. 16.)
22. Readers should remember the distinction made at the beginning between paradisic Abodes, which are such by right of priority, and those which are such by derivation. These lines introduce a description of the latter.
23. This motif of the *well* is a classic example of gnostic anthropology (Mandeism, Suhrawardī, Najmuddīn, Kubrā).
24. All the Shīʿite fervor bursts forth in this last page. The *parousia* of the Imām is awaited as the reign of spiritual liberty, the advent of the Paraclete. But in this eschatology there is still the consciousness that the occultation of the Imām results from the fact that men have become incapable of seeing him, and that the *parousia* of the hidden Imām presupposes first of all the disoccultation of their hearts. Otherwise they would not even recognize him, and that is why, in Shīʿite esotericism, it is obligatory not to talk about him to anyone incapable of recognizing him.

Article XI
SHAIKH ABU'L-QĀSIM KHĀN IBRĀHĪMĪ

1. The chapter extracted from this considerable work forms a commentary on the text of Muḥ. Karīm Khān Kirmānī in Art. x, above. The selection was a result of a quite inept question by a person who, not understanding much of mystical theosophy (*ʿirfān*), did not understand the relation established between the world of Hūrqalyā and the epiphany of the hidden Imām. This chapter is the most suitable to conclude our choice of texts; all the overtones of Hūrqalyā that sound in Shīʿite piety are to be heard here. The limitations of our book prevent us from doing justice to it.

2. Intelligence, of course, refers to the first hypostasis (*Noūs* or *Ennoia*). The *ḥadith* that relates it to the "Muḥammadan Light" (the primordial spiritual entity of the Prophet) offers numerous variations, all of which bore fruit in the meditation of the mystics.
3. Therefore, it is not a question here of perishable "matter" as opposed to "spirit," but of *spissitudo spiritualis*—"spiritual matter" consubstantial with every being (cf. the idea of *Nafas al-Raḥmān* in Ibn ʿArabī).
4. The "cosmic liturgy" celebrated by the Intelligence forms a theme well developed also in Ismāʿīlī gnosis (Nāṣir-i Khusraw, Abū Yaʿqūb Sijistānī); see our *Ṣūfism of Ibn ʿArabī*, pp. 105 ff. (the "prayer of the heliotrope" in Proclus).
5. That is, separated from perishable and corruptible "material matter," while possessing their own consubstantial and incorruptible "spiritual matter."
6. The *logoi spermatikoi*; see above, Art. IX, n. 11; *Safīna*, I, 482; Muḥ. Karīm Khān Kirmānī, *Kitāb al-fuṣūl*, 236; cf. Plotinus, *Enneads*, V.8.13; VI.3.15, and passim.
7. Allusion to the preexistential choice, the decisive event of metahistory; see above, Art. IX, nn. 71, 72.
8. On the pleroma of the Fourteen Very-Pure (the Twelve Imāms around the Prophet and Fāṭima) forming the pleroma of the *lāhūt* in Twelver Shīʿite theosophy, see above, Part One, Ch. II, § 1. Their manifestation in the world of the *Malakūt* is referred to here. Similarly, the theme of the "Earth of the world of the Imperative," found at the beginning of this text of Sarkār Āghā, recalls the theme of Fāṭima as the supracelestial Earth of the *lāhūt*.
9. An idea very close to the endogenous time (*zamān anfusī*) of Simnānī: each soul, each form, *is* its time (not *of* its time).
10. The fundamental importance of the comparison with the mirror has already been noted here. It shows us how what is called docetic metaphysics is in fact a theological critique of knowledge. The spiritual cannot "be materialized" in the natural world: the latter represents the surface of a mirror, nothing more or less. Thus, material history is erased in favor of a realism of the soul.
11. Cf. the theme of the "six Treasuries" in Shaikh Aḥmad Aḥsā'ī (above, Art. IX); on the concept of *materia prima*, see above, n. 3.
12. This is the *Irshād al-ʿawāmm*, several pages of which we have translated above, Art. X.
13. See above, p. 191, the text of Shaikh Aḥmad: "Its lower plane

borders on the convex surface of the Sphere of Spheres," when, emerging from the physical and astronomical cosmos, one enters the "eighth climate," the *quarta dimensio.*

14. On this theme of fundamental Imāmology (presupposing the isomorphism of all the planes of the universe), see above, Part One, Ch. II, § 1.
15. See ibid., for one sees in these lines how the theme of Hūrqalyā and the Shī'ite faith are linked. At the same time as the theme of the "companions of the hidden Imām" there reappears, in a new octave, the Zoroastrian theme of the "companions of the Saoshyant"; this takes place thanks to the entire individual ethic of the Shī'ite adepts. Each of them is in a relationship to the hidden Imām (in Hūrqalyā, on the "green island," and so on) analogous to the relationship of one of the hundred and twenty-four thousand Nabīs to the Prophet. On this *Ecclesia spiritualis*, see our book *En Islam iranien*, I, 35, 119, 132, and IV, 275–445. The theme should also be related to the theme of the Watchers of *al-A'rāf*, the "men of the Invisible world" dwelling in the country of *Yūḥ* (above, Art. IV).
16. We have already encountered here descriptions relating to the inhabitants of the *Var* of Yima or of the cities of Hūrqalyā (above, Part One, Ch. I, § 2 *in fine*, and Ch. II, § 2). The present context emphasizes further that they must be considered as a phenomenology—that is, as a description of the outer things which are the *apparentiae reales* of inner states. As previously suggested, a fruitful comparison with Swedenborg's descriptions could be attempted.
17. The first work cited is the work of Muḥ. Khān Kirmānī, Third successor to Shaikh Aḥmad (d. 1324/1906). The *Biḥār al-Anwār* is the great Shī'ite encyclopedia of Majlisī, cited here many times. The traditions about Jābalqā and Jābarṣā are in Vol. XIV, 78–87.
18. Ibid., p. 80, lines 23–26.
19. This refers to the author's own father, Mawlānā Zaynal-'Ābidīn Khān Kirmānī (d. 1361/1942), Fourth successor of Shaikh Aḥmad; for the work in question, see *Fihrist*, p. 449 (the tenth treatise of the collection described).
20. *Biḥār al-Anwār*, XIV, 81–82 (p. 81: theme of the emerald, which is known to symbolize the cosmic Soul for the Ṣūfīs).
21. The plural "We" designates the pleroma of the Twelve Imāms, in the name of which each Imām speaks—here, the Imām Ja'far Ṣādiq. One sees that the humanity described in these lines is that of the archetypal Imāmites, centered on the Imāms as cosmogonic and soteriologic theophanies.

22. In these lines there is an explicit and stirring demand by the Imām himself for the esotericism which is imposed on faith and on Shīʿite beliefs.
23. This detail suffices to show that the eschatological descriptions, the final battle in which the mystical Knights surrounding the Imām participated, should not be understood as data concerning material events. They translate events taking place now "in Hūrqalyā."
24. This accords with the remark attributed to Jāgir Kurdī, one of the Shaikhs of Rūzbihān of Shīrāz (d. 605/1209): "He has given me a two-edged blade, one for the East, the other for the West; if I pointed it toward the mountains, the high peaks would collapse." See our introduction to the book of Rūzbihān, *Le Jasmin des Fidèles d'amour*, p. 52.
25. For there is no common measure between *zamān anfusī*, endogenous qualitative time, and *zamān āfāqī*, quantitative physical time.
26. This number "encodes" the duration of an astronomical cycle; seven heptads of millennia, each governed respectively by one of the seven planets. It should therefore be taken, as the author suggests, as essentially a symbol of purely *Hūrqalyāvī* duration.
27. That is, in the text translated above, Art. x, 2, and commented on in the present chapter. The symmetry between the configurations of the theme has already been noted: Here the "transportation" upwards to Hūrqalyā; the descent of the "Abode of hymns" (*Garōtmān*) to encounter the Earth, in Mazdean eschatology; the descent of the celestial Jerusalem, in the Apocalypse; see above, Part One, Ch. I, n. 128.
28. On the touching figure of the Eleventh Imām, Ḥasan ʿAskarī, father of the "hidden Imām," who died at the age of twenty-eight (in 260/873), see our study "Le Douzième Imām" in *En Islam iranien*, IV, 301–460. The episode narrated here refers to the annoyances inflicted on him by the ʿAbbāsid Caliph.
29. On this treatise, see above, n. 19.
30. On this qualification of the hidden Imām, see our study cited above, n. 28.
31. An allusion to the theme of the *sodalitas spiritualis* which, with the *tawḥīd*, prophetology, and Imāmology, is one of the "four pillars" of the Shīʿite Shaikhī teaching.
32. This is one of the oldest symbols of Shīʿite gnosis. The alchemist Jābir ibn Ḥayyān already saw the "sun rising in the West" as the symbol of the Imām, the inaugurator of a new cycle.

LIST OF WORKS CITED

Acts of John. See JAMES, *The Apocryphal New Testament*.

Acts of Peter. See JAMES, *The Apocryphal New Testament*.

Acts of Thomas. See JAMES, *The Apocryphal New Testament*; this is the source of the "Song of the Pearl," which is the same as the "Hymn of the Soul."

AFFIFI, A. E. (ABU'L-ʿALĀ' ʿAFFĪFĪ), ed. *Fuṣūṣ al-ḥikam*. 2 vols. Cairo, 1365/1946. (*Fuṣūṣ* I = Ibn ʿArabī's text; *Fuṣūṣ* II = Affifi's commentary.)

AĞA-OĞLU, MEHMET. "The Landscape Miniatures of an Anthology Manuscript of the Year 1398 A.D.," *Ars Islamica*, III, pt. I (1936), 77–98.

ĀGHĀ BUZURG (SHAIKH). *Dharīʿa*. 20+ vols. Teheran.

AḤSA'Ī, (SHAIKH) AḤMAD. Commentary on the *Kitāb al-ḥikma al-ʿarshīya* of Ṣadruddīn Shīrāzī. Tabrīz, 1278/1861.

———. *Jawāmiʿ al-kalim*. 2 vols. Tabriz, 1273–1276/1856/1859.

———. *Kitāb sharḥ al-ziyāra*, II. 2 vols. Tabriz, 1276/1859.

———. *al-Risāla al-khāqānīya*. (This part of his *Jawāmiʿ al-kalim*.)

ARDABĪLĪ, ṢAFĪUDDĪN. *Ṣafwat al-ṣafā'*. Bombay, 1911.

BACHOFEN, JOHANN JAKOB. *Das Mutterrecht: Eine Untersuchung über die Gynaikokratie der alten Welt nach ihrer religiösen und rechtlichen Natur*. Stuttgart, 1861. (See *Gesammelte Werke*. Ed. Karl Meuli. Basel, 1943–.)

BADAWĪ, ʿABD AL-RAḤMĀN. *Ideae platonicae*. Cairo, 1367/1947.

BAILEY, HAROLD WALTER. "Iranian Studies III," *Bulletin of the School of Oriental Studies*, VII (1933–1935), 275–298.

———. *Zoroastrian Problems in the Ninth-Century Books*. Oxford, 1943.

BENVENISTE, ÉMILE. "L'Erān-vēž et l'origine légendaire des Iraniens," *Bulletin of the School of Oriental Studies*, VII (1933–1935), 265–274.

BIDEZ, JOSEPH, and CUMONT, FRANZ. *Les Mages hellénisés: Zoroastre, Ostanès et Hystape d'après la tradition grecque*. 2 vols. Paris, 1938.

BĪRUNĪ, ABŪ RAYḤĀN. *Kitāb al-tafhīm*, ed. Humāyī. Teheran, 1318/1900.

BOUSSET, WILHELM. *Hauptprobleme der Gnosis*. (Forschungen zur Religion und Literatur des Alten und Neuen Testaments, 10.) Göttingen, 1907.

BOUSSET, WILHELM. *Die Religion des Judentums im späthellenistischen Zeitalter*, ed. Hugo Gressmann. 3rd edn., Tübingen, 1926.

BRANDT, A.J.H. WILHELM. *Die mandäische Religion*. Leipzig, 1889.

Bundahishn. The "great *Bundahishn*," an unedited MS, is cited in part in Nyberg, "Questions," I, q.v. The "small *Bundahishn*" is tr. in West, *Pahlavi Texts*, pt. I, pp. 3–151. Unless further identified, references are to the great *Bundahishn*.

CORBIN, HENRY, tr. and ed. *L'Archange empourpré*, by Shaykh al-Ishrāq Sohravardī (=Suhrawardī). Paris, 1976. (Fifteen treatises and mystical recitals, translated from the Persian and Arabic, annotated.)

———. *Avicenna and the Visionary Recital;* tr. Willard R. Trask, New York (Bollingen Series LXVI) and London, 1960. (Orig.: *Avicenne et le récit visionnaire*. 2 vols. Teheran and Paris, 1952, 1954. Bibliothèque iranienne 4–5.)

———. *Creative Imagination in the Ṣūfism of Ibn ʿArabī*, tr. Ralph Manheim. Princeton (Bollingen Series XCI) and London, 1969. (Orig.: *L'Imagination créatrice dans le Soufisme d'Ibn ʿArabī*, Paris, 1958.)

———. "Cyclical Time in Mazdaism and Ismailism." In: *Man and Time* (Papers from the Eranos Yearbooks 3), pp. 115–172. New York (Bollingen Series XXX) and London, 1957.

———. "De la Gnose antique à la gnose ismaelienne," *Atti del XII° Congresso Volta*, Accad. Naz. dei Lincei. Rome, 1956.

———. "Divine Epiphany and Spiritual Rebirth in Ismailian Gnosis." In: *Man and Transformation* (Papers from the Eranos Yearbooks 5), pp. 69–160. New York (Bollingen Series XXX) and London, 1964.

———. *En Islam iranien: aspects spirituels et philosophiques*. (Bibliothèque des Idées.) Vol. I, *Le Shiʿisme duodécimain*; Vol. II, *Sohravardi et les Platoniciens de Perse*; Vol. III, *Les Fidèles d'amour. Shiʿisme et soufisme*; Vol. IV, *L'École d'Ispahan; L'École Shaykhie; Le Douzième Imām; index général*. Paris, 1971–1972.

———. *Étude préliminaire pour le "Livre réunissant des deux sagesses" de Nāṣir-e Khosraw*. Teheran and Paris, 1953. (Bibliothèque iranienne 3a.)

———. *L'Homme de lumière dans le soufisme iranien*. Paris, 1971.

———. "Le 'Livre du Glorieux' de Jābir ibn Ḥayyān: alchimie et archetypes," *Eranos Jahrbuch*, XVIII/1950, 47–114.

———, ed. *Œuvres philosophiques et mystiques de Sohrawardī*, I

(= *Opera metaphysica et Mystica*, II). Teheran and Paris, 1952. (Bibliothèque iranienne 2.) (Contains: *Kitāb ḥikmat al-ishrāq* [Book of Oriental Theosophy]; *Kitāb i'tiqad al-ḥukamā'* [The Symbol of the Philosophers' Faith]; *Qiṣṣat āl-ghurba al-gharbīya* [Recital of the Occidental Exile].)

———, ed. *Opera metaphysica et mystica*, I. Istanbul, 1945. (Bibliotheca Islamica 16.) (Contains the metaphysics of *Kitāb al-talwiḥāt* [Book of Elucidations], *Kitāb al-muqāwamāt* [Book of Oppositions], *Kitāb Mashāri' wa'l-Muṭārahāt* [Book of Conversations].)

———, tr. *Pand Nāmak i Zartusht* (*The Book of Counsels of Zartusht*, tr. from the Pahlavi). In: *Poure Davoud Memorial Volume* II. Bombay, 1951.

———. See also RŪZBIHAN BAQLĪ SHIRĀZĪ; SUHRAWARDĪ, SHIHĀBUDDĪN YAḤYÀ.

Corpus hermeticum. Text established by A. D. Nock. Tr. A.-J. Festugière. 4 vols. Paris, 1945–1954.

CUMONT, FRANZ. "Les Anges du paganisme," *Revue de l'histoire des religions*, LXXII (1915), 159–182.

———. *See also* BIDEZ, JOSEPH, and CUMONT, FRANZ.

DARMESTETER, JAMES, tr. *Le Zend-Avesta.* 3 vols. Paris, 1892–1893. (Annales du Guimet, 21–22, 24.)

Dātistān-i-Dīnīk. In: West, E. W., tr., *Pahlavi Texts*, II, 1–276.

DEFFONTAINES, PIERRE. "The Religious Factor in Human Geography: Its Force and Its Limits," *Diogenes*, II (Spring, 1953), 24–37.

DĒNKART. In: West, E. W., tr., *Pahlavi Texts*, Parts IV and V.

DROWER, ETHEL STEFANA. "Hibil Ziwa and the Parthian Prince," *Journal of the Royal Asiatic Society*, 1954, pts. 3–4, pp. 152–156.

———. *The Mandaeans of Iraq and Iran.* Oxford, 1937.

ELIADE, MIRCEA. *The Forge and the Crucible.* Tr. Stephen Corrin. London and New York, 1962. (Orig.: *Forgerons et alchimistes*, Paris, 1956.)

———. *Images and Symbols: Studies in Religious Symbolism.* Tr. Philip Mairet. New York and Paris, 1961. (Orig.: *Images et Symboles: Essais sur le symbolisme magico-religieux*, Paris, 1952.)

———. *The Myth of the Eternal Return.* Tr. Willard R. Trask. New York (Bollingen Series XLVI) and London, 1954. (Orig.: *Le Mythe de l'éternel retour: Archétypes et répétition*, Paris, 1949.)

———. *Patterns in Comparative Religion.* Tr. Rosemary Sheed.

London and New York, 1958. (Orig.: *Traité d'histoire des religions*, Paris, 1964.)

The Encyclopaedia of Islām. Ed. M. Th. Houtsma, T. W. Arnold, R. Basset, R. Hartmann, *et al.* 4 vols. and suppl. Leiden and London, 1913–1938.

FECHNER, GUSTAV THEODOR. *Über die Seelenfrage. Ein Gang durch die sichtbare Welt, um die unsichtbare zu finden.* Leipzig, 1861; 2nd edn., Hamburg and Leipzig, 1907.

Fihrist. See Ibrāhīmī.

The Gospel According to Thomas. Ed. and tr. Antoine Guillaumont *et al.* New York and Leiden, 1959.

GRAY, LOUIS H. *The Foundations of the Iranian Religions.* Bombay, 1925.

GRESSMANN, HUGO. "Das religiongeschichtliche Problem des Ursprungs der hellenistischen Erlösungsreligion," *Zeitschrift für Kirchengeschichte*, XLI (1922), 154–180.

HASTINGS, JAMES, ed. *Encyclopedia of Religion and Ethics.* 13 vols. Edinburgh and New York, 1908–1926.

HEIMANN, BETTY. *Indian and Western Philosophy, a Study in Contrasts.* London, 1937.

HERTEL, JOHANNES. *Die awestischen Herrschafts- und Siegesfeuer.* Leipzig, 1931.

HERZFELD, ERNST EMIL, ed. *Archäologische Mitteilungen aus Iran*, II. Berlin, 1930.

———. *Zoroaster and His World.* 2 vols. Princeton, 1947.

HERZOG, JOHANN JAKOB, ed. *Realencyklopädie für protestantische Theologie und Kirche.* 3rd edn., 24 vols. Leipzig, 1896–1913. See VI (1899), XVIII (1906).

Hildegarde of Bingen. Physica.

"Hymn of the Soul." *See Acts of Thomas.*

IBN 'ARABĪ, MUḤYĪDDĪN. *Fuṣūṣ al-ḥikam*, ed. A. E. Affifi. 2 vols. Cairo, 1365/1946. (*Fuṣūṣ* I = Ibn 'Arabī text; *Fuṣūṣ* II = Affifi's commentary.)

———. *Kitāb al-futūḥāt al-Makkīya fī ma'rifat al-asrār al-malikīya wa'l-mulkīya.* 4 vols. Cairo, 1329/1911.

——— (attributed). *Tafsīr al-Qur'ān.* Cairo, 1317/1899–1900.

IBRĀHĪMĪ, (SHAIKH) ABU'L-QĀSIM KHĀN (SARKĀR ĀGHĀ). *Fihrist.* Kirmān, 1329/1911.

———. *Tanzīh al-awliyā'.* Kirmān, 1367/1947.

JACKSON, ABRAHAM VALENTINE WILLIAMS. *Zoroaster, the Prophet of Ancient Iran.* 5th edn., New York, 1938.

JAMES, MONTAGUE RHODES. *The Apocryphal New Testament.* Oxford, 1960.

JAMES, MONTAGUE RHODES, and RYLE, HERBERT EDWARD, eds. *Old Testament Apocryphal Books: The Psalms of Solomon.* Cambridge, 1891.

JĪLĪ, ʿABD AL-KARĪM. *Kitāb al-insān al-kāmil.* Cairo, 1304/1886–1887.

JUNG, CARL GUSTAV. *Mysterium Coniunctionis*, tr. R.F.C. Hull. (The Collected Works of C. G. Jung, 14.) New York (Bollingen Series XX) and London, 1963. 2nd edn., Princeton and London, 1970.

———. "Paracelsus as a Spiritual Phenomenon," in *Alchemical Studies*, tr. R.F.C. Hull. (The Collected Works of C. G. Jung, 13.) Princeton (Bollingen Series XX) and London, 1967. Pp. 109–189.

———. "The Philosophical Tree," in *Alchemical Studies*, tr. R.F.C. Hull. (The Collected Works of C. G. Jung, 13.) Princeton (Bollingen Series XX) and London, 1967. Pp. 251–349.

———. *Psychology and Alchemy*, tr. R.F.C. Hull. (The Collected Works of C. G. Jung, 12.) New York (Bollingen Series XX) and London, 1953; 2nd edn., rev., Princeton, 1968.

JUSTI, FERDINAND. *Der Bundehesh. Zum ersten Male herausgegeben, transcribiert, übersetzt und mit Glossar versehen.* Leipzig, 1868.

KĀSHĀNĪ, MUḤSIN FAYẒ. *Kalimāt maknūna.* Lithograph, Teheran, 1216/1801; Bombay, 1296/1878.

———. *Tafsīr al-ṣāfī*, Teheran, 1275/1858.

KIRMĀNĪ, (SHAIKH ḤAJJ) MUḤAMMAD KARĪM KHĀN. Irshād al-ʿawāmm. 3rd edn., 4 vols. in 2. Kirmān, 1353–1355/1934–1936.

———. *Iṣlāḥ al-ajsād.* Manuscript.

———. *Iṣlāḥ al-arwāḥ.* Manuscript.

———. *Islāḥ al-nufūs.* Manuscript.

———. *Kitāb al-fuṣūl.* Kirmān, 1354/1935–1936.

———. *Mir'āt al-ḥikma.*

———. *Risāla-yi naṣīrīya.* Kirmān, 1375/1955.

———. *Risāla-yi sulṭānīya.* Bombay, 1860.

———. *Risāla-yi yāqūtīya.*

KRAMERS, JOHANNES HENDRIK. *The Daēnā in the Gāthās.* Oriental Studies in Honour of Dasturji Saheb Cursetji Erachji Pavry, January 1934. Reprinted in: *Analecta Orientalia*, I, 225–231. Leiden, 1954.

KRAUS, PAUL. *Studien zu Jābir ibn Ḥayyān.* 2 vols. Cairo, 1942–1943.

LĀHĪJĪ, ʿABD AL-RAZZĀQ. *Gawhar-i murād.* Teheran, 1313/1895.

LAHĪJĪ, SHAMSUDDIN MUḤAMMAD. Commentary on the *Gulshan-i rāz* of Maḥmūd Shabistarī. (Edn. of Kayvān Samī'ī.) Teheran, 1378/1958.

LEISEGANG, HANS. *La Gnose*, tr. J. Gouillard. Paris, 1951. (Orig.: *Die Gnosis*, Leipzig, 1924.)

LIDZBARSKI, MARK, ed. and tr. *Das Johannesbuch der Mardäer*. Giessen, 1915; repr. Berlin, 1966.

MAETERLINCK, MAURICE. "Le Vieux qui ne veut pas mourir." In: *L'Autre Monde, ou Le Cadran stellaire*. New York, 1942.

MAJLISĪ, MUḤAMMAD BĀQIR. *Biḥār al-anwār*. 14 vols. Teheran, 1305/1887–1888.

MAMAQANI, 'ABD ALLAH. *Tanqīḥ al maqāl fi aḥwāl al-rijāl*. 3 vols. Najaf, 1349–1352/1930–1933.

MASSIGNON, LOUIS. "Comment ramener à une base commune l'étude textuelle de deux cultures: l'arabe et la gréco-latine." In: *Lettres d'humanité*, II, 122–140. Paris, 1943.

———. *La Mubāhala de Medine et l'hyperdulie de Fāṭima*. Paris, 1955.

———. "La Notion du vœu et la dévotion musulmane à Fāṭima." In: *Studi orientalistici in onore di Giorgio Levi della Vida*. 2 vols. Rome, 1956. Pp. 102–126.

MEIER, FRITZ. "Die Welt der Urbilder bei 'Alī Hamadānī († 1385)" *Eranos Jahrbuch*, XVIII/1950, 115–172.

MĒNŌKĒ-XRAT. In West, E. W., tr., *Pahlavi Texts*, Part III, pp. 1–113. (Same as: *Mainyo-i-Khard* and *Mainog-i-Khirad*.)

MESSINA, GIUSEPPE, ed. and tr. *Libro apocalittico persiano Āyātkār i Žāmāspīk*. Rome, 1939.

———. *I Magi a Betlemme e una predizione di Zoroastro*. Rome, 1933.

MODI, JIVANJI JAMSHEDJI. *The Religious Ceremonies and Customs of the Parsees*. 2nd ed., Bombay, 1937.

MUḤSIN FAYZ. *See* Kāshānī, Muḥsin Fayẓ.

MO'ĪN [MU'ĪN], MUḤAMMAD, ed. *Burhān-i qāṭi'* by 'Alī ibn Muḥammad Ṭabāṭabā'ī. 5 vols. Teheran, 1371–1376/1951–1956; IV, 1376/1956.

———. *The Philosophy of Illumination and the Ancient Iranian Culture*. Teheran, 1370/1950. In Persian.

———. *See also* Rūzbihan Baqlī Shīrazī.

MONNERET DE VILLARD, UGO. *Le Pitture musulmane al soffito della Cappella Palatina in Palermo*. Rome, 1950.

MORE, HENRY. *Enchiridion metaphysicum*. London, 1671.

MOULTON, JAMES HOPE. "It Is His Angel," *The Journal of Theological Studies*, III (1902).

MULLĀ ṢADRĀ. *See* SHĪRĀZĪ ṢADRUDDĪN.

NYBERG, HENRIK SAMUEL. *Hilfsbuch des Pehlevi.* 2 vols. Vol. I, Uppsala, 1928; Vol. II, Glossary, Uppsala and Leipzig, 1931.

———. *Kleinere Schriften des Ibn al-ʿArabī.* Leiden, 1919.

———. "Questions de cosmogonie et de cosmologie mazdéennes," *Journal asiatique* (Paris), CCXIV: 2 (April-June, 1929), 193–310. (*Cited as* "Questions," I.)

———. *Die Religionen des alten Iran.* German tr. H. H. Schaeder. Leipzig, 1938. (Mitteilungen der Vorderasiatisch-aegyptischen Gesellschaft, 43.)

Odes of Solomon. See James, Montague Rhodes, and Ryle, Herbert Edwards, eds.

Pand Nāmak i Zartusht. See CORBIN, HENRY, tr.

PASCHER, JOSEF. *Der Königsweg zu Wiedergeburt und Vergottung bei Philon v. Alexandreia.* Paderborn, 1931.

PAVRY, JAL DASTUR CURSETJI. *The Zoroastrian Doctrine of a Future Life from Death to the Individual Judgment.* 2nd edn., New York, 1929.

The Persian Rivayats of Hormazyar Framarz, the Saddar Bundehesh. Bombay, 1932.

PHILO JUDAEUS. *De somniis.* In: *Philo*, ed. F. H. Colson and G. H. Whitaker. Vol. V. Cambridge, Mass., 1934, pp. 285–579. (LCL.)

PLOTINUS. *The Enneads.* Tr. Stephen MacKenna, rev. B. S. Page. London and New York, 1956.

PLUTARCH. *Isis and Osiris.* In: *Plutarch's Moralia*, tr. F. C. Babbitt. Vol. V, Cambridge, Mass., 1936, pp. 3–191. (LCL.)

POORTMAN, JOHANNES JACOBUS. *Okhēma, Geschiedenis en zin van het hylisch pluralisme.* 2 vols. Assen, 1954–1958.

PORPHYRY [PORPHYRIUS]. *De antro nympharum.* In: *Opuscula Selecta*, ed. A. Nauck. Leipzig, 1886.

PROCLUS. *The Elements of Theology*, ed. and tr. Eric Robertson Dodds. 1933.

QAYṢARĪ, DĀ'ŪD. Commentary on the *Fuṣūṣ al-ḥikam* of Ibn ʿArabī. Bombay, 1881 and 1882.

QUMMĪ, ʿABBĀS. *Safīnat al-biḥā al-anwār.* 2 vols. Najaf, 1352–1354/1934–1937.

RAHNER, HUGO. "Die seelenheilende Blume. Moly und Mandragore in antiker und christlicher Symbolik," *Eranos Jahrbuch*, XII/1945, 117–239.

RĀZI, FAKHRUDDĪN. *Mafātīḥ al-ghayb.* 8 vols. Istanbul, 1307–1308/1889–1890.

REITZENSTEIN, RICHARD. "Gedanken zur Entwicklung des Erlöserglaubens," *Historische Zeitschrift*, CXXVI (1922), 1–57.

———. *Das iranische Erlösungs-mysterium.* Bonn, 1921.

REITZENSTEIN, RICHARD, and SCHAEDER, HANS HEINRICH. *Studien zum antiken Synkretismus aus Iran und Griechenland.* Leipzig, 1926. (Studien der Bibliothek Warburg, VII.)

RINGBORN, LARS-IVAR. *Graltempel und Paradies.* Stockholm, 1951. (Kungl. vitterhets historie och antikvitets akademiens handlingar, 73.)

ROSENBERG, FRÉDÉRIC, ed. and tr. *Le Livre de Zoroastre (Zarātusht-Nāma) de Zartusht-i Bahrām ibn Pajdū.* St. Petersburg, 1914.

RŪZBIHĀN, BAQLĪ SHĪRĀZĪ. *'Arā' is al-bayān.* 2 vols. 1301/1883.

———. *Le Jasmin des Fidèles d'amour (K. 'Abhar al-'Āshiqīn). Traité de Soufisme en persan,* ed. and tr. Henry Corbin and Muḥ. Mo'īn. Teheran and Paris, 1958. (Bibliothèque iranienne 8.)

Saddar Bundehesh. In: *The Persian Rivayats* (q.v.).

Safīna. See QUMMĪ, 'ABBĀS.

SARKĀR ĀGHĀ. *See Ibrāhīmī.*

SCHAEDER, HANS HEINRICH. *See* REITZENSTEIN, RICHARD, and SCHAEDER, HANS HEINRICH.

SHABISTARĪ, MAḤMŪD. *See* LĀHĪJĪ, SHAMSUDDĪN MUḤAMMAD.

Shāyast lā-shāyast. In: West, E. R., tr., *Pahlavi Texts.* Oxford, 1880, Part I, pp. 237–406.

SHĪRĀZĪ, QUṬBUDDĪN MAḤMŪD. *Sharḥ Ḥikmat al-ishrāq.* Lithograph, Teheran, 1315/1898.

SHĪRĀZĪ, ṢADRUDDĪN (MULLĀ ṢADRĀ). *Kitāb al-ḥikma al-'arshīya.* Teheran, 1315/1897.

Sīrōza. In Darmesteter, tr., *Zend-Avesta,* II. *Sīrōza* I, pp. 296–322, *Sīrōza* II, pp. 323–330.

"Song of the Pearl." *See Acts of Thomas.*

SOURIAU, ETIENNE. *L'ombre de Dieu.* Paris, 1955.

SPIEGEL, FRIEDRICH, ed. *Avesta, die heiligen Schriften der Parsen.* 3 vols., Leipzig, 1852–1863; III, Khorda-Avesta, 1863.

STROTHMAN, RUDOLF, ed. *Mizāj al-tasnīm.*

SUHRAWARDĪ, SHIHĀBUDDĪN YAḤYÀ (SHAIKH AL-ISHRĀQ). *Œuvres philosophiques et mystiques de Sohrawardī,* II (= *Opera metaphysica et mystica,* III) Works in Persian, ed. S. H. Nasr. Foreword by H. Corbin. Teheran and Paris, 1970. (Bibliothèque iranienne, 17).

———. *See also* CORBIN, HENRY.

SWEDENBORG, EMANUEL. *De Coelo et ejus mirabilibus* § 156 (orig. publ. in Latin, London, 1758). Tr. Rev. Samuel Noble, *Heaven and Its Wonders, The World of Spirits and Hell: From Things Heard and Seen.* New York, 1864.

ṬABARĪ, MUḤAMMAD IBN JARĪR. *Chronique de Abou-Djafar-Mo'hammed-ben-Djarir-ben Yezid Tabari*, tr. Hermann Zotenberg. 4 vols. Paris, 1867–1874.

ṬABARSĪ, AL-FAḌL IBN AL-ḤASAN. *Majma' al-bayān*. Teheran, 1318/1900.

TABRĪZĪ, M. A. *Rayhānat al-Adab*, I.

VAJDA, GEORGES. "Les Notes d'Avicenne sur la 'Théologie d'Aristote,'" *Revue Thomiste*, LI (1951), 346–348.

Vendidād. In Darmesteter, tr., *Zend-Avesta*, II, 1–293.

Vispered. In Darmesteter, tr., *Zend-Avesta*, I, 443–492.

WENSINCK, ARENT JAN. *The Muslim Creed*. Cambridge, 1932; repr. New York, 1966.

WEST, E. W., tr. *Pahlavi Texts*. 5 vols. Oxford, 1880–1897.

WIET, GASTON. *Soieries persanes*. (*Mémoires de l'Institut d'Egypte*, Vol. 52.) Cairo, 1367/1947.

WOLFSON, HARRY AUSTRYN. *Philo. Foundations of Religious Philosophy in Judaism, Christianity, and Islam*. 2 vols. Cambridge, Mass., 1947.

YĀQŪT IBN 'ABD ALLĀH, AL-ḤAMAWĪ. *Mu'jam al-buldān*. 10 vols. Cairo, 1345/1926.

THE YASHTS. In: Darmesteter, tr., *Zend-Avesta*, II, 331–683.

Yasna. In: Darmesteter, tr., *Zend-Avesta*, I, 1–442.

Zāt-Spram. In: West, E. R., tr., *Pahlavi Texts*, I.

ZELLER, EDWARD. *Die Philosophie der Griechen*. 3 vols. in 6 parts. Leipzig, 1879–1892. III, pt. 2. 3rd edn., 1881.

ZIMMER, HEINRICH. *Philosophies of India*, ed. Joseph Campbell. New York (Bollingen Series XXVI) and London, 1951.

INDEX

Index

Index

light: auroral, 125ff; "victorial," 55, 130
Light of Lights, 129, 132, 134
Logos and *Sophia*, 64
Lotus of the Boundary, 145, 234

Macrobius, 93
Maeterlinck, M., 96, 299 n 64, 318 n 9
Mahler, G., 105
Mahryag-Mahryānag, 47
Maitreya, 89
Majlisī, 258, 309 n 4, 330 n 17
Malakūt (world of sphere of the Soul), 55, 59ff, 130, 148, 165, 177, 191, 192, 207, 208, 211ff, 244ff, 252, 297 n 49, 311 n 5
mandala, 276 n 39
Mandeans, 103, 192
Mandeism, 278 n 47
mandragore, 304 n 3
Manicheism, 280 n 64, 305 n 4, 396 n 45, 327 n 12
Maryam, 136, 177, 309 n 4
Massignon, L., 276 n 40, 293 n 5
matter: "immaterial," spiritual, 78, 169ff, 206ff; material, *see hyle*
matriarchal system, 277 n 46
Mazdaism, 6; *see also* angelology, eschatology
Mehmet Ağa-Oğlu, 281 n 71
Meier, F., 294 n 21
men of the Invisible, 123, 151, 153, 156ff, 314 n 28
mēnōk (celestial, subtle state), 10
Mēnōkē Xrat, 278 n 47
Mēnōkē Yazishn, 272 n 6, n 12
metahistory, 48, 60
metamorphosis, 218–221, 242ff
metals, the seven, 47ff, 69
Michael (archangel), 65, 191, 306 n 9, 314 n 28
Midnight Sun, 71–72, 86, 151
Mīr Dāmād, 69, 113, 306 n 12
Mīr Findariskī, 113
Miʿrāj (the Prophet's assumption), 86, 145, 282–283 n 76, 318 n 8
Mirkhwānd, 283 n 81
mirror: symbol of the, 81, 127ff, 247, 250, 253, 329 n 10; of the Philosophers, 204ff, 323 n 52; of the Wise Men, 99ff
Mithra, 280 n 64, 289 n 107
Mithraic liturgy, 92
Mithraism, 44
Modi, J. J., 282 n 73
Moʿīn (Muḥ.), 282 n 75, 293 n 11, 296–297 n 45
Monneret de Villard, U., xviii
More, Henry, 164
Moses, 132, 145, 314 n 28
Moulton, J. H., 274 n 20
Mshunia Kushta, 103, 278 n 47, 303 n 88, 321 n 21
Mufīd, Shaikh, 149
Muḥammad (the Prophet), 62, 244
Muḥammad Bāqir, fifth Imām of Shīʿism, 259, 314 n 26, 327 n 18
Muḥammad Karīm Khān Kirmānī, 60, 69, 116, 222–239, 263, 293 n 6, 301 n 79
Muḥsin Fayẓ Kāshānī, 83, 101, 114, 176–179, 296 n 37, 309 n 4, 324 n 59
mulk (*ʿalam al-*), the visible sensory world, 191ff, 248ff
mundus imaginalis archetypus, 76, 77, 87, 122, 126, 144–147, 160ff, 172ff, 190, 192, 240ff, 256ff, 262, 267; *see also barzakh*, Hūrqalyā, archetype-Images, *Malakūt*, world beyond
Mutakallimūn (scholastic theologians of Islam), 171, 174
musical relationships, *see* Pythagoras

nafas al-Raḥmān, 174
Najmuddīn Kubrā, 296 n 45, 307 n 18, 308 n 24
Naṣīruddīn Ṭūsī, 286 n 94

Library of Congress Cataloging in Publication Data
Main entry under title:
Spiritual body and celestial Earth.
(Bollingen series; XCI, 2)
Translation of Terre céleste et corps de résurrection.
Bibliography: p.
Includes index.
1. Sufism—Iran. I. Corbin, Henry. II. Series.
BP188.8.I55S6413 297'.4 76-45919
ISBN 0-691-09937-5